Metacognition, Cognition, and Human Performance

VOLUME 2
Instructional Practices

Edited by

D. L. Forrest-Pressley
Department of Psychology
Children's Psychiatric Research Institute
Ontario, Canada

G. E. MacKinnon
Department of Psychology
University of Waterloo
Ontario, Canada

T. Gary Waller
Department of Psychology
University of Waterloo
Ontario, Canada

1985

ACADEMIC PRESS, INC.
(Harcourt Brace Jovanovich, Publishers)
Orlando   San Diego   New York   London
Toronto   Montreal   Sydney   Tokyo

ACADEMIC PRESS, INC.
Orlando, Florida 32887

United Kingdom Edition published by
ACADEMIC PRESS INC. (LONDON) LTD.
24–28 Oval Road, London NW1 7DX

LIBRARY OF CONGRESS CATALOGING IN PUBLICATION DATA

Main entry under title:

Metacognition, cognition, and human performance.

　　Includes indexes.
　　Contents: v. 1. Theoretical perspectives — v.2.
Instructional practices.
　　1. Metacognition.　　2. Cognition.　　3. Cognition in
children.　　4. Performance.　　5. Learning, Psychology of.
I. Forrest-Pressley, Donna-Lynn.　　II. MacKinnon, G. E.
III. Waller, Gary T.　　[DNLM: 1. Cognition—in infancy &
childhood.　　2. Psychomotor Performance—in infancy &
childhood.　　3. Child Development.　　WS 105.5.C7]
BF311.M4487　　1985　　153　　84-21688
ISBN 0-12-262301-0 (v. 1 : alk. paper)
ISBN 0-12-262302-9 (v. 2 : alk. paper)

PRINTED IN THE UNITED STATES OF AMERICA

85 86 87 88　　　9 8 7 6 5 4 3 2 1

Contents

1
Metacognitive Processes: Reading and Writing Narrative Discourse
Christine J. Gordon and Carl Braun

2
Cognitive Monitoring and Early Reading: A Proposed Model
Jana M. Mason

v

3

Metacognition, Instruction, and the Role of Questioning Activities
James R. Gavelek and Taffy E. Raphael

4

Metacognition and Learning Disabilities
Bernice Y. L. Wong

5
Metacognition and Attention
Patricia H. Miller

6
Cognitive Self-Regulatory Training for Underachieving Children
Ann Booker Loper and Donna M. Murphy

7
Children's Ability to Cope with Failure:
Implications of a Metacognitive Approach for the Classroom
Joy L. Cullen

Contributors

Numbers in parentheses indicate the pages on which the authors' contributions begin.

Carl Braun (1), Department of Curriculum and Instruction, University of Calgary, Calgary, Alberta T2N 1N4, Canada

Joy L. Cullen (267), Western Australian College of Advanced Education, Western Australia 6018, Australia

James R. Gavelek (103), Department of Counseling, Educational Psychology, and Special Education, Michigan State University, East Lansing, Michigan 48824

Christine J. Gordon (1), Department of Curriculum and Instruction, University of Calgary, Calgary, Alberta T2N 1N4, Canada

Ann Booker Loper (223), Department of Special Education, University of Virginia, Charlottesville, Virginia 22903

Jana M. Mason (77), Center for the Study of Reading, University of Illinois, Champaign, Illinois 61820

Patricia H. Miller (181), Department of Psychology, University of Florida, Gainesville, Florida 32611

Donna M. Murphy (223), Department of Special Education, University of Virginia, Charlottesville, Virginia 22903

Taffy E. Raphael (103), Department of Counseling, Educational Psychology, and Special Education, Michigan State University, East Lansing, Michigan 48824

Bernice Y. L. Wong (137), Instructional Psychology Research Group, Simon Fraser University, Burnaby, British Columbia V5A 1S6, Canada

Preface

In the short history of research on metacognition, theory and practice have never been very far apart. As the chapters in Volume 1 of *Metacognition, Cognition, and Human Performance* testify, researchers concerned primarily with basic theoretical issues consider demonstrable practical utility a critical source of data in building and evaluating theory. Seminal contributions to theory, moreover, have been made by researchers who have worked more directly in applied settings to develop and test instructional programs. The current status of such work in the field of education is the subject of Volume 2.

In the first chapter, Christine Gordon and Carl Braun describe an instructional program in reading that incorporates training in metacognition. Children were exposed to simplified narrative story structure and guided in posing questions related to story structure prior to reading new stories. The authors provide data that show that such a program is effective not only in facilitating reading comprehension but also in improving the writing of stories. Gordon and Braun conclude their chapter with recommendations, based on their research, for effective instructional methods in the classroom.

The importance of metacognition in the early stages of reading acquisition is discussed by Jana Mason in Chapter 2. Mason argues that planning how to participate, figuring out how to give correct responses, learning what to do in evaluating information, and organizing and keeping track of a lesson are critical in learning to read with comprehension. Mason provides detailed transcripts from a program of instruction for preschoolers that illustrate that such skills can be acquired by children as young as 4 years if the tasks set for them are understandable, can be tied to something they already know, and are clearly modeled for them.

James Gavelek and Taffy Raphael focus, in Chapter 3, on the central role in instruction of asking questions with specific reference to the relationship of both student- and teacher-generated questions to the development of reading comprehension. The authors discuss how the ability of students to ask questions depends on complex interactions between cognitive and metacognitive knowledge. Gavelek and Raphael include in their chapter a critique of the state of the art of instructional systems that have been designed to teach teachers to ask better questions and to enhance students' question-asking abilities.

In Chapter 4, Bernice Wong critically reviews current theory and research on the nature of the disability in learning disabilities. Wong points out the inadequacies of the traditional conceptualizations of learning disabilities, which emphasize deficits in basic cognitive abilities and/or a lack of mastery in specific academic subskills. Wong argues that metacognitive factors must be included in any satisfactory account of learning disabilities and discusses the implications of current research on metacognition for remedial instruction.

Patricia Miller, in Chapter 5, reviews the research on meta-attention. Miller presents a framework drawn from the work of Ann Brown and from the research on social attribution that describes the variables affecting attention and the way in which attention changes during development. Miller then points out how the research on meta-attention may be applied to the training of classroom skills in learning-disabled children.

The growing consensus that children who encounter difficulty in school frequently have deficiencies in metacognition has, over the past decade, led to—and in some sense has even been the result of—the development of a variety of metacognitive intervention programs for teaching self-regulatory strategies to underachieving children. Research on the effectiveness of such programs in enhancing academic skills is reviewed by Ann Loper and Donna Murphy in Chapter 6. In their assessment, while the results of these interventions are very promising, it is much too soon, given the state of the extant literature, to draw firm conclusions. Nevertheless, Loper and Murphy point out several conditions that emerge as potentially critical for effective intervention: matching the form of the treatment to the task targeted for intervention, making explicit for the child the particular strategies that are useful for specific academic tasks, and fitting the intervention to the child's premastery level of skill. Loper and Murphy argue that the careful circumscription of these conditions is the most pressing direction for future intervention research. The outcome of such research would not only lead to better programs but would have major theoretical implications as well.

In the final chapter, Joy Cullen explores the relationship between metacognition and learned helplessness. This chaper reviews studies that suggest that learned helplessness is determined in part by the availability of metacognitive strategies for coping with failure. Cullen argues that the learner's affective response to failure may interfere with efficient metacognitive activity to deal with failure. Cullen points out common classroom procedures that may militate against productive meta-cognitive activity and thus may actually facilitate learned helplessness. Future research on metacognition, Cullen concludes, will need to ad-dress affective variables if it is to explain adequately children's everyday learning behaviors.

The chapters in Volumes 1 and 2 attest to the productive interplay between theory and practice that characterizes current research on metacognition. The two volumes document what we now know about metacognition, indicate the questions that are being investigated, and, more importantly, point out those questions that remain to be addressed. It is clear, however, that, even in its short history, the study of metacogni-tion has already had a significant impact and has provided new and challenging perspectives on many long-standing, diverse issues in both child development and education.

Contents of Volume 1

CHAPTER 1

Metacognitive Processes: Reading and Writing Narrative Discourse*

Christine J. Gordon and Carl Braun

Overview

This chapter attempts to contribute some insights toward the under-standing of processes involved in writing and reading. Both readers and writers share the common goal of making meaning. While the processes employed by one are by no means reflected as a mirror image of the other, readers and writers share at least two critical attributes in the meaning-making process—world knowledge (i.e., knowledge of objects, people, and events); and knowledge of certain rhetorical devices (i.e., varying organi-zational structures for expository text, and story schemata in the case of narrative text). The research reported here is delimited to the latter. More specifically, we investigate the extent to which specific instruction in story schema facilitates awareness of such structure as a metacognitive frame-work for both reading comprehension and writing.

*The study described in this article is based on research supported by funds obtained through the Alberta Advisory Committee for Educational Studies (AACES). The grant was awarded for the purpose of investigating the effects of instruction in story schema on reading and writing.

1

Metacognition

Metacognition refers to an awareness of our own cognitive processes (thinking and learning activities) or knowing about what we know. Further, *metacognition* refers to strategic regulation of our own cognitive processes. To elaborate, Flavell (1976) defined metacognition as follows:

> Metacognition refers to one's knowledge concerning one's own cognitive processes and products or anything related to them, e.g., the learning-relevant properties of information or data. For example, I am engaging in metacognition (metamemory, metalearning, metaattention, metalanguage, or whatever) if I notice that I am having more trouble learning A than B; if it strikes me that I should double check C before accepting it as fact; if it occurs to me that I had better scrutinize each and every alternative in any multiple-choice type task situation before deciding which is the best one; if I sense that I had better make a note of D because I may forget it; . . . . Metacognition refers among other things, to the active monitoring and consequent regulation and orchestration of these processes in relation to the cognitive objects or data on which they bear, usually in the service of some concrete goal or objective (p. 232).

The definition therefore extends beyond awareness of one's cognitive processes (self-awareness) to the deliberate and conscious control of these cognitive actions (self-control).

Flavell and Wellman (1977) report that metacognitive knowledge concerning any learning situation develops through the learner's awareness of how variables interact to influence outcomes of cognitive activities. This complex interaction includes person, task, and strategy variables. Brown, Campione, and Day (1981) view the same variables from a four-point model of learning. In addition to the interaction of person (characteristics of the learner), task (critical task), and strategy (learning activities) in their model, they incorporate the nature of the materials. These variables affect learning in general, and more specifically, the reading, listening and writing activities.

What one knows about oneself and other people as cognitive processors are person variables. Brown, Campione, and Day (1981), state that the learner should consider personal characteristics such as (1) limited short-term memory capacity and (2) store of appropriate background knowledge on the topic. While the learner should not tax his or her memory by attempting to retain too many details and/or large segments of information, the learner should try to integrate text content with prior knowledge (content schemata)—that is, to understand the new in terms of that already known.

Task demands involve knowledge of information made available during the actual performance of the task. The reader must consider the point of the learning activity, the purpose of personal endeavors, and become aware that different outcomes will require different learning activities. Such an awareness is necessary to tailor effort to outcome (Brown, Campione, & Day, 1981).

Strategies invoked to make and monitor progress include both cognitive and metacognitive endeavors. *Cognitive endeavors* refer to the intellectual functioning of the human mind and are characterized by remembering, understanding, focusing, and processing information (Babbs & Moe, 1983). Reading is just such an endeavor. *Metacognitive endeavors* refer to one's knowledge of this cognition as well as one's ability to monitor one's own cognition. In other words, *metacognition* is thinking about thinking. This definition of metacognition suggests that during the act of reading, the reader can choose skills and strategies that are appropriate for the demands of the reading task (Babbs & Moe, 1983). According to Brown, Campione and Day (1981), such learning strategies are both general (e.g., generating hypotheses about text) as well as specific (e.g., story grammar rules).

The final variable relevant to metacognition is awareness of the nature of the materials involved in a reading situation. The form and content of text itself provides cues to meaning and should be examined for headings, topic sentences, redundancies, and summaries as sources of help (Brown, Campione, & Day, 1981).

Metacognition and Reading: Metacomprehension

One specific type of metacognition is metacomprehension. *Metacomprehension* is metacognition (knowledge and control over thinking and learning activities) as it relates to reading. Two separate but closely related phenomena can be distinguished in metacomprehension (Baker & Brown, 1980; Flavell, 1976). The first is one's knowledge about cognition—awareness of one's own resources and capabilities relative to the demands of a variety of thinking situations. For example, in reading it is knowing that if one has not comprehended the meaning of a sentence one can regress and reread the particular sentence or even jump ahead to get the meaning from the surrounding context. Awareness of such facts, however, does not ensure that the reader will take steps to be an active, planful learner.

The second phenomenon of metacognition is one's conscious attempts in regulating cognition, the self-regulatory mechanisms such as checking, planning, monitoring, testing, revising, and evaluating used by an active learner in ongoing attempts at comprehension. Continued use of monitoring strategies enables the process to occur at an automatic level. The self-regulatory activities, however, may become a conscious experience (Brown, 1981) only when comprehension difficulties occur. One example of a monitoring activity is the active slowing down of one's reading when a comprehension failure occurs and/or the self-questioning of the extent of one's comprehension as the troublesome passages are reread.

According to Brown (1981), knowledge about comprehension is that stable cluster of information developed as a result of age and experience. Regulation (control or monitoring) is less stable, as the availability of self-regulating mechanisms depends on the reader's expertise and on the task involved. That is, monitoring activities might be used on some tasks by older children and adults, but not consistently. On simple reading tasks, even young children may monitor their activities.

As in metacognition, skill in metacomprehension generally demands an awareness of the interaction between person, task, and strategy, and the nature of materials. Metacomprehension therefore can be redefined as (1) an awareness of one's level of understanding during reading and (2) the ability to exercise conscious control over cognitive actions during reading, by invoking strategies to facilitate comprehension of a particular type of text. Baker and Brown (1980, p. 4) address the third concern—strategy— in metacognition as it relates to reading:

> Given that a learner has some awareness of his own cognitive processes, and is monitoring his progress sufficiently well to detect a problem, what type of remedial activity will he introduce to overcome that problem? Strategies vary depending on the goal of the activity; for example, reading for meaning demands different skills than reading for remembering (studying). What types of strategies are available to the learner and with what efficiency can they be orchestrated are important developmental questions with obvious implications for the study of reading.

Baker and Brown (1980) state that because readers must exercise some self-awareness and self-control of cognitive activities during reading, most characterizations of reading include skills and activities that are metacognitive in nature. They list the following active reading strategies that result in comprehension:

  a) clarifying the purposes of reading, that is understanding both explicit and implicit task demands;
  b) identifying the important aspects of a message;
  c) focusing attention on the major content rather than trivia;
  d) monitoring ongoing activities to determine whether comprehension is occurring;
  e) engaging in self-questioning to determine whether goals are being achieved; and
  f) taking corrective action when failures in comprehension are detected. (pp. 4-5)

Babbs and Moe (1983) summarize metacognitive activity in reading through a sequence that begins with the reader's focus on his or her own metacognitive knowledge of (1) processes involved and (2) demands imposed by different reading goals and types of materials. The sequence ends with the reader's use of specific behaviors and strategies to regulate and control one's reading. Included in the strategic plans of the reader is the reader's identification of the pattern of text and the search for important ideas in text. Babbs and Moe's (1983) sequence is based on Flavell's model (1979) of cognitive activity.

The pattern or structure of text, in fact, has been found to be a powerful variable in predicting the recall of content from text. The overriding conclusion is that people, through experience with text, develop *schemata* (cognitive structures) not only about the content of text but also about the *structure of text* (the underlying organization of narrative text) and then use these schemata as a conceptual framework for encoding and retrieving information. These structure schemata are an abstraction of the conventions and principles observed by authors when constructing particular types of text. This underlying organization of text is also the *top-level schema* and carries the most important information in discourse. The theoretical assumption is that if the reader is consciously *aware* of the structure of text (this top-level schema) his or her comprehension is facilitated. Self-regulation follows self-awareness. Therefore, in accordance with Baker and Brown's (1980) list of strategies, the reader who is aware of the structure of text will use that knowledge to (1) identify the pattern of text and (2) plan to use it strategically to identify the important aspects of a message [as in strategy b], to focus attention on major content rather than on trivia [as in strategy c], and to predict or generate the sequence of events in a narrative.

Researchers have developed fairly elaborate notions of this top-level schema and the formalisms that describe the structure of narratives (Mandler & Johnson, 1977; Rumelhart, 1978; Stein & Glenn, 1977; Thorndyke, 1977) as well as expository materials (Fredericksen, 1975; Kintsch, 1975a; Meyer, 1975, 1977a, 1977b; Meyer & McConkie, 1973). The latter research, however, is not discussed here, as it is not relevant to the present work, which has been limited to narrative (story materials).

Relevant to the use of text structure as a metatextual framework for understanding information presented in stories is the interaction between task demands (e.g., to read and recall the content of a narrative) and available strategies (e.g., to process and recall story information on the basis of the top-level schema of story organization). A similar interaction between task (e.g., to write a story) and strategy (e.g., to use story schema as a framework for generating story content) variables may occur in the writing process. Therefore, it can be hypothesized that teaching the underlying structure of text as an aid to reading comprehension and to writing facilitates *awareness* of such knowledge and, in turn, *control* over both the reading and the writing processes. Emig (1977), in fact, argues that writing constitutes a unique learning strategy closely linked to the development of thinking (reasoning processes). In this sense, reading and writing (both meaning-making processes) share a cognitive commonality. If specific interdependencies exist among language processes (such as reading and writing), one might hypothesize that learning that capitalizes on the realization of specific links between processes allows the processes to become mutually facilitating. Just such a specific transfer link between language processes may be the knowledge and use of text structure.

Before discussing research and implications of research related to metatextual use of story structure in comprehension and writing, a general understanding of the nature and form of narrative structure is necessary. Thus, the next section of this chapter focuses on story grammars, the psychological counterparts of the abstract organization of text. A brief review of more recent research in the use of text structure as a metatextual aid to reading follows it. After that, we direct attention to the cognitive-process theory of writing, and then review studies related to children's knowledge and use of structural elements in the writing process. Finally, we focus on our present research. This research examines the effect of instruction in story structure on reading comprehension and writing. Subsections address the research method and the results. We end with our conclusions and possible implications of this research for educational practice.

The Structure of Narratives

Several models of reading have incorporated comprehension strategies and monitoring activities (Collins, Brown, & Larkin, 1980; Goodman, 1976; Ruddell, 1976; Rumelhart, 1980). Taken together, these models view reading as a multilevel interactive process. The reader, in addition to processing the explicit features of text, must bring preexisting knowledge to the comprehension process. Preexisting knowledge includes *content schemata* (knowledge about the topic), as well as *structure schemata* (knowledge about the organization of texts).

Essential to comprehension is the interaction of text-based and prior knowledge-based processes at levels of analysis going from single letters to units as large as whole stories. Story comprehension, therefore, results from the interaction of incoming information, preexisting content schemata, as well as schemata containing knowledge about the generic characteristics of stories. These mind *macrostructures* or internalized story schemata potentially act as a framework or set of expectations to predict story information, organize information *during* the reading act, and act as retrieval cues for the recall of information bound to the story structure (Kintsch, 1975b; Van Dijk, 1977).

Several similar formalisms, dubbed story grammars, have been developed to describe the story schema underlying the organization of narrative texts (Mandler & Johnson, 1977; Stein & Glenn, 1977; Rumelhart, 1978; Thorndyke, 1977). Research has shown that readers (and listeners) have well-developed knowledge and recall stories and use this mental schema to understand and recall stories (Bartlett, 1932; Mandler & Johnson, 1978; Rumelhart, 1977; Stein & Glenn, 1977; Thorndyke, 1977; Whaley, 1981). That is, readers have some concept about the constituent elements of stories and the organization of these elements. What readers remember best when they recall a story tends to approximate this organization of elements.

To represent these mind macrostructures, story grammars have been written as sets of rules that define the underlying organization of all narratives. (Folktales, fairytales, legends, and myths most closely approximate this organization.) These rules specify how stories are broken down into their component parts, the types of information that occur at various locations and the type of relationships that connect story parts. These rules specify the important information in a narrative. Using a combination of the story grammars developed by Stein and Glenn (1977) and Thorndyke (1977), the major story categories can be said to include a setting, a theme, a plot, and a resolution. The plot can be broken down further into five subparts: initiating event, internal response, attempt, outcome, and reaction. These categories are defined in Table 1.

The Owl and the Raven, an Eskimo legend, serves to illustrate the division of a story according to the parts and subparts in a story grammar (see Table 2).

The Owl and the Raven

Many years ago, in the land of the Eskimos, lived an owl and a raven. They were fast friends. The raven had made a dress for the owl dappled white and black and the owl planned to do something in return.

One day, the owl made a pair of boots of whalebone for the raven and then began to make a white dress. He wanted the raven to try on the dress to be sure it fit properly. But when he was about to try it on, the raven kept hopping about and would not stand still. The raven continued to hop around until the owl got so angry that he poured oil from the lamp all over the raven. Since that day, the raven has been black all over.[1]

Table 1

Major Story Elements

Setting
1. **Major setting:** information about time, place (locale), characters, also the physical, social, and temporal context in which the story takes place; a habitual state.
2. **Minor setting:** time, place, characters in each episode; habitual state in a single episode.

Theme
3. **Theme:** the stated or implied goal of the main character(s); underlying goal or intent of author in writing the story.

Plot
4. **Starter event (initiating event):** some type of event, action, or natural occurrence that marks a change in the story environment and serves to initiate a response in a character; the beginning of an episode.
5. **Inner response (internal response):** some emotion, cognition, subgoal, or plan of a character.
6. **Action (attempt):** the planful effort to achieve the goal (subgoal).
7. **What happens (outcome or consequence):** the success or failure of the action; an event, action or end state that marks the attainment or nonattainment of a subgoal.
8. **Reaction:** a feeling, thought or action in response to the outcome [or to the attempt, or to the starter event].

Resolution
9. A direct consequence and reaction in an episode; or a statement of the final result of the story with respect to the theme; may express the attainment or nonattainment of the *main goal*; or a response of the main character to the final state of affairs.

Although a story grammar is usually described in terms of a complex tree diagram, a simplified diagram (based on Cunningham and Foster, 1978) was developed for use with intermediate grade level children by Gordon (1980) (see Figure 1). The diagram shows the network of story categories and the main relationships—THEN, CAUSE, AND—that connect episodes or happenings. Terminology was also adapted for classroom use so that story parts and relationships could be discussed in terms more familiar to children.

Figure 2 shows the "general" story diagram completed with story content from *The Owl and the Raven*.

What has been presented, of course, might be considered an "ideal" story grammar or an "average" of several story grammars. However, not all main categories are present in all stories or all subcategories in all episodes. An episode, for example, may contain only a starter event (the beginning), an action, and an outcome (or ending). However, knowledge of the components in a well-organized story may enhance comprehension and recall through inference. For example, in *Goldilocks and the Three*

Table 2

The Owl and the Raven

Category type	Type of information	Story statement
Major setting	Time, place, characters, state	Many years ago, in the land of the Eskimos, lived an owl and a raven. They were fast friends. The raven had made a dress for the owl dappled white and black
Major goal	Plan	and the owl planned to do something in return.
Minor setting	Time	One day,
Starter event	Action	the owl made a pair of boots of whalebone for the raven and then began to make a white dress.
Inner response	Goal	He wanted the raven to try on the dress to be sure it fit properly.
Action	Action	But when he was about to try it on,
Reaction	Action	the raven kept hopping about and would not stand still. The raven continued to hop around until
Reaction	Affect	the owl got so angry
What happened, (outcome)	Action, end state	that he poured oil from the lamp all over the raven. Since that time the raven has been black all over.

Bears, there may be no explicit goals, inner responses, or reactions. But the child can infer "She felt hungry, so she tried the porridge," "She wanted to go to sleep," or "She was glad to get out of the house" and add these during reading or recall. Knowledge or a story schema therefore may cue children to infer content under the omitted story categories.

Furthermore, not all of the subparts of an episode (a happening) always occur in the same order. Episodes differ from the ideal in that an inner response (subgoal, thought, plan or feeling) may occur before the initiating event (some change in the environment or some internal event) that sets the episode in motion. There may be several reactions. Perhaps one reaction occurs after the initiating event, while another one follows the outcome or consequence (what happens as a result of the characters action) at the end of the episode.

How do readers (listeners, writers, speakers) develop these sets of expectations (story schemata) that serve as frameworks for organizing story information? Children's frequent exposure to narratives through listening, speaking (storytelling) and reading activities accounts for much of the learning of what constitutes a story. Further learning occurs as a result of questions asked about stories. Questions are generally directed to the im-

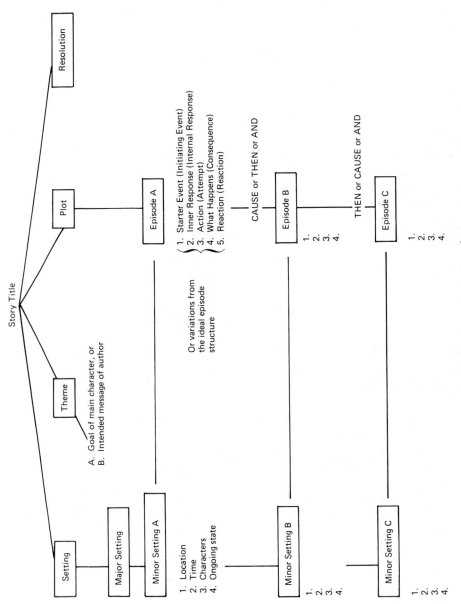

FIGURE 1. Schematic representation of story structure.

10

The Owl and the Raven

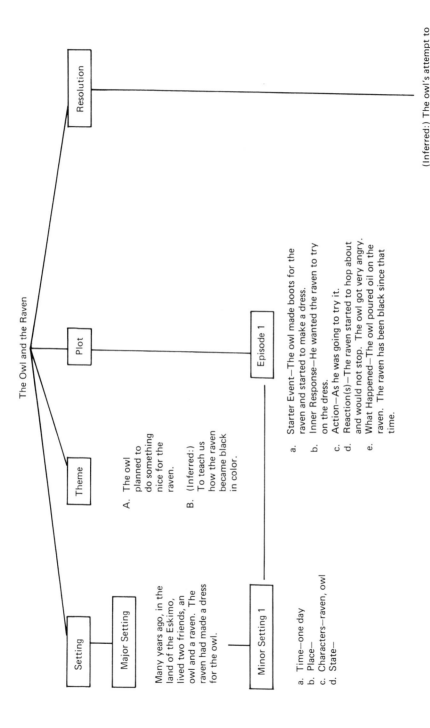

Setting

Major Setting

Many years ago, in the land of the Eskimo, lived two friends, an owl and a raven. The raven had made a dress for the owl.

Minor Setting 1

a. Time—one day
b. Place—
c. Characters—raven, owl
d. State—

Theme

A. The owl planned to do something nice for the raven.

B. (Inferred:) To teach us how the raven became black in color.

Plot

Episode 1

a. Starter Event—The owl made boots for the raven and started to make a dress.
b. Inner Response—He wanted the raven to try on the dress.
c. Action—As he was going to try it.
d. Reaction(s)—The raven started to hop about and would not stop. The owl got very angry.
e. What Happened—The owl poured oil on the raven. The raven has been black since that time.

Resolution

(Inferred:) The owl's attempt to return a favor turned out badly.

FIGURE 2. Complete story summary.

11

portant information in narratives. From these questions, readers and listeners derive a generalized (but implicit) framework for understanding stories. While readers and listeners might utilize their knowledge of story constituents as a scaffolding for comprehension, the effort is not often or usually a conscious one. That is, existence of mental macrostructures does not necessarily guarantee awareness of their existence (Kinstch, 1975b). In fact, studies have shown that people incidently learn aspects of story structures and use them (without conscious awareness of doing so) to recall similarly organized selections (Bower, 1974, 1976; Thorndyke, 1977). The question relevant to the discussion here is the extent to which instruction in structural elements leads to awareness and subsequent use of these elements. Instructional procedures might include making story grammars explicit and then engaging children in some specific metacomprehension procedure. The question of the effect of direct instruction in story grammars on reading comprehension has therefore been the subject of some investigations.

Effects of Training in the Use of Story Structure as a Metatextual Aid to Reading

With one exception (Dreher & Singer, 1980), research into the instructional effects of story structure awareness has shown knowledge and use of text structure to be an important metacognitive strategy in reading (Gordon, 1980; Short and Ryan, in press). The study by Gordon (1980), for example, found that story-structure awareness contributed significantly to story comprehension and recall. In the study, fifth-grade students were taught (over a period of 32 instructional sessions) to apply a simplified story schema (see Figure 1, this chapter) to long and complex basal reader stories that were part of their daily reading instruction. The macrostructure rules were made explicit and a macrocloze technique was used to train the children in the use of the identified story grammars as basic operations involved in comprehending and remembering narratives. Teachers modeled general questions regarding schema linked to specific story components. These questions served as the procedure by which students were directed to use the story grammar in the comprehension process. For example: "On your story diagram, the next thing that happens in this episode is the INNER RESPONSE. Read the next paragraph to find out, "What does the character think, feel or want?" As the stories were read and the questions answered, students filled in certain slots on the story outline with information from the story. Results showed that on the final instructional selection students recalled more high-level information in the story summaries they wrote than did an untreated control group. The categories in which more information was recalled were minor setting, initiating event, reaction, and final resolution—categories frequently omitted in the recalls of children in developmental studies. Children's recall of unfamiliar selections was not tapped. However, no significant differences were found in the Gordon (1980) study between the story schema group and the control group in ability to answer literal and inferential wh- probes following the reading of unfamiliar selections. Thus, the effectiveness of story grammars as metatextual aids appeared to vary under specific task demands in reading (written recall vs. question probes; familiar vs. unfamiliar stories).

Using a technique similar to the one suggested by Cunningham and Foster (1978) and used by Gordon (1980), Dreher and Singer (1980) found, after three instructional sessions, that fifth-grade students who received story structure instruction did not significantly improve their recall of well-structured transfer stories (i.e., simple fables). Dreher and Singer (1980) interpreted their findings to mean that teaching story grammars was not a useful reading strategy. More recently, Singer and Donlan (1982) reported a significant improvement in eleventh-grade students' comprehension of complex short stories after teaching them to generate story-specific questions from general questions regarding schema related to story grammars. They concluded that high-school-level students can acquire not only more adequate story schemata but also an appropriate story-schema-related metacognitive strategy that results in improved comprehension. In addition, they modified their earlier view based on the findings of Dreher and Singer (1980).

Because previous research with poor readers had demonstrated metacognitive deficits (Bransford, Shelton, Stein, & Owings, 1980), Short and Ryan (in press) also utilized a story grammar strategy as part of a metacognitive intervention program to remediate comprehension difficulties of fourth-grade poor readers. The main purpose of the study was to determine if a story grammar strategy and attribution training could decrease or increase comprehension differences between skilled and less-skilled readers. Attribution training consisted of procedures emphasizing the direct relationship between effort and outcome. Story grammar intervention consisted of both improving children's schematic knowledge and their ability to employ existent story schemata through the use of five wh- questions about both the setting and the categories of episodes as described by Stein and Glenn (1977). Attribution training was incorporated into the metacognitive training program to further enhance strategy application. The training procedures consisted of seven sessions. The less-skilled readers participated in all training sessions while the skilled readers were included in only the testing sessions. The two training components were employed with less-skilled readers in three groups: strategy and attribution;

strategy only; attribution only. In addition, a highly skilled group of readers was included for contrast purposes only. The researchers found that strategy training enabled less-skilled readers to utilize story schemata to aid reading comprehension to the extent that they did not differ from skilled readers. Further, without strategy training, attribution did not enhance performance in comprehension. Short and Ryan (in press) concluded that story grammer training remediated comprehension difficulties on the target story. They obtained only partial support for strategy generalization to other reading tasks.

In summary, the research into the instructional effects of bringing story structure to children's conscious awareness has not produced consistent results. However, indications are that such instruction is helpful if instruction occurs over an extended period of time. It appears from the results of these intervention studies that children were making some conscious decisions to use these elements in their recalls of familiar selections that they had read. However, the question of transfer value to unfamiliar narratives, to a variety of reading tasks, and across language components still remained.

While some researchers have focused on the concepts of story schema and story grammars as facilitating cognitive and metacognitive structures in reading comprehension, professional opinion has long held that reading is only one aspect of language. Total language experiences include reading, writing, listening, and speaking—all of which share particular linguistic and cognitive commonalities. Experimental evidence (Shanahan, 1980; Stotsky, 1975; Zeman, 1969) does confirm these opinions. In aggregate, their findings suggest that mental and language processes involved in producing written materials are very similar to those involved in comprehending written materials. Would it be reasonable to suggest, then, that if efficient reading appears to be dependent on knowledge and use of text structure, then efficient writing, too, might be related to awareness and control over text structure? Would knowledge and use of text structure during the reading process serve as a transfer link to writing? We must turn to a brief review of relevant theory and research into the writing process before these questions can be examined.

Related Theory and Research in Writing

The writing process can be viewed as a cognitive activity (Flower & Hayes, 1981a). Writing involves application of specific knowledge that a writer is able to orchestrate in constructing meaning. Underlying this use of knowledge are a number of component processes that interact (rather than occurring in a linear sequence). According to Flower and Hayes, the cognitive process theory of writing consists of three major components: planning, translating, and reviewing. Writers set goals and plans, and they organize the content in the prewriting stage. During planning, writers "form an internal representation of the knowledge that will be used in writing" (Flower & Hayes, 1981a, p. 372). Flower and Hayes (1981b) examined protocols of novice writers. They found that writers included plans for generating ideas (e.g., producing information about a topic in the form of key words) and plans for expressing ideas in text (e.g., organizing information into sequential topically related text and using prototypic structures to frame production). *Translating* is essentially the process of putting ideas (the knowledge about a topic, plans for structuring knowledge) into "a linear piece of written English" (Flower & Hayes, 1981a, p. 373). *Reviewing* involves two subprocesses: evaluating and modifying text. In reviewing, the results of the first two processes are put to the test.

Theory and research (Flower & Hayes, 1981a; 1981b) in writing suggests that just as readers employ structural schemata, novice writers make plans as part of their goal-setting for strategies to be used, for using specific text structures in the production of their text. Because metacognitive abilities of children are not as well developed as those of adults, what evidence is there that children do use (or can use) abstract structural elements in the writing process?

Knowledge and Use of Structural Elements in Writing

Bereiter and Scardamalia (1982) have examined questions about children's knowledge of structure as it applies to writing. Their particular interest in whether children use this knowledge consciously in planning or whether the knowledge is a tacit influence on performance is relevant to our present work.

A series of studies (Bereiter, Scardamalia, & Turkish, 1980; Paris, Scardamalia, & Bereiter, 1980) investigated children's knowledge of discourse structure and its availability for use in planning compositions. Bereiter, Scardamalia, and Turkish (1980), interviewed children of ages 10 to 12 years, to elicit information on the types of elements that they thought belonged in (1) narrative texts, (2) argumentative texts, and (3) direction-giving texts. Children were presented with a story that they were not allowed to read. However, they were asked to speculate about the kinds of things that would be expected in (1) a good story (2) a persuasive argument or (3) a set of good directions. If the child focused on concrete content that might be in a narrative text, for example, a set of prompts was used to encourage each child to focus on the structural elements in narratives. Approximately a month later, students were asked to write in each of the three genres as part of their regular school work. The Stein and Glenn (1979) story grammar was used to classify responses to the probes and to parse the written productions. Generally speaking, the researchers found a discrepancy between students' use of different story elements in their writing and ability to name story elements during prompts.

The researchers concluded that children do have structural knowledge of stories and other texts. Further, this knowledge is accessible to consciousness, but only with much coaxing and effort on the part of a prompter. The question of whether this consciously accessible knowledge has any functional value was pursued by Paris, Scardamalia, and Bereiter (1980). Subjects were asked to arrange the elements of an opinion essay (statement of belief, reason for, elaboration, example, repetition, statement of other side, reason against, conclusion, general statement, personal statement) as though they were going to write the essay. Later, subjects were asked to write two opinion essays following (1) the order conventionally found in children's essays and (2) following an order a mature writer would use. Indications were that children had more difficulty following the mature writer's order. The researchers believe that such data supports the psychological reality of the discourse grammar knowledge that children actually report. They also feel that the second study supports the view that the grammars do have operational significance.

However, do children access and use this knowledge spontaneously? To that question, the same researchers concluded "that children do have structural knowledge of genre other than just narrative and that this knowledge could potentially be put to conscious use by them in planning, but there are no indications that they actually do use it consciously. It must function as implicit knowledge, like their knowledge of sentence grammar, shaping production but has no role in conscious planning" (Bereiter & Scardamalia, 1980, p. 32). Bereiter and Scardamalia (1982) hypothesized that in order for higher-level intentions (use of structure) to be translated into local decisions (what to say next in terms of content), children need to be able to make conscious use of concepts linking language to function. For example, children may need to make decisions such as "I had better give an example."

Bereiter and Scardamalia (1982) report that in the Paris et al. (1980) research, some children indicated that because they had learned to recognize structural elements, they had some control in planning compositions. This belief was not supported by children's actual performance.

The Bereiter, Scardamalia, Anderson and Smart (1980) training study that followed was an attempt to provide children with an executive procedure for bringing structural knowledge into use. Children were given practice in using a simple routine for switching between text generation and making decisions at the structural element level. Discourse elements were embedded into lists of imperatives (e.g., *reason* translated into "give a reason for an opinion"). The routine consisted of (1) choosing a directive, (2) writing a sentence fulfilling it, (3) choosing a next directive, and so on. Specific ordering of elements was discouraged. Rather, children were encouraged to choose elements most appropriate to their own criteria at each point in the composition.

Posttest compositions, representing a test of transfer to typical school settings, were written without access to lists of structural elements or embeddings of these in directives. Posttest composition comparisons of the experimental and control groups (in sixth grade) showed that the experimental group significantly exceeded the control group in (1) the total number of discourse elements used and (2) the different types used. No significant effects were evident, however, on quality or quantity of written work. The researchers interpreted their findings to suggest that while training in the conscious use of structural elements may have had an effect on composition planning, the use of a larger variety of elements cannot be explained simply through exposure to these elements. Bereiter and Scardamalia (1982) concluded, therefore, that "the value of the study . . . . lies mainly in its indication that children's planning processing can be altered by helping them gain access to rhetorical knowledge and by helping them develop executive procedures for using that knowledge as they compose" (p. 33).

For narrative discourse, accumulated research evidence suggests that children may have well-developed schemata of what constitutes a story (Mandler & Johnson, 1977; Stein & Glenn, 1979; Stein & Trabasso, 1982; Whaley, 1981). Such learning possibly accrues from frequent exposure to narratives in listening, speaking, and reading situations. Further, there is some evidence that children can be taught directly what elements constitute a story grammar and then to utilize that knowledge in organizing their written recalls of familiar selections read (Gordon, 1980). In writing, there is evidence that training in conscious use of structural elements may have an effect on composition planning (Bereiter, Scardamalia, Anderson, & Smart, 1980). To date there has been no research representing a test of transfer from one type of reading task to another or from the reading mode to the writing mode. Our research addressed the question: Can explicit instruction in structural elements affect children's reading and writing of narratives?

Effects of Instruction in Story Elements on Reading Comprehension and Writing

The purpose of the study was to investigate the effects of instruction that makes explicit to children the story structure elements. Instructional effects were assessed across several task demands in reading comprehension, across reading and writing modes, and over time. More specifically, it was hypothesized that story schema would serve as (1) a transferable metatextual framework for storing and retrieving information from new and unfamiliar selections read, (2) a framework for answering literal and inferential question probes, and (3) a cue system for planning and generating information in the writing process. Further, the effect of instruction would be durable over time. The first prediction was that direct instruction in story schema would increase the number of text structure categories generally found lacking in children's recall of a narrative used in instruction. Second, such instructional effects would transfer to the reading of unfamiliar but similarly organized narratives. The third prediction was that story schema awareness would contribute significantly to literal and inferential comprehension if prior knowledge on the topic (content schemata) was developed to the same extent in both the control and the experimental groups (the feasibility of equating prior knowledge had been previously ascertained in a pilot study). Fourth, children would utilize their knowledge of story schema to generate information in independently written compositions. Finally, it was predicted that children would continue to employ structure as a metatextual framework for storage and retrieval in reading and for generation of content in writing under delayed test conditions.

Method

Children

The 57 children for the study were drawn from three fifth-grade classes from one school population. Two small Grade 5 classes from split-grade combinations (4–5 and 5–6) were assigned to one class. The other class consisted of an intact group of Grade 5 students. These two classes were then randomly assigned to experimental ($N = 34$) and control ($N = 23$) groups. The mean standardized reading grade equivalent obtained on the *Canadian Tests of Basic Skills* for each group, respectively, was 5.8 and 5.1; the mean IQ was 116.3 and 102.6. Though similar in reading ability, the two groups were significantly different in measured IQ.

Materials

The experimental test materials consisted of four similarly organized unfamiliar fables adapted to include in each 16 story structure categories. In each fable, there was 1 major setting, 1 minor setting, 2 aspects related to theme (a goal and the author's message), 2 initiating events, 2 inner responses, 2 attempts, 2 outcomes consisting of an action, 1 outcome consisting of an end state, 2 reactions, and 1 resolution. These four fables were used to pre- and posttest written recall.

For two other unfamiliar fables, short "scripts" were written to provide children with background content schemata requisite for inferencing from the fables. (Our pilot study had shown that the amount of background information children possessed on a particular story topic could be equated by providing children with the background information required for inferencing prior to reading.) Wh- comprehension questions were constructed for the two fables. These probes were tied to specific text structure categories (e.g., major setting, initiating event). An additional constraint was that probes included textually explicit, textually implicit, and scriptally implicit categories (Pearson and Johnson, 1978). Examples of each question type follow:

Textually Explicit: Question and response are formed from constituents in the same sentence.
  Passage: In the city of Rome, there was once a poor Roman slave whose name was Androclus. His master was a cruel man and so unkind to him that at last Androclus ran away.
  Question: Why did Androclus run away?
  Response: He ran away because his master was cruel and unkind.
Textually Implicit: Question is formed from the constituent in one sentence, the response from a constituent in another sentence. The integration of textual information is required.
  Passage: A lion had come into the cave and was roaring loudly. Androclus was very much afraid, for he felt sure that the beast would kill him. Soon, however, he saw that the lion was not angry but that he limped as though his foot hurt him.
  Question: Why was the lion roaring loudly when he walked into the cave?
  Response: The lion appeared to have hurt his foot.
Scriptally Implicit: The question is based on the passage but requires the use of one's background knowledge in formulating the response. The exact answer cannot be found in text.

Passage: In the city of Rome, there was once a poor Roman slave whose
name was Androclus. His master was a cruel man and so unkind to
him that at last Androclus ran away.

Question: Why did Androclus likely become a slave?

Response: Because he was a Roman, and not a captive, he probably
became a slave because he had debts (or owed someone a lot of
money).

Similarly organized legends and fables were chosen as instructional
narratives. Where necessary, minor modifications were made to have the
stories correspond to a similar organization. The macrostructure of each
narrative was then determined based on an adaption of Stein and Glenn
(1979) and Thorndyke (1977) (see Table 1, this chapter). Three separate
raters validated the categorization of statements in each narrative.

Both the inclusion of specific text structure categories and the taxonomic probe categories were validated by three independent raters. Interrater agreement on the taxonomic probe categories and parsing of the
text and instructional fables into text structure categories was .91.

Instructional materials for writing consisted of story settings as story
starters. The class was given a choice of story starters. The following exemplifies a story setting.

In olden times, there lived a King who enjoyed a good laugh,
especially at the expense of others.
"I really feel like playing a trick on someone," he thought as he
rode.

As well, the class was encouraged to volunteer story settings for writing activities. In most cases, during the instructional sessions, settings, elicited from the class were used in the writing of stories.

For the independent writing pre- and posttests, story starters consisted of brief settings such as:

"Long ago, there lived a wicked old witch named . . . "
or
"Once there was a brave young knight called . . ."

Any number and/or type of specific text structure categories was possible in the independent writing task, depending on the child's concept of
story structure and length of story produced.

Instructional Method

Instruction for both the experimental and the control group consisted of 15 sessions of 30 minutes duration spaced regularly over a 5-week period.

EXPERIMENTAL GROUP. Initial instruction in the experimental group consisted of exposure to a simplified, global organization structure of a narrative. Macrocloze procedures were used (e.g., templates on transparencies were presented with some text-structure categories already completed with story content, while others were left blank for children to complete [see Figure 3]. A priori schema-related questions were used to guide the search for information contained in specific text structure categories. Upon consensus, such information was written by the teacher–investigator on the macrocloze template. Then an inductive approach was used to deal with specific categories in three similarly organized fables before proceeding to all text structure components in one narrative.

Succeeding lessons guided students in posing their own questions (story-specific questions related to story schema) prior to reading unfamiliar narratives. In an attempt to enhance transfer effects, the remaining sessions involved the writing of narratives, first with teacher guidance and then without. These narratives were discussed in terms of text structure components. Table 3 presents an overview of instructional procedures used in the experimental group.

CONTROL GROUP. The control group received teacher-directed discussion, probes, and activities related to drama and literature appreciation. In order to offset any biasing effects of the experimental writing tasks, the control was engaged in the writing of drama and poetry. Table 4 provides an overview of instructional procedures used in the control group.

Dependent Variables

The dependent variables used for pre- and posttests were (1) a written recall of an unfamiliar narrative (one of the four fables); (2) wh- probes following the reading of an unfamiliar narrative; and (3) a creative writing production of a narrative for which a one-sentence starter had been provided. An additional posttest measure consisted of the written recall of a narrative (one fable) that had become familiar, as it was used in an instructional session (Lesson 10) immediately preceding the written recall. Following a 2-month time delay, two more posttests were administered: (1) a written recall of an unfamiliar narrative (a fable), and (2) a creative writing production following a story starter.

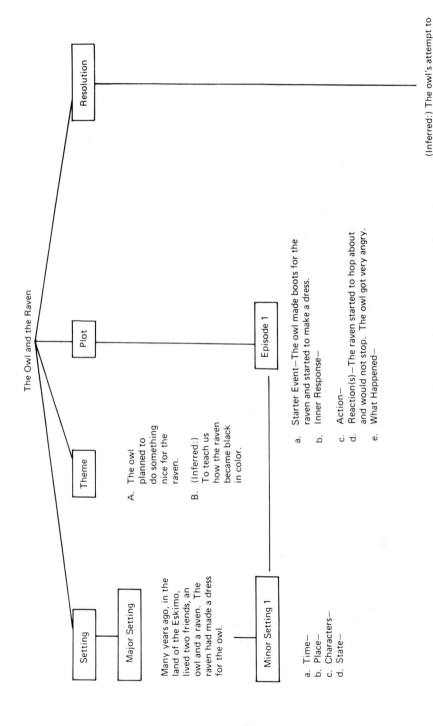

The Owl and the Raven

Setting

Major Setting

Many years ago, in the land of the Eskimo, lived two friends, an owl and a raven. The raven had made a dress for the owl.

Minor Setting 1

a. Time—
b. Place—
c. Characters—
d. State—

Theme

A. The owl planned to do something nice for the raven.

B. (Inferred:) To teach us how the raven became black in color.

Plot

Episode 1

a. Starter Event—The owl made boots for the raven and started to make a dress.
b. Inner Response—

c. Action—
d. Reaction(s)—The raven started to hop about and would not stop. The owl got very angry.
e. What Happened—

Resolution

(Inferred:) The owl's attempt to return a favor turned out badly.

FIGURE 3. Macrocloze example.

22

Table 3

Overview of Instructional Method—Experimental Group

Lesson number	Focus of instruction (cumulative progression)	Example	Rationale
1	a. Expose children to structure of a simple narrative written to conform to an "ideal" story grammar.	a. See Appendix for story example. (The Knight and the Dragon)	a. Provides the children with a global overview of the four main story parts.
	b. Define terms (e.g., major setting).	b. See definitions in text of article.	b. Teaches children meanings of terms.
	c. Pose a priori questions—general questions related to story schema.	c. Read the first paragraph to tell me: 1. What is the major story setting? (time, place, characters, on-going state?)	c. Sets purposes for the story reading by guiding the search for information.
	d. Restate questions and elicit responses. Then fill in story information that fits in under each text structure.	d. Responses to above: 1. 2. 3. 4.	d. Children associate element of structure to story content by categorizing story information.
	e. Paraphrase story content under each text-structure category.	e. "A long time ago in a far away land called Fantasia, a beautiful maiden was captured . . . ." could become "Many years ago a maiden who lived in Fantasia was captured . . . ."	e. Students recognize the equivalence in meaning of statements.
	f. Conclude discussion related to each story component with a restatement of the term.	f. What is this story part called?	f. Summarizes learning.
	g. Proceed as above (c, d, e) for theme (goal), plot, and resolution.		

(Continued)

23

Table 3 *(Cont.)*

Lesson number	Focus of instruction (cumulative progression)	Example	Rationale
2	a. Conduct a detailed analysis of two story components: major setting and theme (goal), by dealing with only two categories across three similarly organized narratives (fables).	a. Deal with only major setting and theme in 1. The Knight and the Dragon 2. 3.	a. Use of the inductive teaching approach to teach specifics by holding constant the structure element, while varying story content.
	b. Begin instruction of each story part with an ideal story.		b. To provide a familiar story (as a review) prior to identifying the same elements in new materials.
	c. Reword prereading schema-related questions so they are story-specific rather than general in form.	c. Let's reread Paragraph 1 of "The Knight and the Dragon." Read to answer: 1. Besides the knight, who is the story about? 2. What was the name of their homeland? 3. When did the story take place? 4. What had happened to the maiden 5. Where was she living?	c. Modeling the method of transposing general questions into story-specific questions.
	d. Use the same procedure as described above to teach the theme (goal).		
3	a. Expose children to the subparts of a plot in an ideal story of two episodes.	a. Use the "The Knight and the Dragon" as the exemplar.	a. To provide a global overview of the five components of the plot.

24

b. Provide story-specific prereading questions related to structure.

c. Use the same procedure as described in Lesson 3 to teach:
1. starter event
2. inner response
3. action
4. what happens, and
5. reaction in Episode 1.

d. Proceed as above for the five subparts of Episode 2 of "The Knight and the Dragon."

4–5

a. Conduct a detailed analysis of the subparts of a plot by dealing with specific categories across two similarly organized narratives.

b. Begin instruction of each plot subpart with the contrived ideal story.

b. Read Paragraph 1 to find out: "What is it that gets the knight moving towards his goal? What news causes a change in how things were?"

a. & b. Deal with
1) Starter Event in each story:
1. The Knight and the Dragon
2.
Then deal with
2) Inner Responses in:
1. The Knight and the Dragon
2.

etc. . . . .

a. Use of the inductive teaching technique to teach specifics of plot structure by holding constant structure while varying story information.

b. Progress from the familiar to the unfamiliar in identifying story information that fits into each category.

(Continued)

25

Table 3 (*Cont.*)

Lesson number	Focus of instruction (cumulative progression)	Example	Rationale
	c. Provide story-specific a priori questions.	c. Read paragraph 2 of "The Knight and the Dragon" to find out the answer to this question: "What does the knight think, want, or feel?"	
	d. Use the same procedure as described in Lesson 3 to teach 1. starter event 2. inner response 3. action 4. outcome 5. reaction, in turn across three stories.		
	e. Proceed as above for each episode in the stories.		
	f. Expose children to theme (author's message) and resolution in the two narratives.		
6–7	a. Introduce stories that vary from the ideal story grammar—stories in which 1. all story parts or subparts are not explicitly stated, and 2. the subparts of an episode do not occur in the same order.	a. Stories such as "The Ant and the Grasshopper" and "The Tricky Fox and the Crow" are examples.	a. To build in an expectation and recognition of variability within stories and among stories, while providing an overview of each story structure.

	b. Introduce an understanding of relationships between story episodes (AND, CAUSE, THEN); provide the type of relationship and point out why it is that type.	b. Episodes 1 and 2 are connected by THEN because one thing happens after the other, not because of it.	b. To show children that stories are connected strings of episodes.
	c. Introduce the macrocloze technique on the transparency and story structure sheet.	c. Complete some story slots for the students by filling in beforehand, for example, theme of the story, minor setting, and reaction for Episode 1, and starter event and action for Episode 2.	c. Provision of correctly slotted content under some text structure categories enables the children to handle the element of structure variability that has been introduced.
	d. Address the complete structure of a story in one teaching session.		
8–9	a. Focus on children generating and asking some schema-related and/or story-specific questions related to text structures and then reading to answer their own questions. Some question-asking continues to be modeled by the teacher. The unfamiliar stories contain structure variation from the ideal story grammar.	a. The teacher states: "Before I start reading Episode 2, I might ask—What event starts this happening in the story? Now, what is another question I might ask before I start reading? Another question?"	a. A stimulus is provided for interaction with text—that is, a stimulus to engage in a very active but independent search for answers. The children now have a metatextual aid (knowledge of a story grammar) on which to develop questions when reading.
	b. Continued focus on children formulating questions and reading to answer the self-constructed questions on a story.	b. Today everyone will jot down their own questions (at least 3) based on story organization before we start reading each episode.	b. Ensures independent search and involvement through writing task.

(Continued)

Table 3 (*Cont.*)

Lesson number	Focus of instruction (cumulative progression)	Example	Rationale
10	a. Focus on reading a story from beginning to end before analyzing the story.	a. Let us read the whole story before talking about its story structure.	a. Provide practice in applying story structure to whole stories (as in real-life reading situations).
	b. Emphasize writing as well as reading by requiring children to write a summary of the discussed story. (The summary is written without access to the story structure or the text.)	b. We will summarize the story we have just finished studying.	b. Using a familiar story provides an easy transition from the reading mode to the writing mode. The summary also demonstrates that by utilizing story structure as scaffolding for story recall and generation, all the important information is included.
11–12	a. Focus on the writing process by writing a short but well-structured class story.	a. "Today we're going to write a story. I will get us started by giving you the time, place, and general situation for the whole story, as well as the major goal. Here it is:	a. Focus on transferring the knowledge of story structure in reading to serve as a scaffolding for information generation in writing.
		Hundreds of years ago in England, two princes claimed the right to the throne. Standing straight, head erect, one of the young princes thought, "I want to be king. The decision must be made soon."	
	b. Provide teacher-guidance in the form of prewriting questions for the story writing.	b. The teacher then poses questions such as	
		1. What can be our minor setting for	

	the first episode? Where is this happening going to take place— near a river, in the forest? 2. We need a starter event or action. What gets our prince moving?	
13–14 a. No teacher guidance for the writing of a well-structured class story.	a. Today we will write another story. I'm not going to help you in any way. But keep in mind what we learned about the organization of stories when you are helping to write this story. Years ago, a daring young soldier galloped through a forest in England. He yearned to find some excitement, and he hoped to show his true worth to his King.	a. Expectation that each student will apply knowledge of story schema to writing.
b. Story statements volunteered by children are written on chalkboard.		
c. Analysis of class-produced story through children-generated questions related to story structure.	c. Child: Do we have an inner response in Episode 1? Do we know the plans, feelings, thoughts of the soldier?	c. Focus on transferring strategies used in reading to written productions.
15 a. Examination of a child-produced story to identify text-structure categories into which story content fits.	a. Let's analyze this story to see if we can slot the information the child wrote down under a story structure. You tell me the questions we should ask as we examine his story.	a. Children will use their knowledge of structure for generating questions in a critical examination of text.
b. Emphasis in the analysis of stories on children posing story-specific questions related to text structure.		

Table 4

Overview of Instructional Method—Control Group

Lesson number	Focus of instruction	Example	Rationale

1–5	1. Focus is on literature appreciation.
	a. Demonstrate oral reading techniques.
	b. Discuss techniques to enhance story reading.
	
	c. Elicit other techniques to be used in story reading or retelling.
	
	d. Pose literal comprehension questions that children answer in writing.
	e. Assign story sections to groups in class. Each group prepares to read or tell a story section incorporating techniques discussed in (b) and (c). Each group is to develop questions on their section. The questions will be answered in writing by class members.
	f. Have groups read or retell story sections next day.
		a. Use folktales such as "The Ashes that Make the Trees Bloom."
		b. What made the reading interesting?
		  1. voice modulation
		  2. showing pictures in book
		  3. use of sound effects
		c. What else can make interesting story listening?
		  1. use of puppets
		  2. background music
		  3. dress appropriate to story locale
		  4. dramatizations, pantomines
		d. How did the wicked old man and woman treat dogs?
		e. Group 1, you will be responsible for Section 2 of the story. You will be the storytellers or story readers. What will you do to make your presentation interesting to us?
		
		f. Group 1, please present your section of the story.
			a. To use the same genre (folktales) as used by the experimental group.
			
			d. To provide opportunities for teacher-pupil interaction as in experimental group.
			e. To offset any biasing effects due to writing, the control group was also given question-answering tasks.

g. Discuss strengths of presentations. Discuss ways to improve presentations.

h. Allow groups to repeat their performance, incorporating suggestions.

i. Have groups pose their questions. Other class members write responses.

g. Did the group use interesting vocabulary in the *retelling*? conversation? include details?

6–9

2. Focus is on drama appreciation.

a. Have the students take the role of stage designer.

b. Read orally the setting of each of the scenes in the play to elicit the props needed for each scene.

c. Discuss how the props will serve to convey mood.

d. Change a story into a play. First divide the story into scenes. Then decide, as a group, on setting, props, and mood to be created in each scene.

e. Using the outline prepared for setting, props, mood, and characters, have groups of class members rewrite the story sections into a play. Demonstrate the format used when writing drama.

a. Use plays such as "Why the Sea is Salt."

b. Have students write the list of props.

d. Use stories such as the Norse tale, "The Apples of Iduna." Let's read orally the first section. Now where will it take place? What props do we need? What mood do we want to set? Who are the characters?

e. Rewrite the story into a play. Set up your play as follows:

a. To observe details of setting and note their effect on the story (create mood of each scene).

c. To note that setting conveys the mood of a play.

d. To deal with narratives without dividing them into episodes (as per story structure).

e. To offset biasing effects, the control group was given writing tasks.

(Continued)

31

Table 4 (*Cont.*)

Lesson number	Focus of instruction	Example	Rationale
10–15	3. Focus is on poetry appreciation. a. Have children listen to poems that try to explain something.	a. Use poems like the "Wind-Wolves" by William Sargent or "Questions at Night" by Louis Untermeyer.	a.–n. Focus in on appreciating the words, visual images, and sounds in poetry through listening, reading, and writing.
	b. Discuss with children what is being explained and the choice of words in the descriptions.	b. What sound does "Wind-Wolves" try to explain? How is the phrase "And drink up the Milky Way" a play on words?	
	c. Have children write poems to provide an explanatin of a phenomenon.	c. Write a poem to explain 1. why the snake has no feet, or 2. why cats have whiskers.	
	d. Have children listen to poems that are full of sounds.	d. Use poems like "Texas Trains and Trails" by Mary Austin.	
	e. Have children read poems that are full of sounds.	e. Use poems like "Policemen on Parade" by J. Garthwaithe.	
	f. Discuss the words imitating sounds.	f. Which part of the poem describes the noises of trains?	
	g. Have children write short poems using words that imitate sounds.	g. Write a poem about 1. a computer 2. a video-game, or 3. ___	g.,k.,l.,m.,n. To offset biasing effects, children wrote a variety of poems.
	h. Have class listen to poems describing sights.	h. Use poems like "The Mountain" by Caroline Wild.	

i. Discuss the sights that have been described.

j. Have children read poems that describe sights.

k. Have children write poems describing things in such a way that the reader can picture it.

l. Follow the same steps (listening, reading, writing) using poems describing both sights and sounds.

m. Follow the same three steps (listening, reading, writing) using poems that tell "why."

n. Have class listen to, read, and write Haiku poems describing feelings. Discuss the Haiku form.

i. What is described? How? Can you "see" it in your mind's eye?

j. Use poems like "White" by Elizabeth-Ellen Long.

k. Let's write a poem describing:
1. a rainbow,
2. a circus, or
3. Mt. Everest

l. Use poems like "Trains" by J. S. Tippett, and "Trains at Night" by Frances Frost. Then have children write a sight-and-sound poem.

m. Examples to use include "Who Has Seen the Wind?" by Christina Rossetti and "Why the Winds Blow" by C. S. P. Wild.

n. Use Haiku poetry collections as sources of poems. Have students think about their feelings and then express them in a Haiku on one of the following:
   i. snow
   ii. chinooks
   iii. lazy cats
   iv. a storm
   v. a tiny mosquito.

Scoring

The following set of criteria was used to score the open-ended responses to the wh- comprehension questions. Interrater reliability was .91.

Textually explicit: Answers were scored as being correct if they were reproductions of, or synonymous to, the appropriate statements in the narrative.

Textually implicit: Answers were given an optimal value score (scored as correct) if there was an appropriate match between the question statement and the response statement, both of which were derived from the text. Such responses required the student to make at least one step of logical or pragmatic inferring in order to get from the question to the response. Reproductions of and/or ideas synonymous to those found in the response statement from the text were both accepted as correct answers.

Scriptally implicit: Answers were scored as correct if they were based on information in the narrative but required information from one's background knowledge to answer the question.

Propositions in subjects' written recalls of each fable were compared to validated macrostructures of each narrative and categorized into specific text structure categories.

Propositions in the creative writing productions were also classified into specific text structure categories (for use in statistical analyses), based on a production scoring system. Because there were no templates against which to compare independent writing productions (as there were in the written recalls), the production scoring system basically involved the following:

1. Comparing story content to the definitions of story elements (see Table 1, this chapter) in order to classify content into text structure categories
2. Attending to syntactic as well as semantic concerns in capturing the essence of categories. For example, "After she threw him off the platform" would be classed as setting (tells when). However, "She threw him off the platform," would be either initiating event, action, or reaction, depending on its position in the episodic sequence
3. Judging the vagueness and clarity of statements in terms of semantic content.

Interrater agreement of three trained raters for scoring 10% of the randomly selected written recalls was .98. For scoring creative writing productions, the average agreement was .89. The written recalls and the creative writing productions were also subjected to a holistic evaluation to gain a more global impression of the quality of writing (see section on the descriptive analysis of reading and writing tasks for the experimental group, this chapter).

Results and Discussion

An overview of statistical analyses is provided in an extended footnote.[2] Further, description of statistical results for individual hypotheses tested are also provided in footnotes.

Pretests

We found that the experimental and control groups did not differ significantly in *total* number of correctly answered wh- probes and in *total* number of text structure categories produced in written recalls and in creative writing productions.[3] These were administered prior to intervention to obtain baseline data. Table 5 reveals the comparable performances of the two groups. Neither did the two treatment groups differ significantly

[2]Because the subjects for the experimental and control group were not randomly selected (random assignment of groups was made to treatment) and found to be different in measured IQ, multivariate and univariate analyses of covariance (MANCOVA and ANCOVA) were used to compare the experimental and control groups. Standardized reading scores (*Canadian Tests of Basic Skills*) and IQ scores (*Otis-Lennon*) were used as covariates in the pretest and posttest analyses. Wherever corresponding pretest measures were administered prior to treatment, the relevant pretest scores were also included as covariates in the posttest analysis (i.e., pretest scores were also included as covariates in the posttest analyses, along with standardized reading and IQ scores on the written recalls, the creative writing productions and the wh- probes). In the ANCOVA of the written recalls and creative writing productions (but not the wh- comprehension or the inferencing ability), the effects of covariates were assessed after the main effects for factors, but before any factor-by-factor interaction. Regression analyses had shown that for the written recalls and the creative writing productions, only corresponding pretest scores (and not standardized reading scores or IQ) were significant predictors of posttest results. For example, posttest results in written recall were predicted well only by the subject's pretest scores in written recall.

[3]A MANCOVA (with IQ and standardized reading scores as covariates) revealed no significant differences between experimental and control groups on the pretest measures administered to obtain baseline data (written recall of an unfamiliar selection, wh- probes, and a creative writing task given prior to intervention). No significant differences between groups were found on the total number of text structure categories produced in the written recall of an unfamiliar selection, in the independent writing task, or in the total number of wh- probes answered correctly on an unfamiliar fable ($F(3, 51) = 0.18$, $p < .91$). Separate ANCOVAs for all the pretests (and on each specific wh- question type) confirmed the multivariate results.

Table 5

Means and Standard Deviations for All Measures

Dependent measures	Pretest measures of treatment groups				Immediate posttest measures of treatment groups				Delayed posttest measures of treatment groups			
	Experimental		Control		Experimental		Control		Experimental		Control	
	$\overline{X}$	(SD)	$\overline{X}$	(SD)	$\overline{X}$	(SD)	$\overline{X}$	(SD)	$\overline{X}$	(SD)	$\overline{X}$	(SD)
Standardized reading	5.8	(0.6)	5.1	(0.7)	—	—	—	—	—	—	—	—
IQ	116.3	(9.3)	102.6	(8.9)	—	—	—	—	—	—	—	—
Reading Tasks												
1. Wh- comprehension questions (Unfamiliar selection)												
Total overall comprehension	10.0	(1.3)	8.8	(2.1)	6.7	(1.8)	4.9	(2.0)	—		—	
Textually explicit comprehension	3.4	(0.6)	3.2	(0.8)	2.2	(0.8)	1.7	(1.0)	—		—	
Textually implicit comprehension	3.4	(0.7)	3.1	(0.8)	2.9	(0.9)	2.1	(1.0)	—		—	
Scriptally implicit comprehension	3.2	(0.8)	2.4	(0.9)	1.6	(1.0)	1.1	(0.8)	—		—	
2. Written recall (unfamiliar selection)												
Total number of text structure categories	5.7	(2.4)	3.7	(2.9)	8.1	(2.0)	4.8	(2.4)	8.6	(1.5)	7.5	(3.0)
3. Written recall (familiar selection)												
Total number of text structure categories	—		—		9.8	(1.6)	6.0	(2.4)	—		—	
Writing Tasks												
1. Creative writing production												
Total number of text structure categories	10.6	(4.3)	11.1	(4.8)	11.4	(4.2)	9.1	(4.5)	11.5	(3.7)	7.5	(3.3)

on each specific question type (textually explicit, textually implicit, and scriptally implicit) in the wh- probes.

However, statistical analyses were not possible to test the hypothesis that the experimental and control groups differed on each *specific* text structure category in the written recalls and creative writing productions.[4] In an attempt to show more graphically how the groups performed in relation to the total number possible (the ceiling) in each text structure category in the reading tasks, the data were plotted. While the total possible is presented for the written recalls (reading), no ceiling was postulated for the creative writing productions. By examining Figures 4 and 5, a comparison of profiles of categories is possible on the reading and writing tasks. The data suggests that

1. Neither group approximated the total possible in each individual text structure category in the written recall except in the number of actions (Figure 4).
2. In the written recall following reading, both groups of children included a comparable number of major settings, minor settings, initiating events, internal responses, attempts, and consequences (actions as well as end states), and reactions. No inferred themes, main goals, or final resolutions were provided (Figure 4);
3. The written production profiles of both groups were very similar (Figure 4).
4. The creative writing production differed from the written recall in that both groups explicitly stated the main goals of their protagonists (Figures 4 and 5);
5. The creative writing production differed from the written recall in that there were generally more specific text structure categories of each type (Figures 4 and 5).

The plotted means of specific text structure categories in the written recalls suggest that while the nature of the reading selection constrained children to the recall of information in the two-episode selection, in the independent writing production, their selections were longer, some containing three, four, and even five episodes. The findings in writing regarding major goals support Applebee's (1978) contention that major goals are salient for even very young children.

[4]Because (1) the total number possible in some of the categories was very small in the written recalls and (2) some categories were not included by the children in their written productions, many empty cells existed. Therefore, multivariate (MANOVA) and univariate (ANOVA) analyses of variance were not possible. One assumption underlying ANOVA and MANOVA is a normal distribution of data which, by virtue of story structure itself, cannot be obtained when dealing with comparisons involving one text structure category.

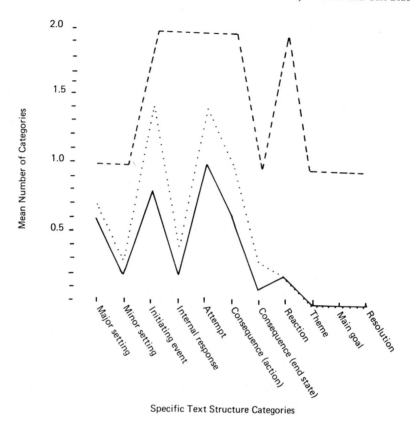

Specific Text Structure Categories

FIGURE 4. Mean number of specific text structure categories recalled by experimental (dotted line) and control (solid line) groups on written recall of unfamiliar reading selection (pretest). Dashed line, total possible.

Immediate Posttests in Reading and Writing

The experimental and control groups were first compared on four posttests administered immediately after intervention.[5] The four posttests consisted of wh- probes, a written recall of a familiar selection, a written recall of an unfamiliar selection, and a creative-writing production.

WH- COMPREHENSION QUESTIONS. Findings were that, as a result of treatment, the experimental and control groups differed significantly on

[5]The total scores obtained on the written recalls, wh- comprehension and creative-writing data immediately after intervention were analyzed using a MANCOVA with group as a factor and intelligence, standardized reading, and corresponding pretests as covariates. A multivariate effect for group was obtained ($F(3, 48) = 4.07$, $p < .004$). Separate ANCOVAS were then computed, with group as a factor, and IQ, standardized reading, and pretests as covariates.

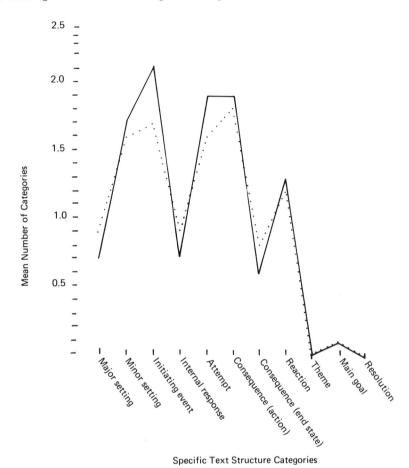

FIGURE 5. Mean number of specific text structure categories produced by experimental (dotted line) and control (solid line) groups on the creative writing production (pretest).

(1) the total number of questions answered correctly, and (2) each specific question type when the total was divided into textually explicit, textually implicit, and scriptally implicit categories (see Table 5).[6]

The results support the hypothesis that the effects of story schema instruction would be observed across several reading tasks. Previous re-

[6]The ANOVA of the total number of questions answered correctly showed that the experimental group significantly outperformed the control group in total overall comprehension ($F(1, 56) = 15.89$, $p < .001$) on the wh- comprehension posttest. Further, separate ANOVAs on each specific question type in the total comprehension score (textually explicit, textually implicit, and scriptally implicit, respectively) revealed significant group effects for treatment: $F(1, 56) = 3.99$, $p < .05$; $F(1, 56) = 12.28$, $p < .001$; $F(1, 56) = 5.21$, $p < .03$).

search (Gordon, 1980) had shown that story schema instruction improved children's comprehension abilities as evidenced by their ability to answer literal and inferential questions on familiar stories (those handled in instructional sessions). However, children's ability to answer literal and inferential questions on unfamiliar stories had not been significantly affected by instruction in story structure.

In the present study, the careful control exercised over the amount of background information (content schemata) children possessed prior to reading, possibly enabled a better tapping of the effect of story structure. In the Gordon (1980) study, no effort was made to equate the groups on prior knowledge. Therefore, the children likely came to the reading and question-answering task with varying amounts of prior knowledge on the topic to be read. The varying levels of prior knowledge may have confounded results in the 1980 study. Several researchers (Anderson, Reynolds, Schallert, & Goetz, 1977; Anderson, Spiro, & Anderson, 1977; Pearson, Hansen, & Gordon, 1979; Pichert & Anderson, 1977) have demonstrated that comprehension recall, generally, and performance on inferential tasks, in particular, are strongly influenced by prior knowledge about the topic addressed in text (content schemata).

In the present study, children in both the experimental and control groups were provided, prior to reading, with a conceptual framework requisite for inferencing. Such a conceptual framework was shown in a pilot study to make groups of children comparable in inferential comprehension scores. Having made the experimental and control group equivalent in content schemata for inferencing, it would appear that the experimental group's stronger performance in ability to answer inferential probes is attributable to the influence of *structural schemata* (knowledge about how texts are typically organized).

Because comprehension is so strongly influenced by the content schemata that readers bring to a text, we need to consider how structural schemata might facilitate inferencing. Knowledge of story structure appears to establish at least the literal comprehension of the story by binding explicitly stated information to the story schema; it provides children with a metatextual plan for comprehension. Because literal comprehension may now be occurring much more readily, we suggest that the reader is better able to shift more attention to (or become more actively involved in) the use of content schemata for processing information. Hence, the increased level of both literal and inferential comprehension may be due to maximal utilization of both content and structure schemata. Knowledge of text structure may, in this manner, facilitate the drawing of implicit relationships while reading. Other than inferring the content of two or three specific text structure categories (i.e., theme, resolution, and, occasionally, major goal) omitted by the author, the treatment group had received no instruction in drawing inferences—neither text-connecting inferences (textually implicit) nor slot-filling inferences (scriptally implicit).

FAMILIAR READING SELECTION. The final instructional story served as the familiar target selection. Children in the control group had previously interacted with the story through a brief-in-class discussion unrelated to story structure. Children in the experimental group had determined the underlying structure (story grammar) as part of their treatment. Significant differences between the experimental and control group were found on the total number of text structure categories recalled following reading[7] (see Table 5).

An examination of Figure 6 suggests that

1. The experimental group recalled more information than the control group in each specific type of text structure category except theme and resolution.
2. In particular, the experimental group performed better on major setting, initiating events, attempts, consequences, and reactions.
3. Internal responses appeared to be least salient for either treatment groups.

Present findings on familiar selections replicate previous results (Gordon, 1980). These findings provide further support for the hypothesis that children who have been trained in story schema awareness will utilize such awareness as a metatextual aid in information retrieval of stories previously read.

UNFAMILIAR READING SELECTION. We found that the experimental group recalled significantly more text structure categories[8] following the reading of an unfamiliar selection than did the control group (see Table 5). Statistical tests were not possible on individual categories. However, the data, plotted into specific text structure categories (see Figure 7), suggested the following:

1. The experimental group recalled more information than the control group in each specific type of text structure category except

[7]Because no pretest was possible on an instructional selection, only reading and IQ scores were used as covariates in the analysis of written recall results of a familiar selection. The ANCOVA revealed significant differences between the experimental and the control group on the total number of text structure categories recalled on an instructional selection ($F(1, 56) = 51.89, p < .001$).

[8]The ANOVA results showed that the experimental group recalled significantly more text structure categories in total than did the control group in the written recall of a new selection ($F(1, 56) = 39.17, p < .001$).

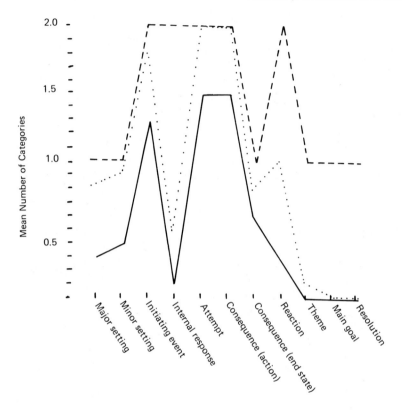

Specific Text Structure Categories

FIGURE 6. Mean number of specific text structure categories recalled by experimental (dotted line) and control (solid line) groups on written recall of familiar reading selection (immediate posttest). Dashed line, total possible.

theme and resolution. The latter two were generally implied, rather than explicitly stated.

2. Following treatment, one category—reactions—appeared to have become particularly salient for the experimental group.

3. A comparison of the experimental group's performance on the pretest (Figure 4) and the posttest (Figure 7) showed that on most of the text categories except two (reactions and main goals), the experimental group's performance is marginally different from pretest to posttest. However, their inclusion of reactions as well as main goals likely contributed to their ability to outperform the control group on the total number of text structure categories.

4. The hypothesis that story structure awareness is a transferable

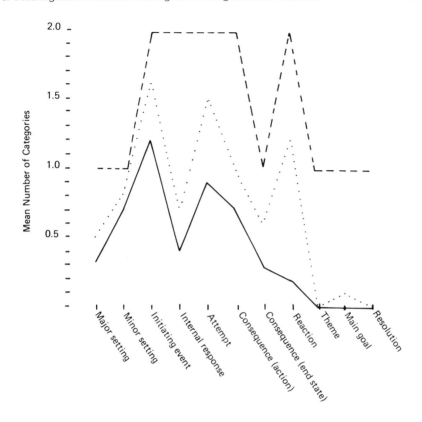

Specific Text Structure Categories

FIGURE 7. Mean number of specific text structure categories recalled by experimental (dotted line) and control (solid line) groups on written recall of unfamiliar reading selection (immediate posttest). Dashed line, total possible.

framework that will facilitate comprehension of a similar organized but unfamiliar narrative has been supported by the results.

The observation that theme (author's message) and resolution were not salient categories following the reading of both familiar and unfamiliar selections suggests that, if not explicitly stated, these categories are not easily inferrable. This finding occurs despite teacher guidance of children in inferring theme and final resolution (as it relates to the major goal) and despite inclusion of these two text structure categories in story diagrams in instructional sessions. Reactions and main goals, on the other hand, were explicitly stated in texts. Hence, they were recalled much more easily on the posttests. We are unable to say, however, whether reactions would be more readily inferred than themes and resolutions.

Present findings also replicate previous findings by Gordon (1980) related to theme. In the 1980 research, recalls of even familiar selections, included no themes (major goal or intended message of author). The two findings (1980 and the present study) differ from that of Stein and Glenn (1979), who suggested that the major goal of a character was likely critical in story recall because children in their study often added the primary goal of the protagonist even though it was not explicitly stated in texts. The difference between our findings and Stein and Glenn's (1979) findings may be due to the more complex nature of selections used in our study.

CREATIVE WRITING. The story schema group included more text structure categories in total than did the control group on the creative writing posttest.[9] An examination of Table 5 shows that the experimental group's productions were longer. That is, they included semantic content that on the average consisted of 9.8 text structure categories, whereas the control group wrote information that averaged 9.1 text structure categories.

Figure 8 displays the differences in the mean number of specific text structure categories produced in the independent writing production, although statistical analyses could not be conducted on individual categories.

The plotted data suggests that

1. The experimental group produced more information classified as minor setting, initiating events, internal responses, attempts, consequences (final action as opposed to the end state), and final resolutions.
2. The control group continued to demonstrate a greater emphasis on describing the major setting. (It had been observed on the pretests that both groups provided lengthy setting descriptions.)

A comparison of Figure 7 and Figure 8 shows that for the control group, reactions were more frequently included in creative writing productions than they were in the written recall of reading selections. For the experimental group, final resolutions were more salient in the writing process (Figure 8), than in the recall of information read (Figure 7). This observation is discussed further later in this chapter.

The data for creative writing support the notion that knowledge of

---

[9]The story schema group significantly outperformed the control group on the total number of text structure categories produced in the creative writing posttest ($F(1, 56) = 4.18, p < .05$).

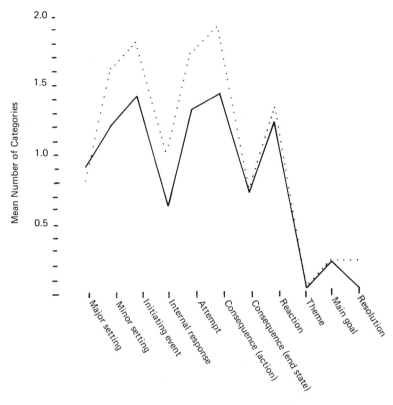

FIGURE 8. Mean number of specific text structure categories produced by experimental (dotted line) and control (solid line) groups on the creative writing production (immediate posttest).

story schema serves as a scaffolding for independently generating information under specific text structure categories. Regarding between-group differences in writing, the experimental group did not appear to generate more information than the control group in the categories of consequence (end state), reaction, theme, and main goal.

Delayed Posttests in Reading and Writing

The experimental and control groups were also compared on reading and writing tasks administered 2 months after intervention. Delayed posttest results in written recall of an unfamiliar selection and a creative writing production were analyzed using separate ANCOVAs. In the analysis, covariates (IQ, standardized reading, and immediate posttest score) were entered after the factor main effect (group).[10]

UNFAMILIAR READING SELECTION. Table 5 shows that over time the experimental group outperformed the control group in total number of text structure categories recalled.[11]

Figure 9 suggests that the superiority maintained by the experimental group was likely due to inclusion of information in the text structure categories of minor setting, initiating event, attempt, consequence (action), and major goal.

Following a 2-month time lapse, the results support the hypothesis that knowledge of story schema serves as a long-term metacognitive guide for regeneration of narratives read. Because comprehension is a long-term process, rather than transitory, training in story schema awareness seems to provide readers with a durable organizational framework within which to encode and integrate new input, and a cue system for the retrieval of story information (Stein & Glenn, 1979).

CREATIVE WRITING. We found that, even after 2 months had elapsed since treatment, the experimental group generated, in total, more text structure categories than did the control group on an independent writing task[12] (see Table 5).

The data are graphed in Figure 10. Particular strengths of the story schema group continued to be, as in the written recalls, the inclusion of more minor settings, initiating events, attempts, consequences (actions), reactions, and major goals. The data suggest that the experimental group continued to utilize story schema as a scaffolding to generate propositions. Over time, story schema maintained its effect as a metatextual aid to the writing process.

Inferred Information in Written Recalls

An observation during the scoring of the written recalls (familiar and unfamiliar selections) led to post hoc comparisons of the experimental and

[10]Regression analyses had shown that the immediate posttest, and not the pretest, was a significant covariate. Therefore, in the ANOVAs, when the effect of the immediate posttest was removed, group differences could be measured in the delayed test data.

[11]The univariate analysis of covariance revealed that the experimental group significantly outperformed the control group in total number of text structure categories produced in the written recall ($F(1, 56) = 4.17, p < .05$).

[12]An ANCOVA revealed that the story schema group outperformed the control group in total number of text structure categories generated in the independent writing task ($F(1, 56) = 19.59, p < .001$).

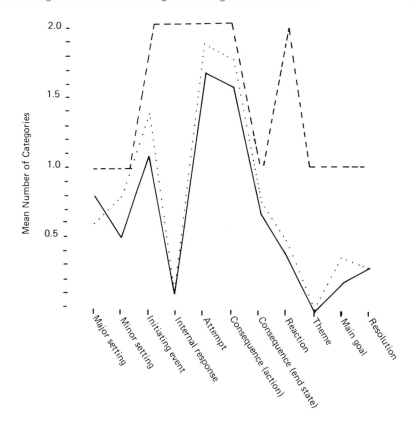

Specific Text Structure Categories

FIGURE 9. Mean number of specific text structure categories recalled by the experimental (dotted line) and control (solid line) groups on written recall of unfamiliar reading selection (delayed test). Dashed line, total possible.

control groups on inferencing ability. It was observed that many of the written protocols included script-based inferences (Pearson & Johnson, 1978). Ideas that were not explicitly stated in text but that were an elaboration of text based on general world knowledge about objects, actions, and events were specified in the recalls. Therefore, the written recalls of both experimental and control groups were rescored according to the number of correct scriptally implicit inferences made. An optimal value of (1) was assigned to each proposition that showed an integration of text and prior knowledge. For example, one of the selections concerned a

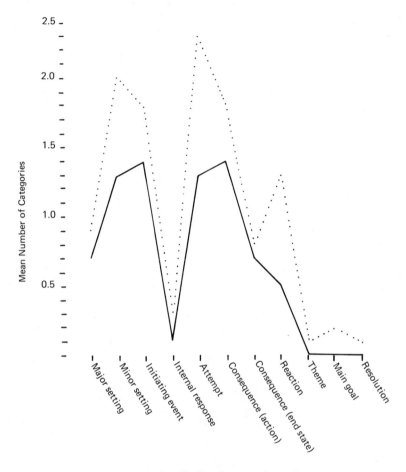

Specific Text Structure Categories

FIGURE 10. Mean number of specific text structure categories produced by experimental (dotted line) and control (solid line) groups on the creative writing production (delayed test).

hunter and hunting dogs. The relevant portion of the selection read as follows:

Suddenly, in the distance, a hunter and his dog were approaching.

A child's recall of the same section consisted of the following statement:

A hunter and his dogs were coming this way. The baying and howling of dogs could be heard in the distance.

A score of (1) would have been assigned to this inference. For inferred items, the average agreement across 10% of the randomly selected selections was .91.

Although the experimental and control group did not differ on script-based inferences made on the unfamiliar selection prior to treatment, they did differ following intervention.[13] However, the differences were negligible over time. Table 6 shows the group means on the various tests. Our findings suggest that story schema awareness may enable children to recall explicit information with ease sufficient to enable them to engage in inferential discourse processing operations. The findings on the probed recall in this research (described later in this Section) also provided support for text structure as a metatextual aid in abstractive processing (selecting important ideas explicit in text and summarizing them) as well as con-

Table 6

Means and Standard Deviations for All Script-Based Inferences

	Treatment groups			
	Experimental		Control	
Inferencing ability	X̄	(SD)	X̄	(SD)
1. Pretest (Unfamiliar selection) Total number of inferences	.88	(.84)	.61	(.83)
2. Posttest (Familiar selection) Total number of inferences	.76	(.78)	.35	(.64)
3. Immediate posttest (Unfamiliar selection) Total number of inferences	.97	(.97)	.17	(.38)
4. Delayed posttest (Unfamiliar selection) Total number of inferences	.53	(.75)	.39	(.66)

[13]ANCOVAs (with standardized reading and IQ scores serving as covariates) were used to compare the experimental and control group on script-based inferences. Main effects for factors were assessed after adjusting for the covariates.

The results revealed that while the two groups were comparable in inferencing ability on the pretest ($F(1, 56) = .61$, $p < .44$), differences were observed on the posttest (after reading familiar and unfamiliar materials) immediately following intervention ($F[1, 56] = 4.22$, $p < .05$, and $F[1, 56] = 14.47$, $p < .001$ respectively). On these posttests the experimental group exceeded control. However, on the delayed posttest (unfamiliar material) there was no evidence that the experimental group maintained its superiority ($F(1, 56) = 0.53$, $p < .47$).

structive processing (using information from the story in association with prior knowledge to construct a meaningful interpretation). Previous research (Brown, Smiley, Day, Townsend, & Lawton, 1977; Tierney, Bridge, & Cera, 1978–1979), however, had shown that while children render inferences during probed recall, they do so much less frequently in free recall situations. Using story schema as a scaffolding for recall appears to account for the greater number of inferences made by the experimental group on the written recall task in this study.

Two possible explanations exist for the lack of differences between the two groups after a time delay. First, an examination of all four test selections suggests that the final one conjures up the barest, or the simplest script. Hence children may have had less interesting background knowledge in their conceptual bases than they had for the other three selections. Secondly, over time, the potency of the story schema itself may have faded to some extent. While it was still a valuable metatextual framework for literal comprehension, less attention could be directed to constructive processing. Unfortunately, no probed-recall delayed posttest was administered. The results might have shed some light on the anomaly.

We now need to examine the findings related to inferencing on the wh- comprehension questions and the written recalls. It is somewhat surprising that children's ability to make text-based and script-based inferences improved following experimental treatment, yet their ability to infer often-omitted categories such as theme or resolution did not. We might have expected the reverse because the focus of instruction was story grammars. Consequently we would agree with Singer and Donlan (1982) that categories like theme may be more dependent on prior knowledge and reasoning resources than on knowledge of story structure. All the themes in our stories were not familiar to students.

While theme (author's message—e.g., "What does the author want to teach us by writing this story?) may not be a compelling aspect of story comprehension (Adams and Collins, 1977), resolution is central in the process of reaching a goal. An examination of the children's recalls suggests that chidren viewed the consequence and reaction in the final episode as the resolution in the story. Without teacher direction (and possibly probes), children did not tie the consequence and reaction back to the goal. For example, having stated that "The owl becomes angry and flies away" children did not explicitly state that "The owl failed to win the love of the ptarmigan" (winning the Ptarmigan was the Owl's main goal).

Experimental Group: Pretest and Posttest Comparisons

Because comparable selections in reading and similar story starters in writing were used as pre- and posttest measures, a post hoc comparison was made to determine growth within the experimental group (story schema group) following the intervention period and following a period of delay.[14] In these analyses, group was not a factor (as the analyses were within the experimental group only).

UNFAMILIAR WRITTEN RECALL. Following the reading of an unfamiliar selection, the children were asked to write a summary of the story. A comparison of the experimental (story schema) group's performance in pre- and posttest can be made by examining Table 5. In total number of text structure categories recalled, significant growth from pretest $(\overline{X} = 5.7)$ to immediate posttest $(\overline{X} = 8.1)$ is shown. From immediate posttest $(\overline{X} = 8.1)$ to delayed posttest $(\overline{X} = 8.6)$ 2 months later, there was no significant deterioration.[15] This finding suggests that instruction in story schema was instrumental in improving children's written recall of unfamiliar stories read. Further, children maintained the use of story schema over time.

In an effort to further examine the growth in specific text structure categories, the data are depicted graphically in Figure 11. From the data, it becomes apparent that, while children initially (in the pretest) focused more on major setting, immediately following instruction there is evidence of growth in recall of information categorized under minor setting, attempt, consequence (both action and end state), reaction, and major goal. Further, delayed test data suggest there is stability in use of text structure as a metacognitive framework.

CREATIVE WRITING PRODUCTION. The experimental group did not lengthen their protocols in total number of categories produced as a result of instruction in story schema.[16] An examination of Table 5 shows $\overline{X}$'s of 10.1, 11.4, and 11.5, respectively, in total number of text structure categories on the pretest, immediate posttest, and delayed posttest. The data were, however, graphically depicted (see Figure 12) to determine if a change in pattern of categories exists within each total score.

---

[14]ANOVAs and t tests were computed when comparing pre- and posttest performance within the experimental group.

[15]An ANOVA of pretest and immediate posttest (unfamiliar written recall) scores within the experimental group revealed a significant growth in the number of text structure categories recalled following the reading of an unfamiliar selection ($F(1, 56) = 20.53, p < .001$), but no significant growth from immediate posttest to delayed posttest ($t(33) = -1.40, p < .17$).

[16]No significant change on the creative writing task was revealed by the univariate analyses and t tests on the total number of text structure categories from pretest to the immediate posttest ($F(1, 66) = 0.55, p < .46$) and then from immediate posttest to the delayed posttest ($t(33) = 0.17, p < .87$).

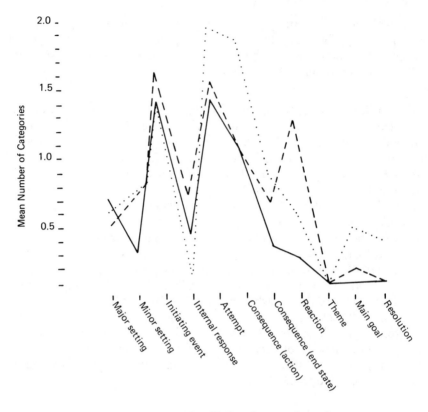

Specific Text Structure Categories

FIGURE 11. Mean number of specific text structure categories produced by the experimental group on written recall of unfamiliar reading selections. Solid line, pretest; dashed line, immediate posttest; dotted line, delayed posttest.

The figure suggests that (despite no significant growth in total number of categories generated)

1. Children increased their awareness of minor settings, attempts, main goals and resolutions as a result of story schema instruction
2. Internal responses and theme appear, in the writing process, to be the least salient of all the text structure categories over time.

Experimental Group: Differences on Reading and Writing Tasks

Once the superiority of the experimental group over the control group had been established, a post hoc analysis was made of the differences in performance on the reading tasks of written recall and the creative writing

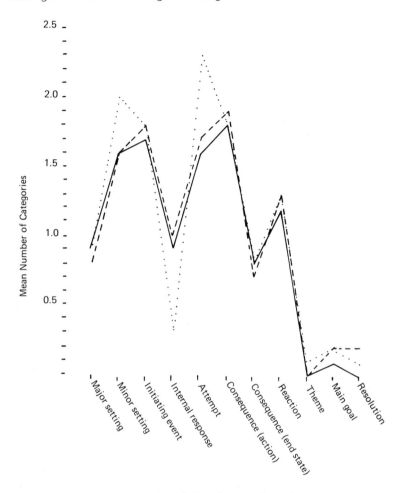

Specific Text Structure Categories

FIGURE 12. Mean number of specific text structure categories produced by the experimental group on the creative writing productions. Solid line, pretest; dashed line, immediate posttest; dotted line, delayed posttest.

productions within the group.[17] The purpose was to determine both the relationship between reading and writing and the nature of the relationship as it applies to story schema awareness. Does story schema transcend modes of processing? How do the children utilize the text structure framework in reading versus writing? What are the differences in utilization?

[17]ANOVAs were computed to compare the performance of the experimental group on reading and writing tasks.

IMMEDIATE POSTTEST (READING VERSUS WRITING). The total number of text structure categories produced by the experimental group in the creative writing task exceeded the total number produced after reading familiar and unfamiliar materials.[18] Table 5 reveals a $\overline{X}$ of 11.4 text structure categories on the immediate posttest in creative writing in comparison to 9.8 and 8.1, respectively, on the familiar and unfamiliar materials read. (Note that recalls of familiar stories were longer than unfamiliar stories.[19] More major settings, initiating events and attempts were recalled on familiar materials, as per Figure 12).

An examination of Figure 13 suggests that children included more statements of minor setting, initiating events, internal responses, main goals and resolutions in their independent writing productions than in written recalls following familiar or unfamiliar reading selections. However, the story schema profiles for reading and writing are quite similar. This observation suggests that knowledge of story schema transcends modes of processing (reading and writing) in a similar fashion. It appears, in fact, that internal responses, consequences (end states), themes, main goals, and resolutions are not included as frequently in reading or writing, while information classed as major and minor setting, initiating events, attempt, consequence (action), and reactions are included in recall following reading, and in independent writing productions.

If one were to examine the slight differences between the reading and the writing profiles, one would find that more initiating events and internal responses are evident in children's independent productions. One reason for the greater number of initiating events and internal responses may be that there was no ceiling in the independent writing. That is, while the reading recall was limited to the two-episode story read, stories produced by children in the creative-writing task were generally longer, containing up to five episodes. Another difference noted was that children, in independent writing, appear, more frequently, to provide a main goal for their protagonist and then to bring the story to a resolution in relation to the main goal. The inclusion of a main goal had also been noted in the creative writing pretests. Any reasons we might put forth for why this same phenomenon was not observed following reading tasks would be purely speculative.

[18]ANOVAs on the immediate posttests showed that the total number of text structure categories produced in the creative writing production exceeded (1) the total number written following the reading of familiar materials ($F(1, 66) = 4.39, p < .05$), and (2) the total following the reading of unfamiliar materials ($F(1, 66) = 16.71, p < .001$).

[19]An ANOVA showed that performance of the experimental group on familiar stories ($\overline{X} = 9.8$) significantly exceeded performance on unfamiliar stories ($\overline{X} = 8.1$) [$F(1, 66) = 14.66, p < .001$].

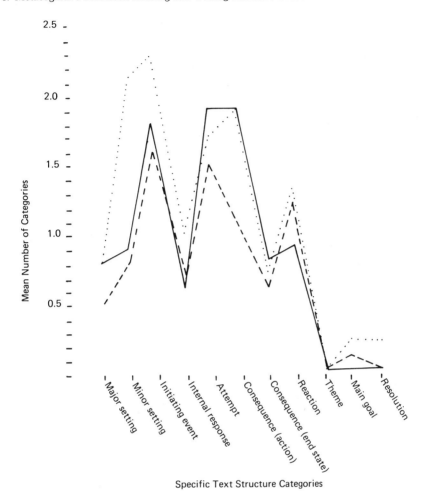

FIGURE 13. Mean number of specific text structure categories produced by experimental group on immediate posttests. Solid line, familiar selection; dashed line, unfamiliar selection; dotted line, creative writing.

DELAYED POSTTESTS (READING VERSUS WRITING). A comparison of unfamiliar reading and writing performance on the posttests shows, again, a larger number of total text structure categories produced on the writing task.[20]

[20]An ANOVA of the delayed posttest in reading and writing showed that the total number of text structure categories on the writing task exceeded the total on the unfamiliar reading task ($F(1, 66) = 13.34, p < .001$).

Graphically depicted in Figure 14, the data suggest that the story-schema profiles for reading and writing continue to be similar with two exceptions. First, reactions and minor settings are more salient in writing. Second, main goals and resolutions are less salient in writing.

One possible explanation for the greater differential in story schema profiles on the delayed reading and writing tasks may be the effect of time on specific categories in recall tasks (reading) versus production tasks (writing).

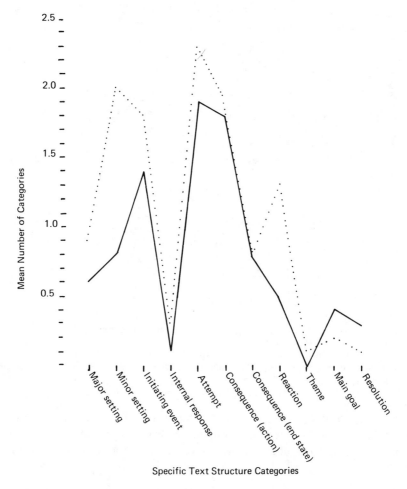

FIGURE 14. Mean number of specific text structure categories produced by experimental group on delayed posttests. Solid line, unfamiliar selection; dotted line, creative writing.

Summary of Major Findings within the Experimental Group

1. Instruction on story schema significantly improved the experimental children's written recalls, and strategy use in reading was maintained over time.
2. While experimental children did not lengthen their creative productions following instruction (not even after a time delay), the pattern of categories changed to suggest a greater awareness of minor settings, attempts, themes, main goals and resolutions.
3. The profiles of specific text structure categories in reading and writing are similar and suggest that knowledge of story schema transcends modes of processing. However, more frequently in independent writing than in story recall, children explicitly state the main goal and the resolution in their stories.

Experimental Group: Descriptive Analysis of Reading and Writing Tasks

In this section, children's written summaries and creative writing productions pre- and post intervention are examined through a holistic (global impression) approach. For the sake of brevity, samples of summaries and creative productions collected after a time delay are not examined here because they were found to be comparable to those immediately following intervention. The holistic evaluation supports and reinforces the results obtained statistically. In the following pages, the changes are traced in one child's (Stephen) summaries. These changes occurred from the pretest to specific posttests administered at various intervals through the research. In addition, there is a description of the changes in the creative writing productions of another child (Nancy). While no formal scheme was employed to evaluate the productions, Cramer's (1982) work provided useful insights in the evaluations.

SAMPLE OF PRETEST SUMMARY OF UNFAMILIAR READING SELECTION. A study of the written-recall sample in Figure 15 reveals several differences from the original selection in Figure 16, in both composing skills and mechanical skills.

First of all, Stephen's recall reflects no sense of story. He provides no overall context or setting for the story and no clear beginning, middle, or ending. The sentences have some meaning individually, but collectively do not reveal the plot of the story. In fact, Stephen has not grasped the main story idea—that in an attempt to win Aquilgieq's love, Okpik killed her husband. Further, Stephen does not bring the story to a satisfactory

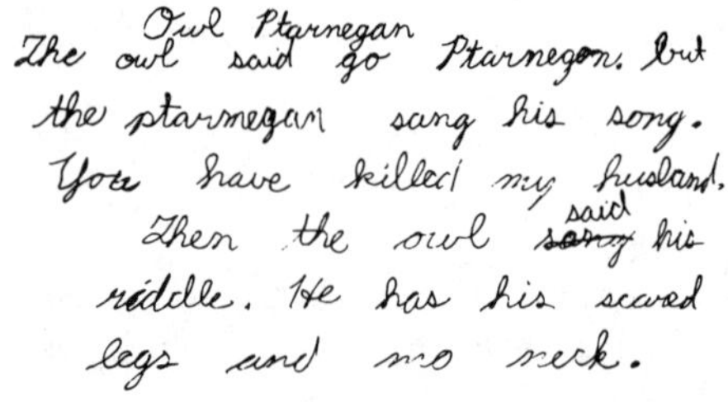

The Owl Ptarmegan
The owl said go Ptarmegon, but
the ptarmegan sang his song.
You have killed my husband.
Then the owl said his
riddle. He has his scared
legs and mo neck.

FIGURE 15. "The Owl and the Ptarmigan" by Stephen.

Okpik, the big owl of the Arctic desert, was in love with Aqilgieq, the little white ptarmigan. However, Aqilgieq already had a husband whom she loved very much.

One evening, Aqilgieq and her husband were doing a ceremonial dance. In a sudden fit of jealousy, Okpik killed his rival and began to woo Aqilgieq in earnest. But the little ptarmigan only cried and cried for her dead husband. Okpik felt disheartened.

Aqilgieq did not love her new suitor and began to sing a song of ridicule.

> Okpik, go away!
> With your big head
> And your two large eyes
> And your sorry-looking legs—
> You are ugly!
> Who would want you for a husband?
> Who would want for a husband
> A being like you?
> With big knitted eyebrows,
> and with lashes that long,
> You big dumpy owl,
> With no feet and no neck!

Okpik became angry and decided to shame Aqilgieq in return so he sang in ridicule and jealousy:

> Eater of owls! Bah!
> I shall leave you.

So saying he flew away. From that time on, the Eskimos enjoy listening to such songs of insult and ridicule.

FIGURE 16. "The Owl and the Ptarmigan"*

*Copyright (c) *Tales from the Igloo*, edited and translated by Father Maurice Metayer. Adapted with permission of Hurtig Publishers.

resolution. Readers of Stephen's story, for example, cannot relate Stephen's "Then the owl sang his riddle" to the series of songs of ridicule that occurred until Okpik flew away, unsuccessful in the courtship. Therefore, in Stephen's recall, most of the important ideas are excluded from the recall but some unimportant details (e.g., "He has his scared legs and mo neck.") are mentioned.

It is interesting to note that Stephen gave little attention to mechanics. There appears to be some attempt at paragraphing, but spelling, capitalization and punctuation errors are evident. Attention to handwriting and neatness is lacking.

SAMPLE OF FIRST POSTTEST SUMMARY OF FAMILIAR READING SELECTION. The first posttest was administered following the intervention period that emphasized using story schema as a scaffolding for the improvement of reading comprehension. The material read was considered familiar because the children had read the story and had categorized story information under each text structure category that occurred in the selection. Then the children were asked to write a summary of the story. The selection that was read, parsed, and summarized is shown in Figure 17.

Figure 18 displays Stephen's written recall following the reading of "The Sea Goddess." Several improvements are noted from Stephen's performance on the pretest. Comprehension has certainly improved because not only is more information recalled, but also it is recalled in comprehensible thought units from beginning to end. Stephen is utilizing the story schema as a framework to present many more of the important ideas explicitly stated in the original text. First, the settings (both major and minor) are depicted. With the exception of internal responses, each of the two episodes in the story contains an initiating event, an attempt, and a consequence. The first episode even contains a reaction. A final outcome

---

Once there were two giants. They existed, living as Eskimos do, by hunting. They had a child, a girl who grew rapidly and always showed a terrifying inclination to seize on flesh and eat it whenever she could find it.

One night, she felt abnormally hungry even for a giant's child. But she knew there was no meat available. She started to eat the limbs of her parents as they slept. They awoke in horror, seized the frightening child and took her in a boat far out into the deeper parts of the sea.

When they threw her overboard, she wanted to save herself by holding on to the sides of the boat. In a panic, the giants cut off her fingers and as the fingers fell into the water, they turned into whales, seals, and shoals of fish.

The demon girl, living under the sea became Sedna, the great mother of all the sea creatures. She now causes the storms on the sea and governs the migration of her myriads of children—the whales, and walruses, the seals, and fish of all kinds. Now the Eskimos believe Sedna, the powerful spirit, was always there and could always be approached by the shaman [priest]. He visits her so she would be favorably inclined towards his people and give them sea creatures for food at the time of the next hunt.

FIGURE 17. "The Sea Goddess."*

*Copyright (c) 1974 Charles Hofmann, From *Drum Dance* by Charles Hofmann. Adapted with permission of Gage Publishing Ltd.

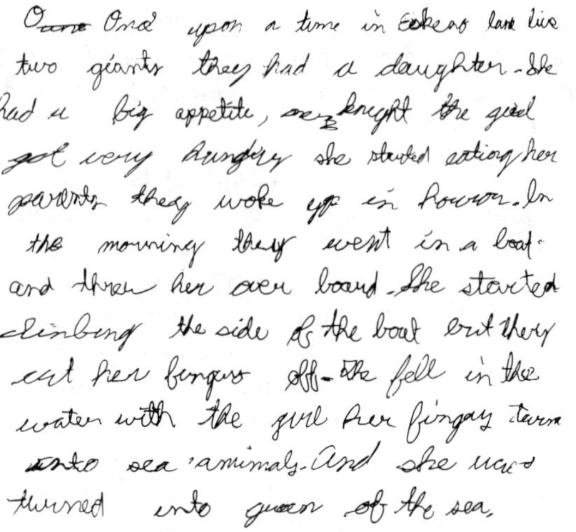
~~Oance~~ Once upon a time in Eskemo land live
two giants they had a daughter. She
had a big appetite, one knight the girl
got very hungry she started eating her
parents they woke up in horror. In
the morning they went in a boat.
and threw her over board. She started
climbing the side of the boat but they
cut her fingers off. She fell in the
water with the girl her fingers turn
into sea animals. And she was
turned into queen of the sea.

FIGURE 18. "The Sea Goddess" by Stephen.

is given. The recall appears well-organized and ideas flow smoothly from one to the next in sequential progression. Vocabulary is more precise than it was on the pretest. For example, Stephen uses such words as "Eskimoland," "horror," and "overboard." Sentence structure is also more varied than it was on the pretest. Note the number of elaborated sentences such as, "She started climbing the side of the boat but they cut her fingers off" in comparison to the simple sentences on the pretest.

While there are distinct thought units in the recall, they are not marked with capitalization and punctuation. Spelling errors are present but handwriting is somewhat improved. At this point it seems apparent that overall comprehension and composition skills have improved to a greater extent than have the mechanics of writing.

SAMPLE OF SECOND POSTTEST SUMMARY OF UNFAMILIAR READING SELECTION. During the writing phase of intervention, emphasis was placed on transferring story schema as a framework from reading to the writing process. No emphasis was placed on teaching the mechanics of writing. Teacher modeling of these skills, however, was inherent in the lessons themselves. Following the writing phase of intervention, another posttest was administered. This time, children were asked to read an unfamiliar selection (not previously read or parsed in class). Following the reading of the story shown in Figure 19, children were asked to "write a summary of the story." Figure 20 shows Stephen's recall of the story.

At the outset, it is evident that story schema instruction has been as instrumental in Stephen's case in improving comprehension of an unfa-

Señor Rooster was a fine bird. He was smart, too, and he liked to take walks beyond the village to see the world. He usually wandered deep into the forest and then flew up into a tall tree to look at the whole world from there.

One day, Señor Fox came walking through the woods. As he passed under the tree on which the rooster was perched, he thought what a fine dinner the fat rooster would make.

"My dear, dear friend, Señor Rooster," cried Señor Fox. "Have you heard the news? Do you know about the new decree now in force in our forest? No animal can eat another; all are to be friends. That's the new law. Anyone who breaks it will be punished severely. I'll be surprised if you haven't heard about it. Everyone knows it."

"Oh, really!" said Señor Rooster. "That is interesting." But still he did not come down. Instead he looked around in all directions.

Suddenly, in the distance, a hunter and his dogs were approaching. This gave Señor Rooster an idea.

"Some fine hunting dogs are running this way, and a man with a gun is behind them," he said to the fox. "They're coming from over that way," he said as he pointed with his wing in exactly the opposite direction from which he saw them

Hearing that, the fox ran off as fast as his legs would carry him.

"Señor Fox, Señor Fox!" called Señor Rooster. "Don't run away! Don't go! You can tell the dogs and the hunter about the new decree among the animals in the forest."

Señor Fox ran into the hunter and his dogs, and Señor Rooster sat in the tree.

FIGURE 19. "The Fox, the Rooster and the Dogs."*

*Version written for story schema study.

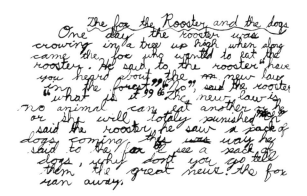

FIGURE 20. "The Fox, the Rooster and the Dogs" by Stephen.

miliar selection as it was in improving the comprehension of a familiar selection. There is a clearly identifiable beginning, middle, and end. The problem is presented and the story is expanded with appropriate conversation and description. The plot is well-developed and an effective ending is provided. Internal responses and reactions are included along with other episode components. Not only are the majority of most important ideas presented, but they are presented in a variety of sentence constructions.

Note the complexity of the first sentence, "One day, the rooster was crowing in a tree up high when along came the fox who wanted to eat the rooster."

The mechanics of writing have improved from the first posttest. Handwriting and spelling are better. An attempt has been made by Stephen to use punctuation such as quotation marks.

CREATIVE WRITING SAMPLES. Following provision of a story starter, children were asked to write a story of their own in the pretest. The story setting provided was, "Once there lived a brave, young knight called . . . ." A sample of one child's (Nancy) writing is shown in Figure 21. One of the first things noticed about Nancy's production was the long description of setting. This finding proved to be typical in the children's writings collected as a pretest. Nancy devoted, as did many others, 7½ lines to a description of time, place, character, and state. The remainder of Nancy's story consists of an initiating event, an internal response, a reaction, and an outcome. After the description of setting, the story line itself is quite brief.

Figure 22 displays Nancy's production following instruction in awareness and use of story schema. The story starter was "Long ago, there lived a wicked old witch called . . . ." A briefer major setting has been produced but a minor setting is given for each episode. The story is longer than the pretest production, as it consists of two episodes. Most striking perhaps is the obvious organization approximating story schema within each episode—in each case, there is an initiating event, an internal response, an action, an outcome. A reaction appears in the second episode.

The examination of the samples obtained from the children in the study supports our statistical findings. Story schema awareness not only enhanced reading comprehension skills but also enhanced the develop-

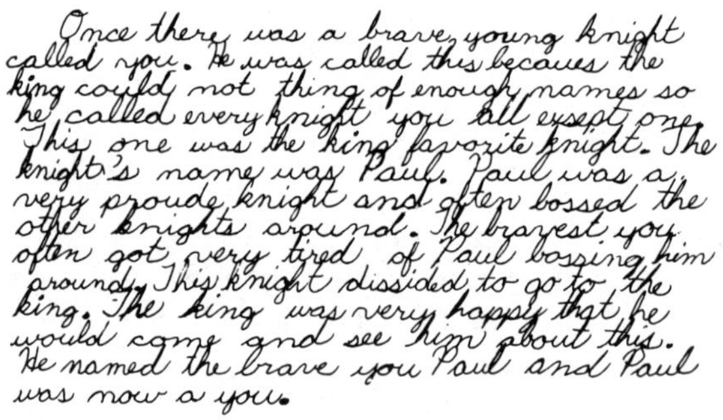
Once there was a brave, young knight called you. He was called this becaues the king could not thing of enough names so he called every knight you all exsept one. This one was the king favorite knight. The knight's name was Paul. Paul was a very proude knight and often bossed the other knights around. The bravest you often got very tired of Paul bossing him around. This knight dissided to go to the king. The king was very happy that he would come and see him about this. He named the brave you Paul and Paul was now a you.

FIGURE 21. Nancy's "Knight" story (pretest).

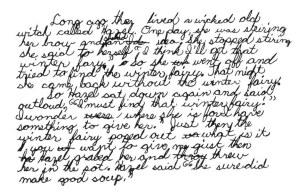

FIGURE 22. Nancy's "Witch" story (posttest).

ment of writing skills. Further, writing activities, which comprised the bulk of activities in the final phase of instruction, continued to maintain and/ or enhance the reading comprehension skills. The results of this study appear to reinforce the notion that an integrated approach to reading and writing instruction has merit (Collins, 1979). A particular linking technique may be the knowledge and use of story structure as a metacognitive strategy in both the reading and the writing process.

Conclusions

Baker and Brown (1980) state that metacognition (i.e., the emergence of self-awareness and self-regulation) is fundamental to effective reading. Further, they write that effective reading can be attained through two major avenues: application of rules and strategies, and development of a sound knowledge base on the topics to be read. These avenues themselves are interdependent, in that knowledge of strategies and requisite knowledge of the world interact in complex ways.

The present research provides support for the postulates presented by Baker and Brown (1980). The research found that sensitizing children to story grammars by explicitly specifying story elements and then having children use the grammars as a composing framework provided children with metacognitive control over comprehension (and writing). The interaction of strategy (story-schema awareness and use) and background knowledge was clearly evidenced on the wh- comprehension task and in the post hoc analysis of script-based inferences made spontaneously. In one respect, the structure of text was found to be independent of text content, but at the same time, the study showed that while story schema provided a framework for understanding the content explicitly presented in text, it also served as an aid in the construction of implicit relationships wherein prior knowledge is a key factor. Earlier work by Gordon (1980) (discussed earlier in this chapter) had provided little support for teaching text structure as a metatextual aid to literal and inferential comprehension of specific story aspects (as determined by wh- probes). The level of content schemata that children brought to the story reading and question answering in the Gordon (1980) study, however, had not been controlled. Varying levels of prior knowledge in the subjects may have confounded the effects of story grammars in explicit and implicit comprehension. The results of the present study, in which very careful control was exercised over content schemata on the wh- probes tests, provide strong evidence that knowledge and use of text structure facilitates not only literal comprehension, but also inferential comprehension. Experimental-group children not only correctly answered more textually implicit and scriptally implicit questions tied to specific text structure categories but also made more spontaneous inferences on their written recalls.

With respect to the second important avenue to effective reading (a sound knowledge base), text structure as a metatextual aid apparently improved children's accessibility to content schemata (prior knowledge). Prior to the reading and answering of the wh- probes, both control and experimental groups had been provided with requisite background knowledge (through development of new schemata) on the topic for inferencing. Yet only the experimental group (story-schema group) accessed the content schema adequately. No background knowledge had been developed prior to the written recalls on which spontaneous script or schemata-based inferences were made. Yet, the story-schema group made more script-based inferences than the control group. Story schemata apparently enabled the experimental group to more easily fit what they were reading into a framework of whatever background knowledge they already had, a strategy previously observed by Anderson (1977) and Brown et al. (1977). The present data appear to support the theoretical assumptions that equipping children with awareness of and control over metacognitive strategies in reading enhances both constructive and abstractive processing of narrative discourse.

Children in the Gordon (1980) study were not given transfer tasks. The generalizability of story-grammar instruction, therefore, could not be adequately addressed. However, the results of the present study suggest that when an instructional method is designed to deliberately enhance and facilitate transfer, children apparently apply their knowledge of the story schema strategy to comprehension of new and unfamiliar, and even less well-organized selections. Teacher guidance and student practice on a variety of materials demonstrated that story schema appears to be a transferable framework that can be used for a variety of comprehension tasks on a variety of materials. Further, story schema transfers as an ideational framework from reading to writing. As stated earlier, professional opinion has for some time held that reading is only one aspect of language and must be viewed within the framework of total language experience. Experimental evidence (Stotsky, 1975; Zeman, 1969) suggests that reading and writing are, in fact, highly related, as both involve similar language processes. The present study reaffirms this strong relationship between reading and writing.

In our study, metacognitive knowledge and use of story grammars appears to have transferred into planning of children's compositions. In other words, the use of structural elements appeared to regulate their thought processes. The question remains: Is this awareness and use conscious or unconscious? Bereiter and Scardamalia (1982) argue that their experimental-training-group children were making some conscious decisions to use structural elements (in opinion essays). They were not prepared to argue that a few training sessions are sufficient for new structural elements to be assimilated into "an unconscious language production system" (p. 33). While one might use the same argument as Bereiter and Scardamalia (1982), it is still speculative. According to Bereiter and his colleagues, children's knowledge of discourse elements varies with different genres. They state that while there is accumulated evidence (Stein & Trabasso, 1982) that children have a well-developed schema of what constitutes a story from frequent exposures to narratives (TV, reading, conversation, etc.), in the genre of argument and opinion essays, children have some knowledge of structural elements, but this knowledge does not correspond well with a mature schema. If we acknowledge that children in our study already had a relatively strong narrative schema, and we maintain that through our intervention we succeeded in developing that schema even further, the question remains: Was the use of story schema automatic or conscious?

In an attempt to at least obtain a partial answer to the question we asked our experimental group children to write down, following posttesting, what they had learned from their lessons. Several examples follow:

Example 1: "I've learned that a story has many parts and now I know them all. I also learned that if you follow these parts you can write a good story."

Example 2: "The thing that I've learned about story structure is that there are important parts to a story. Like major setting, theme, plot, and resolution. The plot usually has episodes. Episodes are then broken into about five parts. The only thing I knew about stories before was that there were paragraphs."

The preceding protocols appear to substantiate both our statistical findings and our holistic analyses of recalls and creative productions that children were aware of structural elements, whereas they had not been prior to intervention. Further, they were using this knowledge consciously to structure their recalls following reading and their compositions in independent writing. It would appear that children likely planned and organized their story content on the basis of the narrative schema. While the evidence regarding use of story grammars in planning is strong, it is not necessarily conclusive. Research investigating the use of story grammar as part of children's internal dialogue in writing (Edmonson, 1983) is continuing. Further, research is being conducted on the effect of story grammar instruction (using a writing model) on reading comprehension and the quality of writing (Braun & Gordon, 1984). Metacognitive probes accompany each of the reading and writing tasks in the Braun and Gordon research. It is hoped that this research will shed more light on the metacognitive nature of story grammars.

Implications for Educational Practice

Based on our research with story grammars in reading and writing, we suggest that instruction should focus on making children aware of the active nature of the meaning-making process. Fostering metacognitive activities is one method of stimulating active involvement in these processes. Awareness of structure inherent in narratives and the importance of consciously using knowledge of structure as an aid in reading comprehension and composition appears to be a type of metacognitive endeavor. While it is necessary to make story grammar rules explicit, it is also necessary to show children how such rules can be applied regularly, to encourage them to apply the rules, and to demonstrate how application of these rules improves their performance. In this respect, a covert process has potential for becoming overt. Active involvement with text can also occur through student-generated questions (Singer, 1978). Questions, especially self-posed questions, prior to reading and writing can be important monitoring strategies. Children can be taught to set their own purposes for reading and writing and then, on the basis of these questions, monitor their progress in comprehension and composition.

Through a variety of techniques in active comprehension, instruction in the Gordon and Braun (1982) research aimed at facilitating transfer of knowledge of story schema to the comprehension of unfamiliar selections and to generation of story content in creative writing compositions. Based on the teaching method used in our research study, instruction would include the following components:

1. Begin with an ideal story (see Appendix for story written to meet ideal criteria) in terms of the story grammar to provide a global overview of structure and to introduce story grammar terminology. Use a diagram of the story (see Figure 23) and fill in story information under each category as content is elicited from the children. The children write the paraphrased story content on their own copies of the diagrammed story.
2. Actively involve students in comprehension by setting reading purposes. Pose schema-related questions prior to requiring children to read a story segment. Elicit responses to the questions following the reading.
3. Utilize well-organized stories initially and use the inductive teaching approach. That is, have children first identify the major setting in each of three different stories, then the starter event of the first episode in each of three different stories, and so forth, before proceeding to identification of all story components in one selection. Thus, the structure element is held constant while story content is varied.
4. Once children have learned to associate story content with specific text structure categories on the diagrammed stories, begin asking story-specific questions. Continue to expect paraphrased story content as answers.
5. To build an expectation or recognition of variability from the ideal structure, gradually introduce less well-organized narratives.
6. To help children to more adequately handle the element of structure variability, use the macrocloze technique on transparencies and individual structure sheets for less well-organized stories. In macrocloze, some categories already contain story content, others are left blank for the children to complete (see Figure 23, this chapter).
7. Provide a stimulus for greater individual interaction with text and for greater monitoring of comprehension by guiding children to start posing their own schema-related or story-specific questions prior to the reading. Have them read to find answers for their orally posed or written self-constructed questions. Knowledge of

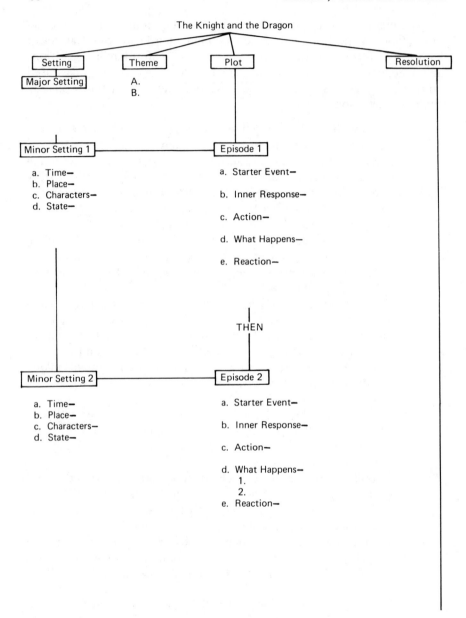

FIGURE 23. Story structure sheets for "The Knight and the Dragon."

story grammar will serve as a framework on which to develop the prereading questions.

8. Transfer the knowledge of story schema as a metatextual aid to the writing process. Children should generate story content in relation to the story grammar. Begin by writing a short but well-structured group story of one or two episodes. Provide a story starter and teacher guidance in the form of schema-related questions.

9. Progress to writing a well-organized group story without teacher guidance. Expect that some children will generate questions (as in reading), while others will volunteer statements for the story content.

10. Analyze a class-produced story by having students identify story components, add omitted components, or revise statements as required in terms of an ideal story grammar.

11. Have children apply their knowledge of story schema by writing stories independently. Encourage children to ask their own questions mentally in the process. Analysis and critique would follow in student pairs.

Before story schema can be taught as a metatextual aid to reading comprehension and writing, several preparational and instructional aspects will require the teacher's attention. First, the teacher has to choose some well-formed stories as models in lessons—not all stories are appropriate due to complexity of the analysis process. Good models often have repetitive elements or refrains. Myths, legends, fables, fairytales, and folktales are good because they are most similar and their structure is fairly clear. "The Owl and the Raven" serves as a good example, though it is shorter than many of the narratives found in folklore. Narratives used by Gordon and Braun (1982), in fact, contained between two and six episodes.

Secondly, the stories that are chosen may require slight modification (rewriting) for story grammar instruction. For example, many fables use the phrase "he said" in situations where there is no audience for the speaker and the story character is unlikely to be speaking aloud. The meaning clearly is "he said to himself," "he thought," or "he decided," an internal response. In such instances, the phrase "he said" can be changed to "he decided," or "he thought," so that the internal response is clearly identified by children.

Thirdly, the teacher has to acquire some expertise in analyzing even well-structured stories (as described earlier in this chapter). Once the story has been parsed into categories, it should be diagrammed for classroom use. The diagram contains, as a story outline, the four main story components (setting, theme, plot, and resolution), any episode subparts explicitly stated in the story (initiating event, internal response, attempt, outcome, and reaction) and the relationships (and, then, cause) between episodes. A diagram enables the teacher to keep the structure elements constant and provides students with a visual image of the various story parts and their relationships.

Finally, all questions can then be keyed to the macrostructure of the story. The questions are derived from the story and help the children develop expectations about the content of the story. Initially, structure schema-related questions can be asked. Later, story-specific questions based on the schema-related questions in each text structure category should be given. The following exemplifies each type of question on "The Owl and the Raven" in a method similar to that coincidentally proposed by Sadow (1982).

Schema-related questions	Story-specific questions
Setting: Where and when did the story take place? Who was in it?	What is a ptarmigan? Who was her friend? Where did they live?
Main goal: What is the main goal?	What did the owl intend to do when the raven made a dress for it?
Starter event: What started the chain of events in the story (first episode)?	What did the owl do for the raven?
Inner response: What does the character think, feel, or want?	What did the raven want?
Action: What does the main character do?	What did the raven do?
Reaction: What are the reactions of the characters?	What does the raven do during the fittings? What are the owl's feelings?
Outcome: What happened as a result of the main character's action? or reaction?	What did the owl do because he was angry that the raven would not stand still? What does the raven look like now?

While such questions will establish the literal comprehension of the story, the design of this research does not suggest that they are the only ones that should be asked. Once the story diagram has been complete and the children have a summary of the text, inferential questions should follow. The expectation is that children, in order to answer inferential questions, interrelate several ideas presented in text, interrelate textual information with prior knowledge, or infer the content of certain text structure categories (i.e., internal responses, reactions, themes, and resolutions) omitted by the author. Inference questions on "The Owl and the Raven" might include

1. How do you think the raven felt after he had oil poured on him?
2. Why were the boots made of whalebone?
3. Why do you think black is a poor color for a raven in Eskimo land?
4. What is the reason that the Eskimos retell this legend? What do they want to teach? (Note inference in Figure 2, this chapter)
5. How does the owl's plan to return a favor turn out? (Note inference in Figure 2, this chapter)

A final aspect of the active nature of comprehension and writing must still be given consideration. That aspect relates to the availability and accessibility of background knowledge prior to reading–writing text on a specific topic. The effect of awareness and use of narrative structure appears to be binary. On the one hand, in reading, it provides a generalized framework for processing explicit information in the story. On the other hand, because children possess this scaffolding, they can more actively engage their prior knowledge to integrate text and content schemata for inferencing. What children require at the outset, along with text-level strategies (such as text structure awareness) for comprehension of what is in the text, is a rich store of information to enhance constructive processing (relating text to their own experiences, insights, knowledge, etc.). Therefore, the importance of improving children's content schemata on the topic prior to reading cannot be overemphasized (Pearson et al. 1979).

Writers, on the other hand, need to write from sound knowledge based on the topic or from experience in a situation (Flower, 1981). It is the writer who determines what from the knowledge base he or she will supply and which inferences to let the readers draw. The creative reader will construct meaning by fitting the new information into an existing framework. The clearer the expectations set out by the writer for the reader and the clearer the structure of a composition, the greater likelihood that the framework the reader builds is the one intended by the writer.

In summary, it would appear from the research that direct instruction in the structure of narrative text has significant impact on the teaching of reading comprehension, writing, and the integration of these two components. Therefore, research-based recommendations for improving reading comprehension and writing can be outlined for classroom use. The teaching technique enhances and facilitates transfer of learnings to comprehension of new and unfamiliar selections through the use of an inductive teaching approach, macrocloze activities, and self-questioning strategies. The technique also provides for the use of story schema as a scaffolding for generating and editing group and individual stories with and without teacher guidance.

Appendix

Story: The Knight and the Dragon*

A long time ago in a far away land called Fantasia, a beautiful maiden was captured by a dreadful dragon. She was forced to live in the dragon's cave miles away from the village. One handsome knight decided that someday he should go to the dragon's cave to rescue the lady.

One day, the knight heard that the fiery dragon was about to kill the damsel. But the knight had no horse. He thought that the first thing that he should do was to go see the King who had stables and stables of horses. Early the next morning he set out on his mission. He begged the King for just one strong steed.

"Of course you may have a horse," replied the King. The knight was most pleased.

When the knight arrived at home, people told him that the dragon could be heard raging and snorting with hunger. Now, he decided was the time to go and ride to the cave and bring back the maiden. He jumped on his horse and galloped to the faraway cave, sword in hand. A vicious battle took place. When it was over, both the dragon and the knight lay dead. The whole village, though saddened by the loss of a life, sighed with relief. Their beautiful damsel was safe and no one had to live in constant fear of the fiery dragon.

*Story written to approximate "ideal" story organization.

References

Adams, M. J., & Collins, A. A schema-theoretic view of reading (Technical Report 37). Urbana, IL: University of Illinois Center for the Study of Reading, April, 1977.

Anderson, R. C. The notion of schemata and the educational enterprise. In R. C. Anderson, R. J. Spiro, & W. E. Montague (Eds.), Schooling and the acquisition of knowledge. Hillsdale, NJ: Erlbaum, 1977.

Anderson, R. C., Reynolds, R., Schallert, D., & Goetz, E. T. Frameworks for comprehending discourse. American Educational Research Journal, 1977, 14, 367–381.

Anderson, R. C., Spiro, R., & Anderson, M. Schemata as scaffolding for the representation of information in connected discourse (Technical Report 24). Urbana, IL: University of Illinois Center for the Study of Reading, March, 1977.

Applebee, A. N. The child's concept of story. Chicago: The University of Chicago Press, 1978.

Babbs, P. J., & Moe, A. J. Metacognition: A key for independent learning from text. The Reading Teacher, 1983, 36, 422–426.

Baker, L., & Brown, A. L. Metacognitive skills and reading (Technical Report 188). Urbana, IL: University of Illinois Center for the Study of Reading, November, 1980.

Bartlett, F. C. *Remembering: A study in experimental and social psychology.* Cambridge, England: Cambridge University Press, 1932.

Bereiter, B., & Scardamalia, M. From conversation to composition: The role of instruction in a developmental process. In R. Glaser (Ed.), *Advances in instructional psychology* (Vol. 2). Hillsdale, NJ: Erlbaum, 1982.

Bereiter, C., Scardamalia, M., & Turkish, L. *The child as discourse grammarian.* Paper presented at the annual meeting of the American Educational Research Association, Boston, 1980.

Bereiter, C., Scardamalia, M., Anderson, V., & Smart, D. *An experiment in teaching abstract planning in writing.* Paper presented at the annual meeting of the American Education Research Association, Boston, 1980.

Bower, G. H. Selective facilitation and interference in retention of prose. *Journal of Educational Psychology,* 1974, *66,* 1–8.

Bower, G. H. Experiments on story understanding and recall. *Quarterly Journal of Experimental Psychology,* 1976, *28,* 511–534.

Bransford, J. D., Shelton, T. S., Stein, B. S., & Owings, R. A. Cognition and adaptation: The importance of learning to learn. In J. Harvey (Ed.), *Cognition, social behavior and the environment.* Hillsdale, NJ: Erlbaum, 1980.

Braun, C., & Gordon, C. J. Writing instruction as a metatextual aid to story schema applications. In J. A. Niles & L. A. Harris (Eds.), *Changing perspectives on research in reading/language processing and instruction.* Thirty-third Yearbook of the National Reading Conference. Washington, DC, National Reading Conference, 1984.

Brown, A. L. Metacognition: The development of selective attention strategies for learning from texts. In M. L. Kamil (Ed.), *Directions in reading: Research and instruction,* Thirtieth Yearbook of the National Reading Conference, Washington, DC: The National Reading Conference, 1981.

Brown, A. L., Campione, J. C., & Day, J. D. Learning to learn: On training students to learn from texts. *Educational Research,* 1981, *10,* 14–21.

Brown, A. L., Smiley, S. S., Day, J., Townsend, M., & Lawton, S. C. Instruction of a thematic idea in children's recall of prose. *Child Development,* 1977, *48,* 1454–1466.

Collins, C. *The effect of writing experiences in the expressive mode upon the reading, self-esteem, attitudes, and academic achievement of freshmen in a college reading course.* Unpublished doctoral dissertation, Rutgers University, New Brunswick, NJ, 1979.

Collins, A., Brown, J. S., & Larkin, K. M. Inference in text understanding. In R. J. Spiro, B. C. Bruce, and W. F. Brewer (Eds.), *Theoretical issues in reading comprehension.* Hillsdale, NJ: Erlbaum, 1980.

Cramer, R. L. Informal approaches to evaluating children's writing. In J. J. Pikulski & T. Shanahan (Eds.), *Approaches to the informal evaluation of reading.* Newark, Del: International Reading Association, 1982.

Cunningham, J. W., & Foster, E. O. The ivory tower connection: A case study. *The Reading Teacher,* 1978, *31,* 365–369.

Dreher, M. J., & Singer, H. Story grammar instruction unnecessary for intermediate grade students. *The Reading Teacher,* 1980, *34,* 261–268.

Edmonson, J. C. *The effect of story grammar instruction on the writing process.* Unpublished Master's thesis, University of Calgary, 1983.

Emig, J. Writing as a mode of learning. *College Composition and Communication,* 1977, *28,* 122–141.

Flavell, J. H. Metacognitive aspects of problem solving. In L. B. Resnick (Ed.), *The nature of intelligence.* Hillsdale, NJ: Erlbaum, 1976.

Flavell, J. H. Metacognition and cognitive monitoring: A new area of cognitive-developmental inquiry. *American Psychologist,* 1979, *34,* 906–911.

Flavell, J. H., & Wellman, H. M. Metamemory. In R. V. Kail & J. W. Hagen (Eds.), *Perspectives on the development of memory and cognition.* Hillsdale, NJ: Erlbaum, 1977.

Flower, L. *Problem-Solving Strategies for Writing.* New York: Harcourt Brace Jovanovich, 1981.

Flower, L., & Hayes, J. R. A cognitive process theory of writing. *College Composition and Communication,* 1981, *33,* 365–386. (a)

Flower, L. & Hayes, J. The pregnant pause: An inquiry into the nature of planning. *Research in the Teaching of English,* 1981, *15,* 229–243. (b)

Fredericksen, C. Representing logical and semantic structure of knowledge acquired from discourse. *Cognitive Psychology,* 1975, *7,* 371–458.

Goodman, K. S. Behind the eye: What happens in reading. In H. Singer & R. B. Ruddell (Eds.), *Theoretical models and processes of reading.* Newark, DE: International Reading Association, 1976.

Gordon, C. J. *The effects of instruction in metacomprehension and inferencing on children's comprehension abilities.* Unpublished doctoral dissertation, University of Minnesota, Minneapolis, 1980.

Gordon, C. J., & Braun, C. *Story schemata: Metatextual aid to reading and writing.* In J. A. Niles & L. A. Harris (Eds.), *New inquiries in reading: research and instruction.* Thirty-first Yearbook of the National Reading Conference. Rochester, NH: National Reading Conference, 1982.

Kintsch, W. Memory representations of text. In Solso, R. L. (Ed.), *Information processing and cognition: The Loyola symposium.* New York: Wiley, 1975. (a)

Kintsch, W. Memory for prose, In C. N. Cofer (Ed.), *The structure of human memory.* San Francisco, CA: W. H. Freeman, 1975. (b)

Mandler, J. M., & Johnson, N. S. Remembrance of things parsed: Story structure and recall. *Cognitive Psychology,* 1977, *10,* 111–151.

Meyer, B. Identification of the structure of prose and its implications for the study of reading and memory. *Journal of Reading Behavior,* 1975, *7,* 7–47.

Meyer, B. The structure of prose: Effects of learning and memory and implications for educational practice. In R. C. Anderson, R. J. Spiro, & W. E. Montague (Eds.), *Schooling and the acquisition of knowledge.* Hillsdale, NJ: Erlbaum, 1977. (a)

Meyer, B. Organization in prose and memory: Research with application to reading comprehension. In P. D. Pearson (Ed.), *Reading: Theory, research and practice.* Twenty-sixth Yearbook of the National Reading Conference. Clemson, SC: The National Reading Conference, 1977. (b)

Meyer, B., & McConkie, G. W. What is recalled after hearing a passage? *Journal of Educational Psychology,* 1973, *65,* 109–117.

Paris, P., Scardamalia, M., & Bereiter, C. *Discourse schemata as knowledge and as regulators of text production.* Paper presented at the annual meeting of the American Educational Research Association, Boston, 1980.

Pearson, P. D., Hansen, J., & Gordon, C. J. The effect of background knowledge on young children's comprehension of explicit and implicit information. *Journal of Reading Behavior,* 1979, *11,* 201–209.

Pearson, P. D., & Johnson, D. *Teaching reading comprehension.* New York: Holt, Rinehart and Winston, 1978.

Pichert, J. W., & Anderson, R. C. Taking different perspectives on a story. *Journal of Educational Psychology,* 1977, *69,* 309–315.

Ruddell, R. B. Psycholinguistic implications for a sytems of communication model. In H. Singer & R. B. Ruddell (Eds.), *Theoretical models and processes of reading* (2nd ed.). Newark, DE: International Reading Association, 1976.

Rumelhart, D. E. Understanding and summarizing brief stories. In D. LaBerge & J. Samuels

(Eds.), *Basic processes in reading: Perception and comprehension.* Hillsdale, NJ: Erlbaum, 1978.

Rumelhart, D. E. Schemata: The building blocks of cognition. In R. J. Spiro, B. C. Bruce, & W. F. Brewer (Eds.), *Theoretical issues in reading comprehension.* Hillsdale, NJ: Erlbaum, 1980.

Sadow, M. W. The use of story grammar in the design of questions. *The Reading Teacher,* 1982, *17,* 166–186.

Shanahan, T. The impact of writing instruction on learning to read. *Reading World,* 1980, *19,* 357–368.

Short, E. J., & Ryan, E. B. Metacognitive differences between skilled and less skilled readers: Remediating deficits through story grammar and attribution training. *Review of Education Research,* in press.

Singer, H. Active comprehension from answering to asking questions. *The Reading Teacher,* 1978, *31,* 901–908.

Singer, H., & Donlan, D. Active comprehension: Problem-solving schema with question generation for comprehension of complex short stories. *The Reading Research Quarterly,* 1982, *17,* 166–186.

Stein, N., & Glenn, C. An analysis of story comprehension in elementary school children. In R. Freedle (Ed.), *Discourse processing: Multidisciplinary perspectives in discourse comprehension.* Hillsdale, NJ: Ablex, 1979.

Stein, N., & Trabasso, T. What's in a story: An approach to comprehension and instruction. In R. Glaser (Ed.), *Advances in instructional psychology* (Vol. 2). Hillsdale, NJ: Erlbaum, 1982.

Stotsky, S. Sentence combining as a curricular activity: Its effect on written language development and reading comprehension. *Research in the Teaching of English,* 1975, *9,* 30–71.

Thorndyke, P. W. Cognitive structures in comprehension and memory of narrative discourse. *Cognitive Psychology,* 1977, *9,* 77–110.

Tierney, R. J., Bridge, C., & Cera, M. J. The discourse processing operations of children. *Reading Research Quarterly,* 1978–1979, *14,* 539–573.

Van Dijk, T. A. Semantic macrostructures and knowledge frames in discourse comprehension. In M. A. Just & P. A. Carpenter (Eds.), *Cognitive processes in comprehension.* Hillsdale, NJ: Erlbaum, 1977.

Whaley, J. F. Readers' expectations for story structure. *Reading Research Quarterly,* 1981, *17,* 90–114.

Zeman, S. S. Reading comprehension and writing of second and third graders. *The Reading Teacher,* 1969, *23,* 144–150.

CHAPTER 2

Cognitive Monitoring and Early Reading: A Proposed Model*

Jana M. Mason

Introduction

Think back to your childhood. Do you have a memory about learning to read? Many of us do. When I ask this question to those who have a distinct memory about when or how they learned, I find that it is often tied to a particular book. For myself, it was Beatrix Potter's book, *Peter Rabbit*. Of course, I have no idea now whether it is an accurate memory and whether it helped me to read in school. Did I actually learn to read the book or was I reciting it from memory? What did I learn by memorizing the story and did it help me read other stories? These are questions none of us who have such memories can answer. Furthermore, because young children might read in ways that are unlike adults or older children, the process probably cannot be extrapolated from models of skilled reading. Nevertheless, while it is difficult to gather reliable retrospective data, it is possible to construct processing models from analyses of children's early attempts to read, recite and interpret printed information, and in so doing to chart the development of their approaches to reading.

What a typical child knows about reading before going to school would seem to be a reasonable question. Yet it is one that is fraught with hazards,

*Portions of this chapter were presented at the Society for Research in Child Development Convention in Detroit, March 1983 and were supported by NIE Grant No. NIE 400-81-0030.

77

influenced not as much by research as by the implicit models we have of reading and by the hidden assumptions we make about how children learn. I describe three hazards to make it more apparent why the question has been difficult to answer. Following this, I propose a model of early reading and then describe data we collected that support some aspects of the model.

Three Hazards to the Study of Early Reading

What Should be Taught

One hazard is that answers to the question are affected by our views of how reading takes place, and extrapolating from that, how it should be taught. Unfortunately, the field is not in agreement about how reading occurs and, as a result, about how to teach children to read. Look, for example, at the number of alternative programs purporting to show effective ways to teach beginning reading (Aukerman, 1971). How can a curriculum supervisor or teacher distinguish among them to choose the best program? One way is to classify them first in terms of their assumed reading-processing model. Then it is apparent that most can be represented by one of two processes; within each, differences are primarily procedural (e.g., on a procedure for introducing letters or sounds).

One set of programs relies on a model of reading in which the beginning reading process is assumed to have a linear quality. The more strictly organized of these is called a code-emphasis program (Beck, McKeown, McCaslin, & Burkes 1979) or a linguistic program (Chall, 1967). Proponents of this model, as evidenced from the following quotes, emphasize that the process is initiated with letters, words, or their sounds and then proceeds to larger units of text. It is a bottom-up model.

> Once a child begins his progression from spoken language to written language, there are, I think, three phases to be considered. They represent three different kinds of learning tasks, and they are roughly sequential, though there must be considerable overlapping. These three phases are: learning to differentiate graphic symbols; learning to decode letters to sounds; and using progressively high order units of structure. (Gibson, 1976, p. 254)

> In the information-processing approach that we have proposed, reading involves the successive recognition of larger and more abstract meaning . . . from the recognition of word meaning to the recognition of the meaning of phrases, sentences and stories. (Venezky, Massaro, & Weber, 1976, p. 695)

> The transformation of written stimuli into meanings involves a sequence of stages of information processing. (LaBerge & Samuels, 1976, p. 551)

The other set of programs assumes that the reading process, as well as its instruction, is not linear but interactive and tightly bound to meaning. Some basal reading programs from the 1940s and 1950s (those that featured a whole-word approach to beginning reading) and, more recently, language experience programs follow many characteristics of this model. In the next quotes, notice the assumption that reading instruction must be formed around understanding and interpreting text. They are top-down approaches.

> Reading is a psycholinguistic guessing game. It involves an interaction between thought and language. (Goodman, 1976, p. 498)
>
> A child learns to read by reading. (Smith, 1980, p. 421)
>
> If learning to read and write is to constitute an act of knowing, the learners must assume from the beginning the role of creative subjects. It is not a matter of memorizing and repeating given syllables, words, and phrases, but rather of reflecting critically on the process of reading and writing itself, and on the profound significance of language. (Freire, 1980, p. 369)

The viewpoint described by the first set of quotes is usually interpreted to indicate that reading has a hierarchical nature. The second emphasizes the interaction between meaning and language and print.

A problem with the first viewpoint is that, while the research does indicate that our eyes read and process small bits of text at a time (see, e.g., McConkie, 1982), it can neither be assumed that the young child reads in the same way as an adult nor that the most effective instruction is first to recognize letters, then words, then larger units of text. One argument against that ordering for instructional purposes is that letters having no intrinsic meaning are not easier to learn than words. Further, words, if placed out of context, often carry very little of their intended meaning (Anderson & Ortony, 1975; Bollinger, 1965). As we showed in a study with children (Mason, Kniseley, & Kendall, 1979), being able to identify printed words (e.g., polysemous words such as *pitch, jam, switch*) does not guarantee that appropriate context-derived meanings are recognized.

A problem with the second viewpoint is that it lacks a clearly formulated instructional approach. The look–say or sight–word approach was rejected as a result of Chall's 1967 survey of instructional effects. Other meaning-oriented approaches either have not been rigorously evaluated (e.g., language experience) or are still being studied (Tharp, 1982). For example, in a 1980 study, I observed and tested children throughout their year in a university nursery school. I found that they began learning to read by recognizing their own name, food labels, and traffic signs. Their early awareness of print was centered on highly meaningful words in context and was followed by active attempts to spell words and to analyze words in terms of their letter sounds. An informal follow-up indicated that they continued to excel in reading. Bissex (1980), who observed her young son from age four years, found that he began learning to read by merging reading and writing with its meaning. Because studies like these do not show a comparative advantage, reading instruction continues to be more influenced by a hierarchical model of reading than by one that focuses on meaning.

While the instructional issue has not been resolved, it can be hedged by taking great care that teachers encourage text understanding and inter-pretation. More specific changes await evidence from long-term investi-gations of young children's developing knowledge of reading. By tracking children's knowledge from or before kindergarten when they more often can choose what and how to spend their time and learn, and then follow them into school, tracking their reading instruction, it might be possible to separate school instructional effects from early home learning effects.

When Children should be Taught

A second hazard to answering questions about what a child knows about reading before going to school is found in assumptions about when children learn. Despite research evidence to the contrary (for example, Brown, 1975; Chi, 1976), many educators appear to believe that what chil-dren are able to learn is profoundly limited by their age or maturity. The field of reading particularly has been influenced by statements that focus on effects of the chronological or mental age of the child. For example, a long-standing statement is that the age of six is the crucial age for learning to read (Heffernan, 1960; Hildreth, 1950; Morphett & Washburne, 1931). Further, research from the 1920s and 1930s often emphasized how intel-lectual endowment affects the age a child can learn to read (e.g., Cox, 1926; Davidson, 1931). What they and others failed to study in the same depth are relationships between age (or intellectual endowment) and home background experience in learning to read. Hence, conclusions that only age and IQ form important ties to reading have misled educators into be-lieving that early instruction is unimportant.

At one point, an even stronger argument was made that early reading instruction could harm children. Here, for example, is the way Gesell stated the issue: "The attempt to force reading [by the age of six] frequently leads to temporary or permanent maladjustment and more or less serious dis-turbance in the course of normal school achievement" (1940, p. 208). Yet there is no evidence for the assumption that children have an inner bio-logical timetable that dictates when they can learn to read or whether there is an optimal time to learn (Coltheart, 1979). Indeed, Clay (1972) argued that *waiting* for the late bloomer to want to read can damage children because important instruction may then be delayed for too long. Despite these contrary arguments, however, some parents and preschool teachers are still wary of teaching young children about reading. This point is discussed in Mason and McCormick (1983) respecting a study in a Head Start preschool where the teacher was using an instructional program that ignored early reading constructs, nearly thwarting our attempts to provide reading experiences to children.

A maturational view is often the basis also for separating children into instructional groups. Placed in the lowest group are children who know little about letters, words, and books, and are given readiness activities rather than early reading tasks. The effect can then be that children entering school with substantial knowledge about reading might be encouraged to read while those with less knowledge might be encouraged to cut, paste, color, and sort pictures. The irony is that early reading instruction is then avoided for chidren who most need it.

To countermand beliefs that children's instruction ought to be based on their maturational level of development, knowledge about reading needs to be shown to be a function not only of natural endowment but also of various experiences of being read to, of learning letters and having signs and labels identified, of printing and spelling letters and words, and of learning that reading is both meaningful and useful. Studies by Durkin (1966), MacKinnon (1959), and Mason and McCormick (1983) support this view. In our study, 22 rural kindergarten children who had received reading materials by mail were matched and compared with their classmates who had not. Not only did end-of-the-year kindergarten tests show significant differences between the two groups, but a year later, there was only one low-achieving reader among the experimental subjects but six among the controls. The availability of easy-to-read materials gave academically marginal children an opportunity to learn about and gain confidence in reading. Unlike their matched controls, they were then able to make average or above-average reading achievement gains through school instruction.

Influences on Learning

A third hazard to answering questions about what preschool children know about reading stems from the extent to which educators believe that reading-readiness test-score differences are more a function of reading and cognitive skills than of social and metacognitive constructs that surround reading tasks and participation in reading lessons. Metacognitive constructs are acquired in part through particular social and cultural experiences (see Cole & Griffin, 1980; Goody, 1982; Heath, 1982; or Resnick, 1981, for elaboration of this point). Yet analyses of reading-lesson structures (Collins & Michaels, 1980; McDermott & Aron, 1978) show that instructional procedures feature individual effort over cooperation, adult-monitored learning over peer learning, and tutorial-type learning interactions over group participation. Minority culture children are, in effect, penalized because they are asked to learn using majority culture social structures when improvements in learning could occur with more familiar social patterns. For example, Au and Mason (1981) showed that when a teacher understood and accepted children's preferred social interactional pattern in a classroom reading lesson, the children gave far more academically relevant responses than when a teacher insisted on using an interactional pattern that was less familiar to the children.

Because of the large number of adjustments all children must make upon entering school, the apparent lack of attention to metacognitive constructs for reading and how the social environment shapes one's expression and ease or ability to perform means that schools are not meeting the needs of many children.

Investigations about the social context effects of reading require comparisons of home and community reading with its use in kindergarten and first grade. We must find out not only how children acquire knowledge about printed information but also what kind of support they obtain as they learn. How is printed information utilized for daily living, working, learning, and recreation among families of diverse incomes, cultures, and geographic areas? How well is home reading matched with school reading activities, materials, and procedures? What kind of community support for reading and writing is there for helping children read and to what extent do schools rely on community support systems? These are some of the questions that need to be answered in order to provide facilitating social contexts for learning to read.

In summary, the question about what children know about how to read has been obscured by beliefs about (1) the process of reading and its instruction, (2) the effect of maturation on learning, and (3) the influence of social structure on metacognitive constructs for reading. We can and must consider how these beliefs have limited an understanding of what children know about reading before they go to school as well as the attempts to establish effective instructional practices. In the following section, I have proposed a processing model of young children's reading that draws on metacognitive constructs and that assumes early reading experience, not merely maturation, lies on the causal path to reading success.

A Theoretical Perspective of Early Reading

Theories about early reading need to be concerned with what children understand as they learn to read and how their understanding is modified through reading and instruction. That is, early reading should be couched foremostly in terms of the learner's understanding rather than how the expert reader processes print; it should emphasize the role of experience rather than maturation; and it should accept that school success stems from metacognitive knowledge about how to approach reading tasks and interact with teachers as well as cognitive knowledge about how to decode and interpret text. These three assumptions are embedded in the following model.

Expanding on an earlier model (Mason, 1981), I propose that children experience and develop concepts about three knowledge domains: (1) the use of print and its relationship to oral language (*function* of print), (2) rules for relating print to speech sounds (*form* of print), and (3) procedures for engaging in the act of reading and for discussing with others what one has read (*conventions* of print and *metacognitive constructs* for doing reading tasks). The third domain is tied to metacognition because children must learn self-regulative functions of planning, monitoring, and evaluating their early reading activities as they learn to read. Thus, while children may not have metacognitive knowledge that enables them to take a cognitive endeavor as its object, they are learning to regulate their activity (distinction from Flavell, 1981). They are developing procedures to organize, keep track of, and check the reading activities in which they are engaged.

Knowledge Domains of Early Reading

Function of Print

This domain regards the tie between the meaning or intent of oral language and comparable written language. It can be supposed that realizing the functional relation of print to meaning occurs through informal, often incidental, occasions of linking print to familiar words, phrases, and stories. This suggests that children begin to learn how print has meaning, how it fits their oral language, and how it can be inferred from its context principally through unsystematic and idiosyncratic learning experiences.

How might children learn about the functional tie between their language and print? A principal way is oral-written referencing. Children are likely to hear TV announcers emphasize a product name and see the printed label displayed on the screen. They could hear a parent announce a trip to a particular store and, accompanying the parent, see the store name displayed in bold letters. The place where a relative works could be pointed out and named. A parent might choose a labeled food product from a grocery or kitchen shelf and name it or even point out the word on the label. Children's own names might be printed for them. Road signs are likely to be pointed out, book words may be identified, and stories may be read over and over until the whole text is known.

Although having words pointed out, named, and read in context ought to help children segment their speech into units that correspond to printed words, and may be similar to early language learning when children begin to recognize meaningful word separations in the stream of speech, it may be complicated by most adults' careless speech habits. Function words and word endings, for example, are often not uttered distinctly. How many of us, as chidren, thought "My country 'tis of thee" was comprised of 3 words (*my country tizathee*) until we saw it printed and could read.

Not only are words difficult to distinguish in speech but objects are often not referenced as they are labeled on packages, making it difficult for children to match spoken words with the printed words. For example, on my kitchen counter were two bags of fruit. One said, "TEXAS GARDEN CITRUS"; nowhere on the package was the word, "grapefruit." Similarly, the bag of apples was labeled, "Belle of Belding." On these packages, as often occurs, the words used to label products are not there or are in small letters to the side of the product name.

Finally, learning to identify print is difficult because stories are not necessarily read to children as they are written. In one of our surveys, one third of the parents reported that they sometimes "tell" a story instead of reading it, an action which could mislead children about how to interpret print (see Bissex, 1980, or Holdaway, 1979, for examples).

If adults are aware of these problems, and if they provide children with many opportunities to try to read, it is clear that many can learn on their own to name and remember printed words. For example, in data collected by colleagues from Vancouver, British Columbia, kindergarten children were asked to read words on labels (e.g., Jell-o, Coca-Cola, baby powder, crayons). When the word included the picture, the average score was 97.5%; when given without the picture it was still high, 79.1%. Thus, even though some printed words are seldom referenced in our labeling and others are hard to find on the object or package, it is apparent that many words, particularly signs and labels (own name, names of important people and objects, food labels, and explicit signs such as STOP) are learned by preschool and kindergarten children.

The concept that print can represent words about events, actions, and objects has not been carefully organized by parents. Hence, it is likely that its development is affected by the amount of print that exists in children's environment, by the uses to which print is put by significant others, by the clarity with which reading experiences are tied to meaning, and by the extent to which opportunities are given for children to test and get responses from adults about their ideas and to identify, interpret, and use printed information.

Form of Print

I refer to the more mechanical domain of print as its form and structure. Initiated by learning to name and recognize letters, it seems to be centered at first on letter shapes and letter distinctions; later it extends to letter–sound recognition. However, because the structure of our graphophonological system is so complex, preschool children can be helped by parents, the community, and preschool teachers. Parents, for example, introduce the alphabet with alphabet posters, alphabet blocks, alphabet books, alphabet cereal, alphabet cookies, alphabet soup, and so fourth. Many also teach an alphabet song and encourage children to watch the TV program (*Sesame Street*) that features letters. Such a concentration on letter information enables most children to recognize, name, and begin printing letters before they reach first grade (we found, for example, an upper case letter naming mean of 90.7% and lower case mean of 85.4% in the Vancouver study). As children learn letters, they figure out what counts (shape, not size, and direction of lines, not color) (Gibson, Gibson, Pick, & Osser, 1962), and learn that each letter can be represented in somewhat different ways. Children usually recognize upper-case letters before lower-case letters, probably because these are what they see on signs and labels (McCormick & Mason, 1981; Olson, 1958). Some children become aware of the relationship between letter names (or the taught letter sounds) and the phonemes or distinguishable sounds within words (Bissex, 1980; Chomsky, 1979; Clay, 1972; Morris, 1981; Paul, 1976; Read, 1971; Soderbergh, 1977).

The fact that there are substantial individual differences in acquisition of letter knowledge (a wide range of scores on a letter-name task is typical; see Calfee, Chapman, & Venezky, 1972; deHirsch, Jansky, & Langford, 1966; McCormick & Mason, 1981) suggests that some parents play an important role here, while others provide much less help for learning letters. For example, in the Vancouver study, 106 (52%) of the children correctly named all 10 lower-case letters we gave them. Twenty children knew fewer than 6 letters and 7 could name no letters. In a spelling task,

68 (34%) correctly spelled 4 3-letter words; 84 spelled half or less, and 16 could not identify a single letter in the words. In a reading task using non-words that resemble real words, 27 children gave the correct sound for all (32) consonants, 18 knew all the short vowel sounds, and 6 knew half or more of the vowel digraph and vowel/silent *e* patterns. At the other extreme, 19 children could identify no consonant sounds, 51 could identify no short vowels, and 148 could identify no complex vowel patterns. While we failed to gather reliable data from parents about their support for reading, we assume that the extent to which parents support naming of letters, spelling, and word reading affected children's knowledge about how to identify letters and words. This conclusion needs to be buttressed by further research.

Conventions of Print

The third domain of early reading deals with metacognitive concepts for talking about and accomplishing reading tasks. Through social interactions with others, through book reading, printing, and schoolwork exercises, children learn how one is supposed to report or talk about what one has read and how to carry out reading and reading-related tasks.

One set of conventions surrounds how to talk about reading to a teacher. This demands not only substantial oral-language competence but also familiarity with the social interaction rules for classroom discourse. When, for example, ought a child speak out or initiate a conversation with the teacher; when is it more appropriate to raise a hand or in some other way request to be called on; and when must one remain silent. These implicit social rules used in classroom lessons have only been studied since the early 1970s (Au & Mason, 1981; Boggs, 1972; Cazden, 1979; Collins & Michaels, 1980; Mason & Au, 1981; Mehan, 1980; Philips, 1972; Sinclair & Coulthard, 1975). What appears to make social interactions hard or easy is the degree of cultural congruence between teacher and student. When the teacher is unfamiliar with students' cultural patterns, smooth communication patterns are often disrupted. For example, in the Au and Mason study, one group of children was observed with two different teachers. One teacher used a social interaction structure where rules for talking were familiar to the Hawaiian children being taught. She allowed the children to initiate talk or to have open turns for 64% of the lesson time. The other teacher never used that approach; instead she required children to raise their hands or wait to be called on for 70% of the lesson time. This profoundly affected students' engagement in reading. The first-mentioned teacher obtained almost twice as many reading-related responses and correct responses and over three times as much discussion of the content of the story being read as did the other teacher.

Another factor affecting social interactions in school lessons is the amount of knowledge children already have about the task. In the Mason and Au study, 4 preschool children from a southern Illinois town practiced letter, letter sound, and word recognition, and story-reciting tasks. A comparison of the second with the fifth lesson determined that while the teacher's remarks to the children decreased, the children's academically related remarks nearly doubled and their violations of turntaking rules (e.g., interrupting or inserting a remark out of turn) diminished from 25% to 8% of their remarks. Further, in a comparison of responses among the four children, the one child who had more knowledge about reading (based on an early reading test we had given before the lesson) responded more often and differently. He made far more academically relevant statements and quickly took on a leadership role in the group (by whispering answers or helping the other children); he began remarking about his plans or accomplishments ("I made a gigantic t"; "I'm goin' to color in the pictures"); and he occasionally commented on the teacher's statements and directives. His leadership was soon reinforced by the teacher. By the fifth lesson she chose him to respond first to the harder tasks and challenged rather than helped ("You have to be very good to find . . ." rather than "There's a couple more left. Let's look through them"). That is, it was apparent that the teacher, after giving only four 20-minute lessons, had picked him to model the task for others. He not only knew more about the reading tasks, but also could talk about the tasks, describe his plans, monitor, and evaluate his success.

The other set of conventions in this third domain are those related to the action of reading or of doing reading-related tasks. It includes (1) knowledge about how to hold a book, turn pages, and direct one's eyes while reading; (2) knowledge of terminology such as book parts (e.g., *front*, *page*), location terms (*top*, *bottom*), actions (*make a circle, underline*), size (a *big* or *little* word), and reading words (*letter, word, sentence*), and (3) knowledge about rules and procedures for school tasks such as reading, printing and writing, spelling, phonics exercises, and test taking. Early manifestations of knowledge about book handling are probably acquired through reading and rereading of books (Chomsky, 1979; Holdaway, 1979; Smith, 1980). Procedures for reading stories, writing, and spelling, when encouraged by parents and preschool teachers, are moderately well-developed without instruction (Bissex, 1980; Clay, 1972; Ferreiro & Teberosky, 1981). Procedures for carrying out phonics exercises and answering reading test questions have not, to our knowledge, been tested but probably are not usually learned until children enter school.

Summary

The model predicts that children can acquire knowledge about three domains of reading before they enter school. Children begin to understand the function of print through opportunities to relate printed information to oral language; in so doing, they refine their understanding of "wordness' in print form and begin to construct ways to derive meaning from print. (Level 1 functioning). With support from adults for letter and word recognition and analysis activities, they notice regular or common letter patterns; they begin to analyze words into letter and sound patterns (Level 2 functioning). As they acquire functional and structural knowledge, they begin to use metacognitive strategies to regulate their reading activity, talk about reading, follow conventions of reading, participate in discussions about reading, and do school reading tasks. Of course, as children receive formal instruction in school, they modify and expand these earlier constructs. Nonetheless, because so much relevant information about reading can be acquired before going to school, it can be predicted that children who arrive in school with some information about the form and function of print are in a better position to use appropriate metacognitive strategies and participate in reading lessons. Those who come to school with little or no knowledge about the function or form of print, will have grave difficulty both in understanding most school reading tasks and in regulating their accomplishment of the tasks.

Two Tests of the Model

A principal goal here was to test the claim that self-regulative behaviors appear in conjunction with tasks that are at an *appropriate level of difficulty* and that *foster reading.* the first study (Mason & McCormick, 1983) included an analysis of videotaped lessons given to low-middle-income preschool children from a small college town attending a church-sponsored day care program. The second study (Mason, McCormick, & Bhavnagri, 1983) focused on an analysis of videotaped story reading lessons of preschool children in a public-school-sponsored Head Start classroom from a low-income region of Illinois. Schools in rural areas and small towns were chosen in order to test and observe children who had very little knowledge about how to read. That was indeed true. They knew few letter names and could not print or recognize any words. Thus, we were relatively confident that the reading lessons we gave them were the first they had ever received and that changes in knowledge about reading were likely to have been initiated by our instruction.

Study 1

One of the lessons given to four children was analyzed in order to determine whether, as hypothesized, Level 2 tasks were harder than Level 1 tasks. After studying the videotapes, three measures of teacher instructional intent were chosen: (1) number of *explicit directives* given to children to carry out a task; (2) number of *implicit directives* to carry out a task; and (3) number of *teacher answers or clues* given (or repeated) to a lesson question. Four types of student responses were counted: (1) number of *correct responses* to lesson questions (answers given simultaneously by more than one child were individually counted; (2) number of *response repetitions,* that is, correct answers already given by the teacher or another child; (3) number of *no responses,* where nothing was said when an answer was requested by the teacher; and (4) number of *wrong responses,* when attempts by children to answer were incorrect. Two raters separately tabulated these activities, settling any disagreements in conference.

The tasks are presented in Table 1, rearranged according to their instructional difficulty. Level 1 tasks at the top of the table were expected to be easier because children who knew little about the structure of print could still participate. They could repeat and remember the words in a simple story, copy letters, and recognize their upper and lower case forms. Level 2 tasks, which are next in the table were expected to be more difficult, because they required children to know that letter sounds could be heard and identified in words.

Children's responses to questions indicated that Level 1 tasks were much easier. There were far more child responses with Level 1 than with Level 2 tasks (78 versus 30), and second, a greater percent were correct (79% versus 3%). The poorer performance of the children with Level 2 tasks could not be ascribed to fewer requests to answer. The teacher issued 27 explicit directives (e.g., "Find a *t*") and 8 implicit directives (gives a nonverbal signal to suggest the task) with Level 1 tasks but made 47 directives with Level 2 tasks. She gave help almost as frequently, giving a clue (e.g., says part of a word that a child is trying to read) or repeating an answer on 56 occasions with Level 1 tasks and on 41 occasions with Level 2 tasks. Finally, because the children did participate when given Level 1 tasks, we knew that a difference in task difficulty, not the teacher, day, or time of day, caused the change in performance.

As we studied the lesson, it was apparent that there were also quali-

Table 1

Instruction for Level 1 and Level 2 Tasks

Tasks	Teacher activity			Student response			
	Answer or clue	Explicit directive	Implicit directive	Correct	Repetition	None	Wrong
Level 1 Tasks							
Identifying own printed name	1	6	0	3	0	1	1
Printing t	1	9	0	4	0	0	0
Finding t in box of letters	2	0	0	13	0	0	1
Reading of story[a] by teacher	19	4	0	—	—	—	—
First reading by children	12	3	0	10	0	0	2
Second reading by children	3	3	3	17	6	0	0
Review story first reading	10	5	1	5	2	0	1
Review story second reading	8	0	4	10	0	0	2
Level 2 Tasks							
Telling words that begin with t	9	10	0	0	3	6	0
Making pictures that begin with t	23	21	0	1	2	2	3
Pointing to t in words in story	9	16	0	0	6	4	3

[a]Each content word in the story that was read or repeated by the teacher was counted as an example. There were 16 content words in the new story and 10 content words in the review story.

tative differences as well between children's responses to the two types of tasks. An analysis of children's unsolicited comments was the key. It showed that when children were asked to carry out tasks that were oriented around their understanding of the task, they monitored the lesson and their performance, commented on the task, and evaluated or solicited help with appropriate questions. Here are examples from the transcript, all of which occurred with Level 1 tasks.

> Hey, my name is on the next card.
> I got 2 big ones (cards, printed with capital letters).
> I know how to make my name.
> There's my whole name.
> Want me to make a smaller m?
> I can't make m's.
> I wanna read that all by myself.
> I don't know what that says (one word under a picture).
> I didn't get a turn.

With Level 2 tasks, there were virtually no metacognitive remarks. Instead, the children remained silent, tried to change the subject, or asked to leave or to do another task. Here are examples from two sections of the transcript (* denotes interruptions or off-topic remarks; T signifies teacher; CH signifies Chris; AN signifies Andy; JE signifies Jean; TO signifies Tony):

(1)   T: Okay. Now, let's think of a picture you could draw and make a T to go with it. What has—what has a T sound? A—

    Ch: Toooo

  *JE: (inaudible)

     T: A toad or a turtle or a turnip.
Who could make $\left[\begin{array}{l}\text{a turnip?}\\\text{What is that—}\end{array}\right]$

  *AN:

  *   What is that thing for up there?

  * T: That's to listen to what we're saying.

  *AN: Oh.

  * T: That's to listen to all your words.
—Or a truck. Are you making a–What are you doing? Let's make a T word. And then we'll put the T with it.

  *CH: Hey, but that's a—

     T: A picture of a T word.

  *CH: But that's a—

     T: A turnip.

   CH: That's a turnip.

     T: Very good. Put a T with it. Make a T that says turnip.

(2)   T: OK Jean put you monster 'n' your mouse 'n' your mud
              in the folder. That's very good. (Teacher has just had
              children draw pictures of objects beginning with m.)
     *AN: I wanna make a flower.
     * T: A flower?
     *AN: Uh uh.
       T: OK, we could make a what? a—
     *CH: I'm gon make a fish.
     *JE: Is that Andy's?
     *TO: I'm goin back outside.

The transcript analyses indicate that task difficulty is an important
factor, not only in overall responsiveness but also in the generation of metacognitive remarks. Comparing children's remarks in Level 1 tasks versus
Level 2 tasks shows that the children made task-sustaining, supportive
comments during the first, but task-obstructive, antagonistic comments
during the second. Not only did the type of task affect the accuracy of the
lesson but also, pertinent to the issue here, it affected the opportunity for
task-sustaining metacognitive statements. Thus, Level 2 tasks generated
more wrong responses and fewer task-sustaining remarks.

Study 2

In this study, a Level 1 task, story reciting, was analyzed in order to
determine whether increases in metacognitive behaviors could be fostered. Videotapes from October and April lessons were transcribed to obtain the teacher's and children's discourse during four lesson phases of
each story: *opening* (introduction), *modeling* (teacher reads the story one
or more times), *tryout* (children take turns reciting the story), and *close*
(teacher ends the lesson). All remarks were categorized, including children's unsolicited comments during each lesson phase. Second, running
transcriptions were made of two of the children—Keith, a child who spoke
less infrequently than the others in the group, and Shawn, a child who
was the most verbal. Both analyses provided evidence of incipient metacognitive behavior.

The October videotape was almost completely bereft of child-initiated remarks, despite the teacher's attempts to engage them in conversation. Groups of 4 or 5 children, dressed in Halloween costumes, lined
themselves stiffly against a wall on a rug where we had told them to sit,
asked no questions about the videotape equipment or why we strangers
were there, and waited silently for our directives. Three groups were read
a Halloween story and given opportunities in chorus and individually to

recite the words. Here are *all* of their self-initiated remarks (Group 2 made none).

(1)	William, Group 1:	I'm a happy ghost (comment made as teacher showed cover of a book)
(2)	Shawn, Group 3:	William used to be a ghost (said just before first reading)
(3)	Shawn, Group 3:	Heh! I am a big boy (said softly during the reading)
(4)	Shawn, Group 3:	Are we going to be done in just a little bit (asked during third tryout)
(5)	Shawn, Group 3:	The big one (said as the teacher read, "A scary ghost")
(6)	Shawn, Group 3:	Ghosts don't say that . . . (comment made after fifth tryout)
(7)	Keith, Group 3:	Do that again (requested after second tryout)
(8)	Keith, Group 3:	You scare me (said after sixth tryout)

Four or five of the remarks (1, 2, 3, 8, and possibly 4) indicate that the children were monitoring the situation but not necessarily the story. One comment (7) indicates planfulness; one (5) is an incorrect attempt to predict the words in the story; and one (6) suggests an evaluation of the story meaning. There were no instances of responses to the teacher's predictive questions. All other remarks were repetitions and answers to simple questions.

The April videotape was made after we had given all the children several copies of little books to take home, had convinced the teacher that the copies we gave her needed to be kept in easy reach of the children (instead of in a loft reached by a ladder), and had encouraged her to read books to the children. The children were now very responsive and made many self-initiated remarks, both on the reading of the new story and on the review story. Tabulation of the three groups' lesson yielded 68 child-initiated remarks and 21 responses to the teacher's request for a prediction, or altogether 89 metacognitive verbalizations.

Planfulness was clearly operating in April, with 13 requests for turns or to "do it by myself" (in comparison to 1 in October). Monitoring of story meaning was much more evident in April in that children initiated 31 comments about the story (rather than 1 in October) and made 21 solicited and 21 unsolicited predictions about the words that would appear on the next page (one prediction had occurred in October). Evaluation of the story content also occurred, but still not often, only three times.

The other kind of evidence of self-regulation was obtained by studying the barely audible verbal and the nonverbal behaviors of several children. Here are the reports of two of them, Keith and Shawn, again comparing the two time periods. These transcriptions indicate that counting audible remarks and responses did not tell a complete story. Even at the first session, the children were not ignoring the lesson but were following and trying out responses that the teacher was modelling. Metacognitive constructs for lesson participation seemed to be emerging.

Keith, October Session, Group 3

Keith has his legs stretched out, back against the wall and hands folded on his lap. He looks in the direction where the teacher is pointing as she introduces the ghost story by reminding them that there is a ghost in the classroom now (the children are dressed in Halloween costumes). He nods his head vigorously and says, "yeah" along with Shawn when the teacher asks, "William was dressed up as a ghost this morning, wasn't he?" As the teacher reads the story, he seriously listens but does not react when the teacher reads the last line "Boo" until the teacher and Shawn began laughing. Then he smiles. On the first tryout, he answers correctly, "Ghosts," when asked what the story was about. He listens in a relaxed fashion, shaking his feet, legs stretched out. He giggles and looks at Shawn when the teacher says, "Boo." He smiles throughout the second tryout, slightly ahead of the teacher when asked to recite one page that says, "Sad ghost." On the last page, "Boo," he says it, grins, intertwines his fingers and brings them to his face, pulls his leg up, tugging at his sneakers, and then requests, "Do that again." He nods his head up and down in agreement when the teacher then asks, "Should we do that once more?" He joins the teacher with the "Sad ghost" page, and raises his eyebrows when the teacher says "Big Ghost." Otherwise he smiles and listens throughout the third tryout, then stretches his hands and turns his hands up when the teacher says, "Boo." To initiate tryout 4, the teacher asks, "Who can remember the story? Do you think you could?" as she points to Keith. He smiles, nods, and answers when the teacher says "What's this about? . . . What's the first one . . . this next one." He hesitates on four of the six pages so that the teacher coaches by saying the words just before he does on all but the pages saying, "Little ghost" and "Boo." On the fifth tryout, as Shawn does the reciting, Keith smiles and watches Shawn demonstrate with hand movements the words big and little. On the sixth tryout, he also demonstrates big and little, now anticipating "Little ghost," by bringing his hands together before the teacher turns the page. He smiles, pulls out his tongue and moves his arm around at the last word, "Boo," then says to the teacher, "You scare me."

Keith, April Session, Group 2

Sitting cross-legged with hands on his lap, Keith whispers to himself, "Eggs," as the teacher shows the cover of the book. When the teacher asks, "What do you think this might be?", he changes his mind and says, "Snowballs." Then as she says, "What else . . .", he smiles as he says confidently to everyone, "Eggs." Later, as the teacher tries to begin reading, he interrupts with, "There's chickens in it," and nods his head when she asked, "You think so?" A second time as she tries to begin reading, he interjects, "How about a giant egg?" She agrees that it might be and begins reading, during which he listens attentively, smiling, and responding along with other children. To the teacher's predictive question, "What's on the next page?" he says correctly, "Four." He responds slightly after the others on the last page when the teacher asks "Who can—Can you make a quack?" However, on the first tryout, when she asks, "Let's see if we can do that—you can do it by yourself." He enthusiastically says promptly, "I can." Then as she sets the rules, "We'll do it one at a time. OK, we'll start with—," he interjects "Me," smiling with dimples as he gets to be first and the teacher responds, "Good." After his turn, he silently mouths some of the words as other children take their turns, looking at the page and then at the child who is responding. On the last page, he joins in with "Quack." On the second tryout the child to his left asks to be first so the teacher begins with her. After three children have turns, he exclaims, "I didn't get mine." While waiting for his turn, he bites his nails and scratches his leg until the teacher says, "OK, Keith, here's your chance. We have one, two, three, four, and then what?" He smiles as he responds correctly "Five." She prompts, "Five baby—" Two other children answer, "Chicks." She prompts again, "How do they go?" Keith answers, "Peep."

The teacher now asks them to read a story that they had in the classroom and have taken home. She introduces it by saying, "Remember this one?" He is the first to respond, "Apples." The fingers of one hand are puckering his lips and his other hand is tugging at his boots but at the same time he listens attentively as the other children respond in unison to the teacher's prompts about the words on each page. As soon as the first reading is over, he anticipates individual participation and so lunges forward, moves his mouth, tilts his head a little back, and points to himself (implying he wants his turn now) as the teacher says, "OK, let's see now." So she turns to him, "What's the first page, Keith?" He responds correctly, "Red apples," and puts each hand on a knee and rocks himself. He says something to himself when the next child responds. When it is again his turn, he responds confidently, "Yellow apples," and rocks back and forward vigorously but listening attentively while others recite the other pages.

Shawn, October Session, Group 3

Shawn nods when the teacher comments on having ghosts in the classroom and looks in the direction the teacher points. He listens with a smile and after the page about the big ghost, comments, "Heh! I am a big boy." On the first and second tryouts, he softly repeats several of the story words after the teacher, giving the word, ghost, when the teacher has said, "A big ghost" and "A little ghost." He watches carefully and imitates her mouth movements, trailing behind the narration. On the third tryout, he asks, "Are we going to be done in just a little bit?" The teacher nods and continues to help children say the story. He participates cheerfully, smiling right away. He shapes his mouth the way he sees the teacher doing it and attempts to imitate her expression. His smile vanishes when the teacher says, "Sad ghost" and makes a rounded mouth and nods when the teacher says, "He's got that scary mouth on him." On the fourth tryout, he continues to monitor and imitate the teacher's words. By the fifth tryout, he has added arm movements, spreading his arms wide after seeing the teacher make the same gesture to denote bigness and putting them down when she says, "Little ghost." At the end, after "Boo," he interjects, "Hey! Ghosts don't say that. They go waah." The teacher retorts, "Yeah, he could go like that. This one goes Boo." As she begins the last tryout, he interrupts, "He goes waah." Then he continues to be a participator, smiling and responding appropriately.

Shawn, April Session, Group 3

Shawn is sitting on his knees, with hands on legs, watching attentively. When the question comes up about what is pictured on the cover, he offers, "Circles." The teacher agrees but suggests that they might also be eggs. He responds to the next question about one of the eggs, saying, "Big" and joins in when they count the eggs. As she begins reading, he softly joins in when they count the eggs. As she begins reading, he softly joins on the "peep" and then initiates a prediction about the second page, "Two baby chicks," and then the next, "Three baby chicks." When the teacher responds, "You think?" he smiles, nods his head with excitement and pops his eyes wide. Then before that page is completed, he predicts the next page, "Four baby chicks, four baby chicks." Before each page, he makes a prediction until the last page, he predicts "six" but when the page is turned and he does not see six eggs, he becomes serious and the smile vanishes. Now he shakes his head and tries to repeat after the teacher the correct line, "One baby duck" but instead says, "Big baby duck." Even though corrected, he smiles and joins in for the last word, "Quack." On the first tryout, the teacher makes an error, saying, "One baby duck," notices her error, at which time Shawn adds, "Yeah, sure, baby duck isn't right." After the teacher agrees, he tries to correct it for her, "Two baby chicks" (instead of one). Throughout this tryout, he predicts the number of chicks to be on the next page before she can say it, with a serious, quick, and alert expression. After the page of five chicks, he forgets and predicts "six" but as the page is turned, he shakes his head and say to himself, "Nope," smiles, and then nods approvingly when the teacher says, "One baby duck." After another child's critical comment about the picture of the duck, he points to the picture and compares the size of the chicks with the duck. The teacher agrees with his remark. On the second and third tryouts, he continues to participate by predicting the number of chicks, no longer making the error of "six chicks."

Next the teacher offers the review book, *Apples,* for them to recite. He points to the book, mumbling about having taken the book home. He participates, saying with the others the color names of the apples. He carefully looks at the pictures when children take their individual turns during the first tryout, smiling and responding correctly on his turn. In response to the last page, "Blue apples, yuk," he comments that he does not like blue apples. He and the teacher chuckle and then he makes a screwed-up face and says, "Yuk." As the teacher announces the second tryout, he interjects the name of the book, "Apples," and then participates in the story reciting. After this reciting, the teacher praises them, "You know that one so well . . . ." He interjects, "Let me, let me do it all by myself." She agrees and he lunges forward and is speedy in saying the words on each page, making only one error which the teacher corrects, "Two apples" instead of "Red apples." When other children get a turn, he listens seriously, mouthing some of the words with them and smiling radiantly when another child says the last word, "yuk."

Interpretation

Two comparisons were made of children's reactions to early reading tasks, one of responses to the teacher's questions and the other of barely audible comments and remarks to themselves. The first comparison indicates that story reading can be initiated with young children. In fact, based on an analysis of task differences, story reading is an effective way to foster lesson participation. The second comparison suggests why story reading can be effective—children are closely monitoring the teacher's behavior, and engaging in private or inconspicuous attempts to behave similarly. These reactions ought to be considered precursors to the more clearly identifiable metacognitive verbalizations that occur in the April lesson. The two studies suggest that planning how to take part in a reading lesson and monitoring the comprehension of the story is fostered in part by opportunities to look at, hear, practice, and recite stories.

Conclusion

Studies that rely on close analysis of a small number of children and on striking comparisons rather than statistical analysis to make their point are held in suspicion by a number of people. Although it is true that they need to be replicated in other settings and with other groups of children before they receive the force of a large survey of children who were selected at random and tested with reliable and valid measures, the results obtained here would not have been noticed in the larger study because the level of detail achieved would not have been practical. What is found contributes in another way to instructional and developmental research.

There are three points to make. First, story reading tasks can foster the use of metacognitive constructs. The tasks can be given to children as young as 4 years if the task is understandable, can be tied to something they already know, and is given in a clearly modeled task situation. Children's verbal responses to the task, remarks that attempt to explain and relate the concepts to their knowledge, and predictive remarks based on the structure they see in the task show the effect. This compares with children's descriptive remarks to tasks that they do not understand as they try to change the subject, modify the task, or avoid participating.

Second, metacognitive constructs appear to be initiated by private monitoring of clearly modeled tasks and inaudible shadowing of correct responses. Children who give little outward indication of monitoring, on close analysis, are evidently watching very closely and practicing responses that the teacher requests or demonstrates with arm and body movements and emphasizes with voice pitch and facial expression.

Third, metacognitive constructs appear to be fostered by repetition of instruction that affords children opportunities to carry out, express, and obtain corrective feedback on their tryouts. This instruction encourages children to plan how to participate, figure out how to give correct responses, and evaluate or criticize information that conflicts with their own knowledge. Learning to do this, I propose, is critical to learning to read with comprehension. That such young children, who were nonreaders when given the lessons, began to organize and keep track of the story reading lesson and its meaningful content attests to the power of tasks that foster metacognitive construction.

The model I have proposed—that early reading ought to be described by aquisition of knowledge about three domains—was considered here only in terms of the third domain, the role of metacognition in obtaining knowledge about social conventions of print. While much more research needs to be carried out to substantiate claims that arise from the three-part construct, it is shown here that metacognition plays a central role in at least one part of early reading.

References

Anderson, R. C., & Ortony, A. (1975). On putting apples into bottles—a problem of polysemy. *Cognitive Psychology, 7*, 167–180.

Au, K., & Mason, J. (1981). Social organizational factors in learning to read: The balance of rights hypothesis. *Reading Research Quarterly, 17*, 115–152.

Aukerman, R. (1971). *Approaches to beginning reading*. New York: Wiley.

Beck, I., McKeown, M., McCaslin, E., & Burkes, A. (1979). *Instructional dimensions that may affect reading comprehension: Examples from two commercial reading programs*. Pittsburgh: University of Pittsburgh, Learning Research and Development Center.

Bissex, G. (1980). *Gnys at wrk: A child learns to write and read*. Cambridge, MA: Harvard University Press.

Boggs, S. (1972). The meaning of questions and narratives to Hawaiian children. In C. Cazden, V. John, & D. Hymes (Eds.), *Functions of language in the classroom*. New York: Teachers College Press.

Bollinger, D. (1965). The atomization of meaning. *Language, 41*, 555–573.

Brown, A. (1975). The development of memory: Knowing, knowing about knowing, and knowing how to know. In H. Reese (Ed.), *Advances in child development and behavior* (Vol. 10). New York: Academic Press.

Calfee, R., Chapman, R., & Venezky, R. (1972). How a child needs to think to learn to read. In L. Gregg (Ed.), *Cognition and learning in memory*. New York: Wiley.

Cazden, C. (1979). Learning to read in classroom instruction. In L. Resnick & P. Weaver (Eds.), *Theory and practice in early reading* (Vol. 3). Hillsdale, NJ: Erlbaum.

Chall, J. (1967). *Learning to read: The great debate*. New York: McGraw-Hill.

Chi, M. (1976). Short-term memory limitations in children: Capacity or processing deficits? *Memory and Cognition, 4*, 559–572.

Chomsky, C. (1979). Approaching reading through invented spelling. In L. Resnick & P. Weaver (Eds.), *Theory and practice of early reading*. Hillsdale, NJ: Erlbaum.

Clay, M. (1972). *Reading, the patterning of complex behavior*. Aukland, NZ: Heinemann.

Cole, M., & Griffin, P. (1980). Cultural amplifiers reconsidered. In D. Olson (Ed.), *The social foundations of language and thought*. New York: Norton.

Collins, J., & Michaels, S. (1980). The importance of conversational discourse strategies in the acquisition of literacy. In *Proceedings of the Sixth Annual Meeting of the Berkeley Linguistics Society*. Berkeley: University of California, Department of Linguistics.

Coltheart, M. (1979). When can children learn to read? In T. Waller & G. Mackinnon (Eds.), *Reading research: Advances in theory and practice*. New York: Academic Press.

Cox, C. (1926). *Genetic studies in genius* (Vol. 2): *The early mental traits of three hundred geniuses*. Stanford University, CA: Stanford University Press.

Davidson, H. (1931). An experimental study of bright, average, and dull children at the four-year mental level. *Genetic Psychology Monographs, 9,* 119–287.

de Hirsch, K., Jansky, J., & Langford, W. (1966). *Predicting reading failure*. New York: Harper & Row.

Durkin, D. (1966). *Children who read early*. New York: Teachers College Press.

Ferreiro, E., & Teberosky, A. (1981). Comprehension of the writing system: The child's original constructions and the specific knowledge of adults. Translated for students by Walter MacGinitie from *Lectura y Vida, 2,* 6–14.

Flavell, J. (1981). Cognitive monitoring. In P. Dickson (Ed.), *Children's oral communication skills*. New York: Academic Press.

Freire, P. (1980). The adult literacy process as cultural action for freedom. In M. Wolf, M. McQuillan, & E. Radwin (Eds.), *Thought, language, and reading*. Cambridge, MA: Harvard Educational Review Reprint Series No. 14.

Gesell, A. (1940). *The first five years of life: A guide to the study of the preschool child*. New York: Harper.

Gibson, E. (1976). Learning to read. In H. Singer & R. Ruddell (Eds.), *Theoretical models and processes of reading*. Newark, DE: International Reading Association.

Gibson, E., Gibson, J., Pick, A., & Osser, H. (1962). A developmental study of the discrimination of letter-like forms. *Journal of Comparative and Physiological Psychology, 55,* 897–906.

Goodman, K. (1976). Reading: A psycholinguistic guessing game. In H. Singer & R. Ruddell (Eds.), *Theoretical models and processes of reading*. Newark, DE: International Reading Association.

Goody, J. (1982). Alternative paths to knowledge to oral and literate cultures. In D. Tannen (Ed.), *Spoken and written language: Exploring orality and literacy*. Norwood, NJ: Ablex.

Heath, S. (1982). Protean shapes in literacy events: Ever-shifting oral and literate traditions. In D. Tannen (Ed.), *Spoken and written language: Exploring orality and literacy*. Norwood, NJ: Ablex.

Heffernan, H. (1960) Significance of kindergarten education. *Childhood Education, 36,* 313–319.

Hildreth, G. (1950). *Readiness for school beginners*. Yonkers, NY: World Book.

Holdaway, D. (1979). *The foundations of literacy*. New York: Ashton Scholastics.

LaBerge, D., & Samuels, S. J. (1976). Toward a theory of automatic information processing in reading. In H. Singer & R. Ruddell (Eds.), *Theoretical models and processes of reading*. Newark, DE: International Reading Association.

McConkie, G. (1982). *Some perceptual aspects of reading*. Paper presented at Michigan State University for a Symposium series, sponsored by the Institute for Research on Teaching and the Center for the Study of Reading.

McCormick, C., & Mason, J. (1981). What happens to kindergarten children's knowledge about reading after a summer vacation? *Reading Teacher, 35,* 164–172.

McDermott, R., & Aron, J. (1978). Pirandello in the classroom: On the possibility of equal educational opportunities in American culture. In M. C. Reynolds (Ed.), *Futures of exceptional students: Emerging structures*. Reston, VA: Council for Exceptional Children.

MacKinnon, A. (1959). *How do children learn to read?* Vancouver: Copp Clark.

Mason, J. (1980). When do children begin to read: An exploration of four-year-old children's letter and word reading competencies. *Reading Research Quarterly, 15,* 203–227.

Mason, J., (1981). *Prereading: A developmental perspective* (Technical Report 198). Urbana: University of Illinois, Center for the Study of Reading.

Mason, J., & Au, K. (1981). *Learning social context characteristics in prereading lessons* (Technical Report 205). Urbana: University of Illinois, Center for the Study of Reading.

Mason, J., Kniseley, B., & Kendall, J. (1979). Effects of polysemous words on sentence comprehension. *Reading Research Quarterly, 15,* 49–65.

Mason, J., & McCormick, C. (1983, April). *Intervention procedures for increasing preschool children's interest in and knowledge about reading.* American Educational Research Association Convention, Montreal.

Mason, J., McCormick, C., & Bhavnagri, N. (1983, March), *How are you going to help me learn? Issues in providing reading instruction to preschool children.* Society for Research in Child Development Convention, Detroit.

Mehan, H. (1980). *Learning lessons.* Cambridge, MA: Harvard University Press.

Morphett, V., & Washburne, C. (1931). When should children begin to read? *Elementary School Journal, 31,* 495–503.

Morris, D. (1981). Concept of a word: A developmental phenomenon in the beginning reading and writing process. *Language Arts, 58,* 659–668.

Olson, A. (1958). Growth in word perception abilities as it relates to success in beginning reading. *Journal of Education, 140,* 25–36.

Paul, R. (1976). Invented spelling in kindergarten. *Young Children, 31,* 195–200.

Philips, S. (1972). Participant structures and communicative competence. In C. Cazden, V. John, & D. Hymes (Eds.), *Functions of language in the classroom.* New York: Teachers College Press.

Read, C. (1971). Preschool children's knowledge of English phonology. *Harvard Educational Review, 41,* 1–34.

Resnick, L. (1981). Social assumptions as a context for science: Some reflections on psychology and education. *Educational Psychologist, 16,* 1–10.

Sinclair, J., & Coulthard, R. (1975). *Toward an analysis of discourse.* London: Oxford University Press.

Smith, F. (1980). Making sense out of reading—and of reading instruction. In M. Wolf, M. McQuillan, & E. Radwin (Eds.), *Thought, language, and reading.* Cambridge, MA: Harvard Educational Review Reprint Series No. 14.

Soderbergh, R. (1977). *Reading in early childhood: A linguistic study of a preschool child's gradual acquisition of reading ability.* Washington, DC: Georgetown University Press.

Tharp, R. (1982). The effective instruction of comprehension: Results and description of the Kamehameha Early Education Program. *Reading Research Quarterly, 17,* 503–527.

Venezky, R., Massaro, D., & Weber, R. (1976). Modelling the reading process. In H. Singer & R. Ruddell (Eds.), *Theoretical models and processes of reading.* Newark, DE: International Reading Association.

CHAPTER 3

Metacognition, Instruction, and the Role of Questioning Activities

James R. Gavelek and Taffy E. Raphael

> *Be patient with all that is unresolved in your heart, and try to love the questions themselves.*
>
> (from Rainer Maria Rilke, Letters to a Young Poet)

Overview

The concept of metacognition has grown to what has amounted to almost "buzzword" proportions. We believe this to be true to some extent because it is a concept that has resonated well with at least two issues of fundamental importance to both cognitive and instructional psychology. The first of these issues relates to the active role of individuals in guiding their own processes of learning. The concept of metacognition addresses this issue directly by maintaining that it is an individual's metacognitive knowledge that enables him or her to function as an independent learner. The second and related issue is concerned with the question of transfer. To what extent are individuals able to apply what and how they have learned across different settings? Again, the concept of metacognition relates to this issue quite naturally, in that its proponents interpret metacognition as the major means whereby the individual is able to adapt or modify cognitive activity across tasks. The learner is viewed as an implicit if not explicit cognitive theorist who through his or her ability to modify

103

performance across various tasks evidences an understanding of the interactive nature of learning.

One form of metacognition—metacomprehension—addresses the
abilities of individuals to adjust their cognitive activity in order to promote
more effective comprehension. We have been interested in a specific aspect of metacomprehension—namely, the manner in which questions generated by sources external to the learner (i.e., from the teacher or text), as
well as those questions generated by learners themselves, serve to promote their comprehension of text.

In this chapter, we focus on the relationship between the concepts
of metacognition, cognition, and comprehension instruction. We do so by
first considering the present intellectual climate within which these concepts are embedded. Next, we discuss metacognition in terms of the concept, its definitions, associated issues and problems, and our working use
of the term. Third, we examine question answering and asking as important comprehension-related cognitive and metacognitive activities, and we
offer a conceptual framework by which to think about the development
of questioning activities in children. Fourth, we use a conceptual model
of instructional psychology suggested by Glaser (1982) as a means of organizing the extant theory and research related to the teaching of question
answering and asking strategies in the service of promoting reading comprehension. Finally, we summarize the area created by the mutual inter-
section of metacognition, instruction, and questioning, and we suggest
some directions that we believe this area might profitably follow.

Introduction: The Intellectual Climate

Much has been made of the heralded cognitive revolution that has
occurred in psychology. As is often the case with revolutions, its partici-
pants initially were swept up in the excesses created by the dogma on
which it was based. Yet while the concept of cognition is alive and well,
we believe that its adherents have begun to move toward a more centrist
position. The assumption of an active learner who is able to control his
or her own input is still a viable one. Indeed, a central focus of this volume,
metacognition, attests to its viability. Similarly, a concern with the structure of knowledge and its relationship to performance is still a major tenet
of cognitive psychology. More recently, however, there has been a recognition that these knowledge structures and the cognitive processes with
which they interact are not unbounded. We speak of the growing recognition among many cognitive psychologists of the contextual nature of
thought and action. We seem to have arrived at a relativity theory of cog-

nition; that is, one which recognizes that *how* we think is to some extent tied to *that* which we are thinking about and the *context* within which all of this occurs.

One of the consequences of the emergence of contextualist theories of cognition has been the granting of equal status to those who would study cognition in ordinary, real-world settings with those who have investigated thinking in the extraordinary environment that characterizes the laboratory. Not all contexts are created equal. Rather than map out the myriad of interactions created by a combined consideration of the universe of persons and situations, it appears more reasonable to begin studying those combinations of persons and settings that naturally group together in ecologically meaningful ways. Perhaps it took an experimental psychologist as respected as Neisser (1976) to wed the concepts of cognition and reality. Whatever the antecedents, it is now appropriate for cognitive psychologists to study basic processes as they occur in natural settings. A related consequence of the concern with context has been the rediscovery of the importance of social influences on cognition. Whether or not the removal of these influences from the study of thinking was a necessary consequence of the adoption of an information-processing model can be debated by philosophers of science. Clearly, the consensus now is that how and what one thinks is influenced by the historical, cultural, and social milieu within which one exists.

One aggregate of everyday contexts worthy of investigation is that concerned with instruction. Unfortunately, the number of contexts needed to characterize the richness of instruction can be overwhelming. A construct that adherents suggest may rescue us from the house of mirrors created by contextualism is metacognition. Although there are many different definitions that have been given to this concept (Brown, 1975; Flavell, 1981), all hold in common that metacognition represents individuals' knowledge of the states and processes of their own mind and/or their ability to control or modify these states and processes. The promise of metacognition is that it addresses the problem of generalization of performance across settings. To the extent that an individual is metacognitively aware, then he or she is a self-correcting system; one who has learned how to learn.

Metacognition

"Metacognition refers to one's knowledge concerning one's own cognitive processes and products or anything related to them" (Flavell, 1976, p. 232). Although the use of the term is relatively recent (Bruner, 1966; Flavell, Friedrichs, & Hoyt, 1970), the view of the learner as one who reflects upon, monitors, and is able to influence his or her own learning has a long history (Dewey, 1933; James, 1890). The term *metacognition* refers to a general concept that subsumes metas for almost any cognitive process imaginable. For example, metamemory is associated with one's awareness of and ability to utilize strategies for enhancing recall of information (Flavell et al., 1970). Metacomprehension has been applied (1) to listeners' abilities to monitor their understanding of oral discourse (Markman, 1979, 1981), (2) to readers' knowledge about the reading process (Myers & Paris, 1978), and (3) to those metacognitive skills associated with questioning activities (Raphael & Pearson, in press; Wong & Jones, 1982). It is the last form of metacognition mentioned that is the focus of this chapter.

There are two important issues concerning metacognition that are necessary to any serious examination of this construct. First, there is an assumption that there will be a substantial and positive relationship between measures of metacognition and their corresponding measures of cognition. That is, it has been predicted that subjects' ability to explain their purposive cognitive activities is an accurate reflection and predictor of the corresponding cognitive performance. All too often however, the metacognitive–cognitive correlations have been modest or nonexistent (e.g., Cavanaugh & Borkowski, 1980). We believe that in part this has been because of the way in which metacognition has been measured.

The second issue then, with respect to metacognition concerns how we go about measuring it. The requirement that we be able to verbalize our metacognitive knowledge is as limiting as it would be were we to apply it to cognition. Much of what we know, we are nevertheless unable to report (Polanyi, 1958). This raises important methodological considerations both of when verbal reports are appropriate and of what other measures are potentially viable. In considering the appropriateness of verbal reports, we wish to emphasize that we do not reject the use of verbal reports per se. Nor do we deny the very important role that verbal information (e.g., explanations of cognitive processes) provided by others serves in mediating children's developing cognitive and metacognitive functioning. Verbal reports of one's declarative (i.e., background) knowledge constitute prima facie data of *what* one knows. Yet, while verbal reports concerning individuals' procedural (i.e., strategic) knowledge may allow us to construct an attribution theory of their belief systems concerning higher-order processes they are for the most part irrelevant to *how* we know.

Our bias in studying metacognition is toward measures grounded in actual performance. Just as there exist performance measures of cognitive outcomes, we believe that there should be such measures of metacognitive performance. The use of strategies is not inherently indicative of purposive, intentional behavior. For example, a child may learn that underlining or highlighting is a useful strategy for facilitating comprehension of text. Yet, if he or she uses it indiscriminately, highlighting irrelevant details or the entire text, it is unlikely that the child is acting metacognitively aware. The implementation of *appropriate* strategy use is as important to measure as is the use of strategies in general. Expressions such as learning-to-learn (Bransford, Stein, Shelton, & Owings, 1981), transfer-appropriate (Bransford, Nitsch, & Franks, 1977), optimal (Lockhart, Craik, & Jacoby, 1976), and differential (Wellman, 1977) processing all capture what we believe to be essential aspects of the concept of metacognition. These are that individuals behave in reflective, planful, and where necessary, self-correcting ways.

We believe that the determination of whether a child is utilizing metacognitive knowledge should be based upon the answers to three questions: (1) Does an individual give evidence of monitoring and/or regulating his or her cognitive performance? (2) Is this individual's performance facilitated as a result of such activity? The determination of whether this criterion has been met necessarily requires the comparison of an individual's behavior with him- or herself. For example, to the extent that the same individual behaves differently (i.e., uses different strategies) in anticipation of different task demands and his or her performance is incremented as result of knowing what these task demands are, then would we be more inclined to ascribe metacognitive knowledge to that individual? (3) Does the individual engage in the metacognitive activity across multiple settings? The determination of whether this last criterion has been satisfied presents some difficult conceptual problems that go to the heart of the issue of transfer with which metacognition has been so closely associated. At one extreme we would maintain that the demonstration of self-monitoring and/or regulative behavior over two relatively similar tasks does not constitute evidence for the presence of metacognitive knowledge. However, neither do we ascribe to the opposite extreme. There is little evidence for pure processes, or in the present case, pure metaprocesses (Rogoff, 1982). Rather, consistent with a contextualist position we believe that an individual's knowledge of cognitive and metacognitive processes is bounded to specific contexts. We have purposely avoided the question of how broad or narrow is the bandwidth of a particular type of metacognitive knowledge. Suffice it to say that we are more confident in maintaining that an individual is behaving metacognitively to the extent that she or he demonstrates that knowledge across a number of settings within a particular content domain.

Metacognition is a construct that can inform the areas of both cognition and instruction. Further, there are a number of metas within the construct of metacognition that can serve to guide our research questions.

We now examine one specific area in which issues of metacognition and of instruction intersect, that of questioning.

Questioning as a Cognitive and Metacognitive Activity

Question answering and asking are among the most commonplace, indeed, most prototypical of instructional activities that occur in the classroom. The single most frequent activity in classrooms involves questioning (Tierney, 1976). Although questioning may be used for many purposes in the classroom we are concerned in the present chapter with the use of questions as they relate specifically to students' comprehension of written text.

The Functions of Comprehension Questions

Questions fulfill two primary functions with respect to reading comprehension. The first function of questions is to promote students' comprehension of text, while the second is to assess students' understanding. When used to promote comprehension, a distinction may be made between questions that derive from some external source such as a teacher or text in contrast to those questions that students generate themselves as a result of their own reading of text. These questions, oral or written, may (1) occur prior to the text to call attention to what is considered important, (2) during the reading of text as a guide to the central theme, or (3) at the end of text as a stimulus for reviewing important points (Pearson, 1981). Self-generated questions may also serve to promote the readers' comprehension of text (André Anderson, 1978–1979). This may occur in two ways. First, students may ask questions of others, one of the most direct ways of enlisting assistance in facilitating their own comprehension. Second, while reading students may ask themselves questions that are internally directed and not necessarily in verbal form (Bransford et al., 1981; Kearsley, 1976; Palincsar, 1983).

The second and currently more common function of questions (Durkin, 1978–1979; 1981) relates to their role in the assessment of comprehension. It is primarily students' ability to answer questions related to material that they have read in formal (i.e., standardized) test-taking situations that determines whether they are judged to be good or poor readers and thus, to no small extent, whether they are thought of as good or poor students. One may draw a distinction between this static role that questions play in formal assessment of comprehension and the more dynamic role that questions may play in less-formal types of assessment. In this latter case, teachers may ask a series of questions graduated in difficulty, the answers of which determine their subsequent instructional activities. Here the distinction between the assessment function of questions and the comprehension-promoting function mentioned earlier becomes fuzzy. Finally, although seldom used formally, the questions asked by students themselves are often used as a basis for informal evaluation of what it is that they know. In a very real sense the questions an individual asks are thought to reflect both the extent and the structure of his or her knowledge. Indeed the title of an article, "To ask a question one must know enough to know what is not known" (Miyake & Norman, 1979), suggests this relationship between question asking and background knowledge.

Characterizing Comprehension Questions

There have been numerous attempts to describe the questions that may be asked of and by students when interacting with text. These taxonomies of questions have sought to categorize questions into groups according to the level of thinking or type of mental activity the question engenders. Many of these have been based on earlier work by Bloom, Engelhart, Furst, Hill, and Krathwohl (1956). The problem with this research is that while various operational definitions have been created for assigning questions to categories, these taxonomies have considered questions in the absence of any context (e.g., Barrett, 1976; Sanders 1966). They have ignored the fact that the same question can require different processing depending upon the background knowledge of the reader, the text to which the question refers (Pearson & Johnson, 1978), and the purpose for which it has been asked. Clearly the goodness of a question (or answer) must be judged relative to the context in which it is embedded. Included as a part of this context are various characteristics of the reader as well as those features of the comprehension task itself (e.g., the nature of the text to be comprehended and how this comprehension is to be demonstrated). One taxonomy that incorporates the preceding dimensions has been developed by Pearson and Johnson (1978). In this taxonomy a distinction is made between questions with answers that are either knowledge or text based and questions categorized in terms of a question answer relationship (Raphael & Pearson, in press). Text-based questions can be further divided into those that have answers explicitly stated within a single text sentence and those with answers requiring integration of text information across sentences or paragraphs.

Questions that occur during comprehension instruction and during dynamic assessment of students' comprehension should reflect a progression from ones with answers clearly stated in text to ones that require more integration of text information and background knowledge (Crowell, Au, & Blake, 1983). Young children often must devote much of their attention and cognitive effort to decoding, thus may have difficulty initially in integrating information. Integration of text information can be promoted through careful questioning practices that guide the reader through the text. As young readers mature, more cognitive effort can be put to the integration of information as decoding skills become more automatic. In fact, this sequence of questioning rarely occurs. Research in the frequency and occurrence of types of questions asked during reading sessions suggest that the predominant type of question is text based and often explicit (Guszak, 1967; Hare & Pulliam, 1979). Questions that ultimately appear on tests of comprehension also tend to be dominated by those text-based questions with answers explicitly stated, with no systematic variation in the proportion of inferential to literal questions (Crowell et al., 1983).

It is important to emphasize that any type of question can be valuable depending upon the context in which it is asked. What we are suggesting is a notion similar to the concept of encoding specificity (Tulving & Thomson, 1973). If on a test of comprehension, one wants a reader to recall detailed information explicitly stated in a text, then the type of questions to ask while reading that text should be ones that address such information (Wixson, 1983, 1983a, 1984). If one wants information recalled such that the text has been integrated, then a question requiring the reader to integrate text information would be appropriate. Accordingly, it is an oversimplification to suggest any questioning taxonomy that fails to take into consideration the purpose for which a question may be asked, as well as the relationship of the question to the sources of information for locating an appropriate answer.

An Information-Processing Analysis of Questioning and Comprehension

As presently conceived, question answering and asking may be thought of as a recursive sequence of organized problem-solving processes that are often socially mediated and have as the ultimate goal or end state the comprehension of a given unit of text. Logically, one may distinguish among a number of different cognitive processes associated with the use of questioning in comprehension:

1. Students must first be sensitive to problems that they are experiencing in comprehending a given unit of text. These problems in comprehension monitoring may be the result of the way in which the text has been written (Anderson & Armbruster, 1984), gaps in the readers' background knowledge (Miyake and Norman, 1979) or some combination of the two. Such problems are likely to be manifested in a lack of clarity, incongruity, inadequacy, and so forth.
2. There must be an accurate characterization of this state (i.e., someone must ask the appropriate question(s)) that brings into focus what the "problem" is.
3. Someone must determine the correct source(s) of information necessary for answering this (these) question(s).
4. This (these source(s) must be searched so that the information is adequately retrieved and integrated.
5. An answer must be constructed.
6. This answer must be compared to some criterion to determine its adequacy.

Several features of this information-processing analysis of questioning deserve mention. First, the preceding description allows for both question answering and question asking by students. On the one hand, explicitly stated questions may be asked by a teacher or may accompany the text that students are reading. Alternatively, students may arrive at their own questions as a result of their reading of the text. Second, these processes are likely to be recursive in that there are apt to be a number of questions asked and answered before it is determined (by either the student or the teacher) that their understanding of a given unit of text is adequate. Finally, although not explicitly indicated, the preceding hypothesized sequence allows for the likelihood that any or all of several steps in the questioning process may be socially mediated. That is, another individual (a teacher or another student) may assist a student's comprehension of text by asking a question, suggesting a source for its answer, formulating an answer, or checking to see whether the answer is correct. In the next section, we maintain that this social mediation constitutes the primary mechanism by which control over the processes of comprehension are transferred from adults to children.

It is the transfer of control from another individual to the learner him- or herself that is one of the primary criteria suggested for determining whether metacognition is involved. Strategic awareness is a necessary but not sufficient condition to behaving metacognitively (Paris, Lipson, & Wixson, 1983). Specifically, with respect to questioning and its relationship to comprehension, students demonstrate metacognitive activity to the extent that they monitor and regulate their own reading comprehension by assuming increasingly greater responsibility in the questioning process. We have conceptualized students' questioning-related knowledge as existing on a continuum ranging from an awareness of both the role and the value of the questioning process in text comprehension to a complete absence of such knowledge. As students move along the continuum, they can be characterized as operating on one of three general levels. The first and highest level of metacognitive activity involves generating and answering one's own questions to promote comprehension in response to reading text. This activity is considered a higher form of metacognitive activity than answering the questions asked by another, the second level of metacognitive activity in questioning. Postman and Weingartner state that "Once you have learned how to ask questions, relevant and appropriate and substantial questions, you have learned how to learn and no one can keep you from learning whatever you want or need to know" (1969, p. 23). In the second level, metacognitive control may be exercised by another individual such as a teacher. By the guidance that he or she provides, the teacher in the forementioned questioning process serves as a metacognitive surrogate for the student. The third level describes the other end of the continuum, the absence of metacognitive activity, evidenced when neither the learner nor the mediator drives the learning process. Rather, it is the task itself that drives student's learning. While a determination of the extent of metacognitive involvement is a relative judgement, the range of behaviors from student control of mediation to no control may be characterized as ranging from the sophisticated to the metacognitively naive learner.

Questioning within the Context of Cognitive and Metacognitive Development

There has been a paucity of theory and research concerned with questioning activities in children and what work there is has often been inconclusive if not inconsistent. What is needed is a conceptual framework or model of how to understand the development of question answering and asking in children and the relationship of these questioning processes to children's eventual comprehension. Because there has been so little theorizing concerning children's questioning activities, much of what we suggest is speculative. However, we believe that our speculations are based on sound principles derived from cognitive development.

In what follows, we examine what is known about cognitive development in general as a conceptual framework for thinking about the development of children's question answering and question asking activities as they relate to the promotion of their comprehension of textual material. The issue of primary concern in this section is how both question answering and asking as cognitive and metacognitive activities develop in children. Of interest specifically, is how the developing learner (1) comes to acquire the requisite processes which comprise question answering and asking, and having done so (2) becomes increasingly able to self-monitor and regulate these processes with the attendant goal of comprehension.

We have treated both question answering and question asking as purposive activities that are utilized in the service of the comprehension of text. Clearly, answering self- or other-generated questions is not necessary for comprehension to occur. The value of questions is that they may increase the likelihood that students will interact with text in a manner known to facilitate comprehension. The value of *learner-generated* questions would seem to be that the learner is able to identify those aspects of text most in need of his or her own individual attention. By our own definition, learner-generated questions involve a high degree of metacognitive involvement because the learner is acting independently in monitoring and regulating his or her own comprehension. However, there is an apparent dilemma here, in that in order for learners to ask questions that promote their own comprehension, they must know enough to know what is not known (Miyake & Norman, 1979). This dilemma is reminiscent of a similar one posed by Plato in his *Meno*. In a famous Platonic dialogue, Meno suggests the following problem for Socrates: "You argue that a man cannot inquire either about that which he knows or about that which he does not know; for if he knows, he has no need to inquire; and if not, he cannot; for he does not know the very subject about which he is to inquire." The problem presented by learner-generated questions is similar to Meno's dilemma in that in order to be able to become more knowledgeable the learner needs to ask questions that promote the acquisition of that knowledge, but in order to ask questions she or he must know enough to know what is not known.

Children often lack both the declarative and the procedural knowledge by which to utilize questions as a means toward the goal of comprehension. On the one hand, they may lack the background knowledge necessary to ask their own questions or even answer the questions of others; On the other hand, they may lack the procedural knowledge for discriminating what it is that they do know from that which they do not know. They may be unable to pose questions that would serve to clarify what it is they don't know; or they may experience difficulty in searching for and constructing answers in response to the questions of others.

What sort of metacognitive knowledge do children acquire with respect to questioning and its relationship to comprehension? We believe that a distinction similar to that made by Flavell and Wellman (1977) with respect to children's knowledge of memory applies equally well to their knowledge of the relationship between questioning and comprehension. Flavell and Wellman suggest two levels of understanding with respect to the development of the purposive utilization of strategies in memory tasks. At an initial level children must become aware of the fundamental fact that a memory task requires that they engage in some activity now that will facilitate the retention of a given set of information at some later time. The second level involves children's developing awareness of the myriad of factors that influence their memory performance. Similarly, with respect to comprehension, children must first become sensitive to the objective need to engage in present activity (e.g., question answering or asking) in a manner that facilitates later comprehension. Initially, one may observe children engaging in a form of *incidental comprehension*—that is, unintended comprehension that comes as a result of meaningful interaction with text induced by someone else's questions and that is demonstrated by an individual's performance on an unanticipated test of comprehension. Next, children must come to understand which variables interact in what ways to affect performance on a comprehension problem.

A major contention in the present chapter is that question asking represents one of the primary means by which individuals are able to foster their own comprehension and as such represents a powerful metacognitive activity. However, before individuals can ask questions they must understand the concept of a question and the fundamental means–ends relationship between answering questions and their subsequent comprehension. To be sure, children learn to answer and ask oral questions well before they have become skilled at reading. However, children must learn the cognitive processes that underlie the answering and subsequent comprehension of text-related questions. As suggested earlier, initially this knowledge may be acquired incidentally—that is, as a consequence of their answering questions asked by another. In this case the use of questions as means has been formulated not by the learner but by some external agent such as a teacher or the text itself. The learner must abstract out the relationship between the cognitive processes engaged by another's questions and the learners' own enhanced comprehension. Apart from their different origins, there are obvious formal similarities between the cognitive processes of answering questions asked by someone else and those questions generated by oneself. Whether the activities associated with answering the questions of others also enhance the ability of individuals to generate their own comprehension-promoting questions could well be the subject of an entire program of research.

How then is it that children come to acquire both the procedural and declarative knowledge that enables them to ask questions that further promote their own comprehension? First, while logically separable, we wish to emphasize the psychological inseparability of *what* we come to know and *how* we come to know it. One does not acquire these two types of knowledge in isolation from one another. There is no such thing as pure process, but rather, process tied to context (Rogoff, 1982). When one is acquiring given content, the opportunity at least exists for the acquisition of procedural (strategic) knowledge.

We believe that the development of cognitive processes associated with question answering and asking as means toward comprehension are socially mediated. In this regard, our thinking has been heavily influenced by the socio-cultural theory of cognitive development formulated by Vygotsky (1978), his students and those in this country who have interpreted and extended his ideas (Brown & French, 1979; Laboratory of Comparative Human Cognition, 1983; Rogoff, 1982; Wertsch & Stone, in press). Basic to Vygotsky's approach is the assumption that social interaction plays a major role in the origin and development of higher mental (e.g., metacognitive) functions. These functions appear first on the interpsychological (i.e., social) plane and only later on the intrapsychological (i.e., individual) plane. Metacognitive processes such as those associated with questioning may be carried out by social groups. For example, adult–child interaction in formal and informal instructional settings such as reading groups often serves to introduce children to metacognitve skills. Independent metacognitive functioning is a direct reflection of these social interaction processes (i.e., is internalized social interaction). The process of internalization of these metacognitive functions is facilitated to the extent that an adult mediator (e.g., teacher or parent) is able to engage children within their zones of proximal development. Vygotsky defined the zone of proximal development "as the distance between the actual developmental level as determined by the independent problem solving and the level of potential development as determined through problem solving under adult guidance or in collaboration with more capable peers." Thus, adult and peer mediators serve a scaffolding function by providing adjustable but temporary strategic assistance and other instructional support to carry out cognitive tasks. Specifically, with respect to comprehension instruction the teacher may serve this social mediating function by: (1) describing the task (e.g., establishing the goal of comprehension and the allowable means for the attainment of this goal); (2) explaining, and where necessary, directing the reader through this task; and (3) monitoring student's levels of comprehension. As suggested earlier, teachers serve to temporarily mediate the higher cognitive processes of children with whom they interact. In effect, teachers carry out the metacognitive functions that their students will (or at least should) eventually come to exercise themselves.

What factors influence whether children abstract out question–comprehension relationships? With respect to the sequence and timing of the acquisition of the various sorts of cognitive and metacognitive knowledge associated with questioning activities we agree with Flavell and Wellman (1977), who have suggested that "those psychological processes of self and others that tend to be relatively more external and therefore more accessible to perceptual inspection ought to become objects of knowledge earlier than those that are relatively less overt" (p. 25). To this we would add that it is important not only that cognitive processes be external, but also that the outcomes of these processes be observable as well. Moreover, it would seem especially important that the learner perceives the two, process and product, as being functionally related to each other.

Two dimensions important to thinking about questioning are suggested by the preceding account. First, the cognitive processes associated with questioning and comprehension should be observable or "out there" for the learner to see. For example, although an adult's search for information sources for answering questions is likely to be largely unobservable, it is essential that this activity be made visible so that children are able to see such thinking in action. Indeed, later in this paper we will describe an instructional program designed to teach children strategies for locating information sources for questions. Second, the relationship between the cognitive means and ends of question answering and asking should be made explicit. Even though a given operation such as locating information in text and its outcome (i.e., enhanced comprehension) may be made observable, their relationship may not be understood unless someone also makes this relationship explicit. Roehler, Duffy, Book, and Wesselman (1983) report the highest gains in reading achievement scores among students who have been taught by teachers observed to be explicit in the explanations they offer for the cognitive processes involved in reading.

A hypothetical sequence such as what follows may represent the typical course of development of children's comprehension-related question activities. As is the case with other problem-solving tasks, children's comprehension activities may initially be largely incidental and nonstrategic. In such instances, questions asked by others serve to direct the learner's attention to important information. Note however, that specifying questions for children does not necessarily guarantee their understanding. Bruner (1966), among others, has cautioned that when children answer a question inappropriately it may simply mean that they have answered a different question than that which we had intended. The extent of involvement by others in conveying the means by which these questions are answered may involve detailed instruction of the various strategies that individuals utilize to access, integrate, and produce an appropriate answer. Indeed, a major tenet of Soviet pedagogical and developmental theory is that before a cognitive operation can function as a means toward some other end it must be learned as an end itself (Smirnov & Zinchenko, 1969). For example, one must first be able to recognize that information for a question may reside in one's head as a part of background knowledge. Once this is learned as an end, it may later be used in the service of other ends (e.g., answering a question). Similarly the ability to answer questions may have been learned initially as an end and may now serve to promote a higher-order end (e.g., comprehension of text). It is important to recognize that whether an activity serves as a means or an end is necessarily bound to the context in which it occurs.

A second level in children's question-related activities may still involve questions provided by an external agent, but with little or no involvement on the part of such an agent in conveying the various means of question answering. This probably represents the typical way in which text-based questions are asked of children in the classroom.

A third level relates to the idea that learners who generate their own questions indicate what they consider to be important. Accordingly, this level in children's questioning activities may involve generating their own questions but again with varying levels of external intervention in the means of answering these questions (e.g., the child asks a question, but an outside agent either answers it or provides the means so the child can answer it).

Finally, a fourth level in question activities for children's text comprehension may occur as a result of their ability both to generate and to answer their own text-related questions. That is, this level would represent the more sophisticated reader who is able to proceed independently through a given selection. This level of question activities may be represented by such behaviors as the reader encountering an unknown word in text, questioning himself or herself as to what it may mean, determining the meaning based on previous context, and proceeding successfully without external guidance through the text.

Questioning and Metacognition
in Instructional Settings

The preceding hypothesized sequence can be considered relative to the specific world of classroom settings. While we have described aspects relating questioning and metacognition, we have yet to prescribe how these factors should be addressed instructionally. In this section, we discuss question answering and asking related to reading comprehension in the context of research on questioning in general, and specifically within a framework of a model of instructional psychology proposed by Glaser (1982).

Glaser's model provides an excellent framework for examining questioning, instruction, and metacognition. His model consists of four components that guide inquiries about the development of skilled performers in a logical sequence within any given domain of knowledge. The four components are (1) the need to understand the competent or skilled performer, (2) the need to identify the initial state of the learner, (3) the need to determine the mechanisms by which the less skilled become skilled, an issue which is the crux of educational concerns, and (4) the need to assess or monitor newly acquired skills.

Competent Performance

In recent years there has been a rash of studies concerned with identifying the differences that exist between experts and novices across a number of content domains (e.g., mathematics, reading, chess playing, medical diagnosis, etc.). A goal of many of these studies has been to determine whether there is knowledge (declarative and procedural) that serves to distinguish experts in general from their novice counterparts. In this section we are interested specifically in whether there are generalizations that can be made characterizing the ability of skilled individuals within their respective areas of expertise to both answer and ask questions related to that area. In a certain fundamental sense, it is these individuals' ability to answer questions that characterizes them as experts in the first place. Less well-documented but certainly supported by reason, is the notion that experts are also better at asking questions related to their domain of expertise (Bransford et al., 1977; Miyake & Norman, 1979). Of interest in the present context, however, are the specific cognitive and metacognitive skills that mediate these question answering and asking abilities.

To begin with, skilled performers should be adept at knowing whether or not they understand the questions asked by others. In the absence of an appropriate definition of the question then no amount of sophistication in the use of subsequent question-answering strategies is likely to be helpful. This is not simply a problem with children's comprehension-related questions. The researcher who fails to determine whether his or her experimental instructions were correctly understood by the subjects is often faced with a study in ruin.

Second, skilled performers are aware of the various information sources available for responding to questions asked of them, and also can evaluate which information would be most appropriate for obtaining an adequate answer (Raphael & Pearson, in press; Raphael & Wonnacott, in press). Skilled performers may recognize that questions asked can be a source for some answer information or serve as a cue for information needed to respond appropriately to the same or to other questions (Kavale & Schreiner, 1979–1980). Students need to understand that the sources of information used in answering questions may reside explicitly in a single source of text or implicitly across several different sources of text. Finally, students should recognize that their background knowledge is relevant in answering a question. As suggested earlier, it is not uncommon to observe students who do not know that they could go to their existing knowledge for an answer. On the other hand there are the few who do report going to their own knowledge only to discover that "there was nothing there" (Raphael, 1984, p. 306).

A third but related skill involves students' abilities to assess the adequacy of their own knowledge states (i.e., whether the sought information is available or not, is complete or partial) (Gavelek & Raphael, 1981; Hart, 1966). This skill is as relevant in test-taking situations as it is in students' preparatory study activities, because in both instances the outcomes of such assessments are likely to influence students' decisions as to how they are to allocate their cognitive resources (Hosseini & Ferrell, 1982).

A fourth area in which more expert behavior is demonstrated through question answering involves the learners' use of questions inserted in text. Their are two dimensions of which competent performers appear to better understand the task of question answering. First, competent performers appear to use these questions as signals for important information, attending to specific types of information suggested by the questions, or to specific pieces of information (Anderson & Biddle, 1975; Reynolds & Anderson, 1982). Second, competent performers, when asked questions during reading, appear to recognize the value of information in the text itself, using text look-backs successfully in locating appropriate response information, and to then recall the information at a later point in time (Garner & Reis, 1981).

A final question-answering skill is concerned with the *criterion prob-*

lem (Bransford et al., 1977).This involves students' recognition of when their answer to a question is complete, as contrasted with accurate, but incomplete (e.g., one part of a three-part answer).

In general, skilled performers show more insight in terms of their knowledge about questioning activities and the variables that influence it (Wonnacott & Raphael, 1982). To possess these skills describes only part of the picture of competent performers in their abilities with respect to question activities. Still to be considered is the nature of the relationship between skilled question asking and competent performance. Indeed, a widely quoted injunction when rewritten for questioning might read: "give a student a question to answer and she will learn the passage she has just read. Teach her how to ask questions and she will learn how to learn for the rest of her life".

We consider competence as it relates to students' question-asking abilities with regard to text they have read. Dillon (1982a) has suggested that learner-generated questions in educational settings are particularly useful if they can be employed when the learner wishes to seek unknown information. Perhaps the first step, or prerequisite to other activities related to skilled performers' questioning, is that they experience a state of disequilibrium, tension, or uneasiness. That is, competent performers must first experience the internal state of tension that something is missing or not right, that signals a need for further explanation or information. The missing something may be defined in terms of the text (e.g., the text is poorly written) or in terms of the individual reading it (e.g., a lack of necessary background knowledge). If this need goes unidentified, a question will not be asked. While it is imperative to know *that* something is missing, an important related step is the ability to determine *what* is missing.

Therefore, a second area of competence necessary for skilled performance is the ability to recognize that known information is relevant to asking the questions that will allow the question askers to gain the information they are seeking. Miyake and Norman (1979) have found that both the quality and quantity of student-generated questions is predicted by the background knowledge that they bring to the question-asking task.

Goodness or quality may be a dimension that characterizes not only students' individually generated questions but also their sequencing of questions. Comprehension involves more than just an accretion of facts. Knowledge is often hierarchically organized. To the extent that students are aware of this organization, they can use it to constrain the universe of information they would consult in seeking answers. Each question builds upon the answer of the one previously asked. Denny (1975) has studied the development of this sequential question-asking in children's play in the "20 questions" game. This game involves at least two players. One thinks of an item, the other can ask up to 20 questions to identify the item the other is thinking about. Denny found that older children are increasingly able to take advantage of the hierarchical organization of knowledge. Unfortunately this ability has not been studied extensively in adults or in tasks in which organized information is presented as connected discourse.

A number of metacognitive strategies are implied by this description of competent performance in questioning. Questions can be asked *of* the learner such that metacognitive knowledge about the purpose of the questions and the strategies for answering them would be important. Questions asked *by* the learner serve two important metacognitive functions: the monitoring of learners' current understanding and the seeking of information in situations where necessary information is not available or part of their knowledge base. The ability to determine the presence, absence, and completeness of the information required are metacognitive skills often required in the comprehension of text.

Initial State of the Learner

Glaser's second component of instructional psychology involves the specification of the initial state of the learner, the point at which instruction should begin. At the simplest level, one might argue that the initial state is merely the absence of those skills described in the preceding section. That is, novices are less adept or are unable to assess their own knowledge states, to recognize various sources of information, to recognize the information available in questions themselves, to understand and to answer questions designed to direct their attention to important information in text, to use appropriate look-back strategies for accessing information provided in text, or to provide complete information when answering questions. In terms of the question asking, they apparently are less likely to recognize the need to question, to ask questions that are sequential, build upon each other, or constrain the world of relevant information, nor are they able to generate spontaneously the kinds of questions that serve to monitor their level of understanding of text.

A more complex analysis of the initial state could consider both procedural and declarative knowledge deficits. For example, research suggests that declarative knowledge affects the quality of questions asked (Miyake & Norman, 1979) as well as the quality of students' responses (Pearson, Hansen, & Gordon, 1979). Novices tend to be identified as such because of a lack of background knowledge within a given domain. When one focuses on mechanisms of transition from novice to expert, concentrating on changing the status of the novices' knowledge base would involve instruction in amount of background knowledge.

Considering the initial state in terms of procedural knowledge would involve examining the learners' awareness of strategies and procedures for asking and answering questions, independent of background knowledge. Areas within procedural knowledge would include the learners' awareness, for example, of the difference in requirements between recognition (e.g., multiple choice or matching) as opposed to recall (e.g., essay) tasks, or the *criterion problem*. It is possible that the novice is destined to remain so unless procedural knowledge can be taught helping him or her to identify information sources, to use text information appropriately, to identify the problem inherent in a question, and so forth. The initial state of the knowledge base is a form of declarative knowledge, while knowledge of strategies for identifying and utilizing this declarative knowledge is procedural. The point is not to dichotomize knowledge, but to recognize that both kinds are part of competent performance.

Learning and State Transformation Processes

Thus far we have described the question-related knowledge that characterizes the performance states of both the competent and the newly initiated learner in any given content domain. We now turn our attention to the sin qua non of instruction: the ways and means by which the newly initiated learner is transformed into a competent learner. We present three areas of research relevant to the development and use of questioning activities: (1) experimental studies of questions as they are used to enhance comprehension of text, (2) instructional studies designed to teach teachers to ask better questions as well as to teach students to answer them, and (3) instructional studies designed to enhance students' question-asking abilities.

As a prescriptive science, the issue that confronts an instructional psychology of questioning is how we can best make use of questions and encourage their generation on the part of students in order to optimize their comprehension. Throughout this chapter we have maintained that if the construct of metacognition is to be useful to instructional psychology it is by virtue of the extent to which this construct has served to focus our attention on how learners come to control their learning in a way that optimizes their performance. A useful way of conceptualizing instruction in general is to look upon it as a continuum from other-generated activities (i.e., provided by teachers, texts, teachers' manuals, etc.) to learner-generated activities. Earlier we suggested a hypothesized sequence of development for children's questioning activities that span this sort of continuum. At one extreme are those situations in which both the question and the strategies for answering it are prescribed by external sources. At the other extreme are those situations in which both the question and the strategies for answering it are controlled by the learner. In the following review of studies, we have ordered the presentation from less to more learner control over the activities associated with questioning.

One heavily researched area of other-generated questions involves studies of the role of adjunct or inserted questions in text. Many studies exist, as well as several critical reviews (e.g., Anderson & Biddle, 1975; André, 1979; Carrier & Fautsch-Patridge, 1981; Faw & Waller, 1976) concerning the effects of adjunct questions in adult populations, while far fewer studies have examined the effect of adjunct questions with younger populations. Generally, the paradigm was made popular by Rothkopf (1965, 1966), who suggested that there exist *mathemagenic behaviors*, or behaviors that induce learning. One such behavior is answering questions related to text, the underlying assumption being that the questions engender activity on the part of the readers, which helps to induce deeper processing and leads to enhanced comprehension.

A typical adjunct-question study involves readers being directed to read a passage that contains questions inserted at various points. The questions relate either to text that has been read or to upcoming text, and require the readers to respond either overtly or covertly as they proceed through the text. Following this activity, readers are given a test concerning the passage, and performances of readers in various question–no question conditions are compared. Conditions vary, including pre- and postquestions, questions massed either before or after text, or interspersed throughout, questions at varying frequencies and of different levels.

Of theoretical interest is the role these text questions play in enhancing text processing. Several theories have been proposed, generally suggesting that questions cue readers to attend to specific upcoming information or types of information, or that the questions induce a review of previously read text (Anderson, in press; Reynolds & Anderson, 1982; Rickards, 1979). André (1979) has suggested that the questions are effective only if the reader would otherwise be operating under a *principle of minimal effort*. That is, readers who are developmentally young, of low ability, or of low motivation are unlikely to attend fully to the text. In this case the questions serve to cue them to the important information. Thus, in testing situations their performance is likely to improve. However, a highly motivated and able reader may find such aids unnecessary or even burdensome.

Developmental considerations have received some attention, though the body of literature at this point is small. These studies parallel the adult studies in design but have had inconsistent results as compared with the adult literature. In the adult literature, consistent direct effects have been found favoring readers who received inserted questions. These effects suggest that when readers are tested directly on information questioned during reading, their performance increases. Less consistent a finding is the incidental effect, which assesses readers' recall of nonquestioned information, though this effect tends to be present more often when questions follow the related information than when they precede it (Anderson & Biddle, 1975). The studies of the effects of different levels of questions have suggested that questions that require application or other higher cognitive processes can enhance memory for text more than lower-level (e.g., verbatim) questions (e.g., Watts & Anderson, 1971). These studies have been criticized, however, on two points. First, comparisons across studies are difficult due to inconsistency of definition of levels (André, 1979; Carrier & Fautsch-Patridge, 1981). Second, whether or not a higher-level question necessarily elicits a higher-level answer has been questioned (Dillon, 1982b).

In children, results of studies within a similar paradigm have yielded findings ranging from a depressive effect on students' performances (Rickards & Denner, 1979) to facilitating performances of students of low ability (Rickards & Hatcher, 1978) to facilitating performances of students in general when testing direct effects (Reynolds & Magleby, 1981) to finding developmental differences in performance (Raphael & Wonnacott, 1981). These inconsistencies could be due to a number of causes. It may be that younger readers who are less adept at answering questions in general find the extra effort of responding to questions during a reading task to be too burdensome. They may be unaware of how to integrate their own knowledge base with the information in the text and therefore do not assimilate the new information. As the Soviet literature suggests, for means to be useful in reaching a higher goal, they must first be learned as ends in and of themselves (Smirnov & Zinchenko, 1969).

The inconsistent results with children suggest that more research is needed to specify exactly when and what type of inserted questions would be beneficial to a younger reader, taking into account the probably interactive nature of the learner characteristics, the materials to be read, the type of test format, and the kinds of activities children are directed to use with the inserted questions (Reynolds & Raphael, 1984). Another possible benefit as yet unexamined is whether students who have been given good questions to answer, as modeled through adjunct questions, may in fact be better able to generate them.

In addition to experimental studies that have investigated ways to enhance comprehension, a number of instructional studies focusing on teacher question-asking and student question-answering have been conducted. Several training programs have been developed that relate to the transformation of unskilled to skilled (1) learners, (2) question askers, and/ or (3) question answerers. Raphael and her colleagues (Raphael & McKinney, 1983; Raphael & Pearson, in press; Raphael & Wonnacott, in press) have developed an instructional program designed to heighten students' awareness of sources of information for responding to other-generated questions. The training period consists of a week of intensive training (four sessions of 40 minutes each) and an optional maintenance practice period of eight weekly lessons. During the training, using modeling and feedback, students were guided through answering postreading comprehension questions wherein much discussion focused upon the location of the response information (e.g., in the text to which the question refers or in the readers' knowledge base). The training was tested under two naturalistic settings. In the first, the first author conducted the lessons with upper elementary school and middle school children in the students' classroom. In the second and third, the lessons were conducted by classroom teachers as part of their developmental reading program. In both experiments, the children who had experienced the training performed at a higher level on comprehension questions following text readings than did a control group.

Often it is the case that children have the requisite background knowledge to answer a question but simply fail to activate it. Another group of instructional studies in children's question answering has focused on teaching children to understand the relationship between their background knowledge and stories or expository texts they are going to read. Au (1979) and Hansen (1981; Hansen & Pearson, 1983) have taught teachers to ask questions of students prior to reading assignments. The questions are constructed such that students are first asked about events, feelings, people, and so forth from their own background of experiences. Then the same information is related to events, people, or character's feelings from the story. Throughout these discussions, children are reminded of how thinking about their own experiences helps them to better understand the passage. These studies focus on the use of other-generated questions to promote efficient and effective understanding of text, yet, the implicit goal is to help children to understand the value of asking themselves questions that relate their knowledge base to the text they are reading.

A third area of research into questioning related to the work of Au and Hansen was developed by Beck and her colleagues (Beck & McKeown, 1981; Omanson, Beck, Voss, & McKeown, 1984). They have suggested that children see arbitrary questioning patterns modeled for them as a result of poorly written teachers' guides to basal manuals. The sequence of questions in these manuals often focuses on less-important details, and the questions often do not build upon one another. This may make the question-answering process an arbitrary task, not background for the development of independent comprehension question/kills. Beck and her colleagues have introduced the notion of *story maps*, which identify the central theme to the story and from which teachers can generate a logical sequence of literal and inferential questions, modeling such a sequence for young readers, and perhaps eventually leading them to create maps and corresponding questions. Initial results have been promising regarding teachers' development and use of the story maps, and should provide the basis for extending the work to instructional studies with children.

Studies in which students were taught question-asking strategies include instruction in question asking based on the story grammars (i.e., the underlying structure of text) of various texts (Singer & Donlan, 1982), instruction in generating questions relative to the main idea of texts (André & Anderson, 1978–1979; Wong & Jones, 1982), and studies that, through reciprocal questioning between an adult and student, model the asking of appropriate text-based questions that demonstrate one's understanding of text (Palincsar, 1983). These learner-generated questions can be categorized as investigations of either content free or content bound. Content-free questions are those that involve self-questioning about how well one has comprehended a passage or section of text that has been read. These questions are of a rather generic nature (e.g., Do I understand this? Who are the main characters?) The same questions can be used with a variety of texts. Meichenbaum and Asarnow (1979) have used modeling to train students to conduct an internal dialogue relative to text, consisting of reminders to remember the main characters, the important details, and characters' feelings and motivations. This modeling has been based on principles of cognitive-behavioral modification. In other training programs, André and Anderson (1978–79) and Wong and Jones (1982) taught students to determine main ideas in passages and to create questions relative to this idea. The general questions (e.g., What is the main idea?) helped secondary as well as learning disabled students in their text comprehension. Content-bound questions are concerned with specific characters or events given their current status in a passage. Palincsar (1983) has trained students to self-question by means of a reciprocal questioning technique in which she modeled for students appropriate questions asking about main ideas in the stories or predicting events based on knowledge of story events. She also modeled for them how one can use summarization to complement the asking of questions. Finally, students themselves created the questions and led discussions about the stories. Again, this self-questioning procedure had positive effects of students' performance. Singer and Donlan (1982) used a different approach in teaching students a problem-solving schema for generating questions specific to a story. Aspects of stories (e.g., characters or goals) were identified based upon research in story grammars and students were taught to generate questions about these aspects specific to a given story. In heightening students' awareness of the process of understanding prose, and in teaching viable strategies to use in this process, students' performance levels improved.

The preceding studies depict empirically tested training programs related to questioning activities. There are also potential areas for further training in questioning skills. In the area of training less-skilled performers to assess their own knowledge states, the research by Hart (1966), suggests that adults are sensitive to the absence or presence of information. Gavelek and Raphael (1981) demonstrated that this knowledge correlates with performance in instructional settings. It would seem reasonable to examine whether or not this skill is amenable to training. A second as yet unexplored area is the application of research using the 20 questions paradigm to understand connected discourse, using the procedure as a means of teaching students to generate questions related to their text.

Instructing students to both ask and answer questions is relevant to metacognitive tasks in two obvious ways. First, teaching children strategies for locating information in response to questions can assist them in recognizing the relationship between their own knowledge base and the information presented in textual materials. In teaching them to ask questions, we are providing them with a tool for seeking new and desired information and for monitoring their level of understanding of texts.

Assessing and Monitoring Acquired Skills

Glaser's fourth component concerns assessing and monitoring those skills that are acquired. The role played by questions can be seen in the numerous reading-comprehension tests consisting of texts and related questions (e.g., Gates-MacGinitie, ITBS), by sampling science texts (Pearson & Gallegher, 1982), and by observing basal readers that have questions at the end of stories and chapters for the express purpose of checking or monitoring students' understanding, and by observations of classrooms sampling the frequency of questions asked by the teachers to assess children's level of understanding. Thus, it is apparent that questions are used for the assessment of content domains or declarative knowledge. Still at issue are the relative merits or (1) using questions to assess this knowledge, (2) providing credit for partial states of knowledge, and (3) recognizing the potential differences between questions of different types (explicit vs. inferential) or different styles (recognition or recall). An intriguing possibility that the authors are presently investigating is whether the quality of learner-generated questions may index their comprehension of text. A common sense expression, "ask a stupid question, get a stupid answer," implies that "smart [i.e., good] questions beget smart answers." Most instructors can identify with the experience of having students who ask a range of quality questions, often finding the questions themselves predict the students' success in the class. Perhaps this situation has potential as a means of assessment.

In considering the research on metacognition and questioning within an instructional framework such as Glaser's, it appears that the picture of instruction or prescription related to questioning activities is incomplete. First, while we can describe a skilled question-answerer with some confidence, we are basing this description on a small number of studies. Further, our knowledge of a skilled question-asker is severely limited. These statements imply a similar position with respect to our knowledge of the novice question-answerer and -asker. Second, there is encouraging evidence that training programs may have a positive effect on students' ability to both answer and ask questions, though again, there is much to learn regarding factors that influence these abilities, particularly in question-asking skills. Third, while much has been investigated regarding the use of questions when testing for recall of information, testing of one's own learning (e.g., monitoring and assessment) using questioning tasks has yet to be examined.

To summarize, it is apparent that the understanding of the role of questions and their related cognitive requirements has a great deal of relevance to classroom settings. It is also apparent that a number of investigations have concerned question-related activities. Yet, the picture remains cloudy and research in some of the aforementioned specific areas is badly needed.

Summary and Conclusions

In this section, a summarization of our major ideas is presented, as well as a critical analysis of the concepts of cognition and metacognition. We make this analysis more concrete by our consideration of these concepts as they serve to help us understand question answering and asking as activities used in the service of reading comprehension.

We have seen that metacognition is a term that embraces as vast an expanse as individuals' knowledge of their own cognitive processes and cognitive states. Metacognition is a vague concept that resists any exact definition and yet is one that has been useful heuristically. We have agreed that such a concept should include individuals' conscious or verbalizable knowledge but at the same time we have suggested that like cognition, much of metacognition may be tacit (Kendall & Mason, 1982; Moroz, 1972; Polanyi, 1958). An attribution theory of individuals' explanations of their own mental events and activities, while interesting in its own right, nevertheless leaves untold the relationship of these explanations to their actual performance. More important, in the present context restricting metacognition to those mental events of which we are aware, the concept is rendered impotent with respect to the psychology of instruction. We maintain that if the concept of metacognition is to be useful to the psychology of instruction it is not because of what students know about their own cognition out of context, but rather it is because such knowledge is manifest in their performance on academic tasks. Or, as Schank (1982) so succinctly puts it: "A child need not 'know that' in order to 'know how'" (p. 56). Expressions such as learning-to-learn, self-correcting systems, and the orchestration of learning perhaps best capture our more performance-based concepts of metacognition.

The concept of metacognition is attractive to cognitively oriented instructional psychologists because it addresses two of its major concerns. First, it goes to the very heart of the cognitivists assumption of the learner as an active organism. It is individuals' metacognitive knowledge that enables them to behave proactively or to influence the input that in turn influences their activity. Second, and related, the concept of metacognition addresses one of the perennial problems of instruction—that of transfer or generalization of what has been learned. It is reasoned that to the extent individuals know what and how they know, such higher-order knowledge should be utilizable across different settings. This knowledge should not have to be relearned in every context. Yet just as there is no such thing as pure process (Rogoff, 1982) we would argue similarly that there is no such thing as pure metaprocess. The questions of how broad- or narrow-banded metacognition is and the factors that influence this band width are among the more important concerns of a theory both of cognition and of instruction.

In the present chapter, a major focus that intersects with our interests in metacognition and instruction has been the role of questions, both student- and other-generated, and their relationship to reading comprehension. In short, question-related activities rely heavily upon both cognitive and metacognitive knowledge and play a role in some of the most important and frequently used tasks in text-based instruction. We have seen that the use of questions in instruction may span a continuum ranging from little to extensive learner control over the reading-comprehension process.

One extreme entails minimal metacognitive involvement: students may be asked questions that direct their attention to *what* is important and may be given instructional support as to *how* to arrive at an acceptable answer to such questions (e.g., assessing their own knowledge, locating and integrating this with text-based information, etc.). The other end of the continuum involves extensive metacognitive knowledge: students are left to their own devices in comprehending what they are reading. That is, students generate and answer their own questions (see also Raphael & Gavelek, 1984).

A number of interesting research questions derive from thinking about the relationship between questions and reading comprehension in this way. An obvious and fundamental issue with implications for a cognitive theory of instruction concerns the relative effectiveness of other- versus learner-generated questions as facilitators of comprehension. It would seem that one can mount a reasonable argument for either side of this issue. One might maintain that other-generated questions are likely to be superior because they have been created by subject matter specialists (e.g., teachers, text authors) who presumably know best what students need to know. The case to be made for other-generated questions as facilitators of comprehension is perhaps best made by this quote of Jenkins (taken from Brown, 1975):

> If we give the head higher order things to do, it retains the analysis of the higher order relations, it extracts and uses these relations to generate products related to the initial activity; it seems to function very efficiently in pursuing such tasks; if on the other hand we give the head stupid things to do by brute force, it can only do relatively stupid things with the task and in the normal case it functions relatively inefficiently (Jenkins, 1971, p. 295).

Whether matching takes place such that good questions beget good answers has hardly been addressed with respect to text-based questions.

The other position that we might label the "wisdom of the learner" maintains that students are more likely to ask questions which optimize their own comprehension. Throughout the literature there is either stated or implied an epistemic motivation to know; this results in the learner asking questions of external sources (e.g., teacher, text) or him- or herself. With respect to the latter, the assumption that learners engage in this sort of private interrogation when confronted with text material has gone largely untested. A number of issues with respect to this assumption come to mind. What constitutes a questioning state? How shall these states be measured? In what way do they influence an individuals' comprehension? A number of concepts in cognition and development seem to posit similar or related concepts. (e.g., epistemic motivation, problem finding, disequilibrium). When applied to reading, all of these concepts suggest that when students encounter anomalies in text they analyze these anomalies and ask questions of themselves or others which promote their own comprehension. Dewey (1933) recognized in his treatment of reflective thought that understanding oftentimes does not occur automatically but must be evoked by the disequilibrium inherent in a situation in which incompatibility exists between two or more sources of information. With respect to reading, this disequilibrium may result from a disparity between what individuals know as a part of their background knowledge and what they are presently reading, or it may be indicated by sensing that two different ideas in the same text are not congruent with each other. Feuerstein (1980) suggests that the inadequate recognition and definition of a problem (i.e., an incongruity in what has been read) may underlie many of the difficulties that children with learning problems experience. Bransford et al. (1981) make a similar argument with respect to children with problems related to text comprehension.

The arguments for both other-generated and learner-generated questions have their rejoinders. For example, other-generated questions are typically targeted for the average child, presented to groups of children, and in a linear sequence, the result being that such questions are optimal for no one. On the other hand learners-as-questioners may suffer from their own primary and/or secondary ignorance (Brown, 1975). That is, they may not know enough to know what is important or they may not know what they do and do not know.

There is an apparent paradox involved in the use of learner-generated questions to promote comprehension. On the one hand, students need to ask questions to acquire more knowledge, but on the other, they need the background knowledge to ask these comprehension-promoting questions. There may well be a third position—the Socratic method of teaching—which is informed by this dialectical nature of questioning activities. An integral skill of the Socratic method encouraged by its teacher-student dialogue involves the student learning to ask the right questions when there is not enough information to make a prediction with respect to some line of thought (Collins, 1977). With the advent and already widespread purchase of microcomputers for the classroom, it is now feasible to design Socratic tutorial systems that promote the comprehension of text (Collins, 1977).

Clearly, the issue of which is better with respect to learner- and other-generated questions is more profitably addressed by considering the moderator variables of which comprehension is a function. Because we are interested in questioning activities, we have tended to act as though they are all important and can be decoupled from the rest of what a learner does to comprehend text. Both of these notions we disclaim. We close this chapter with a variation on the quote with which it began. Be patient with all that is unresolved in your heart, and try to love the questions themselves—but not too much.

References

Anderson, R. C., & Biddle, W. B. On asking people questions about what they do when they are reading. In G. Bower (Ed.), *Psychology of learning and motivation* (Vol. 9). New York: Academic Press, 1975.

Anderson, R. C. Allocation of attention during reading. In A. Flammer & W. Kintsch (Eds.), *Discourse processing*. Amsterdam: North Holland Publishing Company, in press.

Anderson, T. H., & Armbruster, B. B. Content area textbooks, In R. C. Anderson, J. Osborne, & R. J. Tierney (Eds.), *Learning to read in American schools: Basal readers and content texts*. Hillsdale, NJ: Erlbaum, 1984.

André, T. Does answering higher level questions while reading facilitate productive learning. *Review of Educational Research*, 1979, 49, 280–318.

André, M. D. A., & Anderson, T. H. The development of a self-questioning study technique. *Reading Research Quarterly*, 1978–1979, 14, 605–623.

Au, K. H. Using the experience–text–relationship method with minority children. *The Reading Teacher*, 1979, 32, 677–679.

Barrett, T. C. Taxonomy of reading comprehension. In R. Smith & T. C. Barrett (Eds.), *Teaching reading in the middle grades*. Reading, MA: Addison-Wesley, 1976.

Beck, I. L., McCaslin, E. S., & McKeown, M. G. Basal readers' purpose for story reading: Smoothly paving the road or setting up a detour? *Elementary School Journal*, 1981, 81, 156–161.

Bloom, B. S., Engelhart, M. D., Furst, E. J., Hill, & W. H., & Krathwohl, D. R. (Eds.), *Taxonomy of educational objectives: Cognitive domain*. New York: David McKay, 1956.

Bransford, J. D., Nitsch, K. E., & Franks, J. J. Schooling and the facilitation of knowing. In R. C. Spiro, R. J. Spiro, W. E. Montague (Eds.), *Schooling and the acquisition of knowledge*. Hillsdale, NJ: Erlbaum, 1977.

Bransford, J. D., Stein, B. S., Shelton, T. S., & Owings, R. A. Cognition and adaption: The importance of learning to learn. In J. H. Harvey (Ed.), *Cognition, social behavior, and the environment*. Hillsdale, NJ: Erlbaum, 1981.

Brown, A. L. The development of memory: Knowing, knowing about knowing, knowing how to know. In H. W. Reese (Ed.), *Advances in child development and behavior* (Vol. 10). New York: Academic Press, 1975.

Brown, A. L., & French, L. A. The zone of potential development: Implications for intelligence testing in the year 2000. *Intelligence*, 1979, 3, 253–271.

Bruner, J. S. *Toward a theory of instruction*. New York: W. W. Norton & Company, 1966.

Carrier, C. A., & Fautsch-Patridge, T. Levels of questions: A framework for the exploration of processing activities. *Contemporary Educational Psychology*, 1981, 6, 365–381.

Cavanaugh, J. C., & Borkowski, J. G. Searching for metamemory–memory connection: A developmental study. *Developmental Psychology*, 1980, 16, 441–453.

Collins, A. Processes in acquiring knowledge. In R. C. Anderson, R. J. Spiro, & W. E.

Montague (Eds.), *Schooling and the acquisition of knowledge.* Hillsdale, NJ: Erlbaum, 1977.

Crowell, D., Au, K. H. & Blake, J. Reading comprehension questions: Differences among standardized tests. *Journal of Reading*, 1983, 26(4), 314–319.

Denny, D. R. The effects of exemplary and cognitive models and self-rehearsal on children's interrogative stategies. *Journal of Experimental Child Psychology*, 1975, 19, 476–488.

Dewey, J. *How we think.* Boston: Heath & Co., 1933.

Dillon, J. T. The multidisciplinary study of questioning. *Journal of Educational Psychology*, 1982, 74, 147–165. (a)

Dillon, J. T. Cognitive correspondence between question/statement and response. American Educational Research Journal, 1982, 19, 540–551. (b)

Durkin, D. What classroom observations reveal about reading comprehension instruction. *Reading Research Quarterly* 1978–79, 14, 481–533.

Durkin, D. *Reading comprehension instruction in five basal reader series* (Reading Education Report 26). Champaign, IL: Center for the Study of Reading, University of Illinois, July 1981.

Faw, H. W., & Waller, T. G. Mathemagenic behaviours and efficiency in learning from prose materials: Review, critique and recommendations. *Review of Educational Research*, 1976, 46, 691–720.

Feuerstein, R. *Instrumental Enrichment.* Baltimore, MD: University Park Press, 1980.

Flavell, J. H. Cognitive monitoring. In W. P. Dickson (Ed.), *Children's oral communication skills.* New York: Academic Press, 1981.

Flavell, J. H., Friedrichs, A. G., & Hoyt, J. D. Developmental changes in memorization processes. *Cognitive Psychology*, 1970, 1, 324–340.

Flavell, J. H. Metacognitive aspects of problem solving. In L. B. Resnick (Ed.), *The nature of intelligence.* Hillsdale, NJ: Erlbaum, 1976.

Flavell, J. H., & Wellman, H. M. Metamemory. In R. V. Kail, Jr. & J. W. Hagen (Eds.), *Perspectives on the development of memory and cognition.* Hillsdale, NJ: Erlbaum, 1977.

Garner, R., & Reis, R. Monitoring and resolving comprehension obstacles: An investigation of spontaneous text lookbacks among upper-grade good and poor comprehenders. *Reading Research Quarterly*, 1981, 16, 569–582.

Gavelek, J. R., & Raphael, T. E. *The relationship between one's feeling of knowing and performance on comprehension questions.* Paper presented at the National Reading Conference, Dallas, Texas, 1981.

Glaser, R. Instructional psychology: Past, present, and future. American Psychologist, 1982, 37, 292–305.

Guszak, F. J. Teacher questioning and reading. *The Reading Teacher*, 1967, 21, 227–234.

Hansen, J. The effects of inference training and practice on young children's comprehension. *Reading Research Quarterly*, 1981, 16, 391–417.

Hansen, J., & Pearson, P. D. An instructional study: Improving the inferential comprehension of good and poor fourth-grade readers. *Journal of Educational Psychology*, 1983, 75, 821–830.

Hare, V., & Pulliam, C. A. Teacher questioning: A verification and an extension. *Journal of Reading Behavior*, 1979, 12, 69–72.

Hart, J. T. Memory and the feeling of knowing experience. *Journal of Educational Psychology*, 1966, 56, 208–216.

Hosseini, J., & Ferrell, W. R. Detectability of correctness: A measure of knowing that one knows. *Instructional Science*, 1982, 11, 113–127.

James, W. *The principles of psychology.* New York: Holt, 1890.

Jenkins, J. J. Second discussant's comments: What's left to say? *Human Development*, 1971, 14, 279–286.

Kavale, K., & Schreiner, R. The reading process of above average and average readers: A comparison of the use of reasoning strategies in responding to standardized comprehension measures. *Reading Research Quarterly*, 1979-1980, *15*, 102-127.

Kearsley, G. P. Questions and question asking in verbal discourse: A cross-disciplinary review. *Journal of Psycholinguistic Research*, 1976, *5*, 355-375.

Kendall, J. R., & Mason, J. M. Metacognition from the historical context of teaching reading. *Topics in Learning and Learning Disabilities*, 1982, *2*, 82-89.

Laboratory of Comparative Human Cognition. Culture and cognitive development. In P. H. Mussen & W. Kessen (Eds.), *Handbook of Child Psychology* (Vol. 1). New York: Wiley, 1983.

Lockhart, R. S., Craik, F. I. M., & Jacoby, L. L. Depth of processing, recognition, and recall. In J. Brown (Ed.), *Recognition and recall*. London: Wiley, 1976.

Markman, E. M. Realizing that you don't understand: Elementary school children's awareness of inconsistencies. *Child Development*, 1979, *50*, 643-655.

Markman, E. M. Comprehension monitoring. In P. W. Dickson (Ed.), *Children's oral communication skills*. New York: Academic Press, 1981.

Meichenbaum, D., & Asarnow, J. Cognitive-behavioral modification and metacognitive development: Implications for the classroom. In P. C. Kendall & S. D. Hollon (Eds.), *Cognitive-behavioral interventions: Theory, research, and procedures*. New York: Academic Press, 1979.

Miyake, N., & Norman, D. A. To ask a question one must know enough to know what is not known. *Journal of Verbal Learning and Verbal Behavior*, 1979, *18*, 351-364.

Moroz, M. The concept of cognition in contemporary psychology. In J. R. Royce & W. W. Rozeboom (Eds.), *The psychology of knowing*. New York: Gordon & Breach, 1972.

Myers, M., & Paris, S. G. Children's metacognitive knowledge about reading. *Journal of Educational Psychology*, 1978, *70*, 680-690.

Neisser, U. *Cognition and reality*. San Francisco, CA: 1976.

Omanson, R. C., Beck, I. L., Voss, J. F., & McKeown, M. G. The effects of reading lessons on comprehension: A processing description. *Cognition and Instruction*, 1984, *1*(1), 45-67.

Palinscar, A. S. The quest for meaning from expository text: A teacher guided journey. In G. Duffy, L. Roehler, & J. Mason (Eds.), *Comprehension instruction: Perspectives and suggestions*. New York: Longman, 1983.

Paris, S. G., Lipson, M. Y., & Wixson, K. K. Becoming a strategic reader. *Contemporary Educational Psychology*, 1983, *8*, 293-316.

Pearson, P. D. *Asking stories about questions* (Occasional Paper 15). Ohio: Ginn & Company, 1981.

Pearson, P. D., & Gallegher, M. Paper presented at the National Reading Conference, Clearwater Beach, Florida, December, 1982.

Pearson, P. D., & Johnson, D. D. *Teaching reading comprehension*. New York: Holt, Rinehart & Winston, 1978.

Pearson, P. D., Hansen, J., & Gordon, C. The effect of background knowledge on young children's comprehension of explicit and implicit information. *Journal of Reading Behavior*, 1979, *9*, 201-210.

Polanyi, M. *Personal Knowledge*. Chicago: University of Chicago Press, 1958.

Postman, N., & Weingartner, C. (1969), *Teaching as a subversive activity*. New York: Delacorte Press.

Raphael, T. E. Teaching learners about sources of information for answering questions. *Journal of Reading*, 1984, *27*, 303-311.

Raphael, T. E., & Gavelek, J. R. Question-related activities and their relationship to reading comprehension: Some instructional implications. In G. Duffy, L. Roehler, & J. Mason

(Eds.), *Comprehension instruction: Perspectives and Suggestions*. New York: Longman, 1984.

Raphael, T. E., & McKinney, J. An examination of fifth and eighth grade children's question answering behavior: An instructional study in metacognition. *Journal of Reading Behavior*, 1983.

Raphael, T. E., & Pearson, P. D. Increasing students' awareness of sources of information for answering questions. *American Educational Research Journal*, in press.

Raphael, T. E., & Wonnacott, C. A. Heightening fourth grade students' sensitivity to sources of information for answering comprehension questions, *Reading Research Quarterly*, in press.

Raphael, T. E., & Wonnacott, C. A. *The effect of type of response and type of post test on understanding of and memory for text*. Paper presented at the National Reading Conference, Dallas, Texas, 1981. (ERIC Document Reproduction Service #ED212 898).

Reynolds, R. E., & Anderson, R. C. Influence of questions on the allocation of attention during reading. *Journal of Educational Psychology*, 1982, 74, 623–632.

Reynolds, R. E., & Magleby, L. B. *Developmental effects of question position and question type on children's learning of prose material*. Paper presentation at the National Reading Conference, Dallas, Texas, 1981.

Reynolds, R. E., & Raphael, T. E. *The effect of inserted questions on childrens comprehension: A new look at an old paradigm*. Unpublished manuscript, University of Utah and Michigan State University, 1984.

Rickards, J. P. Adjunct postquestions in text: A critical review of methods and processes. *Review of Educational Research*, 1979, 49, 181–196.

Rickards, J. P., & Denner, P. R. Depressive effects of underlining and adjunct questions on children's recall of text. *Instructional Science*, 1979, 8, 81–90.

Rickards, J. P., & Hatcher, C. W. Interspersed meaningful learning questions as semantic cues for poor comprehenders. *Reading Research Quarterly*, 1978, 13, 539–553.

Roehler, L. R., Duffy, G. G., Book, C., & Wesselman, R. *Direct teacher explanation during reading instruction: A pilot study* (Research Series 132). East Lansing, MI: Institute for Research on Teaching, April, 1983.

Rogoff, B. Integrating context and cognitive development. In M. E. Lamb & A. L. Brown (Eds.), *Advances in developmental psychology* (Vol. 2). Hillsdale, NJ: Erlbaum, 1982.

Rothkopf, E. Z. Some theoretical and experimental approaches to problems in written instruction. In J. D. Krumboltz (Ed.), *Learning and the educational process*. Chicago: Rand-McNally, 1965.

Rothkopf, E. Z. Learning from written instructive materials: An exploration of the control of inspection behavior by test-like events. *American Educational Research Journal*, 1966, 3, 241–249.

Sanders, N. *Classroom questions: What kinds?* New York: Harper & Row, 1966.

Singer, H., & Donlan, D. Active comprehension: Problem-solving schema with question generation for comprehension of complex short stories. *Reading Research Quarterly*, 1982, 17, 166–186.

Schank, R. C. *Reading and Understanding: Teaching from the perspective of artificial intelligence*. Hillsdale, NJ: Erlbaum, 1982.

Smirnov, A. A., & Zinchenko, P. I. Problems in the psychology of memory. In M. Cole & I. Maltzman (Eds.), *A handbook of contemporary Soviet psychology*. New York: Basic Books, 1969.

Tierney, R. J. A comparison of Australian and American reading teachers. In J. E. Merritt, (Ed.), *New horizons in reading*. Newark, DE: International Reading Association, 1976.

Tulving, E., & Thomson, D. M. Encoding specificity and retrieval processes in episodic memory. *Psychological Review*, 1973, 80, 353–373.

Watts, G. H., & Anderson, R. C. Effects of three types of questions on learning from prose. *Journal of Educational Psychology*, 1971, 62, 387–394.

Wellman, H. M. The early development of intentional memory behavior. *Human Development*, 1977, 20, 86–101.

Wertsch, J. W., & Stone, C. A. The concept of internalization in Vygotsky's account of the genesis of higher mental functions. In J. V. Wertsch (Ed.), *Culture, communication, and cognition: Vygotskian perspectives*. New York: Cambridge University Press, in press.

Wixson, K. K. Postreading question-answer interactions and children's learning from text. *Journal of Educational Psychology*, 1983, 30, 413–423. (a)

Wixson, K. K. Questions about text: What you ask about is what children learn. *The Reading Teacher*, 1983, 37, 287–293. (b)

Wixson, K. K. Level of importance of postquestions and children's learning from text. *American Educational Research Journal*, 1984, 21, 419–433.

Wong, B. Y. L., & Jones, W. Increasing metacomprehension in learning disabled and normally-achieving students through self-questioning straining. *Learning Disabilities Quarterly*, 1982, 5, 228–240.

Wonnacott, C. A., & Raphael, T. E. *Comprehension monitoring: An investigation of children's question-answering strategies*. Paper presented at the National Reading Conference, Clearwater, Florida, December 1982.

Vygotsky, L. S. *Mind in society: The development of higher psychological processes*. Cambridge, MA: Harvard University Press, 1978.

CHAPTER 4

Metacognition and Learning Disabilities

Bernice Y. L. Wong

Metacognition and Learning Disabilities

The theme of this chapter is the connection between metacognition and learning disabilities. In pursuing this theme, three questions are addressed. (1) What is the relevance of metacognitive theory and research to the learning disabilities field? (2) Why is the learning disabilities field so receptive to metacognitive theory? (3) What is the impact of metacognitive theory and research on the learning disabilities field? Before addressing these questions, some clarification of concepts, for example, metacognition, learning disabilities, ability deficits, appears to be necessary.

Clarification of Concepts

Metacognition: Definition

Flavell (1976, p. 232) stated that "metacognition refers to one's knowledge concerning one's own cognitive processes and products of anything related to them, e.g., the learning-relevant properties of information or data." Included in that statement are two clusters of activities: Knowledge about cognition and regulation of cognition (Baker & Brown, 1984a).

Knowledge about cognition concerns a person's knowledge about personal cognitive resources, and the compatibility between himself or herself

137

as a learner and the learning situation. Specifically, Flavell (1982) proposes three categories of knowledge about cognition: person variables, task variables and strategy variables. *Person variables* refer to an individual's acquired knowledge and beliefs concerning human beings as cognitive organisms. Thus, an individual may believe she or he is good at processing verbal materials, but poor at spatial materials. She or he may judge himself or herself to be brighter than his or her parents, but realize the parents in turn are brighter than some of their friends. Then there is some universal knowledge that one gains in the course of attaining maturity. For example, the knowledge–intuition that human short-term memory is fallible and of limited capacity (Flavell, 1982). The preceding examples correspond to the three subcategories of person variables proposed by Flavell (1982): Intraindividual, interindividual, and universal.

Knowledge about task variables refers to the individual's learning from experience that different kinds of tasks exert different kinds of information processing demands on us, for example, one's knowledge that learning the gist of a story is much easier than learning it verbatim (Flavell, 1982). Learning the implications of different task demands on us enables us to take account of them, and to incorporate them into our subsequent plans and actions to complete the task successfully.

Strategy variables refer to those strategies for monitoring an individual's cognitive progress. For example, to find the sum of a list of numbers, one simply adds them up. Here, adding is the cognitive strategy used to fulfill the goal. A metacognitive strategy in that situation would be repeating the adding process to ensure the sum is correct. Here the purpose is no longer reaching the goal—that is, deriving a sum (cognitive strategy). Rather, the purpose is to ensure that the goal has been reached through self-checking (metacognitive strategy) (see Flavell, 1982).

Flavell (1982; Flavell & Wellman, 1977) emphasizes the interactions among persons, task, and strategy variables. We develop intuitions about interactions among these variables. For example we become aware of the superiority–inferiority of certain strategies, given our own particular cognitive constitution and the particular task (Flavell, 1982).

The regulation of cognition concerns the self-regulatory mechanisms used by an active learner during an ongoing attempt to solve problems (Brown, 1980; Baker & Brown, in press 1984a, 1984b). The metacognitive activities here include planning, checking, monitoring, testing, revising, and evaluating. Brown (1980) captured the intricate orchestration of these metacognitive activities in the good reader. She wrote that the efficient reader deploys the following activities:

> (1) clarifying the purposes of reading, that is, understanding the task demands, both explicit and implicit; (2) identifying the aspects of a message that are important; (3)

allocating attention so that concentration can be focused on the major content area rather than trivia; (4) monitoring ongoing activities to determine whether comprehension is occurring; (5) engaging in review and self-interrogation to determine whether goals are being achieved; (6) taking corrective action when failures in comprehension are detected; and (7) recovering from disruptions and distractions—and many more deliberate, planful activities that render reading an efficient information-gathering activity. (Brown, 1980, p. 456)

The two aspects of metacognition: Knowledge about cognition and regulation of cognition are important determinants of successful learning, efficient reading, and effective studying (Brown, 1980; Baker & Brown, 1984a, 1984b). Although they are very closely related, the two aspects of metacognition have different characteristics. Knowledge about cognition is "stable, statable but fallible, and late-developing" (Brown, 1982, p. 6). It is fallible in the sense that a child or an adult may believe herself or himself to know some facts about something, for example, reading, that are untrue. Regulation about cognition, on the other hand, is "relatively unstable, rarely statable and relatively age independent" (Brown, 1982, p. 8). The regulating activities stated earlier, are unstable and age independent, in that although used more often by older children and adults, they are *not* always used by them. Even young children monitor their activities on a simplified task (Patterson, Cosgrove, & O'Brien, 1980). Moreover, adults and fluent readers may only be aware of their regulating activities when they encounter a reading comprehension failure (Anderson, 1980). Thus, active comprehension monitoring is often an unconscious, hence, unstatable experience (Baker & Brown, 1984a, 1984b). The preceding brief introduction to the term metacognition should suffice because other excellent sources are available (cf. Brown, 1978, 1980, 1982; Flavell, 1976, 1982).

Learning Disabilities: Definition

The term *learning disabilities* was originally created to procure recognition and political influence for a particular group of children. These children showed developmental delays in speech and language facilities, problems in visual/auditory perception, problems in visual–motor coordination, and academic difficulties. Yet they had intact intelligence and absence of sensory handicaps, (e.g., blindness–deafness). Hence, they did not fit into the existent categories of exceptionality. Consequently, they did not qualify for special educational services funded by the U.S. federal government (Kirk, 1972; Kirk & Gallagher, 1979). Parent groups lobbied for creating a category of exceptionality for learning-disabled children in order to obtain educational services for them. These parents adopted the term *learning disabilities*," which was coined by Kirk (1963). Kirk used the term to focus on the learning difficulties of these children, and to deemphasize the etiology of learning disabilities (Cruickshank, 1972; Kirk, 1972).

The characteristics of these learning disabled (LD) children include academic learning difficulties, disorders in receptive and/or expressive language, disorders of perception (e.g., visual/auditory discrimination problems), disorders of motor activity (e.g., hyperactivity, hypoactivity, or incoordination), attentional problems, memory problems, and socioemotional problems (Mercer, 1979; Myers & Hammill, 1982; Wallace & McLoughlin, 1979). Because of their heterogeneity, LD children may either show various combinations of the aforementioned problems, or specific problems in one area—for example, arithmetic. The heterogeneous nature of their problems is such that given two LD children with difficulties in a specific subject (e.g., arithmetic), it is rare that the sources of their difficulties would be identical or that the remedial methods for instructing them would be identical (Kinsbourne & Caplan, 1979; Myers & Hammill, 1982).

The nature of the academic difficulties in LD students is *selective* and *specific* (Kinsbourne & Caplan, 1979; Kirk, 1972; Kirk & Gallagher, 1979). Unlike the general learning problems in retardates, the learning disabilities in LD students are located in a more limited/specific area. The source of a student's learning disabilities is psychological process problems. These process problems impede the LD child's normal development in reading, spelling, mathematics, and writing (Kirk, 1972; Kirk & Gallagher, 1979). The formal definition of learning disabilities follows:

> "Specific learning disability" means a disorder in one or more of the basic psychological processes involved in understanding or in using language spoken or written, which may manifest itself in an imperfect ability to listen, think, speak, read, write, spell, or to do mathematical calculations. The term includes such conditions as perceptual handicaps, brain injury, minimal brain dysfunction, dyslexia, developmental aphasia. The term does not include children who have learning problems which are primarily the result of visual, hearing, or motor handicaps, of mental retardation, of emotional disturbance, or of environmental, cultural, or economic disadvantage (National Advisory Committee on Handicapped Children [NACHC], 1968).

The preceding definition was incorporated into the recent 1977 U.S. Public Law 94-142. Additionally PL 94-142 states that an assessment team may decide a child has a specific learning disability if:

1. The child does not achieve commensurate with his or her age and ability levels in one or more of seven specific areas when provided with learning experiences appropriate for the child's age and ability levels.

2. The team finds that a child has a severe discrepancy between achievement and intellectual ability in one or more of the following areas: (1) oral expression, (2) listening comprehension, (3) written expression, (4) basic reading skill, (5) reading comprehension, (6) mathematics calculation, (7) mathematics reasoning.

The definition of learning disabilities has always been problematic to professionals both within the field and without. Among learning disabilities professionals, debates over its formulation have continued from the beginning of the field to the present. Two specific parts of the NACHC (1968) definition have been widely criticized. The first criticism concerns the clause that states learning disabilities cannot occur jointly with other handicaps (e.g., deafness) or cultural or economic disadvantage. Basically the interpretation of this clause is that learning disabilities cannot be the *direct* result of conditions of sensory handicaps and cultural–environmental disadvantage. However, learning disabilities can co-occur with those conditions. For example, the research on the relation between malnutrition and learning (Cravioto, 1972) suggests that learning disabilities can occur in children from impoverished homes where they do not have balanced and nutritious diets. Second, the definition of learning disabilities is obscured by the list of conditions for which the term serves as an umbrella (i.e., "perceptual handicaps, brain injury, minimal brain dysfunction, dyslexia, and developmental aphasia"). Other criticisms of the current (PL 94-142) definition concern the word *child*, which does not provide for LD adolescents and adults, and the phrase, *basic psychological processes*. A detailed discussion of these weaknesses of the current definition of learning disabilities can be found in Hammill, Leigh, McNutt, and Larsen (1981).

In an attempt to redress the criticisms on the current official definition of learning disabilities, the National Joint Committee on LD (NJCLD) worked on and eventually produced a new definition of learning disabilities. The representatives for NJCLD consisted of members from each of the following organizations: The American Speech–Language–Hearing Association (ASHA), the Association for Children & Adults with Learning Disabilities (ACLD), the Council for Learning Disabilities (CLD formerly DCLD), the Division for Children with Communication Disorders (DCCD), the International Reading Association (IRA), and the Orton Dyslexia Society. This new definition states that

> Learning disabilities is a generic term that refers to a heterogeneous group of disorders manifested by significant difficulties in the acquisition and use of listening, speaking, reading, writing, reasoning or mathematical abilities. These disorders are intrinsic to the individual and presumed to be due to central nervous system dysfunction. Even though a learning disability may occur concomitantly with other handicapping conditions (e.g., sensory impairment, mental retardation, social and emotional distur-

bance) or environmental influences (e.g., cultural differences, insufficient/ inappropriate instruction, psychogenic factors), it is not the direct result of those conditions or influences (National Joint Committee on LD, 1981).

Currently, the preceding definition has been endorsed by the governing boards of all the organizations excepting ACLD. Thus, the proposed new definition of learning disabilities has not yet been accepted by all learning disabilities professionals.

The significant advance of this new definition of learning disabilities over previous ones lies in the removal of the list of inclusive conditions for learning disabilities and in its allowance for co-occurrence of learning disabilities with other handicapping or environmental conditions. However, the deletion of the phrase *basic psychological processes* produces a *functional* definition of learning disabilities, which may prove insufficient. Some suggestion for the mechanisms/psychological processes responsible for the LD student's academic difficulties needs to be made for theoretical and empirical purposes.

Ability Deficit

Children with learning disabilities are defined in part, as having disorders in one or more of the basic psychological processes needed for school learning (Lerner, 1981; Torgesen, 1977a). Because of this definitional clause, much research effort had been directed at pinpointing the particular disorder(s) in basic psychological processes which are responsible for the child's learning difficulties (Torgesen, 1977a). The findings of earlier learning disabilities research indicated that LD children performed poorly on a wide range of experimental tasks (Torgesen, 1975).

A pertinent observation is that researchers designed tasks that they assumed would directly measure basic psychological processes. Thus, failure on the part of LD children on these tasks led to the inference that these children lacked the particular basic ability—that is, the particular psychological process required for successful task performance (Lerner, 1981; Torgesen, 1977a). For example, if LD children failed in a memory task, they would be seen as demonstrating an *ability deficit* in memory processes. A different way of expressing the same inference would be: The LD children had *process problems* in memory. This kind of inferential perspective, coupled with the LD children's poor performance on a wide variety of experimental tasks, resulted in the creation of a catalogue of discrete ability deficits that purportedly underlie LD children's poor learning (Senf, 1974; Torgesen, 1977a). Eventually labels were used interchangeably by researchers: Ability deficits, process problems, processing dysfunctions, deficits in psychological processing functions (Lerner, 1981, pp. 170–178; Torgesen, 1977a). So pervasive was the deficits perspective that one prominent theory of learning disabilities was based on children's ability deficits in a particular cognitive area. Specifically, the proponents of the perceptual deficits hypothesis of learning disabilities believe that deficient perceptual functions in visual discrimination and visual memory cause learning disabilities (Bender, 1957; Cruickshank, 1972; Frostig, 1966). They considered disordered visual perception, as in persistent letter reversals, to be the root of reading disability. However, this theory has been soundly criticized on theoretical and empirical grounds by Vellutino, Steger, Moyer, Harding, and Miles (1977). Consequently, it no longer holds sway in the LD field.

What Is the Relevance of Metacognitive Theory and Research to the Learning Disabilities Field?

The relevance of metacognitive theory and research to the LD field lies in providing a more complete understanding of academic difficulties/ failures in LD students. It will be shown that the ability-deficits theory of LD students' academic difficulties is inadequate, and the opposing theory of task-analysis insufficient. Metacognitive theory redresses the insufficiency in the task-analysis theory. Together, task-analysis and metacognitive perspectives provide a satisfactory conceptual perspective on the academic difficulties of LD students, by pointing to the twin foci of LD students' instructional needs—namely, cognitive *and* metacognitive skills.

Contrasting the Ability-Deficits Theory with the Metacognitive Theory

There have been several models of psychological processing proposed to interpret LD. Among these, Kirk and Kirk's (1971) psycholinguistic model is the best known (Lerner, 1981, pp. 170–173). These models represent a particular theoretical orientation in LD—namely, the ability-deficits theory. Their basic tenet is that certain children fail to learn well in school because of deficits in processing functions—that is, ability deficits. For example, the theory suggests that children with ability deficits in auditory processing will have difficulty with primarily auditory instructional approaches, such as phonics. For these particular children to learn, the theory suggests special instructional methods are necessary. Specifically, three different instructional plans are espoused by the ability-deficits theory. The first centers on deficit training. The goal here is to develop and build in the LD child those areas in which ability deficits have been diagnosed. Thus, in the case of a child diagnosed to have ability deficits in auditory processing, she or he will be given exercises in auditory processing, in the hope of strengthening that area of function. The second instructional plan centers on teaching to the child's preferred modality of strength. The goal here is to capitalize on the child's intact–strong abilities by basing instruction on them, thus circumventing his or her ability deficits. In the case of a child with ability deficits in auditory processing but intact abilities in visual processing, teaching to the intact/strong abilities in reading would mean using a sight method to teach reading. The third instructional plan is simply a combination of the first two.

The Inadequacies of the Ability-Deficits Theory

There are serious problems with the ability-deficits theory and the instructional methods that this theory supports. First and foremost is the lack of a demonstrated relationship between LD students' ability deficits and their academic problems. Without documented empirical relationships between the two, we may not justifiably use ability deficits to explain academic problems in LD students. Although Kirk and Gallagher (1979) alluded to the critical issue under discussion, it appears to have been virtually ignored by practitioners in the LD field. Excepting Torgesen (1984), the same vital issue has seemingly attracted little interest among researchers.

Using comprehension measures in one study and story recall of important thematic ideas in another, Torgesen (1984) found no performance differences among normally achieving children, LD children with normal performance on the digit span of the WISC-R, and LD children with severe problems on the digit span. The results led him to conclude that short-term memory limitations as measured by the digit span on the WISC-R did not impair LD children's listening comprehension of meaningful narrative. Although Torgesen's findings are restricted to memory processes and to his particular methodology, they nevertheless challenge the tacit assumption held by many professionals in LD that LD students' ability deficits necessarily impair their academic learning–performance.

Second, studies on deficit training involving auditory or visual processes indicated little transfer to reading (Myers & Hamill, 1982). The consistent findings of negative transfer suggests that bridging between deficit training on the one hand and the reading tasks on the other, is required. More importantly, and on a broader level, the negative transfer in deficit training studies highlights the *simplistic* analysis of LD students' academic failures in the ability-deficits theory. By focusing exclusively on the child's ability deficits, the proponents of this theory failed to grasp the complexity of the total learning situation, in which multiple and interactive factors determine the learner's learning outcome (cf. Brown, 1982; Jenkins, 1979). Among these multiple and interactive determinants of successful learning, the student's abilities and/or ability deficits stand as *one* mere factor.

Jenkins' (1979) tetrahedral model (TM) outlines four basic sources of influence in a learning situation. These include (1) the characteristics of the learner, (2) the nature of the materials to be learned, (3) the criterial task, and (4) learning activities engaged in by the learner. Jenkins' TM of memory was borrowed and modified for use by Bransford (1979). It was subsequently borrowed from Bransford by Brown (1982). Because Brown's modified TM is more suited for the educational scene, it is used here, and is referred to simply as the TM. Figure 1 depicts the aforementioned four major sources of influence on the outcome of learning in the TM.

The *characteristics of the learner* refers to the cognitive and strategic repertoires the individual brings to the learning situation. Individual differences in these repertoires affect how the individuals learn (Brown, 1982). The *nature of the materials* to be learned refers to the organizational nature of the materials, materials that match the readers' prior knowledge and so forth. The nature of the materials to be learned affects the individual's learning outcome. For example, materials that match subjects' prior knowledge are more easily understood by subjects (Anderson, 1982; Brown, 1980). *Criterial task* is the end product in any learning. The efficient learner is aware of this end product; and tailors his or her learning activities accordingly (Baker & Brown, in press-a). The criterial task is what sets the learner's purpose in learning, as well as providing him or her with standards for evaluating his or her learning (Anderson, 1980; Brown, 1980). *Learning activities* refer to the activities the subject engages in while learning. The subject could spontaneously deploy suitable learning activities. She or he could be trained to do so, or even tricked into doing so by means of well-designed incidental orienting tasks. As children grow older, they gradually learn a repertoire of learning activities. With extensive use, these learning activities/strategies become automatic and their deployment unconscious (Brown, 1982). Engaging in appropriate learning activities influences significantly student learning outcome. For example, failure to categorize items into discrete categories of food, clothing, furniture, and vehicles impaired LD children's recall. Unobstrusively prompting them to put related items into suitable categories remarkably improved their recall (Wong, 1978).

The literature in cognitive psychology and developmental psychology

CHARACTERISTICS OF
THE LEARNER

Skills

Knowledge

Attitudes

and so forth

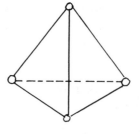

LEARNING ACTIVITIES   CRITERIAL TASKS

Attention   Recognition

Rehearsal   Recall

Elaboration   Transfer

and so forth   Problem Solving

and so forth

NATURE OF THE
MATERIALS

Modality

(visual, linguistic, etc.)

Physical Structure

Psychological Structure

Conceptual Difficulty

Sequencing of Materials

and so forth

FIGURE 1. A. L. Brown's adaptation of Jenkins's (1979) tetrahedral model of memory experiments. Reprinted with the permission of the publishers of *Human Development*, S. Karger Publishers, Inc.

has shown us clearly how each of the sources/factors labelled in the TM governs the likelihood of a student's successful learning. To demonstrate the point that the individual factors in the TM are important determinants of learning, some of the research on learner's learning activities is described. Learner's learning activities are chosen because this factor is in line with cognitive psychology's current emphasis on the learner's own role in his or her learning. The following research by Bransford and his colleagues focused on a particular learning activity, namely, learner's self-questioning activities.

Recently, Bransford, Stein, Vye, Franks, Auble, Mezynski, and Perfetto (1982) conducted three sets of studies. In their first set, they found that less-successful fifth graders could not write continuations to sentences that would make the events depicted in the individual sentences match particular types of men. For example, the sentence, "The tall man bought some crackers," appears to contain arbitrary information. To make the attribute of tallness in the man relevant to the event of buying crackers, a continuation or an elaboration of the sentence could have been "from the top shelf." Less-successful fifth graders wrote meaningful continuations such as "from the store" to the previous sentence. Only successful fifth graders produced elaborations that clarified the significance of the various attributes of the men in respective sentences (Stein, Bransford, Franks, Owings, Vye, & McGraw, 1982). Stein et al. called the elaborations produced by successful students, precise elaborations.

In analyzing the performance of less-successful students, Stein et al. (1982) reasoned that these students failed to generate relevant elaborations because they did not ask themselves the significance of the given attributes of the men. Referring to the preceding example, they did not ask themselves, "Why does it have to be a tall man who bought some crackers? Why not a short man?" In an earlier paper, Bransford, Stein, Shelton, and Owings (1981) observed that successful fifth graders spontaneously generated self-questions and evaluations in studying passages on boomerangs and rings around the moon. They used self-questions to activate their prior knowledge, which facilitated their comprehension and studying (Bransford et al., 1981). Thus self-questioning appears to be *instrumental* in activating one's prior knowledge.

Stein et al. (1982) also showed that training less-successful students to ask themselves relevant questions to activate prior knowledge helped them generate successfully precise continuations to given sentences. Specifically, Stein et al.'s training focused on making the students aware that they needed to clarify and make significant the attribute of each man to the corresponding event in the sentence. Training also increased sentence recall in less-successful students. Thus, the work of Bransford et al. (1981, 1982) highlighted the role of the learner's strategy of active self-questioning in sentence comprehension and retention.

Using children from Grades 5 to 7, Wong and Sawatsky (1984) have recently replicated the results in the first set of studies in the series of studies reported by Bransford et al. (1982). Unlike Stein et al., however, Wong and Sawatsky found that even average readers needed training in activating relevant prior knowledge through self-questioning. Specifically, Wong and Sawatsky gave good, average, and poor readers 12 sentences on which to write continuations/elaborations. They instructed the children that they should write continuations that would help them understand and remember which man did what particular action in the sentences. The investigators found $\frac{8}{15}$ average readers and $\frac{13}{15}$ poor readers could not generate precise elaborations. They then trained all of them systematically to ask a series of questions designed to help them write precise elaborations to the respective sentences.

The training used by Wong and Sawatsky differed from that used by Bransford et al. (in press). In the case of Bransford et al., the individual child was prompted to ask himself or herself questions that would facilitate seeing the arbitrary relationship between "tall man" and "buying crackers." The experimenter would ask, "Is there any more reason to mention that a kind man bought milk than a tall man? a mean man?" This prepared the child for the next step, which was to prompt him or her to activate prior knowledge that would make the relationship between "tallness" and "buying crackers" less arbitrary. For example, the experimenter would ask, "Why might a tall man be buying crackers?" The last step was prompting the child to evaluate the self-generated elaboration. The purpose here was to help the child check the precision of the elaboration generated. Wong and Sawatsky's training procedure reflects the influence of Meichenbaum's (1977) cognitive behavior modification. The investigators modelled a set of five self-questions and answers for the individual child. These were (1) What do I have to do? (Write a continuation of this sentence.) (2) What kind of a continuation? (One that makes me understand why *this* kind of man did *that* action in the sentence.) (3) How do I begin? (Think: What do I know about being tall? being bald? being strong, etc.? Why would a tall man do that action?) (4) Check my continuation. (Does it really make it clear why that kind of man did that action?) (5) I give myself a pat on the back. (I did it. I wrote a good continuation.) These questions and answers were typed clearly on an index card measuring 20.3 cm (8 inches) × 12.8 cm (5 inches). This cue card was present throughout the two separate individualized training sessions, each lasting about 20–30 minutes. The trainer modelled the self-questions and answers for the child for the first two practice sentences. Thereafter the child was prompted only when necessary. Few children needed much help. Each child practiced the questions and answers for 10 sentences. To ensure that the children were generating the questions during training, each child had to verbalize his or her thoughts while attempting to write an elaboration for a practice sentence. The practice sentences were taken from the pretest of 12, on which all of the trainees had failed miserably to write precise elaborations.

Training was very effective. On the posttest of 12 new sentences, all trained children produced precise elaborations. The following example gives some flavor of the kind of precise elaborations the children generated after training. Given the sentence "The strong man helped the woman," one child gave this elaboration, "out of the ditch." He did so with alacrity. Moreover, training increased the children's recall substantially. The results in Wong and Sawatsky therefore replicated those in the first set of studies of Bransford et al. (1982). Together, these two sets of results underscore the important effects of learning strategies generated by learners themselves on the learning outcome. Specifically, self-questioning has been shown to be an important learning strategy learners must use to activate relevant prior knowledge in order to comprehend and retain new information.

The influence of knowledge of criterial task on students' performances and perception of the ease/difficulty in task learning was shown by Wong, Wong, and LeMare (1982). In two experiments involving normally achieving and LD children, Wong, Wong, and LeMare (1982) investigated the hypothesis that poor comprehension and recall in LD children might stem from vague perception of the criterion tasks, and that provision of clear knowledge of criterion tasks would enhance their performance. This performance enhancement comes from students focusing on relevant parts of the task, in light of knowledge of criterion task.

Fifty-seven children (28 normally achieving; 29 LD) participated in the first experiment. The children were randomly assigned to treatment and control conditions, staying for both comprehension and recall tasks. Treatment referred to knowledge of criterion task. In the comprehension task, children given knowledge of criterion task were told explicitly to attend to preparagraph questions in the two expository passages because they modelled test questions the children would receive later. In the recall task, the children in the treatment condition were told to study the two expository passages for subsequent recall. Within the comprehension and recall tasks, the passages were counterbalanced in presentation.

The results in the comprehension task substantiated the hypothesis under investigation. Wong, Wong, and LeMare (1982) found that both normally achieving and LD children given knowledge of criterion task correctly answered more questions than their respective counterparts in the control condition. However, the results in the recall task did not indicate reliable differences between treatment and control groups. The investigators attributed this outcome to the imprecision in the instructions given to the treatment groups. It is recalled that these children were simply told to expect a recall test. Unlike the comprehension task, they were not guided on which parts of the text to focus on in studying.

Post experimental interview confirmed the investigators' analysis of the recall data. Children in the treatment condition viewed the recall task as being harder than the comprehension task, whereas the opposite view was held by children in the control condition. The treatment groups of normally achieving and LD children received very specific focusing preparagraph questions in the comprehension task, and the subsequent test items were equally specific. Thus they tended to perceive the task demands matched the test. In the recall task, however, the instruction was very global—namely, that they would get a recall test. Because they did not know which parts of the passages the experimenter wanted them to focus on, the children in the treatment condition reported they studied the entire passages. Consequently, they felt the processing load was too heavy. To them, the recall task was understandably harder.

As for children in the control condition, they felt the nondirective instruction in the recall task matched the demands of the free recall test. But they thought the specific comprehension test questions did not match the global instructions they were given in the reading comprehension task. It is recalled that they were simply told to read for understanding. Consequently, they felt the comprehension task was harder.

In a follow-up experiment involving 20 normally achieving and 20 LD children, Wong, Wong, and LeMare (1982) improved the methodology in the recall task. They instructed the children in the treatment condition to study the passages for subsequent recall, and to attend specifically to certain important parts of the passages in their study. The children in the control condition were simply told to study the passages for subsequent recall. The results clearly indicated that given explicit knowledge of criterion task, both normally achieving and LD children recalled substantially more of the passages than their respective control groups. In sum, Wong, Wong, and LeMare (1982) showed that the explicit knowledge of criterion task induced appropriate studying activities in children. The children were able to focus their attention on relevant contents in the passages, because of knowledge of criterion task.

Equally important influences on a student's successful learning are exerted by the interactions between the factors in the TM. Miyake and Norman's (1979) study illustrates the interactive influences between the nature of the materials to be learned (in this case, conceptual difficulty) and learning activities employed by students. Miyake and Norman (1979) investigated the effects of prior knowledge on student's questioning behavior. They used two groups of college students: one group was ignorant of computers and text editors; the other group was given sufficient training in the use of a text editor. The criterion in training was the students' editing one text unaided. Subsequently both groups were instructed to learn to operate a different text editor by following either an easy, nontechnical manual or a hard, technical manual. The students were further instructed to think out loud their thoughts and questions as they tackled the new text editor. Miyake and Norman (1979) found an interesting interaction in their study: Novice students in computer science asked more questions on the easy manual but very few on the hard manual. The reverse pattern of questioning was obtained for the trained students. Miyake and Norman interpreted the findings to suggest that to ask a question, you have to have an *optimal* amount of prior knowledge for the *particular* subject matter at hand. Because educators have long stressed the importance of cultivating questioning behaviors to facilitate learning in students, Miyake and Norman's findings imply that teachers should attend to students' existent prior knowledge as a concomitant condition in teaching students to generate questions. The preceding study of Miyake and Norman (1979) presents a mere glimpse into the web of interactions of various parameters underlying successful learning.

Against the backdrop of the dynamic portrayal of the interactional nature of learning given by Jenkins (1979) and Brown (1980), it is difficult to accept ability deficits as the *sole* determinant of an LD student's state of learning. For example, knowledge deficiencies, strategic deficits, and their interactions appear to pose as equally important sources/factors as ability deficits in influencing LD students' academic success (Hagen & Barclay, 1981). I submit that a more profitable way of addressing LD students' ability deficits is to investigate how they interact with those four basic sources of variables that influence importantly the student's learning outcome.

Metacognition and the Tetrahedral Model

One impetus responsible for the development of metacognitive theory and research is that within a learning situation, it is insufficient for any individual to have background knowledge or learning strategies. Equally important, if not more so, the individual must be able to use his or her background and strategic knowledge effectively during learning (Brown, 1980). If an individual is unaware of his or her strategic repertoire, she or he would be unlikely to deploy suitable strategies flexibly and precisely in tune with task demands. Occasionally, children and adults fail to use appropriate strategies for learning despite having them in their repertoire of strategies (Brown, 1980). The term *production deficiencies* has been applied to those occasions by Flavell (1976).

Thus efficient learning does not consist merely of acquiring the necessary background knowledge and strategic knowledge. It consists also of sufficient use and control of the background knowledge and strategies available to the individual (Brown, 1980). For the learner to be able to use and control his or her appropriate background and strategic knowledge, she or he needs metacognitive skills (Baker & Brown, 1984a; Brown, 1980).

It is recalled that metacognition refers to the awareness of knowledge and control/regulation of knowledge (Baker & Brown, 1984a, 1984b). The distinction between cognition and metacognition is the "distinction between knowledge and the understanding of knowledge in terms of *awareness and appropriate use*" (Brown, 1980, p. 453, emphasis added). Metacognitive skills are those that have been attributed to an executive process in numerous theories of human memory and artificial intelligence. These metacognitive skills include "predicting, checking, monitoring, reality-testing, and coordination and control of deliberate attempts to study, learn, or solve problems" (Brown, 1980, p. 454). These are the essential characteristics of efficient thinking in a broad range of learning situations, including efficient reading and effective studying (Anderson, 1980; Baker & Brown, 1984a; Brown, 1980). The following example gives some flavor of how fluent readers/good students deploy metacognitive strategies in their reading. Given a reading assignment, good students seek to understand both the explicit and the implicit task demands of the criterial task. They are also aware of the strengths and limitations of their repertoires in the background and strategic knowledge regarding the given task. Their understanding of the task demands, together with their awareness of their own background knowledge and strategic repertoires result in their deployment of suitable reading strategies. These reading strategies are goal oriented (i.e., on target vis-à-vis the criterial task) and flexibly employed. For example, if instructed to read for pleasure, better readers would scan or read faster than if instructed to read for more detailed information (Forrest-Pressley & Waller, 1980). Moreover, they monitor, regulate, and evaluate their reading progress against the standards of the criterial task. When they make good progress in reading comprehension, good students continue reading. However, when they encounter comprehension difficulties, good students would slow down, focus their attention on the parts of the text that present difficulties, or backtrack in their reading (Anderson, 1980; Brown, 1980; Whimbey & Whimbey, 1975). These debugging strategies are also flexibly employed. Good students appear to use a cost–benefit analysis approach in their debugging of comprehension difficulties. Sometimes, for the sake of economy in effort, rather than backtracking they may decide to continue reading for clues to enlighten a previous comprehension difficulty (Anderson, 1980).

The preceding description shows how fluent readers/good students *consciously* and *deliberately* coordinate their efforts in reading. The skills they have mobilized in coordinating and regulating their efforts in reading are metacognitive skills. What they have coordinated and regulated are (1) their own knowledge, (2) their own learning activities, and (3) the criterial task. These are factors depicted in the TM. Thus, it can be seen that metacognitive skills are essential in effective coordination of the various factors in the TM that significantly affect the success of learning outcomes.

Advantages of a Metacognitive Perspective over the Ability-Deficits Theory of Learning Disabled Students' Academic Difficulties

In light of the criticisms of the ability-deficits theory, the advantages of a metacognitive perspective to understanding LD students' academic difficulties are readily discernable. First, it is recalled that the relationship between LD students' ability deficits and their academic failures has yet to be researched and established. In contrast, it has been shown that efficient reading and effective studying require important metacognitive skills (Baker & Brown, 1984a, 1984b; Brown, 1980). Baker and Brown (1984a) have presented excellent summaries on the research literature on metacognitive skills in reading. Hence, only a brief mention is made of findings in metacognitive research that support the point under discussion.

In general, studies found that younger and poorer readers are less aware of reading as a process of extracting meaning. Because they are less aware of the purpose of reading, it is less likely that they will read for meaning. Indeed, younger and poorer readers perceive reading as a decoding process (cf. Clay, 1973; Forrest-Pressley & Waller, 1980; Myers & Paris, 1978; Reid, 1966; Strang & Rogers, 1965). Young children are also poor at detecting ambiguity–inconsistency in oral and/or written messages (Markman, 1977, 1979). However, providing them with explicit standards for evaluating their comprehension substantially increased children's comprehension monitoring (Markman & Gorin, 1981). Regarding reading strategies, Smith (1967) found that good readers adjusted reading behaviors according to reading purposes—reading for general impressions versus reading for details. Poor readers showed no differential adjustment in reading behaviors. Moreover, poor readers used no debugging strategies in resolving comprehension difficulties (Strang & Rogers, 1965). However, Olshavsky (1976–1977) found no differences in good and poor readers' comprehension monitoring. She found both groups could use context cues, inferential reasoning, and rereading as strategies for resolving comprehension difficulties. In sum, older and better readers have more metacognitive skills than younger and poorer readers. These differential metacognitive skills explain a sizeable portion of their different reading skills. The remaining portion is likely explained by poorer decoding skills in younger and poorer readers.

Second, it is recalled that deficit training in the LD children had consistently failed to induce transfer to reading (Myers & Hammill, 1982). In contrast, instructional research inculcating various cognitive and metacognitive strategies in LD students, poor readers, and students with lower verbal ability significantly improved their reading comprehension and summarization skills (Andre & Anderson, 1978–1979; Garner, Hare, Alexander, Haynes, & Winograd, 1982; Palinscar, 1982; Wong & Jones, 1982). Compared to the ability-deficits theory, instructional research ensuing from a metacognitive perspective clearly elucidates substantially more of our understanding of LD students' academic failures.

Third, multiple and interactive factors underlie successful learning. Moreover, metacognitive skills play a crucial role in coordinating those factors (Bransford, 1979; Brown, 1982; Jenkins, 1979). Within the complex and dynamic learning situation, the LD students' ability deficits constitute merely one factor. It is therefore difficult to accept ability deficits as the *sole* determinant of LD students' learning outcome. Other factors such as knowledge and strategic repertoires, knowledge of criterion tasks and their interactions should receive equal focus in influencing LD students' successful learning (Hagen & Barclay, 1981).

Contrasting the Academic-Skills Mastery Theory with the Metacognitive Perspective

The academic-skills mastery theory has been proposed as an alternative to the ability-deficits theory. Proponents of this theory reject the idea that prerequisite abilities and ability deficits cause students' academic failure. Instead, they consider school failures to reflect skills deficits. Hence, they suggest educators should focus on teaching the academic skills a child needs to learn, and not concentrate on the child's ability deficits (Lerner, 1981, pp. 173–176; Wallace & McLoughlin, 1979; Ysseldyke, 1978; Ysseldyke & Salvia, 1974).

The teaching approach espoused by this theory consists of analyzing the academic task in terms of the underlying skills needed to accomplish the task—that is, performing a task analysis (Bateman, 1971). The subskills from the task analysis are sequenced logically according to certain criteria, for example, teaching concrete subskills before teaching more abstract subskills; teaching subskills with less memory load before teaching those with heavier memory load. The child is tested to ascertain which subskills from the task analysis are possessed and which ones must be acquired. Teaching consists of getting the child to acquire subskills that are not yet learned, or learned but not yet mastered (Lerner, 1981, pp. 173–176).

The skills-mastery theory has been criticized on two grounds. First, there is the question of whether learning is composed of a series of separate and discrete skills. The crux of the matter is the view that the whole is greater than the sum of its parts (Lerner, 1981, p. 175). Second, the skills-mastery theory assumes that a hierarchy of subskills in reading has already been empirically substantiated, rather than being a topic of continuing research.

But the Achilles' heel in the skills-mastery theory is its neglect of the importance of the understanding of knowledge in terms of awareness and appropriate use (Brown, 1980, 1982). Acquisition of knowledge/skills is insufficient. One must also be aware of what one does and does not know, and one must regulate the use of one's knowledge appropriately (Baker & Brown, 1984a, 1984b; Brown, 1980; Hagen & Barclay, 1981). Such self-awareness and self-regulation are the individual's metacognition. Clearly, a metacognitive perspective overcomes this very problem of understanding knowledge in terms of awareness and appropriate use, which remains a thorny problem in the skills-mastery theory. It complements the task-analysis theory. Together, they provide a satisfactory conceptual framework for analyzing academic difficulties in LD students.

Why Is the Learning Disabilities Field So Receptive to Metacognitive Theory?

Prior to the development of metacognitive theory, there were research findings in LD that support a strategic-deficits rather than an ability-deficits explanation of LD children's poor task performance. The research findings come from two areas: research on LD children's selective attention and research on their memory processes. In essence, investigators initially found that LD children performed more poorly than non-LD children. However, brief training on using a task-appropriate strategy in aid of learning typically resulted in substantially improved performances in the LD children. Because of the remarkable ease in inducing performance improvements in LD children, researchers concluded that the LD children's initially poorer performance reflects their failure to apply spontaneously a strategy that already exists in their strategic repertoire. This strategic-deficits view culminates in the conceptualization of the LD student as a maladaptive learner, someone who does not participate actively in his or her own learning through the use of efficient strategies, who lacks self-awareness and awareness of task demands, or who may use strategies inappropriate for the given task (Torgesen, 1977a). Moreover, Torgesen

(1977a) alludes to meta variables and motivational variables as the under-lying explanatory mechanisms of LD chidren's inactivity in learning. Con-sequently, when metacognitive theory arrived on the scene in cognitive psychology, supporters of the maladaptive learner framework readily em-braced and incorporated it into that framework. In the following section, the research supporting a strategic-deficits rather than an ability-deficits explanation of LD children's poor task performance is summarized.

Research on Selective Attention

The work by Hallahan and his associates on selective attention con-stitutes one major source of support for the hypothesis that LD students fail spontaneously to employ suitable strategies in the learning/experi-mental setting (Dawson, Hallahan, Reeve & Ball, 1979; Tarver, Hallahan, Cohen & Kauffman, 1977; Tarver, Hallahan, Kauffman & Ball, 1976). Bas-ically, these investigators found deficient selective attention and verbal rehearsal in their LD subjects.

Using Hagen's Central Incidental Learning Task, Tarver et al. (1976) investigated the development of verbal rehearsal strategies and selective attention in 8- to 13-year-old LD children. Central information was des-ignated by the experimenter as the material to be remembered. Tarver et al. found that LD children remembered substantially less central infor-mation than a group of the same-aged nondisabled peers. There were no reliable differences between the groups in recall of incidental information. These results suggest deficient selective attention in the LD group (Hagen & Barclay, 1981). The results also suggest that LD children are slow to develop efficient encoding strategies such as verbal rehearsal. This lack of verbal rehearsal in the LD children was inferred from their failure to show primary effects in the recall (Tarver et al., 1976, 1977).

However, in a second experiment, when LD children were induced to rehearse, substantial improvement in recall of central information was obtained in the older children (Tarver et al., 1977). Similar positive effects on LD children's selective-attention performance were obtained by Dawson et al. (1979), who instructed their LD subjects on the use of a verbal-rehearsal strategy in the serial recall task. Such improvement in per-formance subsequent to a brief instruction in the use of a specific task strategy suggests that failure to apply spontaneously the relevant strategy may explain the originally deficient task performance in the LD subjects (Torgesen, 1977a).

Tarver et al. (1977) again found deficient selective attention in LD boys. Moreover, strong support for the hypothesis of developmental lag in verbal rehearsal strategies was obtained on data pooled from two studies (Tarver et al., 1976, 1977). The investigators suggest that the lag in verbal rehearsal strategies underlies the lag in selective attention.

Another study by Hallahan, Tarver, Kauffman, and Graybeal (1978) investigated the effects of incentives on the selective-attention performance of LD children. They found that positive reinforcement (delivery of pennies) led to increased selective attention in LD children. Moreover, an analysis of the subjects' recall at different serial positions led the investigators to conclude that the superior selective attention of the group that was reinforced for recall had been mediated by their adoption of a verbal-rehearsal strategy. This conclusion suggests that incentives induced LD children to apply a strategy that was already existent in their strategic repertoire. Alternatively, the conclusion suggests that in the course of the experiment, the LD children came to develop the task-appropriate strategy. Hallahan et al.'s conclusion that positive reinforcement for recall resulted in the use of more efficient strategies by LD children is consistent with the results from a study by Haines and Torgesen (1979) in which rehearsal was directly observed. Haines and Torgesen found second-grade children with reading problems rehearsed more when they were rewarded for recall than when they were not.

Although the preceding findings by Hallahan et al. (1978) are interesting, they should be taken cautiously. This is because a follow-up study by Dawson et al. (1979) using LD children, and another by Gelabert, Torgesen, Dice, and Murphy (1980) using non-LD children found no effects of incentives on the use of verbal rehearsal to facilitate selective attention–memory.

Nevertheless, excepting replication problems over Hallahan et al. (1978), the findings on LD children's selective-attention abilities have been very consistent. The interpretation of these findings is that LD children have a strategic deficit.

> At this time, it appears that the most parsimonious explanation for the LD child's tendency to have problems in attending to relevant cues and ignoring irrelevant cues is his inability to bring to the task a specific learning strategy . . . . Apparently then, it is not so much the LD child's inability to attend selectively that is his basic problem so much as it is his inability to analyze the task in terms of the best strategies needed for performing it. (Hallahan & Reeve, 1980, p. 32)

Research on Memory Processes

The following summaries of research on memory processes supports the hypothesis that LD children engage in less-efficient strategies in memorizing meaningful and nonmeaningful materials (Torgesen & Kail, 1980).

Torgesen (1977b) asked fourth-grade children of different reading levels to study 24 pictures of common objects that could be grouped into four categories. During a 2-min study period, the children were encouraged to move the pictures, and/or to do anything which they thought would help them remember the pictures better. Torgesen found that good readers were more likely to organize the material into categories during the study period, and recalled more pictures. A brief training in using categorizations as a mnemonic strategy eliminated recall differences between the two groups of good and poor readers. The finding that poor readers were less likely than good readers to capitalize on categorical relationships among stimuli in studying for recall, had also been replicated by Torgesen, Murphy, and Ivey (1979) and by Wong (1978).

Another study by Torgesen and Goldman (1977) also supports a strategic-deficits explanation of poor readers' poor recall performance. Torgesen and Goldman (1977) found that good readers in the second grade recalled sequences of familiar stimuli better, and rehearsed them more than did children with reading problems. They also found that when children were told to name the stimuli aloud as they were presented, differences between groups in both recall and rehearsal disappeared.

On the basis of processes assumed to be operative in immediate free recall, Bauer reasons that if elaborative encoding is deficient in LD children, the primacy effect in immediate free recall would be lower in LD than in non-LD children. Similarly, in delayed free recall, both primacy and recency effects would be lower in LD children. These predictions were substantiated (Bauer, 1977, 1979). Torgesen (1977b) also reported that LD children in his study had fewer observable lip movements than nondisabled children while trying to retain verbal information. This confirms Bauer's hypothesis that LD children are less likely to use elaborative strategies to retain information.

More recently, Newman and Hagen (1981) investigated the effects of instruction on both serial and free recall in LD children. The children ranged in age from 7 to 13 years and were divided by age into a younger and an older group. Neither group was found to produce spontaneously a verbal-rehearsal strategy. However, the serial recall of the older group was somewhat higher than that found for the younger children. Moreover, neither group produced an effective organizational routine on the free recall task, in which categorizable items were used. Interestingly, with instructions the older children's clustering and recall improved. But the performance of the younger children was not affected by the training. Conceivably, the instructions were not powerful enough to elicit an effective mnemonic in the younger children. Alternatively, these younger children had a mediational deficiency. Newman and Hagen (1981) concluded that the children were not actively involved in learning (Torgesen, 1977a).

Taken together, the preceding studies on memorization processes in children argue against an ability-deficits explanation of poor recall in LD children. Rather, the results suggest that deficient use of active elaborative strategies (e.g., rehearsal and/or organization) among LD children was responsible for their inferior recall. This strategic-deficits interpretation is supported by the ease with which LD children's performance level was raised to the level of non-LD children.

The preceding strategic-deficits perspective of memorization processes in LD children led Torgesen (1977a) to conceptualize them as maladaptive/inactive learners. Specifically, within a learning situation, LD children are seen as failing to deploy appropriate learning strategies that would be in tune with task demands. Such a strategic deficit does not necessarily mean that LD children lack the particular learning strategy in their store of strategic knowledge. That minimal prompting could induce them to apply the task-appropriate strategy suggests otherwise (Torgesen, 1977b; Torgesen & Goldman, 1977; Torgesen et al., 1979; Wong, 1978). What the LD children's strategic deficits suggest is their lack of awareness of task demands, the lack of awareness of what they do or do not know regarding strategies, and their lack of awareness of which learning strategy to deploy in order to match the task demands. In short, LD children's strategic deficits reflect their lack of metacognitive skills. Clearly, the research highlighting both the maladaptive learner framework and the strategic deficits in LD children are in accord with what metacognition conceptually embodies (awareness and self-regulation). Understandably, supporters of the inactive learner framework are very receptive to metacognitive theory.

What is the Impact of Metacognitive Theory and Research on the Learning Disabilities Field?

The impact of metacognitive theory and research on the LD field can be seen in the research on and remediation of LD students. Concerning research, there is a budding area of research into the metacognitive processes of LD students, and intervention studies designed to increase metacognitive skills in LD students. Concerning remediation, there is a growing awareness of the importance of building self-monitoring behaviors into individualized instructional programs of basic skills training, such as phonics instruction, addition–subtraction facts, and so forth.

Impact of Research on Metacognitive Skills
in Learning Disabled Students

Research on metacognitive skills in LD students generally falls into two lines of inquiry. The first line of inquiry focuses on metacognitive processes in LD students, for example, meta-attention, metamemory. The second line of inquiry focuses on intervention—ways to improve meta-cognitive skills in LD students. Studies on LD students' metacognitive processes consistently indicated metacognitive deficiencies in LD children. The intervention studies indicated that LD students profited from attempts at increasing their sensitivity to important textual units, and at increasing their metacomprehension. They also profited from training in other important comprehension strategies. The beneficial effects of the various interventions were manifested in LD students' improved reading comprehension. However, attempts at increasing LD children's predictive accuracy in spelling performance had been less successful.

Meta-attention in LD and non-LD children was investigated by Loper, Hallahan, and Ianna (1982). These investigators compared the performances of two age groups of LD and non-LD children on a specially designed meta-attentional task. This meta-attentional task comprised six cards on which line drawings depicted either positive or negative situations for three attentional variables: interest, reward, or noise level. Verbal descriptions accompanied each card. For example, for the card depicting a smiling boy, the verbal descriptions were "Imagine a child who is very interested in what he is doing." The six cards (three positive situations and three negative situations) were variously paired with each other to form 12 forced-choice items. The descriptions for each card were repeated for each item, and the children were asked to decide, "Which of these two children do you think will better pay attention?"

The results indicated that regardless of educational status, older children scored higher on the interest variable and scored lower on the reward variable than younger children. Interestingly, the meta-attentional task did not differentiate between LD and non-LD children. Moreover, among the LD children, no significant relationships were found between reading achievement and performance on the meta-attentional task. However, among non-LD children, a significant relationship was found between reading achievement and interest. A significant but inverse relationship was found between reading achievement and reward. These findings among non-LD children suggested that they had a mature understanding of the relationship between two meta-attention variables (interest and reward) and reading achievement.

In Study 2 Loper et al. (1982) explored the possibility that successful remediation would effect more synchrony of meta-attention and academic achievement in LD children. Fifty-four LD children were given (1) the meta-attentional task used in Study 1, and (2) the pre- and posttest in reading in the fall and subsequent spring, respectively.

The LD children were divided into two groups: high-gain and low-gain groups, by subtracting fall reading achievement from spring reading achievement. The reading scores of the high-gain and low-gain groups differed only at posttest. The results indicated no significant correlations between meta-attentional scores and reading achievement for either group at pretest. At posttest however, the high-gain LD group showed a significant correlation between reading achievement and interest, and a significant but inverse correlation between reading achievement and reward. For the low-gain group, similar findings were not obtained.

The findings in Loper et al. (1982) indicated that non-LD children had a mature understanding of the relationship between attention and reading achievement. As they grew older, they appeared to realize that intrinsic motivation (interest) weighs more in reading achievement than does extrinsic motivation (monetic reward). The awareness/understanding of such a relationship was not shown in LD children of comparable age. However, those LD children who achieved substantial remedial progress did show the same awareness or mature understanding of the relationship between meta-attention and reading achievement.

Knowledge about memory and memory processes—metamemory—in good and poor readers were investigated by Torgesen (1979). Adapting questions devised originally by Kreutzer, Leonard, and Flavell (1975), Torgesen asked the children seven questions in a fixed order. These questions concerned (1) the child's awareness of his or her own memory capacity as a rememberer; (2) the knowledge that relearning what one has previously learned yields savings in remembering over learning something entirely new; (3) the differential ease in retention between immediate and delayed recall; and (4) the knowledge of mnemonic and retrieval strategies. Torgesen (1979) found that the most reliable differences between good and poor readers involved the number of different solutions generated to three metamemory questions on mnemonic and retrieval strategies. Examples of the three questions were: "How could you be really certain that you didn't forget to bring your present along to school in the morning (for the school Christmas party)?" "How would you go about finding a lost jacket (at school)?" "Suppose your friend has a dog and you ask him how old he is. He tells you he got his dog as a puppy one Christmas but can't remember which Christmas. What things could he do to help him remember which Christmas he got his dog?" Moreover, Torgesen (1979) found that more good readers described using verbal rehearsal as a mnemonic strategy if they could not write down what they had to remember. Good readers consistently were able to provide a wider range of solutions to the memory problems than poor readers. Torgesen (1979) interpreted his findings to indicate that rather than being limited to their capacity to learn to read, many reading-disabled children may have difficulty in management of their capacities.

Strategic behaviors in selecting retrieval cues in gifted, average, and LD children were investigated in a study by Wong (1982). Specifically, the study investigated whether LD children differed from gifted and average children in their organization and self-checking in selecting retrieval cues that would aid a subsequent story recall.

Within each educational category, there were 10 children, each from Grades 5, 6, and 7. The stimulus was a Japanese folk story called "How to Fool a Cat," originally used by Smiley, Oaken, Worthen, Campione, and Brown (1977), and previously parsed into pausal units–idea units. The children were randomly divided into treatment and control conditions and were seen in groups of three. Those in the treatment condition were read the story, as they simultaneously followed it on their own copies of the story. Subsequently they recalled it by writing it down. Verbatim recall was not mandatory and spelling errors were waived. After recall, each child received the story typed on small index cards, one idea unit of the story per card. The children read the whole story again on the individual cards. Then they were asked to select 12 cards representing 12 idea units that they would like to have as retrieval cues if they were asked to remember the story.

The children in the control condition received the same treatment except that they did not experience story recall prior to cue selection. The manipulation of the variable of prior recall was to see if it would induce more choice of important idea units as retrieval cues. Three categories of behavior were used to analyze the patterns of cue selection in the children. The first was organization/planfulness in search behavior, operationally defined by the child's demonstration of some form of systematic search behavior, for example, a verbalized plan prior to cue selection, or a non-verbalized plan that was clearly observable in its effects on the child's cue-selection behavior (described subsequently). The second was exhaustiveness of cue selection. The focus here was whether or not the child examined the whole pile of cards in his or her selective search. The third concerned presence of self-checking behavior. The focus here was whether or not the child checked through the 12 cards she or he selected as retrieval cues.

The results indicated that LD children lacked self-checking and tended to be less thorough or exhaustive in their cue selection. Both gifted and average children, however, spontaneously engaged in an exhaustive search for retrieval cues and in self-checking behaviors. Interestingly, contrary to expectations, LD children did operate with some form of plan in their search behavior. It consisted of examining carefully each of the idea units. Gifted children, on the other hand, tended predominantly to operate by a nonverbalized plan in their cue selection. They were observed to scan rapidly the contents of the idea units on the cards, simultaneously making two piles of them. One pile was bulky, containing discarded cards. The other pile was noticeably smaller, containing the potential retrieval cues. To this smaller pile, gifted children returned when they finished with the last card. They then carefully examined this smaller pile, eliminating unwanted cards. Finally, they checked through the contents of the retrieval cues, and counted them to ensure they numbered 12.

Doubtless, the LD children's laborious reading of each card reflected their lack of reading fluency. Nevertheless, their decoding problem does not obfuscate the qualitative differences between the organization/planfulness of LD children's cue selection and the aforementioned cue selection of gifted children. However, there were no substantial differences between the organization/planfulness in cue selection of (1) average and LD children; and (2) average and gifted children. In light of the latter findings, a feasible interpretation of the data on planfulness in cue selection is that compared to gifted children, LD children appeared to operate with a less efficient plan. The results also indicated that compared to gifted and average children, LD children lacked self-checking and were less exhaustive in selecting retrieval cues. Lastly, prior experience in recall resulted in all the children choosing significantly more idea units rated to be the most important. Devoid of such experience, the children chose significantly more idea units rated to be less important. Although gifted children chose more items of 4-point importance as retrieval cues than average and LD children, the latter groups of children benefitted equally from the experience of prior recall. Their patterns of recall of important and unimportant idea units were similar.

In three studies, Gerber (1982) investigated the accuracy of predicting one's spelling performance in LD and non-LD children. The task consisted of a 14-word, written spelling test. In the first two studies, the children spelled words illustrative of various phonetic features such as vowels, doubled consonants, and so forth. These words were high in familiarity but low in frequency of occurrence in elementary curriculum materials. In the third study, the words in the spelling test were chosen from those above each child's testing ceiling on a standardized spelling test. This procedure was used to equate difficulty items for all the children. Also, in the third study, half of the LD and non-LD children were taught verbally self-guided proofreading and self-correction procedures. Specifically, children were taught to imitate overtly those questions designed to focus attention on potentially proofreading information.

The results of the first study showed that the LD children were aware of their deficient skills in spelling. They predicted fewer correct spellings than the non-LD children. However, LD children seriously overestimated their spelling ability, in that less than 20% of all their spellings were accurate. In contrast, even the youngest non-LD children tended to underestimate their skill. More than 82% of all spellings produced by the non-LD children were correct.

Equally seriously, the LD children also underestimated their likely errors. Again the non-LD children were very accurate in predicting what they could not spell correctly. The results of the second study replicated those of the first. The results of the third study indicated that (excepting for older LD children) all LD and non-LD children overestimated their ability to spell correctly and underestimated the likelihood that they would spell incorrectly. Interestingly, non-LD children also overestimated their spelling ability. It is recalled that the children were given difficult words on which to predict their spelling performance. These words were the ones selected from those that each child previously could not spell on a standardized spelling test. Lastly, training in self-monitoring produced little effect in prediction accuracy for any group. However, training improved older LD and non-LD students' quality of errors. These children produced better approximations to conventional spellings than their untrained counterparts.

Sensitivity to important textual information is an important metacognitive skill in reading and studying (Brown, 1980; Smiley, Oaken, Worthen, Campione, & Brown, 1977; Winograd, 1982). Smiley et al. (1977) found that Grade 7 poor readers in Title I–funded remedial educational services did not recall as many idea units judged to be thematically most important. From the authors' description, some or all of these children may fall in the LD category. One possible explanation for the authors' findings may be the children's insufficient awareness of important idea units in the passage. If this were the case, focusing LD children's attention on important idea units through preparagraph questions should increase their retention of those units. Reasoning thus, Wong (1979) tested the preceding hypothesis.

Thirty LD and 30 non-LD children were randomly divided evenly into two groups: questions and no-questions conditions. In the questions condition, the experimenter read a Japanese folk story, "Dragon's Tears," to the children as they follow the printed story visually on their individual copies. The experimenter read aloud each preparagraph question before reading the respective paragraphs. These preparagraph questions were also typed on the children's copies of the story. Immediately after the experimenter finished reading the story, the children were asked to write out their recall of it. In the no-questions condition, the children received the same treatment, except that there were no preparagraph questions on their copies of the story.

The results indicated clearly facilitative effects of preparagraph questions on story retention for LD children *only*. Their recall was comparable to that of non-LD children in the same treatment condition. Moreover, for the LD children, the facilitative effects of questions were very specific. Questions substantially increase their recall of idea units rated to be thematically most important. LD children in the no-questions condition recalled the least of story idea units. Regarding non-LD children, the effects of preparagraph questions on their story retention were unremarkable.

These results were taken to suggest that LD children lack awareness/sensitivity to story elements that are most important. Not being sensitive to important elements would result in an inability to focus attention or to engage in active comprehension and study efforts on those elements (Winograd, 1982). Consequently, retention would suffer. The results indicated that directing LD children to important textual elements through preparagraph questions helped them overcome their metacognitive deficiency. Consequently their recall of thematically most-important story elements improved. On the other hand, non-LD children did not profit from preparagraph questions. The results suggested that they had already developed the metacognitive skill of being sensitive to important textual elements (Hare & Borchardt, 1982; Winograd, 1982; Wong, 1979).

Another metacognitive skill pertinent to efficient reading and studying is the awareness of one's state of reading comprehension—metacomprehension. Failure to monitor one's state of reading comprehension may have serious consequences. One may assume one has understood the text when in fact one has not. Or, one may not deploy needed debugging strategies to deal with comprehension difficulties (Baker, 1979). It is possible that insufficient self-monitoring of one's state of reading comprehension may be one causal factor in reading comprehension problems in LD students.

To investigate the preceding hypothesis, Wong and Jones (1982) compared the performances on several variables of LD and non-LD students who received self-monitoring training and those without training. Specifically, Wong and Jones (1982) trained LD and non-LD students on monitoring their comprehension of main ideas through self-questioning. The self-questioning training focused on the students' purpose-setting in reading, on identifying the main ideas in the paragraphs, on changing the identified information into questions, on checking that the questions were targetted on the main ideas, and on an integrative review at the end of reading the given passage.

The self-questioning training spanned 2 days. Prior to the phase of self-questioning training, the children were taught to mastery level, the concept of a main idea. Subsequent to the self-questioning training, the students were given 4 days of testing involving new passages. The results clearly showed that training substantially increased LD students' awareness of important textual units, as well as their ability to formulate good questions involving those units. Moreover, training facilitated their reading comprehension. However, the training effects on non-LD students were less substantial. Training did not increase substantially their awareness of important textual units or their reading comprehension.

Wong and Jones (1982) interpreted their findings to indicate that insufficient awareness of one's state of reading comprehension—insufficient metacomprehension—is *one* cause of LD students' poor reading comprehension. Training LD students to self-monitor systematically their reading comprehension appears to have been an effective solution to their problem.

Palincsar (1982) improved reading comprehension in seven LD students by teaching them specific cognitive and metacognitive strategies. These students had adequate decoding skills, but deficient reading comprehension skills. In 18 successive daily sessions, Palincsar (1982) individually taught them summarizing (a cognitive skill); detecting textual anomalies (a metacognitive skill), and two kinds of questioning: (1) to predict what authors might discuss next in the passage, a metacognitive skill; and (2) to construct questions teachers might ask in testing their knowledge of the text, a task involving both cognitive and metacognitive skills. Palincsar used modelling and corrective feedback to teach the four strategies.

The results clearly indicated that teaching LD students those four cognitive and metacognitive strategies substantially improved their reading comprehension scores on the daily criterion tests. The LD students' improvement in reading comprehension was well maintained during maintenance test and follow-up tests. Moreover, moderate gains were observed in transfer measured by classroom probes.

Palincsar (1982) replicated her first study in a second experiment, in which 21 poor comprehenders from Grades 6 to 8 were taught the same four strategies in small groups ranging from 4 to 8 students. Five experienced teachers were trained in using reciprocal teaching to teach the four strategies of questioning, predicting, summarizing, and clarifying (detecting anomalies). Teaching spanned successive daily sessions ranging from 16 to 20 sessions. Similar positive effects on students' reading comprehension were obtained during intervention, maintenance, and follow-up. Because no probes were given in the classroom, generalization of training to students' classroom performance was not obtained. However, results on transfer measures designed by Palincsar parallelled results in her first study.

Summary

The results of research on metacognition in LD students support a metacognitive perspective of LD students' poor task performance and academic difficulties. This additional metacognitive perspective is *particularly* important in light of the ambiguous, empirically untested role of ability deficits in explaining LD students' academic difficulties. The impact of a metacognitive dimension on remediation in the learning disabilities field is described in the next section.

Impact on Learning Disabilities Remediation

The impact of the metacognitive theory and research on the learning disabilities field is also evident in the development of specific prescriptive approaches in remediation. There is the cognitive-strategies approach developed by Alley and Deshler (1979). They design specific remedial procedures and curricula consistent with their particular framework. A prototypical example of their work is the COPS error-monitoring strategy used in teaching LD adolescents to monitor errors in their written assignment. COPS stands for capitalization, overall appearance, punctuation, and spelling. Similarly, the 5-step self-questioning procedure used in Wong and Jones's (1982) study induced systematic self-monitoring in LD adolescents and consequently enhanced their reading comprehension. The self-questions in Wong and Jones's study were (1) "What are you studying this passage for?" (So you can answer some questions you will be given later); (2) "Find the main idea or main ideas in the paragraph, and underline it"; (3)

"Think of a question on the main idea you have underlined. Remember what a *good* question should be like." (Look at the prompt you are given); (4) "Learn the answer to your question"; (5) "Always look back at the questions and answers to see how each successive question and answer adds more information to you." There are also the strategic intervention studies by Hallahan, Lloyd, Kosiewicz, Kauffman, and Graves (1979) and Hallahan, Lloyd, Kosiewicz, and Kneedler (1979), in each of which an LD boy was trained to monitor his own attentional or on-task behavior.

It appears that metacognition has generated a new orientation in remedial instruction of LD students in which self-monitoring procedures appear to receive equal emphasis as basic skills building. Implicit in this remedial orientation is the adoption of the basic tenet in cognitive psychology—namely, the centrality of the students' active participation in and responsibility for his or her learning (Brown, 1980; Wittrock, 1980). More important but unmentioned is the reason for training LD students self-monitoring skills. That LD students must improve in their academic deficiencies is indisputable. But this statement glosses over the relevance for self-monitoring training. The point is that we need to improve not only LD students' academic skills, but also the extent that they could function as autonomously as their normally achieving peers. To attain such a remedial criterion for LD students typically lacking in autonomy, we must include a self-monitoring component within any remedial program for them. In designing self-monitoring training, learning disabilities researchers and practitioners can draw on the theory and research in cognitive behavior modification (Meichenbaum, 1977; Meichenbaum & Asarnow, 1978).

Criticisms of a Metacognitive Perspective of Learning Disabilities

This section addresses two frequently made criticisms of the usefulness of a metacognitive perspective of learning disabilities. The first is that a metacognitive perspective does not explain ubiquitous decoding problems in LD students. The second is that one's knowledge of an appropriate strategy does not guarantee its use.

The first criticism is that a metacognitive perspective may apply only to LD students' difficulties in higher-order cognitive tasks such as reading comprehension. However, regarding LD students' more basic decoding difficulties, a metacognitive perspective is of little use. For their decoding difficulties, training in more basic skills rather than in metacognitive strategies appears more appropriate (Baker, 1982; Torgesen, 1982).

It is erroneous to assume that metacognition plays a role in reading comprehension and studying, but not in basic skills such as decoding. Such an assumption neglects the research on metalinguistic awareness. Metalinguistic awareness is the ability to reflect on the phonemic, syntactic, and semantic aspects of one's language (Baker, 1982). While difficulties with syntactic and semantic aspects of language contribute mainly to comprehension problems, difficulties with the phonemic aspect of language contribute to decoding problems. The manifestation of deficiency in phonemic awareness comprises the child's difficulties in analyzing phonemes in words. Put differently, the child has difficulties segmenting words into their component sounds (Fox & Routh, 1976; Hook & Johnson, 1978).

LD children have problems in all three aspects of language—phonemic, syntactic, and semantic (Hook & Johnson, 1978). Their problems in phonemic segmentation interfere with the process of phonological recoding (Shankweiler, Liberman, Mark, Fowler & Fischer, 1979). Their phonemic segmentation problems also interfere with the establishment of grapheme–phoneme correspondences (Snowling, 1980). The two skills of phonological recording and the establishment of grapheme–phoneme correspondences are vital to beginning reading (Baker, 1982).

There is some research that suggests that training children to segment and blend words promotes their learning to read. Olofsson and Lundberg (1982) successfully trained kindergarten children to segment and blend two-phoneme and three-phoneme words. Their training program contained an orderly sequence of seven steps that were gradated in difficulty. The instructional steps began with recognition of rhymes and nonsense words, then segmentation of words into syllables, locating initial phonemes of words, and eventually ending in segmenting two- and three-phoneme words into individual phonemes and blending phonemes into words.

Williams (1980) designed and conducted a 2-year training and evaluation program for LD children in the classroom setting. The program components included skills in phonemic analysis, blending, and decoding. Initially, the LD children were taught to analyze syllables and short words into phonemes and then to blend the phonemes into syllables and words. When mastery was reached in phonemic analysis and synthesis, the children were taught to decode.

The results were impressive because effects of training and transfer were observed. The LD children who successfully completed the training program could decode regularly spelled one-syllable and multisyllabic words and nonsense combinations, regardless of whether or not they had previously seen the particular combination of letters. The results of Olofsson and Lundberg (unpublished manuscript) and Williams (1980) support the view that phonemic awareness promotes the child's learning to read.

In sum, it can be seen that metacognition contributes to the child's learning to read, in the form of phonemic awareness. Hence, the role of metacognition may not be restricted to LD students' higher-cognitive functions. However, this is *not* to say that metacognitive deficits underlie all the heterogeneous reading problems of LD children, for example, reading problems that may arise from slower processing speed (Maisto & Sipe, 1980). Indeed a metacognitive intervention would have little effect on reading problems caused by structural problems, be they slower processing speed (Maisto & Sipe, 1980) or severe memory problems (Torgesen & Houck, 1980). For reading-disabled children with such structural problems, one would be hard put to develop effective remedial programs.

A second criticism is that attempts to find a one-to-one correspondence between metacognition and appropriate action in any domain have met with little success (Cavanaugh & Perlmutter, 1982). Specifically, research interest in metamemory stems partly from the assumption that what the child knows about memory mediates his or her actions/strategies in memory tasks. Yet existent research has shown little correlation between memory knowledge and memory behavior. For example, children who know that categorized lists are easier than uncategorized lists may not significantly categorize items as an aid to recall (Salatas & Flavell, 1976). Similarly, children may describe appropriate study strategies, yet fail to use them (Garner & Reis, 1981).

The existent research certainly questions the effects of the individual's metacognition in directing/governing his or her appropriate use of knowledge. Yet it may be argued that it is naive to expect a perfect correlation between metacognition and appropriate action in a particular domain. There may well be other variables in the individual's perception or conception that may outweigh his or her awareness of an appropriate strategy or route of action. One such variable is effort (e.g., Wellman, Collins, & Glieberman, 1981). Wellman et al. (1981) found effort was a powerful variable in young children's estimates of memory performance. Specifically, for preschoolers, the amount of to-be-remembered information plays a lesser role in their conception/estimation of memory performance, whereas how hard the rememberer tries plays a weighty role.

Wellman et al. think that the young child's concern with effort may explain previous findings in Yussen and Levy's (1975) study, in which preschoolers persisted in predicting future success on the same task, despite having experienced failure with recall for 9 or 10 items. Wellman et al. consider those young children's performance to be very understandable if they were introducing effort as a relevant variable, predicting that they could increase their effort and, therefore, increase recall.

Another variable that affects the correlation between metacognition and appropriate strategy is the individual's cost-plus analysis in using the appropriate strategy. Anderson (1980) pointed out that students may not use an appropriate studying strategy if they consider that the benefits do not match the time/effort involved in using it.

Thus the criticism that existent research does not substantiate the assumed relationship between metamemory and memory performance reflects our simplistic conception of that relationship. As Wellman et al. succinctly stated, "an understanding of how metamemory influences memory performance awaits an understanding of the child's overall conception of information processing, as reflected in an understanding of the combined influences of many variables" (Wellman et al., 1981, p. 1317). Wellman et al.'s statement applies equally to other meta domains.

Future Directions

This section focuses on questions in metacognition and learning disabilities for future research. However, before discussing these research questions, it appears appropriate to consider the issues underlying such research. The basic issues appear to be twofold: (1) precisely how do existent metacognitive problems affect LD children's academic learning and performance, and (2) what prescriptive implications for their instruction/ remediation can be drawn from an understanding of the influences of their metacognitive problems (cf. Baker & Brown, 1984a, 1984b; Brown, 1980; Brown & Palincsar, 1982; Forrest-Pressley & Waller, 1982).

Regarding future research directions, the first question concerns instructional research in learning disabilities. It appears that researchers are forging ahead with instructional research, designed to increase cognitive and metacognitive functions in LD students. The instructional foci ranged from handwriting and spelling to reading comprehension (Gerber, 1982; Kosiewicz, Hallahan, Lloyd, & Graves, 1982; Palincsar, 1982; Wong & Jones, 1982). However, the benefits in inculcating various strategies in LD students may be short-termed without more attention being paid to increasing the students' knowledge base in conjunction with teaching them the appropriate learning strategy or strategies (Chi, 1981; Voss, 1982) and observing the effects of increased knowledge on the learned strategies. For example, in Palincsar's (1982) study, LD students were taught questioning strategies, summarization skills, and detecting inconsistencies. The training increased their reading comprehension skills, and transfer to the content area of social studies was observed. It would be instructive to research the effects of increased social studies knowledge on the trained LD students' use of learned strategies. Specifically, as the academic year continued, and the LD students gained in content knowledge of social studies, which of the strategies (questioning, summarization, and detecting anomalies) becomes most used, or evolves into more sophisticated forms?

The point is, there is an intricate relationship between the use of any cognitive and metacognitive strategy and the amount and structure of the content knowledge to which the strategy is to be used (Chi, 1981). Hence, it is insufficient for learning-disabilities researchers and practitioners to focus exclusively on strategy training. In their design of instructional research, they must attend *equally* and *concurrently* to the LD students' acquisition of knowledge in the *specific content area* to which they want the LD students to apply the learned strategy or strategies. Understanding the effects of knowledge on LD students' strategy use is therefore an important issue for future research in learning disabilities.

A second question that may interest researchers concerns investigations of metacognitive processes in LD students. The research on LD students' metacognitive processes, for example, metattention and metamemory, suggests that LD children's metattentional functions resemble those of younger children, rather than those of their peers, and that they showed less rehearsal strategies in memorization. This information has been instructive. A logical extension of such research appears to be investigations on variables that promote LD children's metacognitive development.

Flavell (1982) has given some thoughts to variables/sources that contribute to metacognitive developments. He contemplates two sources: (1) cognitive-developmental changes in the child (e.g., the child's increase in planning capacity), and (2) experiences the child might have that could promote metacognitive development (e.g., classroom teachers modelling self-monitoring in reading comprehension by questioning and attention-focusing, Schallert & Kleinman, 1979; and parents teaching self-regulatory behaviors to their children, Wertsch, 1978).

Let us illustrate one way of researching the kinds of experiences that could promote LD children's metacognitive development. It is recalled that younger and poorer readers typically are less aware of the purpose of reading. To them, reading is a decoding process, rather than a process of extracting meaning from what is read (cf. Forrest-Pressley & Waller, 1980; Myers & Paris, 1978). A relevant research question here would be whether or not successful remediation of LD children's decoding problem would promote their awareness that reading is much more than decoding. The congruity of this research question is clarified by the remedial practice of teachers and reading-disabled children. In remedial instruction of LD children with reading problems, teachers very often provide exercises in passage/story reading jointly with drills in phonics. As the LD children gain in decoding fluency and apply their improved skill in reading exercises or in repeated reading (Samuels, 1982), would they develop the metacognition to read for understanding?

A third question for interested researchers concerns the literature indicating that younger and poorer readers do not monitor their listening and/or reading comprehension as well as older and better readers. Specifically, younger and poorer readers more often accepted as correct, sentences that are grammatically incorrect (Forrest-Pressley & Waller, 1982). However, even good readers in Grade 6 do not always detect inconsistencies in paragraphs (Markman, 1979, 1977; Paris & Myers, 1981).

The pertinent question here concerns the parameters of the poor reader's difficulty in monitoring his or her own listening/reading comprehension (Forrest-Pressley & Waller, 1982). We are only beginning to piece together bits of information toward understanding the complexity of children's comprehension monitoring. Thus far, there is evidence indicating that very young children (age 3 years) would demonstrate comprehension monitoring, given a task involving familiar play activities (Revelle & Karabenick, 1981). Similarly good comprehension monitoring in 6-year-olds was obtained by decreasing the complexity of task demands (Patterson, O'Brien, Kister, Carter, & Kotsonis, 1981). Moreover, standards for evaluating given texts and explicit information on text inconsistency resulted in older children's success in detecting falsehoods or inconsistencies (Markman, 1979; Markman & Gorin, 1981). Further, knowledge of language concepts related to reading (e.g., words and sentences) is related to the child's monitoring of words and sentences (Forrest-Pressley & Waller, 1982). Forrest-Pressley and Waller suggest that such knowledge may be a necessary prerequisite in the poor reader's ability to monitor his or her reading errors and to remediate them. Wong and Jones (1982) indicate the importance of teaching LD students the concept of a main idea prior to teaching them self-monitoring skills in reading comprehension. The results of an earlier study by Wong (1979) suggested that LD children might well be deficient in the knowledge of a main idea.

One parameter governing children's monitoring of reading comprehension or detection of inconsistency appears to be very little understood. This concerns how children and adults successfully reconcile inconsistent information through their own reasoning (Baker & Anderson, 1982; Collins, Brown & Larkin, 1977; Markman & Gorin, 1981; Winograd & Johnson, 1980). Because of this idiosyncratic tendency in children and adults, one may not conclude that a person's (e.g., a child's) failure to mention an inconsistency in the text indicates his or her failure in detecting it. This point bears emphasis in light of evidence that older children detected more inconsistencies when explicitly instructed to locate them (Markman, 1979) or given explicit standards for evaluating what they were reading (Markman & Gorin, 1981).

The preceding brief review highlights the respective roles of certain parameters in children's cognitive monitoring. To understand more fully the processes of cognitive monitoring, we need to research, aside from other parameters, the role of relevant self-questions (cf. Andre & Anderson, 1978–1979; Bransford et al., 1981, 1982; Stein & Bransford, 1979), information processing style of poor readers (Garner, 1981), the bridge between detection of comprehension failure and appropriate debugging strategy (Anderson, 1980; Brown, 1980), and the use of debugging strategies (e.g., look-backs) (Alessi, Anderson, & Goetz, 1979; Garner, in press; Garner & Reis, 1981).

Epilogue

In this chapter, the connection between metacognition and learning disabilities has been explicated. Essentially, metacognitive theory and research contribute importantly to the advancement of the learning disabilities field theoretically, empirically, and in remedial instruction. We have analyzed the inadequacies in two dominant theoretical approaches in learning disabilities, namely, the ability deficits and the task-analysis approaches, and shown how metacognitive theory redresses their insufficiencies. The task-analysis approach, complemented by a metacognitive dimension, currently provides the most satisfactory conceptualization of LD students' academic difficulties.

Metacognitive theory and research has stimulated research on LD students' metacognitive processes and instructional research to enhance their metacognition. In future research, we may profitably concentrate on researching conditions that promote metacognitive development in LD students, and on intervention research that focuses on increasing LD students' content knowledge concurrently with training them on the use of strategies relevant to that content area.

Lastly, metacognitive theory entails equal emphasis on self-regulatory training and basic skills training in the remedial programs of LD students. In the final analysis, the proposal and significance of an additional metacognitive dimension in learning disabilities stem from the possibilities of an increased and more comprehensive understanding of the reasons underlying LD students' academic failures. And through more thorough understanding of their academic failures, we might achieve substantially more effective remediation.

References

Alessi, S. M., Anderson, T. H., & Goetz, E. T. An investigation of lookbacks during studying. *Discourse Processes*, 1979, *2*, 197–212.

Alley, G., & Deshler, D. *Teaching the learning-disabled adolescent: Strategies and methods.* Love Publishing Company, 1979.

Anderson, R. C. Role of the reader's schema in comprehension, learning and memory. In R. C. Anderson, J. Osborn, R. J. Tierney (Eds.), *Learning to read in American schools: Basal readers and content texts.* Hillsdale, NJ: Erlbaum, 1982.

Anderson, T. H. Study strategies and adjunct aids. In R. J. Spiro, B. C. Bruce, & W. F. Brewer (Eds.), *Theoretical issues in reading comprehension: Perspectives from cognitive psychology, artificial intelligence, linguistics, and education.* Hillsdale, NJ: Erlbaum, 1980.

Andre, M. E. D. A., & Anderson, T. H. The development and evaluation of a self-questioning study technique. *Reading Research Quarterly*, 1978–1979, *14*, 605–623.

Baker, L. *Do I understand or do I not understand: That is the question.* (Reading Education Report 10). Champaign, IL: University of Illinois, Center for the Study of Reading, July, 1979.

Baker, L. An evaluation of the role of metacognitive deficits in learning disabilities. *Topics in Learning and Learning Disabilities*, 1982, *2*, 27–36.

Baker, L., & Anderson, R. I. Effects of inconsistent information on text processing: Evidence for comprehension monitoring. *Reading Research Quarterly*, 1982, *17*, 281–294.

Baker, L., & Brown, A. L. Metacognitive skills of reading. In D. P. Pearson (Ed.), *Handbook on Research in Reading.* New York: Longman, 1984.(a)

Baker, L., & Brown, A. L. Cognitive monitoring in reading. In J. Flood (Ed.), *Understanding reading comprehension.* Newark, DE: International Reading Association, 1984.(b)

Bateman, B. D. *The essentials of teaching.* San Rafael, CA: Dimensions Publishing Company, 1971.

Bauer, R. H. Short-term memory in learning-disabled and non-disabled children. *Bulletin of the Psychonomic Society*, 1977, *10*, 128–130.

Bauer, R. H. Recall after a short delay and acquisition in learning-disabled and non-disabled children. *Journal of Learning Disabilities*, 1979, *12*, 596–608.

Bender, L. Specific reading disability as a maturational lag. *Bulletin of the Orton Society*, 1957, *7*, 9–18.

Bransford, J. D. *Human cognition: Learning, understanding and remembering.* Belmont, CA: Wadsworth Publishing Company, 1979.

Bransford, J. D., Stein, B. S., Vye, N. J., Franks, J. J., Auble, P. M., Mezynski, K. J., & Perfetto, G. A. Differences in approaches to learning: An overview. *Journal of Experimental Psychology: General*, 1982, *111*(4), 390–398.

Bransford, J. D., Stein, B. S., Shelton, T. S., & Owings, R. A. Cognition and adaptation: The importance of learning to learn. In J. Harvey (Ed.), *Cognition, Social Behavior and the Environment*. Hillsdale, NJ: Erlbaum, 1981.

Brown, A. L. Learning and development: The problems of compatibility, access and induction. *Human Development*, 1982, *25*, 89–115.

Brown, A. L. Metacognition, executive control, self-regulation and other even more mysterious mechanisms. In F. E. Weinert & R. H. Kluwe (Eds.), *Learning by thinking*. West Germany: Kuhlhammer, 1982.

Brown, A. L. Metacognitive development and reading. In R. J. Spiro, B. Bruce, & W. F. Brewer (Eds.), *Theoretical issues in reading comprehension*. Hillsdale, NJ: Erlbaum, 1980.

Brown, A. L. Knowing when, where, and how to remember: A problem of metacognition. In R. Glaser (Ed.), *Advances in instructional psychology*. Hillsdale, NJ: Erlbaum, 1978.

Brown, A. L., & Palincsar, A. S. Inducing strategic learning from texts by means of informed, self-control training. *Topics in Learning & Learning Disabilites*, 1982, *2*, 1–18.

Cavanaugh, J. C., & Perlmutter, M. Metamemory: A critical examination. *Child Development*, 1982, *53*, 11–28.

Chi, M. T. H. Interactive roles of knowledge and strategies in development. In S. Chipman, J. Segal, & R. Glaser (Eds.), *Thinking and learning skills* (Vol. 2). Hillsdale, NJ: Erlbaum, 1981.

Clay, M. M. *Reading: The patterning of complex behavior*. Auckland, New Zealand: Heinemann Educational Books, 1973.

Collins, A., Brown, J. S., & Larkin, K. M. *Inference in text understanding* (Technical Report No. 40). Urbana: University of Illinois, Center for the Study of Reading, December, 1977.

Cravioto, J. Nutrition and learning in children. In N. S. Springer (Ed.), *Nutrition and mental retardation*. Ann Arbor, MI: Institute for the Study of Mental Retardation and Related Disabilities, 1972, 25–44.

Cruickshank, W. M. Some issues facing the field of learning disability. *Journal of Learning Disabilities*, 1972, *5*(7), 380–383.

Dawson, M. M., Hallahan, D. P., Reeve, R. E., & Ball, D. W. The effect of reinforcement and verbal rehearsal on selective attention in learning-disabled children (Technical Report No. 8). Virginia Research Institute on Learning Disabilities, University of Virginia, 1979.

Flavell, J. H. Speculations about the nature and development of metacognition. In F. E. Weinert & R. H. Kluwe (Eds.), *Learning by thinking*. West Germany: Kuhlhammer, 1982.

Flavell, J. H. Metacognitive aspects of problem solving. In L. B. Resnick (Ed.), *The nature of intelligence*. Hillsdale, NJ: Erlbaum, 1976.

Flavell, J. H., & Wellman, H. M. Metamemory. In R. V. Kail & J. W. Hagen (Eds.), *Perspectives on the development of memory and cognition*. Hillsdale, NJ: Erlbaum, 1977.

Forrest-Pressley, D., & Waller, T. G. Knowledge and monitoring abilities of poor readers. Unpublished manuscript, University of Waterloo, 1982.

Forrest-Pressley, D. L., & Waller, T. G. What do children know about their reading and study skills? Paper presented at the American Educational Research Association, Boston, April, 1980.

Fox, B., & Routh, D. K. Phonemic analysis and synthesis as word attack skills. *Journal of Educational Psychology*, 1976, *68*, 70–74.

Frostig, M. Education of children with learning disabilities. In E. C. Frierson & W. B. Barbe (Eds.), *Educating children with learning disabilities*. New York: Appleton-Century-Crofts, 1966.

Garner, R. Resolving comprehension failure through text lookbacks: Direct training and practice effects among good and poor comprehenders in grades six and seven. *American Educational Research Journal*, in press.

Garner, R. Monitoring of passage inconsistency among poor comprehenders: A preliminary test of the "piecemeal processing" explanation. *Journal of Educational Research*, 1981, 74, 159–162.

Garner, R., Hare, V. C., Alexander, P., Haynes, J., & Winograd, P. Inducing use of a text lookback strategy among unsuccessful readers. Unpublished manuscript, University of Maryland, 1982.

Garner, R., & Reis, R. Monitoring and resolving comprehension obstacles: An investigation of spontaneous text lookbacks among upper-grade good and poor comprehenders. *Reading Research Quarterly*, 1981, 16, 569–582.

Gelabert, T., Torgesen, J. K., Dice, C., & Murphy, H. The effects of situational variables on the use of rehearsal by first grade children. *Child Development*, 1980, 51, 902–905.

Gerber, M. M. Effects of self-monitoring training on spelling performance of learning-disabled and normally-achieving students. Paper presented at AERA meeting, New York, 1982.

Hagen, J. W., & Barclay, C. R. The development of memory skills in children: Portraying learning disabilities in terms of strategy and knowledge deficiencies. *The Best of ACLD*, Rochester: Syracuse University Press, 1981.

Haines, D. J., & Torgesen, J. K. The effects of incentives on rehearsal and short-term memory in reading-disabled children. *Learning Disability Quarterly*, 1979, 2, 18–55.

Hallahan, D. P., & Cruickshank, W. M. *Psychoeducational foundations of learning disabilities*. Englewood Cliffs, NJ: Prentice-Hall, 1973.

Hallahan, D. P., Lloyd, J., Kosiewicz, M. M., & Kneedler, R. D. *A comparison of the effects of self-recording and self-assessment on the on-task behavior and academic productivity of a learning disabled boy* (Technical Report 13). Charlottesville, VA: University of Virginia Learning Disabilities Research Institute, 1979.

Hallahan, D. P., Lloyd, J., Kosiewicz, M. M., Kauffman, J. M., & Graves, A. W. *Self-monitoring of attention as a treatment for a learning-disabled boy's off-task behavior* (Technical Report 10). Charlottesville, VA: University of Virginia Learning Disabilities Research Institute, 1979.

Hallahan, D. P., & Reeve, R. E. Selective attention and distractibility. In B. K. Koegh (Ed.), *Advances in Special Education* (Vol. 1). Greenwich, CT: JAI Press, 1980.

Hallahan, D. P., Tarver, S. G., Kauffman, J. M., & Graybeal, N. L. Selective attention abilities of learning-disabled children under reinforcement and response cost. *Journal of Learning Disabilities*, 1978, 11, 42–51.

Hammill, D. D., Leigh, J. E., McNutt, G., & Larsen, S. C. A new definition of learning disabilities. *Learning Disability Quarterly*, 1981, 4, 336–342.

Hare, V. C., & Borchardt, K. M. Direct instruction of summarization skills. Unpublished manuscript, University of Illinois at Chicago-Circle, 1982.

Hook, P. E., & Johnson, D. J. Metalinguistic awareness and reading strategies. *Bulletin of the Orton Society*, 1978, 28, 62–78.

Jenkins, J. J. Four points to remember: A tetrahedral model and memory experiments. In L. S. Cermak & F. I. M. Craik (Eds.), *Levels and processing in human memory*. Hillsdale, NJ: Erlbaum, 1979.

Kinsbourne, M. L., & Caplan, P. J. *Children's learning and attention problems*. Boston: Little, Brown and Company, 1979.

Kirk, S. A. Behavioral diagnosis and remediation of learning disabilities. In *Proceedings of the Conference on Exploration into the Problems of the Perceptually Handicapped Child, First Annual Meeting* (Vol. 1). Chicago, April 6, 1963.

Kirk, S. A. *Educating Exceptional Children* (2nd ed.). Houghton-Mifflin, 1972.

Kirk, S., & Gallagher, J. *Educating exceptional children.* Boston: Houghton Mifflin, 1979.

Kirk, S. A., & Kirk, W. D. *Psycholinguistic learning disabilities: Diagnosis and remediation.* Urbana: University of Illinois Press, 1971.

Kosiewicz, M. M., Hallahan, D. P., Lloyd, J. W., & Graves, A. W. Effects of self-instruction and self-correction procedures on handwriting performance. *Learning Disability Quarterly,* 1982, *5,* 71–78.

Kreutzer, M. A., Leonard, C., & Flavell, J. H. An interview study of children's knowledge about memory. *Monograph of the Society for Research in Child Development,* 1975, *40*(1, Serial No. 159).

Lerner, J. *Learning disabilities: Theories, diagnosis, and teaching strategies* (3rd ed.). Boston: Houghton Mifflin, 1981.

Loper, A. B., Hallahan, D. P., Ianna, S. O. Meta-attention in learning-disabled and normal students. *Learning Disability Quarterly,* 1982, *5,* 29–36.

Maisto, A. A., & Sipe, S. An examination of encoding and retrieval processes in reading disabled children. *Journal of Experimental Child Psychology,* 1980, *30,* 223–230.

Markman, E. M. Realizing that you don't understand: Elementary school children's awareness of inconsistencies. *Child Development,* 1979, *50,* 643–655.

Markman, E. M. Realizing that you don't understand: A preliminary investigation. *Child Development,* 1977, *48,* 986–992.

Markman, E. M., & Gorin, L. Children's ability to adjust their standards for evaluating comprehension. *Journal of Educational Psychology,* 1981, *73,* 320–325.

Meichenbaum, D. *Cognitive-behavior modification: An integrative approach.* New York: Plenum, 1977.

Meichenbaum, D., & Asarnow, J. Cognitive-behavioral modification and metacognitive development: Implications for the classroom. In P. Kendall & S. Hollon (Eds.), *Cognitive-behavioral interventions: Theory, research and procedure.* New York: Academic Press, 1978.

Mercer, C. D. *Children and adolescents with learning disabilities.* Columbus, OH: Charles E. Merrill, 1979.

Miyake, M., & Norman, D. To ask a question, one must know enough to know what is not known. *Journal of Verbal Learning and Verbal Behavior,* 1979, *18,* 357–364.

Myers, P., & Hammill, D. D. *Methods for learning disabilities* (2nd ed.). New York: Wiley, 1982.

Myers, M., & Paris, S. G. Children's metacognitive knowledge about reading. *Journal of Educational Psychology,* 1978, *70,* 680–690.

National Joint Committee on LD (NJCLD), 1981.

Newman, R. S., & Hagen, J. W. Memory strategies in children with learning disabilities. *Journal of Applied Developmental Psychology,* 1981, *1,* 297–312.

Olofsson, A., & Lundberg, I. Can phonemic awareness be trained in kindergarten? Unpublished manuscript, University of Umea, Sweden, 1982.

Olshavsky, J. Reading as problem-solving: An investigation of strategies. *Reading Research Quarterly,* 1976–1977, *12,* 654–674.

Palincsar, A. S. *Improving the reading comprehension of junior high students through reciprocal teaching of comprehension-monitoring strategies.* Unpublished doctoral dissertation, University of Illinois, 1982.

Paris, S. G., & Myers, M. Comprehension monitoring, memory and study strategies of good and poor readers. *Journal of Reading Behavior,* 1981, *13,* 5–22.

Patterson, C. J., Cosgrove, J. M., & O'Brien, R. G. Nonverbal indicants of comprehension and noncomprehension in children. *Developmental Psychology,* 1980, *16,* 38–48.

Patterson, C. J., O'Brien, C., Kister, M. C., Carter, D. B., & Kotsonis, M. E. Development of comprehension monitoring as a function of context. *Developmental Psychology,* 1981, *17,* 379–389.

Reid, J. F. Learning to think about reading. *Educational Research*, 1966, 9, 56–62.

Revelle, G. L., & Karabenick, J. D. Comprehension monitoring in preschool children. Paper presented at the meeting of the Society for Research in Child Development, Boston, April, 1981.

Salatas, H., & Flavell, J. H. Behavioral and metamnemonic indicators of strategic behaviors under remember instructions in first grade. *Child Development*, 1976, 47, 81–89.

Samuels, J. Invited address, Society for Learning Disabilities and Remedial Education, Kansas City, Missouri, October, 1982.

Schallert, D. L., & Kleinman, G. M. *Some reasons why teachers are easier to understand than textbooks* (Reading Education Report 9). Urbana: University of Illinois, Center for the Study of Reading, June 1979.

Senf, G. M. Issues surrounding classification in learning disabilities. Paper presented at Annual National Convention, Association for Children with Learning Disabilities, 1974.

Shankweiler, D., Liberman, I. Y., Mark, L. S., Fowler, D. A., & Fischer, F. W. The speech code and learning to read. *Journal of Experimental Psychology: Human Learning and Memory*, 1979, 5, 531–545.

Smiley, S. S., Oaken, D. D., Worthen, D., Campione, J. C., & Brown, A. L. Recall of thematically relevant material by adolescent good and poor readers as a function of written versus oral presentation. *Journal of Educational Psychology*, 1977, 69, 381–387.

Smith, H. K. The responses of good and poor readers when asked to read for different purposes. *Reading Research Quarterly*, 1967, 3, 53–84.

Snowling, M. J. The development of grapheme–phoneme correspondence in normal and dyslexic readers. *Journal of Experimental Child Psychology*, 1980, 29, 294–305.

Stein, B., & Bransford, J. Constraints on effective elaboration: Effects of precision and subject generation. *Journal of Verbal Learning and Verbal Behavior*, 1979, 18, 769–777.

Stein, B. S., Bransford, J. D., Franks, J. J., Owings, R. A., Vye, M. J., & McGraw, W. Differences in the precision of self-generated elaborations. *Journal of Experimental Psychology: General*, 1982, 111(4), 399–405.

Strang, R., & Rogers, C. How do students read a short story? *English Journal*, 1965, 54, 819–823.

Tarver, S. G., Hallahan, D. P., Cohen, S. B., & Kauffman, J. M. Visual selection attention and verbal rehearsal in LD boys. *Journal of Learning Disabilities*, 1977, 10, 491–500.

Tarver, S. G., Hallahan, D. P., Kauffman, J. M., & Ball, D. W. Verbal rehearsal and selective attention in children with learning disabilities: A developmental lag. *Journal of Experimental Child Psychology*, 1976, 22, 375–385.

Torgesen, J. K. Factors related to poor performance on rote memory tasks in reading-disabled children. *Learning Disabilities Quarterly*, 1979, 2, 17–23.

Torgesen, J. K. The learning-disabled child as an inactive learner: Educational implications. *Topics in learning and learning disabilities*, 1982, 2, 45–52.

Torgesen, J. K. Listening comprehension in LD children with adequate or poor short-term memory. Unpublished manuscript, State University of Florida, 1984.

Torgesen, J. K. Memorization processes in reading-disabled children. *Journal of Educational Psychology*, 1977, 69, 571–578. (b)

Torgesen, J. K. Problems and prospects in the study of learning disabilities. In E. M. Hetherington (Ed.), *Review of Child Development Research* (Vol. 5). Chicago: University of Chicago Press, 1975.

Torgesen, J. K. The role of nonspecific factors in the task performance of learning-disabled children: A theoretical assessment. *Journal of Learning Disabilities*, 1977, 10, 27–34.(a)

Torgesen, J. K., & Goldman, T. Rehearsal and short-term memory in reading-disabled children. *Child Development*, 1977, 48, 56–60.

Torgesen, J. K., & Houck, G. Processing deficiencies in learning-disabled children who per-

form poorly on the digit span task. *Journal of Educational Psychology*, 1980, 72, 141–
160.

Torgesen, J. K., & Kail, R. V. Memory processes in exceptional children. *Advances in Special Education* (Vol. 1). Greenwich, CT: JAI, 1980.

Torgesen, J. K., Murphy, H. A., & Ivey, C. The influence of an orienting task on the memory performance of children with reading problems. *Journal of Learning Disabilities*, 1979, 12, 396–401.

Vellutino, F., Steger, B. M., Moyer, S. C., Harding, C. J., & Miles, J. A. Has the perceptual deficit hypothesis led us astray? *Journal of Learning Disabilities*, 1977, 10(6), 375–385.

Voss, J. F. Knowledge and social science problem solving. Paper presented at AERA meeting, New York, March 1982.

Wallace, G., & McLoughlin, J. A. *Learning disabilities: Concepts and characteristics* (2nd ed.). Columbus, OH: Charles E. Merrill, 1979.

Wellman, H. M., Collins, J., & Glieberman, J. Understanding the combination of memory variables: Developing conceptions of memory limitations. *Child Development*, 1981, 52, 1313–1317.

Wertsch, J. W. Adult–child interaction and the roots of metacognition. *Quarterly Newsletter of the Institute for Comparative Human Development*, 1978, 1, 15–18.

Whimbey, A., & Whimbey, L. S. *Intelligence can be taught*. Stanford, CN: Innovative Sciences, 1975.

Williams, J. P. Teaching decoding with an emphasis on phoneme analysis and phoneme blending. *Journal of Educational Psychology*, 1980, 72, 1–15.

Winograd, P. N. Strategic difficulties in summarizing texts. *Reading Research Quarterly*, 1984, 19 (4), 404–425.

Winograd, P., & Johnson, P. Comprehension monitoring and the error detection paradigm (Technical Report 153). Urbana: University of Illinois, Center for the Study of Reading, January, 1980.

Wittrock, M. C. The cognitive movement in education. *Educational Psychologist*, 1980, 13, 15–29.

Wong, B. Y. L. Strategic behaviors in selecting retrieval cues in gifted, normal achieving and learning-disabled children. *Journal of Learning Disabilities*, 1982, 15(1), 33–37.

Wong, B. Y. L. Increasing retention of main ideas through questioning strategies. *Learning Disability Quarterly*, 1979, 2, 42–47.

Wong, B. Y. L. The effects of directive cues on the organization of memory and recall in good and poor readers. *Journal of Educational Research*, 1978, 72, 32–38.

Wong, B. Y. L., & Jones, W. Increasing metacomprehension in learning-disabled and normally-achieving students through self-questioning training. *Learning Disability Quarterly*, 1982, 5(3), 228–240.

Wong, B. Y. L., & Sawatsky, D. Sentence elaboration and retention of good, average and poor readers. *Learning Disability Quarterly*, 1984, 7(3), 229–236.

Wong, B. Y. L., Wong, R., & LeMare, L. J. The effects of knowledge of criterion tasks on the comprehension and recall of normally-achieving and learning-disabled children. *Journal of Educational Research*, 1982, 76, 119–126.

Ysseldyke, J. Remediation of ability deficits: Some major questions. In L. Mann, L. Goodman, & J. Wiederholt (Eds.), *Teaching the learning-disabled adolescent*. Boston: Houghton Mifflin, 1978.

Ysseldyke, J., & Salvia, J. Diagnostic–prescriptive teaching: Two models. *Exceptional Children*, 1974, 40, 181–186.

Yussen, S. R., & Levy, V. M. Developmental changes in predicting one's own memory span of short-term memory. *Journal of Experimental Child Psychology*, 1975, 19, 502–508.

CHAPTER 5

Metacognition and Attention

Patricia H. Miller

Introduction

A 6-year-old sits at his desk in his classroom, staring dreamily into space. Before him lies his untouched math worksheet. His teacher startles him out of his reverie with, "Greg, you're not paying attention." The child seems unaware of his lengthy inattention. Such behavior, common in a young child, traditionally has been considered immature attention. Young children are called "easily distracted" or "unable to sustain attention."

A recent area of research, metacognition, offers a new perspective on attentional difficulties, whether a normal phase of development in a young child or a deficit in an older child. *Metacognition* refers to knowledge about any aspect of mental functioning and to the directing of this functioning. Meta-attention, a subset of metacognition, refers to two areas: (1) knowledge about attention and (2) the control of attention. The first area, knowledge about attention, includes attention as the content of cognition. Just as one's reasoning can be directed toward physical events, it can also be directed toward mental events such as memory, comprehension, and attention. In the opening vignette, the child may not know that attention to a task sometimes must be effortful rather than automatic, that humans have a limited attentional capacity, and that attention is affected by variables such as motivation, noise level, and age of the attender. In other words, a child may lack knowledge about attention in the same way that he or she might lack knowledge about number concepts or about situations requiring moral judgments. Knowledge about attention is important because a child without this knowledge probably is not likely to make an active effort to attend.

The second area of meta-attention involves the control of attention. It could be the case the the forementioned young child can attend efficiently once attentional processes are activated, that is, he does not have a deficit in attention per se. However, his problem may be that it does not occur to him to actively manage his attention. Or, he may try to manage his attention but have difficulty accessing the skills that are appropriate for attending in that particular situation. These skills include monitoring one's current attentional state, analyzing the attentional demands of the task, selecting an attentional strategy, and evaluating the attentional strategy. These skills are among those general processes of executive control that Brown (1978) suggested are central in problem solving. The control aspect of meta-attention is closely related to the knowledge aspect. For example, a child may not use a particular strategy to control attention unless he or she understands that the situation requires selective attention and knows that attention would be facilitated by strategies.

In short, a metacognitive perspective, rather than focus on deficits in attention itself, focuses on a child's underlying knowledge about attention and the child's ability to access attention-directing skills. Research on meta-attention is complementary to, rather than an alternative to, the long line of research on developmental changes in attentional behavior. Developing attentional skills and applying them appropriately is a multifaceted achievement, of which metattention is one component.

This chapter begins by reviewing meta-attentional research on attending to a task and ignoring distractions, selectively attending to relevant stimuli within a task, and attending during visual search. Next appears a classification system for variables affecting attention, followed by three theoretical orientations for meta-attentional problems, a critique of methods of assessment, and suggestions for future research. There is much less research on meta-attention than on metamemory and less, in fact, than on most areas of metacognition. Thus, certain questions can only be answered in a sketchy way. In fact, it is only beginning to become clear what the important questions are.

Changes in Attention during Development

The results of studies of children's understanding of attention can best be interpreted if they are prefaced by a description of children's attention. Attention has many aspects—alertness, capacity, overt exploration by the sense organs, and the selection of certain stimuli for further processing from among the total set of stimulation while ignoring other information. Most of the research on meta-attention involves selective attention.

During development, children play an increasingly active role in their own attention (see a review by Lane and Pearson, 1982, and various chapters in a volume on attention edited by Hale and Lewis, 1979). That is, compared to younger children, older children are flexible in that they can adjust their attention to meet the needs of each task. They attend to part of the stimuli in some tasks and attend to all the stimuli in other tasks, depending on which strategy is more efficient. At the same time, children become less susceptible to distraction. In addition, their overt visual and tactual exploration is increasingly orderly, systematic, and, when appropriate, exhaustive. Also, they learn to detect the distinctive features that differentiate members of a stimulus group. These various components of attention play an important role in how children solve the academic and nonacademic tasks they encounter. The ability to concentrate one's information-processing capacity on the relevant input often is a prerequisite for learning.

Meta-attention concerning Attending to a Task and Ignoring Distractions

An Initial Study of Meta-attention

The first study of meta-attention (Miller & Bigi, 1979) explored first, third, and fifth graders' understanding of a wide range of familiar situations involving attention at home or at school. In one session most of the questions were open ended. Because of the high verbal demands of this session, in a later session, children were given several possible answers from which to choose the one they considered the best.

Certain knowledge about attention was already acquired by even the youngest children. Most children knew that they do not always attend well and, furthermore, could identify certain factors that cause attentional difficulties. In Session 1, most children indicated that they sometimes have trouble paying attention (75%, 79%, and 87% of the children in Grades 1, 3, and 5, respectively), usually because other children distract them or they are bored or it is noisy. These distractions sometimes were described quite vividly, as in the following protocol from a third grader: "Because when it's noisy, I can't read; it seems as though everything around me is moving around and dropping on the floor and breaking or something, so when I'm reading I just can't stand it."

In Session 2, when asked directly about the effect of certain variables on attention, nearly all the children in all grades knew that it is easier to pay attention when it is quiet, when interest is high, and when one is not doing something already. Most children were also aware that children are less attentive than adults and they often attributed this to the fact that children's behavior interferes with attention (e.g., "Children mess around, adults listen," "Adults don't have anything to fool around with like paper airplanes"). Adults' greater experience and knowledge also were mentioned: "Adults know more," "When they (adults) went to school nobody made noise and they learned to pay attention."

This knowledge about age differences in attentional ability may develop fairly early. A study by Shatz and Gelman (1973) suggests that even preschoolers know that younger children are less attentive. They found that 4-year-olds adjusted their speech to 2-year-olds in order to elicit and maintain the younger child's attention. The children added words such as *hey, see, look, watch, no,* and the listener's name.

Another vignette in the Miller and Bigi study described a teacher who was giving important instructions concerning painting with special paints. Nearly all the children knew that some children listen more carefully than others. In addition, in Session 2 when asked directly what the effects of certain variables were, they recognized that a child could listen more carefully if he or she looked at the teacher rather than at other children, did not talk to anyone, was interested in what the teacher was saying, and did not fool around.

This vignette, however, also revealed that certain meta-attentional knowledge was not yet acquired by the younger children in the study. Fifth graders were significantly more likely to suggest that inattention in this situation could be due to the child's lack of interest in the painting activity. Younger children usually mentioned causes such as talking to friends, being noisy, and not sitting and listening.

Another vignette revealing strong developmental differences concerned the effect, on doing homework, of having a television or radio on or being near a big window through which the child could see his or her friends playing in the park. Older children were more likely than younger to assert that these temptations could affect the child's concentration. Children in Grades 1 and 3 thought that the radio and television were more distracting than the view of children playing. The opposite was true of fifth graders. Anecdotal evidence suggests that it is not uncommon for older grade schoolers and teenagers to do homework while listening to rock music or watching television. These children, if not their parents, apparently believe that this is not a distracting situation.

Finally, age differences in meta-attention were revealed in another item, which examined children's knowledge concerning what one can do to remove distractions. If a child is reading a book in the library and some children come over and talk loudly, older children were more likely than younger to suggest reasonable strategies, for example, that the child move elsewhere or tell the children to be quiet or to move elsewhere. A few of the children even offered rather subtle strategies; for example, one diplomatic girl suggested, "I could just tell them real nice, 'if you need help on your reading, just read silently, then if you get stuck on a word then I'll help you.'"

As illustrated in the aforementioned results, the most general developmental trend in this study was that with increasing age, children were more likely to mention psychological factors and less likely to mention noise level. That is, the older children usually attributed inattention to psychological factors such as a lack of interest or concentration, temptations in the environment, the desire to be doing another activity, or lack of knowledge or experience. Although the younger children also mentioned these factors, over half of their answers referred to the interfering effects of noise and, to a lesser extent, interfering behavior on the child's part. Thus the initial report of this study was subtitled "You know I can't hear you when the water's running." These age differences are nicely illustrated in a vignette in which a child is in her room and her mother calls her name from the door of the child's room. Younger children usually attributed failure to hear the call to the noise level, for example, a radio playing loudly. In contrast, older children could consider psychological barriers to hearing the call, for example, being engrossed in a book: "When I'm really getting into something, everything just stops and I can't hear anything except what I'm doing."

It should be noted that this developmental trend appeared primarily when children were asked to give reasons for attention or distraction or to describe situations or events when attention or distraction would occur. When children were presented with alternative reasons, situations, or events, or merely had to answer "yes" or "no," the age differences usually were greatly reduced or even eliminated. Thus, it appears that most of the developmental change in meta-attention has to do with the accessibility of this knowledge. Young children know that psychological factors affect attention but they do not often spontaneously access such factors by themselves.

This knowledge about psychological influences on attention may be less accessible in younger children for at least two reasons. First, younger children may find it difficult to express their knowledge verbally. That is, they may have an intuitive, but relatively unarticulated understanding, which remains unexpressable until after additional development of the integration of language and thought. More specifically, unobservable mental events such as interest or boredom may be more difficult to convert into language than observable events such as noise or rowdy behavior. A second way in which meta-attentional knowledge might be less accessible in young children is that they may have a general deficiency in detecting which of the information they have is relevant for the situation in question. Thus, it might not occur to a young child to think about a person's motivation level when explaining lack of attention, even though if asked directly about the effects of motivation on attention the child would see its relevance immediately. There is not yet research that would allow us to prefer one of these explanations over the other, but we return to the issues of access later.

Knowledge concerning the Effects of Noise and Interest

The different levels of knowledge detected by the two procedures in the Miller and Bigi study stimulated a more careful look at methods of assessment. This line of research examined the developmental change from concepts of attention based on noise level to those based on psychological variables, especially level of interest.

Miller and Zalenski (1982) asked whether very young children, 3- and 4-year-olds, have any understanding of the effects of noise level and degree of interest on attentional performance. It was critical, of course, to develop nonverbal procedures appropriate for children this young. Two procedures were used, one a forced-choice procedure requiring a child to choose between two arrays and one giving a child the opportunity to remove noisy objects from a room. In the former, on each trial there were two arrays, each consisting of a miniature room containing small Fisher-Price toy people, furniture, and other props. These toys were intended to heighten the children's motivation and ensure their understanding of the episodes described. The arrays illustrated situations familiar to preschoolers—a child listening to his mother telling him how to play new games (on half of the trials) and a child writing numbers (on half the trials). The two arrays differed only in noise level on two trials and the child was asked which room would be a better place for the boy to listen to his mother (or to learn about numbers). On two trials the arrays differed only in the interest level of the toy child (as illustrated in a happy or sad face) and the subject was asked which child would listen to his mother more (learn about numbers more). The two arrays differed in both noise and interest on two trials and consequently pitted one against the other to reveal which the child considered more important—that is, the interested child was in the noisy room and the uninterested child was in the quiet room. As each pair of arrays was presented, the experimenter described the critical difference or differences between them.

Performance was significantly greater than chance (50%) on all trials. The children chose the quiet room on 75% of the trials in which noise level differed and the interested child on 92% of the trials in which interest varied. Both these trials and the trials pitting noise against interest indicated that interest level was considered a more powerful variable than noise level. In the latter trials, the interested child in a noisy room was chosen over an uninterested child in a quiet room on 84% of the trials. Both the understanding of the effect of noise and interest and the preference for interest over noise were replicated in a study (Miller, in press) that examined preschoolers' understanding of a broad range of internal and external variables that could affect performance.

The other assessment procedure in the Miller and Zalenski study further examined the understanding of noise. There were a number of noisy and quiet objects (e.g., appliances, furniture) in the room in which the toy child was sitting. The subject was asked to take objects out one-by-one, in order of importance, to help the pretend child work on his numbers (or listen to his mother). There was a significant tendency to remove noisy objects first, suggesting that the young children understood their interfering effect.

This study indicated that children as young as 3 years appear to understand that noise and lack of interest hinder cognitive activities, and consider interest more influential. The testing conditions were, of course, optimal for eliciting any understanding of attention because no verbalization was required, the two values depicting each variable were extremes of that variable (e.g., quiet vs. very noisy), and interesting materials illustrating familiar situations were used. As in the forced-choice session of the Miller and Bigi study, the children did not have to spontaneously select these variables as relevant. They had to decide whether the presented variables of noise and interest levels are relevant and whether the two end points of each variable facilitate or hinder performance. Still, some early knowledge about attention clearly is present. Wellman (1977), also using a forced-choice procedure but in the area of metamemory, found that many preschoolers knew that a noisy situation decreases memory performance.

It should be noted that the children's performance on the interest trials does not seem to depend on the use of happy or sad faces to depict interest and a lack of interest. An additional sample of 3- and 4-year-olds correctly chose the interested child when facial expressions did not vary— that is, the variable was described only verbally.

As mentioned earlier, early knowledge about noise and interest revealed by Miller and Zalenski may be rudimentary because only the extreme ends of each variable were presented. That is, the difference between a child who likes to learn about numbers and a child who does not like to learn about numbers is rather salient. With slightly older children it is possible to use more complex assessment procedures, which can detect children's concept of a variable as a quantitative, differentiated dimension rather than a bipolar attribute. The assessment still need not require a verbal response. Miller and Shannon (1984) accomplished this goal by having the children, aged 4 to 7 years, use a scale to indicate how many items a hypothetical child would learn under various levels of noise and interest. For example, on one trial the subject would point to the number of new games a child would learn from a book if several children are reading very loudly near by and if he or she is moderately interested in learning new games. A factorial combination of three levels of interest and three levels of noise generated nine situations for the subject to judge. On each trial, the levels of interest and noise were illustrated in line drawings. With respect to interest level, on the child's face the corners of the mouth turned downward, slightly upward, or extremely upward. With respect to noise level, a drawing of the volume knob of the tape recorder, which had been used to demonstrate the various levels of noise, pointed with an arrow to the left, straight up, or to the right to indicate low, medium, or high noise. The experimenter described the level of each variable as the line drawings were presented. As in the Miller and Zalenski study, two stories were used.

In addition to detecting the understanding of levels of noise or interest, this procedure has another advantage. It can systematically examine whether children can think about two variables at the same time and, if so, examine how they combine the two pieces of information to form a judgment. In real-life settings there usually are several variables simultaneously affecting attention rather than just one variable. To clarify the performance on the trials with two variables, there were three additional trials with information only about noise (low, medium, or high) and three trials with information only about interest (low, medium, or high).

Whether children understand the effect of each variable and how they combine them can be detected by analyses of variance (ANOVAs) on the trials on which information about both noise and interest appear. The significant main effect of the interest variable indicated that children judged that the greater the hypothetical child's interest, the better the performance. This outcome is illustrated in the steep slopes of the curves in Figure 1. Interest level significantly affected judgments in both age groups, regardless of whether the trials with only interest information were presented before or after these trials with information about both noise and interest level.

By the same logic, a significant main effect of the noise variable would indicate that children understand the effect of noise—that is, the more noise, the less learning. The three curves would be separated on a graph. As can be seen in Figure 1, noise level significantly affected judgments only in the older group and even then only if the noise-only trials had been presented before these trials with information about both noise and interest. The analyses of the noise-only trials revealed that even when noise level was presented alone, only the older children's judgments were affected. (See Anderson, 1980, for a discussion of how rules for using and

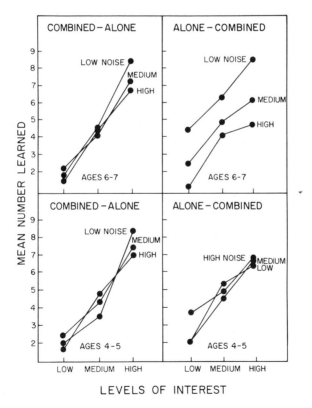

FIGURE 1. Subjects' mean judged number of items learned at each level of noise and interest on the noise-plus-interest trials in each order of presentation.

integrating information can be inferred from ANOVAs and comparisons of graphs.)

In summary, both of the preceding studies suggest that young children understand the effect of interest and think that interest affects performance more than does the amount of noise. The knowledge about noise is less clear. The earlier understanding of noise in the Miller and Zalenski study than the Miller and Shannon study probably reflects the greater difficulty of the procedure in the latter study. It used a rating scale and presented three levels of two variables rather than a simple two-choice procedure.

Young children's greater understanding of interest than noise and their preference for interest over noise was unexpected, given the finding of the Miller and Bigi study that young children are more likely to mention noise level than psychological variables in their explanations. Thus, Miller and Shannon conducted a second study, using second graders, to examine whether the stimuli had inadvertently produced a greater perceived difference between the levels of interest than between the levels of noise. They changed the description of the variables and the drawings illustrating the variables so that the levels of noise were more distinct. Despite these changes, the children still based their judgments on interest level much more than noise level.

The next study by Miller (1982) examined two questions, using the same procedure. First, does the preference for interest continue during later development? Second, are there later developmental changes in how children combine information about noise and interest to make their judgments? The latter question begins to examine the issue of whether there are general cognitive changes during development that underlie changes in metattentional thought.

As illustrated by the steep slopes of the curves in Figure 2, children from kindergarten, Grades 2 and 5, and college students thought that the amount learned would be greatly affected by the child's degree of interest in the task. There was also a significant, but much smaller, effect of noise level on their judgments, as seen in the separation of the three curves, particularly in the older groups. Thus, in answer to the first of the preceding questions, interest was weighted more heavily than noise level at all ages, but this preference decreased among the older subjects.

The answer to the second question, concerning how children combine the two variables, came from an ANOVA performed on each age group. The significant interaction of the noise and interest factors for Grades 2, 5, and college students, but not the kindergarteners, suggests the following: The youngest children were simply adding together the two pieces of information when judging how much the hypothetical child

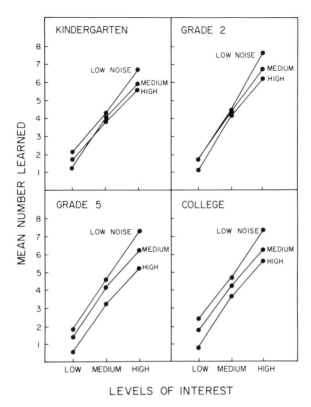

FIGURE 2. Subjects' mean judged number of items learned at each level of noise and interest on the noise-plus-interest trials at four ages.

would learn. This is illustrated by the fact that their curves in Figure 2 do not significantly deviate from parallelism. In contrast, the older three groups were combining the information in more complex ways. There was interaction between the two variables. Although their curves in Figure 2 deviated significantly from parallelism, this deviation clearly is not large in an absolute sense. The largest contribution to the significant interaction is the fact that noise level is considered more important when interest is high than when it is moderate or low. One interpretation of this is that children think that a highly motivated person is most likely to take advantage of a quiet setting.

A final measure taken in the Miller and the Miller and Shannon studies brings us back to a comparison of these studies requiring nonverbal responses and the Miller and Bigi interview study. After all the nonverbal measures were completed, children were asked whether how interested a child is or how quiet it is would be more important for learning. The surprising finding was that in all three studies, children younger than Grade 1 or 2 tended to choose quiet as being more important, despite the fact that their nonverbal choices had indicated a strong preference for interest. Thus, this verbal measure elicited young children's strong concern with noise level, as had the Miller and Bigi verbal measure. However, it should be noted that the verbal requirements were not great in these later studies—that is, the children merely had to say "quiet" or "interest." Thus, it seems unlikely that the demands on verbal production could account for the contradictory results. Perhaps the differing results with the two types of measures may be due to the fact that any type of verbal questioning, even forced-choice questions, is more abstract and less tied to concrete referents than nonverbal measures. One study, however, is at odds with this argument. Loper, Hallahan, and Ianna (1982), also using a choice procedure, found that with increasing age, normal and learning-disabled grade school children put increasing emphasis on interest, but maintained their heavy emphasis on noise. It is not clear why the results deviate from the others reviewed here that used the choice procedure, but the results could have been affected by the inclusion of a third variable on the choice trials: amount of reward for attending.

In conclusion, the belief that interest level greatly affects performance and has more effect than noise level appears to have some generality. The belief is maintained over vignettes depicting seven different activities, including both auditory activities (e.g., a child listening to his mother) and nonauditory activities (e.g., silently reading a book). The same results appear regardless of whether the hypothetical child's activity is a laboratory attention task (Miller & Weiss, 1982) or familiar, real-life situations. Variations from study to study in how the two variables are presented (e.g., drawings vs. toy people, extreme vs. moderate differences between the levels, the type of noise, the way of visually illustrating noise level) have little or no effect. Although it is still possible that noise level was inadvertently made less salient than interest level in these studies, it is unlikely, given the replication despite the many variations.

The perceived importance of motivation also was observed in a study of metamemory by Wellman, Collins, and Gleiberman (1981). Young children considered degree of effort more important than number of objects to be remembered. Effort has also been identified as a salient variable in children's attributions concerning success and failure (Kun, Parsons, & Ruble, 1974).

Children's strong belief that interest in a task influences attention more than does the surrounding noise level is somewhat surprising. Interest is unobservable, abstract, and psychological, whereas noise can be directly perceived and therefore should be easier to comprehend. The social cognitive literature demonstrates a developmental trend from making judgments based on observable, concrete events or characteristics to unobservable, psychological events or characteristics (Shantz, 1983). One possible explanation for the emphasis on a person's interest is Piaget's (1929) finding that young children have an exaggerated sense of personal causality. They believe that wanting something to happen can cause it to happen and that people are responsible for their behavior.

The children in fact are probably correct in their judgments. It is likely that motivation affects performance on most or all tasks, whereas there is evidence that noisy surroundings do not always hinder performance (Christie & Glickman, 1980; Douglas & Peters, 1979).

Understanding the Effects of Other Variables on Attention

Although most of the meta-attentional research has examined the variables of interest and noise, there is work on other variables as well. Yussen and Bird (1979) examined whether young children understand the effects of four variables—length of list (number of items), noise, age, and time allowed—on attention, memory, and communication. The attention task required the hypothetical child to monitor, through a window, several animals "which have escaped from the zoo" (p. 306). The animals could be monitored by shifting attention among them. On each trial the experimenter described the critical difference between two drawings depicting the variable—for example, monitoring 10 animals versus 3 animals. The subject had to decide which child had the harder job. The 6-year-olds understood the effects of all four variables. The 4-year-olds had a greater understanding of the effects of noise and length than age and time. Yussen and Bird suggest that the children may have had more prior experience with variations in noise and length of problems or that these variables are more concrete than others.

Another variable, the amount of reward (i.e., money), is weighted differently at different ages (Loper et al., 1982). Normal and learning disabled children put less emphasis on the effect of reward on attention with increasing age, from 7 to 11 years.

Knowledge about Attentional Strategies for Resisting Temptations

The Miller and Bigi interview study revealed a developing awareness that external events can be distracting not only because they are noisy but also because they pose a temptation for the child. For example, seeing one's friends playing outside or playing the radio or television tempt a child to leave his or her homework. There was little evidence for the awareness of this psychological process working against attention until approximately age 10 years. A relevant line of research, conducted by W. Mischel and H. Mischel, examines the development of children's knowledge of strategies for resisting temptation.

W. Mischel first conducted a series of studies on what conditions facilitate children's ability to delay gratification. For example, viewing a photograph of the reward rather than viewing the actual reward facilitates delay. In general, children are most likely to delay if they control their attention by shifting it away from the object of gratification and toward self-generated cognitive distractions. Particularly effective is ideation that focuses on abstract, nonconsummatory attributes of the reward (e.g., its color rather than its taste) or on the delay task itself (Miller, Weinstein, & Karniol, 1978; Mischel & Baker, 1975). Mischel then began to examine children's knowledge about these conditions.

In an initial set of studies (Yates & Mischel, 1979), children were placed in a delay-of-gratification situation in which they could receive a desirable reward (e.g., pretzels) if they waited for the reward until the experimenter returned. Children received a lesser reward if they could not wait. During the delay the children controlled the amount of time they viewed a delay-facilitating stimulus (e.g., an object unrelated to the reward) and a delay-hindering stimulus (e.g., real pretzels). Children in Grades 1, 2, and 3, when waiting for a reward, preferred to view stimuli unrelated to the reward, apparently correctly realizing that looking at the reward would simply make them want it even more. Thus, grade school children have some understanding of the nature of temptation and what attentional strategies they can employ to reduce this temptation. In contrast, the younger children simply looked at the stimuli they enjoyed looking at, without considering the fact that they were trying to delay gratification. Younger children are "trapped in a delay-defeating cycle, attending to the consummatory qualities of what they want and becoming increasingly frustratively aroused, thereby making it even harder to wait successfully" (Yates & Mischel, 1979, p. 299).

The metacognitive assessment was expanded in a more recent series of studies (Mischel & Mischel, 1983). First, the children were asked whether it would help more to wait for marshmallows if the marshmallows were covered or uncovered. The developmental progression was as follows: no preference (3:0 [3 years, 0 months] to 4:0), preference for having the reward uncovered (4:0 to 4:5), no preference (4:5 to 5:11), and preference for having it covered (6:0 to 11:11), a preference that was stronger in the older children. This latter increasing preference parallels Miller and

Bigi's finding that third and fifth graders were more likely than first graders to say that when studying they would close the curtain of a window through which they could see their friends playing. Next, the children were asked what they could say to themselves to help them wait if the marshmallows were left out in front of them. Only a very few of the youngest children could suggest strategies (e.g., "I would talk to the wall"), but the number steadily increased with increasing age. Through age 7 years, children mainly suggested self-distraction strategies. In fact, many of the young 4-year-olds, who earlier had said that the reward should be uncovered, suggested distraction as a strategy. They seem to think that they can look at the rewards, but still overcome this temptation by distracting themselves. The older children had more variety in their answers. In order of decreasing frequency, the strategies were as follows: focus on the demands of the waiting situation (e.g., "I have to wait for the marshmallow"), think about something other than the waiting situation, mentally transform the rewards to remove their desirability (e.g., "The marshmallows are filled with an evil spell"), and think about positive aspects of the marshmallows (e.g., "It looks good and fluffy").

Next, the children were asked to choose the one of two statements that would be more helpful: "The marshmallows taste yummy and chewy" (consummatory ideation) versus "I am waiting for the two marshmallows" (task-oriented ideation) or "The marshmallows are puffy like clouds" (abstract ideation). Preschoolers showed no preference, but the older children preferred the task-oriented ideation over the consummatory ideation. However, not until the sixth grade was abstract ideation preferred over consummatory ideation. Thus, knowing that thinking about the "cool" properties of a reward poses less temptation than thinking about its "hot" properties is a relatively late acquisition. It is interesting that most sixth graders have this knowledge but none spontaneously suggested this strategy earlier. Many of the grade-school children could support their answers by referring to how the strategy would help motivation, provide distraction, reduce temptation, avoid the arousal of consummatory ideation, etc. Finally, there is evidence that the knowledge of useful strategies for delay is significantly related to how long the child actually can delay (H. Mischel, 1983).

The preceding series of studies and the interview study by Miller and Bigi describe a developing awareness of an understanding of the psychological nature of temptation and of the strategies that facilitate attention away from these temptations. Children learn that tempting objects or events can undermine self-control with respect to waiting for a reward, doing homework, reading in the library, listening to the teacher, and so forth. They also learn that resistance to these tempting objects and events can be facilitated by covering them up, moving away from them, removing them from the environment, or increasing concentration on the activity. They also learn to create an emotional distance by thinking about the desirable object's abstract, "cool" qualities, about the task itself, or about something irrelevant. More generally, this research suggests that it is rather arbitrary to separate attention from social-personality development, including self-control, motivation, and emotion. The latter constantly affect attention in real-life situations.

Meta-attention concerning Selectively Attending to Relevant Stimuli

The first major section of this chapter has examined children's knowledge about variables that affect attending to the task at hand and ignoring distractions. The present section examines metattention regarding an additional attentional requirement of many tasks—namely, selectively attending to certain stimuli within the task while ignoring other stimuli. Unlike the tasks in the previous section, the potential distractors are within the task itself rather than in the surrounding environment or the person.

To study selective attention in children, investigators most commonly have used the incidental-learning task. In a typical version of this task (Hagen, 1967), the child views a row of cards, one card at a time. Each card has a line drawing of an animal and a household object, one above the other. The same cards are used on each trial, but their spatial position in the row varies from trial to trial. The child's task is to remember the locations of the objects designated as relevant by the experimenter, for example, animals. On each trial, after the child views the array he or she is shown a drawing of one of the animals and is asked to point to the card, now face down, that contains that animal. The child's recall of the location of the animals on several trials is a measure of attention to and memory of the relevant stimuli. At the end of these trials the child is unexpectedly asked to try to match up each animal with the household object that always appeared with it. This procedure assesses attention to irrelevant stimuli, termed *incidental learning*. Low incidental learning and high recall of relevant (central) stimuli would indicate selective attention. The results are that with increasing age the recall of central stimuli improves, whereas incidental learning stays the same or increases slightly until approximately age 13 years, when it begins a decline that continues for several years. Thus, selective attention on this task is clearest after age 13 when attentional capacity is allocated mainly to central stimuli.

Because much of the information about children's selective attention comes from the incidental-learning task, the research on meta-attention in this area has incorporated this task. It should be noted, however, that questions have been raised as to whether this task provides an adequate assessment of selective attention (Lane, 1980). Miller and Weiss (1982) examined children's and college students' understanding of the effect of 11 variables known to affect attention. Following Flavell and Wellman's (1977) classification system for metacognitive variables, there were three categories of variables: (1) *Person variables* included age, degree of interest in the task, whether the child is thinking about other objects in the room, and whether the child is listening to the activities next door; (2) *task variables* included the relative salience of relevant and irrelevant stimuli, noise level, number of task-irrelevant objects, and the distance between relevant and irrelevant objects; (3) *strategy variables* were how selectively the person looked at the relevant stimuli, how systematic the order of looking at relevant objects was, and labeling. The subjects used a rating scale to indicate how many relevant objects a child would recall under each of the two conditions illustrating extreme ends of each variable. For example, on the selective-looking trial, one drawing showed a child looking only at the relevant objects and the other drawing showed a child looking at both the relevant and the incidental objects. If subjects indicated that significantly more relevant objects would be recalled in the former situation than the latter, then it was inferred that they understand that this variable would affect performance. Such significant differences were found at all ages (K, 2, 5, college) for 4 of the 11 variables: labeling, order of looking at relevant objects, interest level, and age. In addition, the second and fifth graders showed significant understanding of 5 of the 7 remaining variables. One variable, the task variable of salience, was not significant until college age, and 1 variable, the task variable of distance between objects, was not significant at any age.

Several conclusions emerge. First, even 5-year-olds understand the effect of several variables on selective attention. They do not, however, understand the effect of all relevant variables. Second, most of the increase in meta-attentional knowledge concerning attention on the incidental-learning task comes between kindergarten and Grade 2. In the studies of meta-attention concerning interest and noise described earlier, this also was the transition period for considering the effect of noise when a similar rating scale procedure was used. Third, the study suggests that the understanding of task variables develops later than the understanding of person or strategy variables. This broadens the conclusion of the previous section that an understanding of interest—a person variable—develops before the understanding of noise—an external variable. Miller and Weiss' replication of the study regarding the early concern with person variables is particularly interesting because the task variables were depicted in a concrete salient manner. For example, they varied the numbers of distracting objects and the use of color to manipulate the salience of the relevant objects. Still, the younger children usually did not think such differences had an effect on performance.

Two additional assessments in the aforementioned study involved open-ended questions. In one, the subjects were asked to explain their judgments concerning the effects of the variables. Few of the kindergarteners or second graders were able to give adequate explanations, despite the fact that their judgments often were correct. In particular, there was a dramatic developmental increase in the ability to offer psychological explanations—that is, to note that the variable would confuse or distract the hypothetical child, would hurt concentration, would make him or her forget, and so forth. The proportion of subjects offering at least one psychological explanation, given six opportunities to do so, was .05, .25, .85, and .91 for grades K, 2, 5, and college students, respectively. Thus, the growing ability during the elementary school years to spontaneously refer to psychological variables, as revealed by this verbal assessment, is consistent with the results of the Miller and Bigi verbal interview study.

The other verbal assessment in the Miller and Weiss study examined subjects' ability to suggest strategies useful for selective attention. Few subjects younger than college age proposed useful strategies, despite the fact that they later showed considerable knowledge about the usefulness of strategies when the rating scale was used. Even by Grade 5, only about half of the children gave answers rated as adequate.

Two studies examined some of the strategy variables of the preceding studies. Miller and Weiss (1981) reasoned that if children understand that only relevant stimuli should be attended to, then when given a choice of what stimuli to look at during the brief period for memorization, they should choose only relevant stimuli. Children who do not have this knowledge should choose stimuli randomly. To test this hypothesis, Miller and Weiss developed the following procedure: The top of a wooden box contained two rows of six doors—that is, six aligned pairs of doors. Opening any door with a drawing of a cage on it revealed a drawing of an animal underneath and lifting any door with a drawing of a house revealed a household object. On each trial children were given 25 seconds to open doors of their own choosing in order to remember where the relevant objects (e.g., animals) were. The youngest children, the second graders, tended to open doors either randomly or in a row, following the spatial layout of the apparatus. In either case, they opened relevant and irrelevant doors equally often. In contrast, the majority of eighth graders and many fifth graders opened relevant doors all or most of the time. Thus, there is a growing awareness that one's limited attentional capacity is utilized most efficiently by directing it to relevant information.

Comparing these results with the Miller and Weiss (1982) study (conducted at the same elementary school) described earlier reveals a noteworthy developmental lag. Although Miller and Weiss (1982) found that second graders understand that it is helpful to look only at the relevant stimuli, they do not use this knowledge when deciding what doors to open until Grade 5 or later (Miller & Weiss, 1981). They apparently do not see the connection between the goal of the task and the strategy of attending selectively. Again, as in the research on noise and psychological variables reviewed earlier, we find a lag in meta-attention between accurately judging the effect of a variable presented by the experimenter and spontaneously accessing this knowledge.

Another lag appears later with respect to actual performance on the incidental-learning task. Although the majority of fifth graders opened relevant doors all or most of the time, in another session when given the standard incidental learning task they did not attend selectively. Thus, even after children are able to use the strategy spontaneously, they may not use it in all situations requiring this strategy. The control over one's attention increases during development.

There were two verbal measures of meta-attention in the Miller and Weiss (1981) study. In one, children predicted how many incidental objects they would match up correctly with relevant objects on the incidental-learning task and, after attempting this recall, estimated how many they actually matched correctly. This measure assesses children's knowledge of their current state of knowledge. The other verbal measure was a posttest interview concerning strategies used during the incidental learning task. Second graders' prediction scores and estimation scores after the attempted matching were significantly higher than their actual matching. In contrast, fifth and eighth graders were fairly accurate. A similar developmental change has been identified in metamemory studies in which children predict how many items they will recall (e.g., Flavell, Friedrichs, & Hoyt, 1970).

In the posttest interview, an initial open-ended question about their strategies elicited very little awareness of using strategies among the second graders. In contrast, all but 15% of the fifth and eighth graders mentioned a strategy, such as naming the objects or looking at the objects. When asked directly whether they had labelled the objects, .35, .60, and .70 of Grades 2, 5, and 8, respectively, reported naming the relevant, but not the incidental, objects. When asked directly which objects they had looked at, .16, .25, and .40 of Grades 2, 5, and 8, respectively, reported looking only at the relevant objects. Thus, the older children used more strategies and/or were more aware of the strategies they used.

The generality of the developmental changes in allocation of attention identified by Miller and Weiss (1981) was examined by Miller and Jordan (1982), using a Puerto Rican sample. Several cross-cultural investigators (e.g., Wagner, 1978) have concluded that cultural factors such as schooling, living in an urban environment, and experience with testing situations affect whether children use strategies such as verbal rehearsal, the categorization of stimuli, and the systematic gathering of information. If this is true, then one would expect variation from culture to culture in the use of strategies. If, on the other hand, structural physiological changes such as those underlying changes in capacity are responsible for the growing use of strategies, then there should be similar developmental patterns across cultures. Although development in some cultures may be delayed, the pattern should remain the same.

The Puerto Rican children did not show the same developmental changes as the Florida children in the Miller and Weiss study. Instead, for Puerto Rican children, the period from age 7 to 14 years appears to be a time of little change in attention allocation or selective attention in an incidental-learning situation. There were no significant age differences on either task. Puerto Rican second graders had better strategies of attention allocation than Florida children—that is, 47% opened only relevant doors as opposed to 6% of the Florida second graders. However, the Florida fifth and eighth graders had better strategies than their Puerto Rican counterparts. On the incidental-learning task, the Florida children were more selective in their attention than the Puerto Rican children.

One possible conclusion is that there are different developmental patterns with respect to metattention and attentional behavior in the two cultures. These different patterns suggest that the development of strategies is not simply a function of a growing capacity brought about by physical maturation. Rather, cultural influences apparently act on meta-attention in complex ways. The specific causes of the different developmental patterns could not be identified in this study. A second possible conclusion is that the incidental learning task is not equally sensitive for measuring metattention in the two cultures. For example, in cross-cultural studies there is always the possibility that the instructions are interpreted differently in different cultures.

Meta-attention concerning Visual Search

In addition to attending to a task or selectively attending to components within a task, children often face a third type of demand on their attentional abilities—searching for a particular object among a group of objects. Children search for a particular toy in their room, for a favorite cereal in the supermarket, and for a certain friend on the playground. For efficient search, there is an attentional set for the target and rapid attention to each object in order to reject it or recognize it as the target. In the tasks described in earlier sections, the critical meta-attentional knowledge was that attentional capacity is limited, that a number of internal and external variables affect attention, and that attentional strategies can facilitate performance. Although this knowledge is also relevant for situations involving visual search, an additional piece of knowledge of critical importance concerns what aspects of stimuli can cause visual confusions. An example of this knowledge is that it is easier to find a particular doll among a shelf of board games than among a pile of dolls. The latter situation requires a slow, careful search. Similarly, children may know that they have to look more carefully when hunting for Nebraska than when hunting for Florida on a map because the former is surrounded by other objects and consequently is less salient.

If the assessment task is simple and interesting, even preschoolers demonstrate a rudimentary understanding of the effect of stimulus variables on visual search. Miller, Haynes, and Weiss (1982) used a two-choice forced-choice procedure in which preschoolers judged which one of two stimulus arrays would make it easier to find the targets—cutouts of two identical Teddy bears. The accompanying story described a child who had to quickly find his twin Teddy bears in his toy box before going to bed. Thus, each of the two arrays represented a toy box and contained cutouts of the targets and other toys. On four trials the pair of toy boxes differed in only one way—that is, in the number of objects (5 or 18), distance between the two targets (.5 or 27 cm), color of the objects (brown like the targets or other colors), or shape (Teddy bears of various shapes or boats and balls). There is evidence from other research that visual search becomes more difficult when the surrounding objects are similar in color or shape, when there are many objects to look through, and when the targets of the search are far apart. On 11 additional trials the arrays differed along two, three, or four of the preceding dimensions. It should be noted that the children's own search time could not serve as a clue for their judgments because as the experimenter presented each array, the location of the two targets was pointed out.

The results were as follows: Over the 15 trials, the number of correct choices was significantly better than chance for 62% of the younger preschoolers and 94% of the older preschoolers. Thus, by age 4 or 5 years, most children can identify certain stimulus characteristics as troublesome or facilitative for visual search. This was particularly true if the arrays differed along more than one stimulus dimension. An analysis of individual trials indicated that the children were sensitive to the effect of differences in number, color, and shape but not distance between the targets. Approximately half of the children's explanations for their choices were judged as adequate—that is, they referred to the stimulus dimension differentiating the two arrays.

Another condition examined preschoolers' ability to generate ways to vary the difficulty of visual search. This condition should be more demanding than the other condition, in which children did not have to spontaneously produce the stimulus differences. The children were asked to choose toys to construct arrays that would make it difficult or, on another trial, easy to find the two twin Teddy bears. The objects available were the same as or different from the two twin Teddy bears in color and shape. If children understand that stimulus variables affect the difficulty of visual search, they should differentiate their two toy boxes according to these variables. That is, a toy box creating a difficult search should have numerous brown Teddy bears because the targets are brown Teddy bears.

The preschoolers put significantly more objects into the array intended to be harder. None of the other potential stimulus variables were used to a significant extent. Thus, although the preschoolers could recognize the negative effect of having colors and shapes similar to the targets, as shown in the forced-choice condition, they did not make use of this knowledge to construct arrays themselves. Finally, fewer than half of their explanations were adequate.

Another study (Miller & Zalenski, 1981) further examined preschoolers' awareness of perceptual confusions when colors and/or forms are similar. Children were asked to place a paper cutout of an Easter egg (or, on some trials, a block) in a collection of objects that would make the egg easy to find. On each trial there were four arrays where the egg could be placed. This task fell between the construction and the choice procedures of the previous study in terms of its level of difficulty. Four-year-olds, but not 3-year-olds, placed the egg with objects that differed in color and/or shape from the egg. Thus, this study suggests, as did the preceding one, that knowledge about the task variables of color and form is just beginning to emerge in the preschool years. The knowledge is fragile and not always elicited.

Research also has examined metacognitive knowledge regarding visual search in older children. Miller and Bigi (1977) asked first, third, and fifth graders to rank order three arrays according to how difficult they would make a search for two identical red triangles. Consistent with the Miller, Haynes, and Weiss study with preschoolers, most of the children at all ages (Grades 1, 3, and 5) could rank order the three arrays that differed in number and could construct arrays that differed in number. The majority were also sensitive to distance between the targets. There was less knowledge about the effect of color and shape, especially among the younger children. The use of three arrays, rather than two, apparently masked the emerging knowledge about color and shape revealed in the study with preschoolers.

In summary, the preceding studies reveal that an early piece of knowledge about visual search is the simple fact that it takes longer to look through many objects than few objects. Most children at all ages used this knowledge to construct arrays that differed in difficulty. Other variables, particularly color and shape, apparently are understood only in a rudimentary way, that is, mainly in choice tasks, until well into the elementary school years. The effect of color and shape is less easily inferred than that of number of objects because the former involve a more subtle psychological process—perceptual confusion when the surrounding objects look like the target. A large and small number of objects is a more concrete and salient difference. Another reason for the later acquisition of metattention concerning color and form confusions may be the fact that grade-school children are still developing the ability to analyze a multidimensional object into its dimensions, such as color, shape, and size (Smith & Kemler, 1977).

The next study (Miller et al., 1982, Experiment 2) examined, in greater depth, the growing understanding of the effects of color and shape confusions in grade-school children. The procedure was the same as in the preceding Miller and Bigi (1977) study, except that the number of objects in the arrays was constant and there was only one target rather than two, in order to prevent children from using the variables of number and distance between targets. The arrays differed in how similar the objects were to the target in color on some trials and in shape on other trials. Because perceptual confusions concerning letters are an important part of learning to read, letters instead of toys were the stimuli on some trials.

The kindergarteners and first graders showed very little understanding of the effects of color or shape similarities in the choice or construction task. In contrast, older children (third and fourth graders) showed considerable understanding on the choice task—that is, correct choices significantly greater than chance on nearly all types of trials. Their performance, however, was still far from perfect. On the construction task, consistent with the results in the earlier studies, these older children made significant, but moderate, use of color or shape confusors to manipulate the difficulty of the search task.

In conclusion, the complete understanding that similar shapes or colors can cause perceptual confusions and slow visual search is a relatively late-developing metattentional skill. It is not complete even at the end of the elementary school years. Like other meta-attentional knowledge, there is an extended period of development of this knowledge, beginning with preschoolers' recognition of the effect of certain stimulus variables under very simple and interesting testing procedures.

An additional measure in the Miller, Haynes, and Weiss study with elementary-school children ties the present section back to the earlier section examining the effects of interest and noise. The forced-choice condition contained four trials that examined children's understanding of whether a hypothetical child's (1) degree of interest in the search task or (2) degree of overall attention to the task would affect performance. The number correct was near ceiling for the older children and highly significant for the younger. Thus, in contrast to the poor or moderate understanding of the effect of stimulus variables, there was considerable understanding of person-psychological variables. As in the studies reviewed earlier, nonverbal procedures revealed young children's emphasis on psychological variables.

A Classification System for Variables Affecting Attention

Much of meta-attentional knowledge involves knowing the effect of various variables on attention. As a way of summarizing and giving coherence to the research reviewed here, a classification system for variables affecting attention is proposed. It is an expansion of the categories outlined by Flavell and Wellman (1977) with respect to metamemory.

Person variables relevant to attention include both competence characteristics (e.g., the limits to capacity) and motivational characteristics (e.g., the effect of interest level). Another distinction is universal characteristics of human attentional systems (e.g., the need to avoid information overload, perceptual confusions) versus individual differences (e.g., the self versus others, people of different ages). Finally, there are both enduring attentional characteristics—what attention usually is like in the self or others—and temporary attentional characteristics—for example, the current focus of one's attention.

Task variables often refer to the type of materials. Are the salient features relevant for problem solving? Are the objects easy or difficult to tell apart? Are the materials, such as food, arousing and therefore distracting? Are the materials familiar or unfamiliar? How many potential distractors within the task are there? Another task variable is the goal of the task—that is, how the goal determines whether selective attention, divided attention, or continual monitoring is needed.

Strategy variables can involve physical strategies such as removing distractions or leaving a distracting situation. Other strategies are psychological, such as concentrating or thinking about the "cool" properties of a tempting object. Another distinction is that some are verbal, such as the rehearsal of relevant material, whereas others are nonverbal, such as controlling what is looked at, controlling the visual similarity of objects.

Situation variables, a fourth category, was not part of the Flavell and Wellman system, but is an essential part of metattention. Distractions in the environment may be social (e.g., presence of friends or tempting social events) or physical (e.g., noise, visual distractions). Situations may be academic or nonacademic (playful or interpersonal), with their differing cultural rules. For example, loud talking is not allowed in a library or classroom because it distracts others' attention. When one is relaxing, one's attention can wander without control.

These variables and their dimensions are not exhaustive and are sometimes overlapping, but the classification serves to illustrate the complexity of the attender-in-context. The complexity becomes even more obvious when one considers that these variables interact. For example, if a consideration of the task variables leads the child to conclude that the task is quite difficult and if the child, in particular, is not good at that sort of task (a person variable), he or she is likely to carefully select an appropriate strategy (strategy variable). Not surprisingly, there is growing knowledge in all the categories with increasing age.

Theoretical Frameworks for Meta-attention

The Universal Novice and Problems of Accessibility and Self-Regulation

This chapter began by delineating two aspects of meta-attention—*knowledge about* attention and *control of* attention. One useful theoretical framework for conceptualizing both knowledge and control is Ann Brown's model of general metacognitive deficits in children (1978). Brown refers to children as "universal novices" (Brown & DeLoache, 1978, p. 14) because they have very limited experience with most problem-solving situations they encounter. This limited experience, along with other factors, may lead to limitations in knowledge, not only in the amount of information a child has or the organization and internal consistency of that information, but also in the accessibility of the information. The studies reviewed in this chapter clearly reveal an increase during development in the accessibility of information about attention. Young children typically display a great deal of passive, receptive knowledge—that is, they can evaluate the effects of noise, interest, certain stimulus variables, strategies, and so forth when these variables are presented to them. However, they have a great deal of difficulty spontaneously producing this information or explaining their judgments. The knowledge is in the system, but not readily accessible. This gap is much less evident in older children.

With respect to control, Brown proposes that because of limited experience with a variety of problem-solving situations, children have limited control over their problem-solving activities. They lack "self-conscious participation and intelligent self-regulation of their actions" (Brown & De-Loache, 1978, p. 13). Several metacognitive processes are relevant to the control of problem solving: (1) analyzing the problem to be solved, (2) thinking about what one knows or does not know that may be needed to solve the problem, (3) developing a plan for approaching and solving the problem, and (4) monitoring progress toward a solution. If we applied Brown's model to the area of meta-attention in young children we would note the lack of executive functions such as the following:

1. Analyzing the task demands and goals
2. Predicting one's attentional capacity and the consequences of different ways of allocating attention such as attending exhaustively versus selectively or engaging in long versus short visual fixation of each part
3. Planning how much attention to allocate to the task and how to allocate it within the task
4. Coordinating and controlling the various attentional behaviors such as actively shutting out distractions, concentrating on part or all of the materials, and moderating the speed of scanning the materials
5. Monitoring one's ongoing attention (Am I paying attention?)
6. Checking to see whether the attentional strategy chosen actually is facilitating performance
7. Reality testing by checking answers on the basis of common sense or internal consistency.

Most research on metattention has not been designed to examine separately each of these executive functions. Such research would clarify the locus of developmental differences in metattention.

Even in older children, whether or not these executive functions occur in a particular situation depends on several factors, including the difficulty of the task, the child's motivation, and the familiarity of the task to the child (Brown & Campione, 1980). Brown proposes that these executive functions themselves require some of the child's capacity. Therefore, they are most likely to occur when the attentional activities that they control are familiar and therefore automatized, and consequently do not require much capacity. In the Miller and Weiss studies (1981, 1982) second graders could recognize that the strategy of opening only doors exposing the relevant objects (those to be remembered) was the most appropriate strategy but could not spontaneously produce this strategy when actually involved in a selective-memory task themselves. Within Brown's framework, the task itself (understanding instructions, attempting to remember, etc.) may have required so much of the child's capacity that there was not enough remaining to devote to the control processes that would have selected the appropriate attentional strategy. Fifth graders spontaneously generated the appropriate strategy, perhaps because the processes of attending and remembering were more automated than in the second graders. However, these fifth graders could not spontaneously generate the strategy when the selective memory task was presented without the doors—that is, with both relevant and irrelevant information already exposed. Perhaps having to deal with this large amount of information left little capacity for the functioning of the control processes. Only the eighth graders could use the appropriate selective-attention strategy in both situations, perhaps because both the attentional-memory skills and the control processes were highly practiced and thus made only moderate demands on the available capacity.

Of course, there are other plausible interpretations of the same set of results. However, given the demonstrated critical role of capacity demands and automaticity in children's performance in other areas of cognition (e.g., Case, 1978), Brown's model appears to be a fruitful framework for future metattentional research. Other investigators (e.g., Flavell, 1981a; Lawson, 1980; Sternberg, 1979) have also developed models of monitoring and other control processes that could be applied to the area of metattention.

The issue of the accessibility of knowledge and control have important implications for one central question in metacognitive research: What is the relationship between metacognition and actual cognitive behavior? For example, do children who understand that a particular strategy facilitates problem solving actually use that strategy when faced with problem-solving tasks? Few studies find significant correlations between metacognitive knowledge and performance (see Cavanaugh & Perlmutter, 1982, and Wellman, 1981, for reviews). Both Brown's theoretical arguments and the findings regarding the growing accessibility of knowledge indicate that a child might or might not apply his meta-attentional knowledge. Consider a child who has only passive, difficult-to-access knowledge of a particular variable and does not attend well. If a forced-choice procedure is used, the child would appear to have the relevant meta-attentional knowledge, but not the attentional behavior. In contrast, if the assessment of meta-attention required the spontaneous production of this knowledge, the child would appear to have neither the meta-attentional knowledge nor the attentional behavior. The conclusion about the knowledge–performance relationship would be different in the two cases. More generally, there will appear to be no relationship, a moderate relationship, or a strong relationship between meta-attentional knowledge and performance, depending on when in the extended development of meta-attentional knowledge the measures are taken. During the lags, correlations will be low. By the end of the extended period of development of an item of meta-attention knowledge, the correlations should be higher. In other words, only highly accessible knowledge is likely to be reflected in performance. Of course, low accessibility is not the only reason why metacognitive knowledge might not be immediately applied to performance. Other chapters in this volume can be consulted for other influences.

The Development of Social Attribution

A second theoretical approach that provides a useful framework for the area of meta-attention is social attribution. Social attribution theory was developed primarily from research on adults' *causal schemata*—perceptions of what causes their own behavior and that of others (Heider, 1958; Kelley, 1973; Weiner, 1980). Recently, there has been a great deal of interest in the development of these causal schemata. As yet, however, this research has not been tied systematically to metacognition (but see Flavell, 1981b, for a discussion of monitoring social cognitive enterprises). A common feature of the two areas is that they both involve children's growing understanding of what factors affect mental events and overt behaviors.

Attribution theorists usually classify causes as internal or external. *Internal causes* might include effort, ability, and other motivational variables, whereas *external causes* might include task difficulty, rewards, or commands from others. In certain situations, adults tend to overestimate the influence of internal variables and underestimate the influence of external variables (Ross, 1978). The studies of the understanding of interest, an internal variable, and noise level, an external variable, reviewed earlier, suggest that the overattribution of internal causes may sometimes occur with children as well. Interest appeared to be understood before noise did and at all ages interest level was considered more important than noise level. The preference for internal causes appears to be somewhat general at certain ages, appearing across various types of internal and external causes and various activities (Miller, in press). This apparent trend needs further evaluation, however, because there is always the possibility that a preference for internal causes merely indicates that these causes were inadvertently presented in a more salient way or that the particular internal causes included in the studies happen to be more powerful than the external variables chosen. Also, work on grade-school children's attributions of the causes of their academic success and failure (Bar-Tal, 1978; Dweck & Goetz, 1978; Weiner, Kun, & Benesh-Weiner, 1980) indicates that children refer to both internal and external causes, depending on their age, gender, and whether they do well or poorly on a task.

One important finding of attribution research is that children's attributions have an effect on their emotions, self concept, and subsequent behavior (e.g., Weiner et al., 1980). For example, attributing success to effort leads to feelings of pride, confidence, and general self esteem, which lead to subsequent achievement behavior. With respect to attention, the prediction would be that attributing one's inattention to not making an effort to attend, not having the ability to attend, or to task difficulty would have different effects on subsequent attempts to attend. For example, a child who attributes inattention to his or her own lack of trying should be more open to a teacher's request to try to pay attention than should a child who attributes inattention to lack of ability. These hypotheses generated from attribution theory have not yet been tested, but are of obvious importance for an adequate theory of meta-attentional development and for attempts to train inattentive children to monitor their own attention.

The categories of internal variables and external variables have been further divided into permanent, stable variables and temporary, unstable variables (Weiner, 1980). For example, ability is a stable variable and effort is an unstable variable. This distinction has not yet influenced metacognitive research, but may be quite important because attributing success or failure to a stable factor causes greater changes in expectancy (greater expected success after achieving success and decreased expectations after failure) than does attributing outcomes to unstable causes (Weiner, Nierenberg, & Goldstein, 1976). Thus, children's predictions about their attention or the attention of others may depend on the types of previous attributions made concerning attention. A third, and final, dimension of attributions identified by Weiner (1980) is perceived control—that is, whether the variable can be controlled. For example, effort to attend is controllable, but ability to attend is not. It is important to know whether children think that their attention is due to factors under their control.

Attempts to train a child to control attention are unlikely to be successful if the child perceives inattention as something beyond his or her control.

One way that social attribution and meta-attention research are similar and are different from work in other areas of metacognition is in their emphasis on motivational variables and social and physical situational variables—for example, personal motivation, social pressure, temptations in the environment, and the surrounding noise level. It seems clear that the social and physical environment, so important outside of the laboratory, must be given more attention by any serious attempt to understand metacognitive development.

The emphasis here is on how social attribution theory can serve as a heuristic for metacognitive research. In particular, the classification of variables into internal and external, stable and unstable, controlled and uncontrolled, provides an alternative to the typical classification of variables that has guided metacognitive research—that is, person, task, and strategy variables. In turn, however, metacognitive research can broaden social attribution theory. Children conceptualize others as cognitive beings as well as social beings. People attribute not only intentions, kindness, and attitudes to others, but also attentiveness, preoccupation, comprehension, and mental effort to recall.

An Organizational Model of Meta-attention

It is proposed here that the best framework for conceptualizing meta-attention would emphasize the *organization* of this knowledge, while drawing heavily from both Brown and the social attribution theorists. Brown's work describes the increasing orchestration of the control processes and the greater integration of knowledge as it becomes more accessible. Social attribution theorists have identified various dimensions of causal variables that might be related to how children organize variables cognitively. The work on meta-attention reviewed in this chapter is consistent with both approaches. What follows is an attempt to draw from both approaches as well as previous work on metacognition and general cognitive development in order to outline a useful framework for studying meta-attention.

One of the main conclusions from recent years of research on cognitive development, particularly research stimulated by Piaget's theory, is that knowledge is an organized system rather than a random collection of facts. Although there is controversy as to the degree of organization, there is agreement that some organization exists. Investigators in the metacognitive area, however, have been slow to incorporate a consideration of organization into their research and theorizing. Wellman (1981) has recently argued that metamemory is a "highly integrated set of notions, propositions, and concepts" (p. 7). He refers to the child's "integrated theory of mind" (p. 8). Because most studies have examined only one piece of knowledge in isolation, they have missed the organization among the parts.

It is proposed here that there are at least four aspects to this organization. One could examine organization (1) among the various pieces of knowledge concerning attention, (2) among the various control processes specific to attention, such as orchestrating various attentional strategies, (3) between knowledge concerning attention and knowledge concerning other aspects of cognitive functioning, for example, metamemory, metacomprehension, and metalinguistics, and (4) between control processes specific to attention and control processes specific to other aspects of cognitive functioning, for example, memory, comprehension, and linguistic processing. Developmental changes in the type of organization and degree of organization would be expected in all four of these aspects. To make this process even more complex, there would also be developmental changes in the relationships between the first two aspects (organized knowledge and control with respect to attention) and between the latter two aspects (organized knowledge and control with respect to the cognitive system).

Thus far, the small amount of research on the issue of organization has been directed primarily to the first aspect, the relationship among the various pieces of knowledge concerning attention. Three studies described earlier (Miller, 1982; Miller & Shannon, Experiments 1 and 2, 1984) examined children's knowledge of the combined effects of two variables—noise and interest. Two general results speak to the issue of organization. First, the fact that interest level is weighted more heavily than noise level suggests that when variables considered weak by the children are operating in the situation, other, more powerful variables may be sought and used by them (see a similar argument by Wellman, 1981). Thus, young children may discount the effect of noise on concentration if they know that they are interested in the activity. One implication is that young children, who in some studies did not appear to understand the effects of noise level when it was presented alone, may have spontaneously inferred that their high interest or strong effort or some other heavily weighted variable could overcome the effects of the variable presented by the experimenter. In effect, the single-variable studies may give a distorted view of the child's knowledge because they ignore the unknown, more powerful variables in the child's organized metattentional knowledge that are connected to the variable presented by the experimenter. Wellman notes that this process may sometimes underlie the low correlations between a specific piece of metacognitive knowledge and a specific behavior. Even if a child knows that noise can interfere with performance, when placed in a noisy situation, he or she may rely on extra effort to concentrate rather than attempt to remove the noise or shut it out as a way to attend well. In this case, meta-attentional knowledge and behavior, with respect to the noise variable, would erroneously appear to be unrelated.

The second result of interest from these studies is that the organization of knowledge appears to become more complex with increasing age. Young grade-school children simply added together the effects of the noise and interest levels, whereas older children combined them in an interactive way—that is, the influence of a particular level of one variable depended on the particular level of the other variable with which it was paired. Social attribution research has identified a number of causal schemas that children use to combine information in complex ways: only one of two causes is necessary and sufficient, both causes must be present, one cause inhibits the other, one cause compensates for the other, and so forth. These general ways of combining causes mentally may also be applied in situations involving attention.

One issue concerning the organization of meta-attentional knowledge is how, if at all, attention-relevant variables are clustered from the child's point of view. That is, organizing variables into person, task, strategy, and situation categories or according to the dimensions of internal–external, stable–unstable, controllable–uncontrollable may be sensible from an adult's point of view, but quite different from the way children of various ages organize the variables. For example, because young children often use spatial proximity as a basis for inferring physical causality, they may view the causes of attention in the same way. In this case, a person's interest would be seen as a stronger cause of attention to a task than is noise level because the psychological event, interest, is perceived as spatially closer to the child's activity than are the noise-producing objects. This suggestion, though speculative, illustrates the sort of interesting developmental changes in organization that might emerge in this line of research.

There appears to be no research on the second aspect of organization, the relationships among the various control processes specific to attention. For efficient problem solving, the various attentional strategies must be initiated at the appropriate time and must work in harmony to achieve the goal. One study in progress, an extension of the Miller and Weiss (1981) procedure, examines the relationships among attentional strategies. There are measures of children's attempts to regulate their attentional strategies—that is, to switch from one attentional strategy to another as the nature of the task changes.

Only one study addresses the third aspect, the relationship between meta-attention and other areas of metacognitive knowledge. Yussen and Bird (1979) examined knowledge about the effect of four variables on attention, memory, and communication. The fact that the children showed about the same level of knowledge concerning a particular variable across all three domains suggests that meta-attention, metamemory, and metacommunication are not three independent, isolated sets of knowledge. Another possible design is to teach a new item of metattentional knowledge and to assess its generalization to relevant situations in other areas of metacognition. Such generalization would be evidence that these areas are closely connected in the child's metacognitive knowledge.

The final aspect of organization, the organization of the control processes governing various cognitive skills, is of critical importance for cognitive development. Brown sees the regulation and integration of the various control processes as a central part of the development of general problem-solving skills. Although there are several facets of attentional control processes that pertain to several cognitive processes, perhaps the most important is the allocation of processing capacity. There are developmental changes in the allocation of capacity in many types of tasks, ranging from studying texts (What does the child underline?) (Brown & Smiley, 1978) to practicing the piano (Does the child practice difficult passages the most?) (Gruson, 1980). A child has a limited capacity that must be divided among strategies for visual and auditory selective attention, verbal or nonverbal encoding, comprehension, long-term recall, language, and so forth. Because these processes often occur simultaneously and because, in new or difficult tasks, they cannot all receive as much capacity as is needed for optimal performance, a decision must be made regarding how the capacity should be allocated. Children, because of their limited metacognitive knowledge, may not conduct this allocation well. For example, the second graders in the Miller and Weiss (1981) study, who chose to look at both relevant and irrelevant stimuli, may have decided to allocate their processing capacity to memorizing rather than to strategies of selective attention, even though they know that selective attention would facilitate performance. Although this decision might be appropriate for some tasks, it is not appropriate for a task containing a level of information that exceeds the child's capacity. The general point here is that meta-attention cannot be studied in isolation from other areas of metacognition. In fact, the division of the metacognitive system into areas may exist only in the minds of researchers, not of children.

Applications

Research on metacognition is providing a new perspective on the attentional and memory problems of children with learning disabilities (LD). There is growing evidence that problems with staying on task in some of these children reflect, to some extent, difficulties with bringing useful strategies to bear on the task at hand (Torgeson, 1980). That is, they approach learning situations passively. Furthermore, it has been argued, this production deficiency with respect to strategies may reflect poor metacognitive knowledge or poor utilization of this knowledge, compared to their peers.

Loper et al. (1982) found no difference in the meta-attentional knowledge of normal and LD children, matched on age and IQ (normal range). However, LD children were deficient in their use of this knowledge. More specifically, meta-attentional knowledge was correlated with reading achievement scores for the normal sample but not for the LD sample. Of course, because of the nature of correlations, it is not clear which factor is causal. Further support for the argument that LD children simply fail to use their meta-attentional knowledge comes from a follow-up study in which the LD children of Study 1 were retested after a school year of academic intervention. After this intervention, the LD children, particularly those who made the most gains in reading scores, showed the same pattern as the normal children in the first study—that is, significant correlations between meta-attention and reading achievement.

If LD children have the ability to understand attention (the first aspect of meta-attention) but fail to use it to control attention (the second aspect of meta-attention), then meta-attention training should focus on the latter. Because many LD children have trouble maintaining their attention on the task at hand and are seemingly unaware of their inattention, several investigators have conducted intervention studies designed to increase self-monitoring. For example, Hallahan, Lloyd, Kosiewicz, Kauffman, and Graves (1979) taught a bright 7-year-old LD boy, with a strong tendency to daydream, to self-monitor his on-and off-task behavior. A tape recording of a series of tones (ranging from 10 to 90 seconds apart) provided cues for on-task behavior during seatwork activities in the classroom. After each tone, the child recorded on a sheet whether or not he was paying attention. This procedure should have heightened the child's meta-attention by making him more aware of when he was not attending to the task. The 49 days of training began with this procedure and, in the last phases, removed the prompts (the tape recorder) and the recording sheet.

The training dramatically increased on-task behavior (eyes on the work sheet) and maintained it through the later phases designed to fade the child's reliance on external cues. A high level of attention was still apparent at a 1-month follow-up. Academic productivity (number of correct answers per minute for math, number of words copied per minute for handwriting) also increased and was maintained, though less dramatically than for on-task behavior. It should be noted that the training is more appropriate for situations in which children are having difficulty in applying the skills they already have than for situations in which the academic task itself is difficult for the child.

Another training program based in part on metacognition is cognitive-behavior modification, particularly work on self-instruction by Meichenbaum. Children are taught to use their own verbalizations to guide themselves through the steps involved in solving a problem or completing a task. The self instructions are tailored to the child's particular problem—for example, slowing down and working carefully for hyperactive children or staying on task for inattentive children. These self-instructional programs are successful with certain children in certain academic areas, though the training may not generalize (see Meichenbaum & Asarnow, 1979, for a review). One reason for the effectiveness of these self-monitoring and self-instruction programs may be that they change passive learners with an external locus of control (Hallahan, Gajar, Cohen, & Tarver, 1978) into active learners who view themselves as the controller of their attention. Student-directed rather than teacher-directed on-task behavior should also have the advantage of operating in situations in which the teacher is not present.

Critique of Methods

The conclusion that meta-attentional knowledge changes from a state of relative inaccessibility to accessibility during development is based to a great extent on the fact that some methods of assessment reveal more mature knowledge than other methods, using the same children. Thus, it is important to evaluate the various methods used in meta-attentional studies.

The most demanding (of the child) method is the open-ended interview, which requires the child to introspect about attention and describe variables that affect attention or give reasons for his judgments. The main advantage of this method is that the child's answers are relatively unconstrained by the question. Because the child is not limited to certain alternatives, the answers can be very rich and complex. The disadvantages of verbal methods are well known. Young children's difficulties with comprehending verbal material and putting their thoughts into words and the inaccuracy of their responses because of poor ability to introspect can lead to an underestimation of their knowledge. Furthermore, there are demand characteristics such as perceived pressure to give some answer even if it does not refer to what one actually thinks or does. Interviews are particularly difficult for children because they are usually rather abstract—that is, they refer to hypothetical situations or general tendencies regarding attention. Children, having no concrete immediate referent to provide a context for their introspections, may not relate their knowledge to the question. Using drawings may lessen this problem. After the data are collected, there is the further difficulty of scoring the answers because of their richness and ambiguity. There are, however, ways to reduce some of these problems (see Cavanaugh & Perlmutter, 1982, and Meichenbaum, Burland, Gruson, & Cameron, 1985, for a description of these procedures). For example, verbal reports can be obtained while children are actually performing the task in question or viewing videotapes of their performance.

A second type of assessment uses forced-choice, rank-ordering, or rating-scale procedures. These procedures have advantages and disadvantages that are the mirror image of those of verbal reports. The advantages are that the procedures are less demanding verbally and usually provide a concrete referent in the form of drawings or toys depicting the situation in question. In addition, responses are easy to score. When rating scales are used, it is possible to detect how variables interact in the child's judgments and how heavily the child weights each variable. Thus, the method may provide precise, quantitative information. One disadvantage is that the response may be ambiguous. That is, it sometimes is not clear *why* children think that one situation is more conducive to attention than another. Thus, children's choices may indicate that they understand the effect of the variable, when in fact judgments are based on an irrelevant reason. In contrast to self-reports, the most likely assessment error is that knowledge is overestimated. Another disadvantage is that children are constrained in what responses they can produce. Children may know that noise hinders attention and make the appropriate choice, but this variable may in fact be much less important to them than many other variables that were not presented.

A final method involves inferring the child's meta-attentional knowledge from the child's behavior. Examples include removing noisy or quiet objects to enhance attention in a setting and requiring children to construct arrays that make visual search easy. The advantages and disadvantages of the forced-choice procedure also apply here—that is, it is less verbally demanding, more concrete, easier to score, and more quantitative, but produces constrained and sometimes ambiguous responses. An additional advantage is that engaging the child in the procedure may make it clearer to the child what the task involves. It may, however, have the disadvantage of using up some of the child's limited processing capacity to perform the task. The child may have little, if any, remaining capacity to reflect on his or her thoughts or behaviors. Thus, this method could either overestimate or underestimate the child's knowledge.

It is obvious that no one method is clearly preferable. Each has its own advantages and disadvantages. The choice depends on the age of the child and the goals of the study. For very young children, because verbal demands may be the overriding concern, forced-choice procedures or inferences from behavior may be preferable. For an exploratory study of a new area of meta-attention, using older children, verbal reports may be a better choice. Rating-scale procedures are particularly useful for examining one or two variables in depth. As other reviews have concluded, multiple measures may be the best solution (Cavanaugh & Perlmutter, 1982; Meichenbaum et al., 1985.

Concluding Comments and Directions for Future Research

The clearest conclusion is that knowledge about attention and the control of attention undergo a lengthy period of development. Even preschoolers can recognize the importance of certain variables that affect attention. Certain concepts, however, are not acquired until much later—for example, that certain task variables affect incidental learning and that attending to an object's tempting qualities makes it more difficult to resist. The control of the allocation of attention also appears rather late. Meta-attentional knowledge, once acquired, gradually becomes more accessible. One starting point for future research is a careful analysis of the conditions, within the child and the situation, that elicit meta-attentional knowledge.

As argued earlier, the general focus of future research should be on changes in the organization of meta-attentional knowledge, rather than on single variables in isolation. Another limitation of previous research is that it has ignored the causes of the growth of metattention. Nearly all of the research has been descriptive, with only an occasional hint of explanation. Of course, the first task in any new research area is to describe the phenomena of that area. However, there now is a large enough data base to begin some studies of the process of change.

One promising line of explanation-oriented research examines how adults help young children develop the ability to regulate their own cognitive abilities (Wertsch, McNamee, McLane, & Budwig, 1980). Wertsch et al. find that, consistent with Vygotsky's view that regulation by others leads to self regulation, mothers supply strategic assistance during problem-solving tasks, thus preparing their children to eventually use these strategies on their own. Although many aspects of cognition are involved here, some are largely meta-attentional in nature. In a task requiring the child to copy a puzzle piece by piece, the mother helps the child orchestrate attention by telling or showing the child by her gaze or by pointing where to look (at the model, at corresponding pieces) and to which attributes to selectively attend (e.g., shape or color of the needed puzzle piece).

A suggested focus for future research in all areas of metacognition is the social, motivational, and personality context of metacognition. Meta-attentional research has included these factors—for example, distractions from peers, degree of interest in the task, self-monitoring, and social temptations, much more than other areas of metacognition. The developing awareness of and control of one's own attention or cognitions is merely one part of the development of a much broader awareness of the self and the control of the self.

References

Anderson, N. H. Information theory in developmental psychology. In F. Wilkening, J. Becker, & T. Trabasso (Eds.), *Information integration by children*. Hillsdale, NJ: Erlbaum, 1980.

Bar-Tal, D. Attributional analysis of achievement-related behavior. *Review of Educational Research*, 1978, *48*, 259–271.

Brown, A. Knowing when, where, and how to remember: A problem of metacognition. In R. Glaser (Ed.), *Advances in instructional psychology* (Vol. 1). Hillsdale, NJ: Erlbaum, 1978.

Brown, A. L., & Campione, J. C. Inducing flexible thinking: The problem of access. In M. Friedman, J. P. Das, & N. O'Connor (Eds.), *Intelligence and learning*. New York: Plenum, 1980.

Brown, A. L., & DeLoache, J. S. Skills, plans, and self-regulation. In R. Siegler (Ed.), *Children's thinking: What develops?* Hillsdale, NJ: Erlbaum, 1978.

Brown, A. L., & Smiley, S. S. The development of strategies for studying texts. *Child Development*, 1978, *49*, 1076–1088.

Case, R. Intellectual development from birth to adulthood: A neo-Piagetian interpretation. In R. Siegler (Ed.), *Children's thinking: What develops?* Hillsdale, NJ: Erlbaum, 1978.

Cavanaugh, J. C., & Perlmutter, M. Metamemory: A critical examination. *Child Development*, 1982, *53*, 11–28.

Christie, D. J., & Glickman, C. D. The effects of classroom noise on children: Evidence for sex differences. *Psychology in the Schools*, 1980, 17, 405–408.

Douglas, V. I., & Peters, K. G. Toward a clearer definition of the attentional deficit of hyperactive children. In G. A. Hale & M. Lewis (Eds.), *Attention and cognitive development*. New York: Plenum, 1979.

Dweck, C. S., & Goetz, T. E. Attributions and learned helplessness. In J. H. Harvey, W. Ickes, & R. F. Kidd (Eds.), *New direction in attribution research* (Vol. 2). Hillsdale, NJ: Erlbaum, 1978.

Flavell, J. H. Cognitive monitoring. In W. P. Dickson (Ed.), *Children's oral communication skills*. New York: Academic Press, 1981. (a)

Flavell, J. H. Monitoring cognitive enterprises: Something else that may develop in the area of social cognition. In J. H. Flavell & L. Ross (Eds.), *Social cognitive development*. Cambridge: Cambridge University Press, 1981. (b)

Flavell, J. H., Friedrichs, A. G., & Hoyt, J. D. Developmental changes in memorization processes. *Cognitive Psychology*, 1970, 1, 324–340.

Flavell, J. H., & Wellman, H. M. Metamemory. In R. V. Kail, Jr., & J. W. Hagen (Eds.), *Perspectives on the development of memory and cognition*. Hillsdale, NJ: Erlbaum, 1977.

Gruson, L. *Piano practicing: What distinguishes competence?* Unpublished doctoral dissertation, University of Waterloo, 1980.

Hagen, J. W. The effect of distraction on selective attention. *Child Development*, 1967, 38, 685–694.

Hale, G. A., & Lewis, M., (Eds.). *Attention and cognitive development*. New York: Plenum, 1979.

Hallahan, D. P., Gajar, A. H., Cohen, S. B., & Tarver, S. G. Selective attention and locus of control in learning disabled and normal children. *Journal of Learning Disabilities*, 1978, 11, 231–236.

Hallahan, D. P., Lloyd, J., Kosiewicz, M. M., Kauffman, J. M., & Graves, A. W. Self-monitoring of attention as a treatment for a learning disabled boy's off-task behavior. *Learning Disabilities Quarterly*, 1979, 2, 24–32.

Heider, F. *The psychology of interpersonal relations*. New York: Wiley, 1958.

Kelley, H. H. The process of casual attribution. *American Psychologist*, 1973, 28, 107–128.

Kun, A., Parsons, J. E., & Ruble, D. N. Development of integration processes using ability and effort information to predict outcome. *Developmental Psychology*, 1974, 10, 721–732.

Lane, D. M. Incidental learning and the development of selective attention. *Psychological Review*, 1980, 87, 316–319.

Lane, D. M., & Pearson, D. A. The development of selective attention. *Merrill-Palmer Quarterly*, 1982, 28, 317–337.

Lawson, M. J. Metamemory: Making decisions about strategies. In J. R. Kirby & J. B. Biggs (Eds.), *Cognition, development, and instruction*. New York: Academic Press, 1980.

Loper, A. B., Hallahan, D. P., & Ianna, S. O. Meta-attention in learning disabled and normal students. *Learning Disability Quarterly*, 1982, 5, 29–36.

Meichenbaum, D., & Asarnow, D. Cognitive-behavioral modification and metacognitive development: Implication for the classroom. In P. C. Kendall & S. D. Hollon (Eds.), *Cognitive-behavioral interventions: Theory, research, and procedures*. New York: Academic Press, 1979.

Meichenbaum, D., Burland, S., Gruson, L., & Cameron, R. Metacognitive assessment. In S. R. Yussen (Ed.), *The growth of reflection in children*. New York: Academic Press, 1985.

Miller, D. T., Weinstein, S. M., & Karniol, R. Effects of age and self-verbalization on children's ability to delay gratification. *Developmental Psychology*, 1978, 14, 569–570.

Miller, P. H. Children's and adults' integration of information about noise and interest levels in their judgments about learning. *Journal of Experimental Child Psychology*, 1982, *33*, 536–556.

Miller, P. H. Children's reasoning about the causes of human behavior. *Journal of Experimental Child Psychology*, in press.

Miller, P. H., & Bigi, L. Children's understanding of how stimulus dimensions affect performance. *Child Development*, 1977, *48*, 1712–1715.

Miller, P. H., & Bigi, L. The development of children's understanding of attention. *Merrill-Palmer Quarterly*, 1979, *25*, 235–250.

Miller, P. H., Haynes, V. F., & Weiss, M. *Metacognitive components of visual search in children.* Presented at the meeting of the Southeastern Conference on Human Development, Baltimore, April, 1982.

Miller, P. H., & Jordan, R. Attentional strategies, attention, and metacognition in Puerto Rican children. *Developmental Psychology*, 1982, *18*, 133–139.

Miller, P. H., & Shannon, K. Young children's understanding of the effect of noise and interest level on learning. *Genetic Psychology Monographs*, 1984, *110*, 71–90.

Miller, P. H., & Weiss, M. G. Children's attention allocation, understanding of attention, and performance on the incidental learning task. *Child Development*, 1981, *52*, 1183–1190.

Miller, P. H., & Weiss, M. G. Children's and adults' knowledge about what variables affect selective attention. *Child Development*, 1982, *53*, 543–549.

Miller, P. H., & Zalenski, R. *Preschoolers' awareness of perceptual confusions.* Unpublished manuscript, 1981.

Miller, P. H., & Zalenski, R. Preschoolers' knowledge about attention. *Developmental Psychology*, 1982, *18*, 871–875.

Mischel, H. N. *From intention to action: The role of rule knowledge in the development of self regulation.* Presented at the meeting of the Society for Research in Child Development, Detroit, Michigan, April, 1983.

Mischel, H. N., & Mischel, W. The development of children's knowledge of self-control strategies. *Child Development*, 1983, *54*, 603–619.

Mischel, W., & Baker, N. Cognitive appraisals and transformations in delay behavior. *Journal of Personality and Social Psychology*, 1975, *31*, 254–261.

Piaget, J. *The child's conception of the world.* New York: Harcourt Brace, 1929.

Ross, L. Afterthoughts on the intuitive psychologist. In L. Berkowitz (Ed.), *Advances in experimental social psychology* (Vol. 10). New York: Academic Press, 1978.

Shantz, C. U. Social cognition. In J. H. Flavell & E. M. Markman (Eds.), *Cognitive development* (Vol. 3) in P. H. Mussen (Ed.), *Handbook of child psychology* (4th ed.) New York: Wiley, 1983.

Shatz, M., & Gelman, R. The development of communication skills: Modifications in the speech of young children as a function of listener. *Monographs of the Society for Research in Child Development*, 1973, *38* (5, Serial No. 152).

Smith, L. B., & Kemler, D. G. Developmental trends in free classification: Evidence for a new conceptualization of perceptual development. *Journal of Experimental Child Psychology*, 1977, *24*, 279–298.

Sternberg, R. The nature of mental abilities. *American Psychologist*, 1979, *34*, 214–230.

Torgeson, J. K. Conceptual and educational implications of the use of efficient task strategies by learning disabled children. *Journal of Learning Disabilities*, 1980, *13*, 19–26.

Wagner, D. A. Memories of Morocco: The influence of age, schooling, and environment on memory. *Cognitive Psychology*, 1978, *10*, 1–28.

Weiner, B. A theory of motivation for some classroom experiences. In D. Gorlitz (Ed.), *Perspectives on attribution research and theory.* Cambridge, MA: Ballinger, 1980.

Weiner, B., Kun, A., & Benesh-Weiner, M. The development of mastery, emotions, and morality from an attributional perspective. In W. A. Collins, *Development of cognition, affect, and social relations*. Hillsdale, NJ: Erlbaum, 1980.

Weiner, B., Nierenberg, R., & Goldstein, M. Social learning (locus of control) versus attributional (causal stability) interpretations of expectancy of success. *Journal of Personality*, 1976, *44*, 52–68.

Wellman, H. M. Preschoolers' understanding of memory-relevant variables. *Child Development*, 1977, *48*, 1720–1723.

Wellman, H. M. *Metamemory revisited*. Presented at the meeting of the Society for Research in Child Development, Boston, April 1981.

Wellman, H. M., Collins, J., & Gleiberman, G. Understanding the combination of memory variables: Developing conceptions of memory limitations. *Child Development*, 1981, *52*, 1313–1317.

Wertsch, J. V., McNamee, G. D., McLane, J. B., & Budwig, N. A. The adult–child dyad as a problem-solving system. *Child Development*, 1980, *51*, 1215–1221.

Yates, B. T., & Mischel, W. Young children's preferred attentional strategies for delaying gratification. *Journal of Personality and Social Psychology*, 1979, *37*, 286–300.

Yussen, S. R., & Bird, J. E. The development of metacognitive awareness in memory, communication, and attention. *Journal of Experimental Child Psychology*, 1979, *28*, 300–313.

CHAPTER 6

Cognitive Self-Regulatory Training for Underachieving Children*

Ann Booker Loper and Donna M. Murphy

Introduction

The dictum to "Know Thyself" is ancient and revered. Throughout our society numerous examples can be found of the belief that by better understanding our own abilities we will become richer, holier, better looking, saner and smarter than we were during our uninformed existence. Most of us can recount personal examples from our own lives which testify to the validity of the premise. However, most of us also may voice skepticism that introspective treatments, whether of a religious, medical, or psychological nature, will always give us exactly that for which we were looking. Depending upon what our goals are, self-awareness treatments have limitations. For certain purposes self-rumination may be counterproductive: where automatic response is necessary, self-inspection may be a nuisance; certain individuals may not be at the appropriate intellectual level to comprehend or appreciate the essential aspects of the particular introspective treatment; the treatment itself may be superficial, imparting an enhanced sense of confidence without any observable change in ability to perform relevant tasks; the treatment effects may vanish when the individual is no longer under the obvious influence of the treatment.

*Preparation of the manuscript was supported by a Federal Contract (300–80–0623) to the Learning Disabilities Research Institute from Special Education Programs, United States Department of Education.

223

These same limitations apply to the employment of self-awareness treatments for the purpose of educating children. A considerable interest has been generated in teaching children by emphasizing an understanding of their own personal role in the learning process (Thomas, 1980). This notion fits well with our societal enchantment with self-awareness. However, in order for these educational treatments to be most effectively used, it is important to determine the reasonable limits of the programs.

The present chapter attempts to offer evidence concerning such benefits and limitations. The focus is on empirical investigations of underachieving children, for whom such treatments are intended to increase academic performance; for purposes of conceptual clarity, investigations that target underachieving children with attentional difficulty (e.g., hyperactive children) are distinguished from those that do not make note of specific attentional problems.

The umbrella term that is identified as the important underlying construct in all of these self-awareness treatments is *metacognition*. Multiple definitions of this construct have been offered (Brown & Palincsar, 1982; Flavell, 1979; Hagen, Barclay, & Newman, 1982). Central to most of these views is an emphasis on two features: an awareness of one's own cognitive skills and abilities, and the efficient use of this self-awareness to self-regulate cognitive activity. For purposes of the present review, metacognitive training is defined as a systematic attempt to induce enhanced levels of cognitive performance in a child through the training of self-awareness and/or self-regulatory skills.

This chapter is divided into four main sections. The first section briefly reviews evidence from laboratory research concerning the cognitive performance of underachieving children. Unlike the studies concerning academic behavior described in the second and third sections, the research described in the initial section deals with the performance of underachievers on nonacademic psychological tasks. Typically, these investigations contrast the performance of underachievers with that of normally achieving children in an effort to discern the cognitive deficits in the underachievers. The second section addresses specific metacognitive deficiencies in underachieving children. Both of these lines of research provide a valuable conceptual rationale for the design of self-regulatory interventions with academic material. The third, and major, section of the chapter reviews these academic self-regulatory programs in some detail. Unless otherwise noted, the subjects for the studies reviewed in the second section are all academic underachievers; the studies considered are limited to those that attempt to induce change in academic performance through self-regulatory training. The final section of this chapter draws conclusions

from the literature reviewed, and makes recommendations for future research directions.

Research concerning the Nonacademic Cognitive Behavior of Underachievers

The notion that academically deficient children may profit from self-
regulatory training is not a case of isolated inspiration. The notion is
grounded in considerable basic research concerning the cognitive characteristics of underachievers. A conceptual rationale for employment of
the intervention with these children is derived from a body of research
concerning the development of impulsivity, selective attention, memory,
and problem solving.

Impulsivity

Much of the literature concerning impulsivity in academically deficient children operationalizes the construct with the Matching Familiar
Figures Test (Kagan, Rosman, Day, Albert, & Phillips, 1964). This task
consists of several match-to-sample items for which a child is shown a figure drawing and asked to find another exactly like it from several variants,
only one of which is identical to the standard. Children are evaluated in
terms of the number of errors made, and the average length of time between seeing an item and responding. Children who tend to respond slowly
and have few errors are designated as having a reflective cognitive tempo.
Children who tend to respond quickly and with many errors are seen as
having an impulsive tempo.

Several investigations have suggested that academic achievement is
related to impulsivity as measured by this task (Messer, 1976). These investigations are consistent in indicating that a reflective disposition is associated with improved academic performance. Relative to normally
achieving children, academically deficient children are more likely to exhibit impulsivity. This is evident with learning disabled (LD) children (Cullinan, Epstein, & Silver, 1977; Hallahan, Kauffman, & Ball, 1973; Loper
& Hallahan, 1980), and with hyperactive children (Douglas, Parry, Marton,
& Garson, 1976).

Several investigators have attempted to modify impulsivity (for reviews, see Digate, Epstein, Cullinan, & Switsky, 1978; Messer, 1976). These

training efforts can be categorized according to whether they attempt to implement change by inducing children to take more time before respond-ing (forced delay), by providing reinforcement, or by training children how to scan or analyze the task efficiently. The results of these investigations are relatively uniform in demonstrating that training children in strategies for scanning or analyzing the task is most effective in reducing errors on the task. When underachieving children are given strategies for perform-ing the task, their performance quickly improves (Egeland, 1974; Zelniker & Oppenheimer, 1973; Zelniker, Jeffrey, Ault, & Parsons, 1972). Moreover, when given a strategy for employing self-instruction of the appropriate strategy, underachievers demonstrate an impressive maintenance of effect (Meichenbaum & Goodman, 1971).

Three very significant products emerge from this body of evidence. The first is the demonstration that self-instruction is an effective way of improving cognitive performance by impulsive children. The sequence of steps outlined by Meichenbaum and Goodman (1971) serves as a model for a large portion of the metacognitive training that has been attempted with underachieving children. The second is the demonstration that du-rable change can require more than correcting the observable global be-havior. Having children wait to respond may make them slow down but may not have any consistent effect on accuracy of performance. This sug-gests that making children cease in undesirable inattentive behaviors is effective only if instruction is imparted concerning what to do instead. This finding is also relevant in light of the present emphasis on making academic performance the final criterion of training-program success. Cognitive self-treatments that emphasize only on-task behavior, as mea-sured by such things as time in seat, may miss the more critical variable of cognitive performance. The third important conclusion from this re-search is that, unlike other nonimpulsive children who may spontaneously know how to organize and plan their own activities, impulsive children need specific instruction in how to plan and monitor their own perfor-mance.

Selective Attention

The second line of laboratory inquiry relevant to the present discus-sion concerns selective attention. Most inquiries into selective attention target a child's ability to focus appropriately upon relevant information while filtering out external distractors. Although a variety of tasks have been employed, most are designed such that a child is instructed to learn specific material (central information). The central information is combined with irrelevant or incidental information. Selective attention is assessed in terms of the amount of central information recalled, as well as in terms of the proportion of central to incidental information learned. Selective-attention investigations with normally achieving children have generally indicated a developmental trend whereby, with maturity, children evidence greater central and less incidental recall (Hagen & Sabo, 1967).

Selective attention has been investigated in both LD and hyperactive children (Douglas & Peters, 1979; Hallahan & Reeve, 1980). Hallahan and his associates have extensively investigated the phenomenon in LD children using the Hagen selective attention task (Hagen, 1967; Hagen & Sabo, 1967; Maccoby & Hagen, 1965). Hallahan was attracted to this method of investigating the attentional performance of LD children because unlike other measures, which give unitary indexes of attention, the selective-attention task lends itself to inspecting the manner in which LD children attend (Hallahan & Reeve, 1980). He observes that the attentional performance of LD children is marred because they do not spontaneously employ the appropriate strategy to help them competently recall information (i.e., verbal rehearsal of items). Moreover, when they are given instruction in how to use such a strategy, their performance rapidly improves. The fact that their performance can so quickly be modified suggests that the appropriate strategies are within the ability range of the LD children, but are not being efficiently accessed.

Peters and her associates have intensively investigated attentional behaviors in hyperactive children. In a review of selective attention in hyperactive children, Douglas and Peters (1979) argue that the literature is insufficient to support a conception of hyperactive children as being either unable to filter out extraneous stimuli or incapable of distinguishing central from incidental information. They point out the lack of evidence that stimulus-reduced environments reduce hyperactivity or that hyperactive children attend to more irrelevant information than nonhyperactives; their evidence suggests that hyperactives can successfully ignore disruptive information. As a final "nail in the coffin," they note that some investigations have suggested that low-stimulus environments have been observed to increase activity levels.

Douglas and Peters (1979) thus contend that distractibility is not the major problem in hyperactivity. Rather they suggest that the major disability involves "a failure to apply sufficient strategic effort to the task of thoroughly processing and using information available to them" (p. 201). Once again, the conclusion is made that the attentional problems are a reflection of an inability to know when to use the appropriate cognitive strategies, and that interventions that focus on external restraints will be ineffective if children are not given training in how to substitute their own internal cognitive resources.

Memory and Problem Solving

Other lines of inquiry have led to similar interpretations. Investigations concerning memory processes have indicated that poor readers (Torgesen, 1977; Torgesen and Goldman, 1977) and LD children (Bauer, 1977, 1979) are less likely to employ active recollection strategies (e.g., categorization); however, simple instruction in appropriate procedures can rapidly improve memory performance.

Investigations into the efficient use of questioning in order to solve cognitive problems have suggested that simple instruction can rapidly improve the problem-solving performance of impulsive and LD children (McKinney, Haskins, & Moore, 1977; McKinney & Haskins, 1980; O'Connell & McKinney, 1979). Hyperactive children's difficulty in developing efficient questioning strategies has been attributed in part to the difficulty they have in developing self-conscious control over their own cognitive processes (Tant & Douglas, 1982).

Common to all of these diverse lines of inquiry with LD and hyperactive children is the conclusion that seemingly structural psychological process deficiencies, such as impulsivity, poor attention, or poor memory, are remediable. The facility with which this remediation is enacted, as well as qualitative differences in the pattern of performance after treatment, suggests that the underperforming children have cognitive skills that they do not spontaneously employ. The structural problems seem, in part, to be problems of cognitive access, rather than cognitive ability. A production deficiency is implied (Flavell, 1970): children have appropriate structural mediators, but do not successfully produce them at the right time and place. The logical conclusion of these investigations, impressive in its generality across underachievers, is that training children how to understand and spontaneously use their own abilities is a key to their effective performance. Moreover, instruction is optimal when it goes beyond inducing the children to perform overt attentional behavior, offering instruction in how to perform tasks.

Metacognitive Deficits

Parallel to, and to some degree in response to, the preceding investigations has emerged an interest in examining the metacognitive performance of children. The progression of research reviewed thus far indicates a probable deficiency in metacognitive sophistication in underachieving children. A number of investigations were conducted to directly test the hypothesis that academically deficient children are less capable in meta-cognitive performance than are normally achieving children. Research comparing these children on the basis of their effective utilization of various self-regulatory strategies has focused primarily on reading comprehension. Most of these studies can be classified according to the academic tasks examined: (1) identifying the main idea of a passage, (2) detecting logical inconsistencies in a passage, (3) utilizing contextual clues in a passage, and (4) spelling.

Main Idea

Wong (1982) assessed the organizational strategies and self-checking behaviors of 30 LD, 30 nondisabled, and 30 gifted fifth graders who had listened to a story while silently reading the script. The students were then asked to select 12 of 54 main idea cards as retrieval cues for remembering the story. She found that although the groups did not differ in their use of random or primitive organizational schemes, the LD students demonstrated significantly less exhaustive searches of main-idea cards and significantly less checking of their selections. In an earlier study, Wong (1979) had found that only those LD students who were cognitively activated to attend to thematically important information by being given directive questions before each segment of a story recalled as many main ideas as the nondisabled group.

Logical Inconsistencies

The equalizing effect of cognitive activation on the comprehension monitoring of LD and nondisabled students was also demonstrated in an investigation of seventh graders described by Bos and Filip (1982). Students read two passages containing major interpropositional inconsistencies; prior to reading one of the passages, they were told that something in it did not make sense. Upon being questioned about the general logic of the stories, the LD students, in contrast to their peers, correctly reported the inconsistencies only after prior cuing.

In addition to underreporting logical inconsistencies in the absence of prior cuing, underachieving children demonstrate deficient comprehension monitoring and inadequate strategy modification when asked to discriminate difficult from easy stories on the basis of such inconsistencies. In contrast to their academically successful peers, they have been found to make little distinction between the understandability of consistent and inconsistent passages (Garner, 1980; Owings, Peterson, Brans-ford, Morris, & Stein, 1980), provide insufficient justification for their judgments, and fail to adapt their study effort accordingly (Owings et al.).

Contextual Clues

Investigations of academically underachieving students' identifica-tion and utilization of various kinds of contextual clues support the notion that these children are deficient in their application of self-monitoring strategies. In a study of 132 sixth through eighth graders of five levels of reading ability, DiVesta and his colleagues (1979) found that the lower a student's reading level, the less likely she or he is to refer to succeeding text to locate information when completing a cloze test. The authors con-cluded that "poor readers are hindered when they must monitor their comprehension and seek subsequent information for contextual ele-ments" (p. 103).

Willows and Ryan (1981), employing an oral cloze procedure with 96 fourth through sixth graders, determined that the poor readers did not use syntactic and semantic clues to the extent that the skilled readers did, even when differences in automatic word decoding were controlled. Similarly, Sullivan (1978) reported that sixth- and eighth-grade poor readers "ne-glected to use various clues to confirm their predictions" (p. 713) con-cerning the veracity of statements following a passage; they tended instead to focus on isolated words rather than meaningful qualitative phrases.

Spelling

Gerber and Hall (1981) undertook an extensive series of investigations into the development of spelling in 7- to 12-year-old LD children, most of whom had attention problems. (These studies are described in depth in the intervention section of this chapter.) Their results indicate that LD children, relative to their normally achieving peers, are (1) less accurate predictors of their spelling ability (they tend to overestimate their ability to spell given words), (2) less accurate evaluators of their spelling perfor-mance (they are less able to identify their incorrect spellings), and (3) less likely to self-correct their spelling upon review (even when they have rated a word as being most probably misspelled).

In addition, upon examining metacognitive awareness of the per-sonal, task, and strategy variables affecting spelling, Gerber and Hall (1981) report that LD children do have a fundamental knowledge and under-standing of these factors. Compared to competent spellers, however, they are less likely to view spelling ability from more than one perspective, to search and organize information and strategies about spelling, or to express the need to use their basic knowledge strategically. The authors conclude that the "ineffective *use* of spelling rather than *lack* of information" explains the spelling problems of LD children.

Summary

These investigations support the current characterizations of academically underachieving children as inactive learners who do not spontaneously apply task-appropriate strategies (Torgesen, 1979, 1980; Wong, 1979, 1980). Moreover, relative to their more successful peers, academic underachievers have been found to exhibit metacognitive deficiencies at all levels of task performance: they are apparently less adept at (1) evaluating their ability to successfully undertake a task (Gerber & Hall, 1981); (2) planning effective organizational schemes for approaching the task (Wong, 1982); (3) applying successful strategies (DiVesta, Hayward, & Orlando, 1979; Garner & Reis, 1981; Gerber & Hall, 1981; Sullivan, 1978; Willows & Ryan, 1981); (4) monitoring their progress on or ongoing understanding of the task (Bos & Filip, 1982; Garner, 1980; Garner & Reis, 1981; Owings et al., 1980; Willows & Ryan, 1981; Wong, 1979, 1982); (5) identifying and correcting their errors or modifying their effort as they proceed (Garner & Reis, 1981; Owings et al., 1980; Wong, 1982); and (6) evaluating their overall performance when finished (Wong, 1982).

The studies presented thus far—those specific to academic performance as well as those concerned with related cognitive behaviors—demonstrate that academic underachievers are not adept at regulating their cognition. In addition, limited evidence exists suggesting that such children may not be aware of the need to strategically utilize the basic metacognitive knowledge that they do seem to possess (Gerber & Hall, 1981; Torgesen, 1979). The implications of this combined body of research for intervention with academically underachieving children is discussed in the following section.

Metacognitive Training Interventions

Various lines of inquiry into the cognitive behavior of academically deficient children have lead to a common conclusion: such children do not spontaneously employ appropriate cognitive strategies; however, when they are given simple instruction, their performance on cognitive tasks improves quite rapidly. Investigations that specifically target metacognitive performance are relatively consistent in demonstrating differences on a wide variety of metacognitive tasks between the performance of normally achieving children and that of children with school-related problems. The hypothesis that naturally emerges from these investigations is that training children who are academically deficient in metacognitive self-regulatory activities will lead to improved academic performance.

The training studies reviewed in this section serve to evaluate this hypothesis. In each of the investigations chosen for review, training is designed to enhance academic performance of underachieving children through instruction in self-regulatory skills.

Rationale for Focus on Academic Achievement

Academic performance is one of the most important activities in which children engage. If we assume that academic performance involves a critical cognitive component, then cognitive and metacognitive interventions should be effective in remediating academic underachievement.

The precise role of cognition in academic achievement, however, is unclear. Fundamental to much of the educational literature concerning poor academic achievement is the issue of psychological processes. Two broad schools of thought regarding this topic can be identified. The first view maintains that problems in psychological processes should be the primary focus of any cognitive treatment program. The entire field of learning disabilities traces its history to a conception that learning disability is caused by organic disorders that are manifest in imperfect perception, integration, or expression of information (Hallahan & Kauffman, 1976). With emphasis on the importance of psychological processes comes a contention that unless cognitive training programs attend to the underlying cognitive defects that are mediating the flawed performance, treatment benefits will be superficial and brief.

The other school of thought traces its history to a classical behavioral scheme and considers the existence of underlying, essentially unobservable, cognitive constructs to be irrelevant. Failures of children to perform are seen as the result of inadequate instructional techniques. Engelmann, a staunch behavioral pedagogist, suggests that emphasis be placed on "diagnosing instruction" (Engelmann, Granzin, & Severson, 1979). Within the behavior-therapy community there is continuing debate over whether cognitions can properly be considered appropriate for behavioral intervention (Lewidge, 1978; Locke, 1979; Mahoney & Kazdin, 1979).

There is good reason for skepticism about purely process-oriented views of remediating children. Arter and Jenkins (1977; 1979) have delineated the many difficulties inherent in the view that learning disability is remediable by training children in the processing skills in which they are assumed to be deficient. They present considerable evidence indicating that a variety of training programs that were designed to compensate for assumed psychological process dysfunctions have not been effective in improving academic performance. For example, a commonly accepted practice in LD education is to match academic treatment to processing-modality strengths: a child who is weak in auditory perception would receive reading instruction that emphasizes the visual aspects of a word, while a child with visual perceptual problems would be assigned phonetic instruction (deHirsch, Jansky, & Langford, 1966; Johnson & Myklebust, 1969; Wepman, 1967). Arter and Jenkins reviewed several studies that systematically tested the efficacy of this trait–treatment assignment, and determined that in all but one case, the assumed interactive effect was not present: visual learners did not perform appreciably better in an auditory program, and auditory learners were not detectably aided by visual curricula.

Clearly, any cognitive treatment program worth its salt should, when used with academically underperforming children, improve academic performance. By selecting only training programs that target academic improvement, we anticipate that a case can be made for the benefits and limitations of such treatment. The underlying construct that is interpreted as the key to the success or failure of a program will undoubtedly be affected by the orientation of the individual reader. Staunch instructionalists may contend that the effects are due to the enhanced instructional program, and that the particular cognitive makeup of the individual child is largely irrelevant. Process-oriented individuals may see the benefits as reflecting the successful marriage of cognitive deficiency and cognitive training.

The limitation that the only studies considered are those that target underachievement in academically deficient children narrows the acceptable range of training studies considerably. The vast bulk of cognitive-training studies have not been included. Cognitive self-instruction has been widely investigated as a method of controlling inappropriate social behaviors, such as *talkouts* (talking at inappropriate times), out-of-seat behavior, and aggressive behavior (see O'Leary & Dubey, 1979). In adults, self-regulation has been used to control smoking, eating, and other well-known vices (see Nelson, 1977). Several investigations have examined the effectiveness of self-guiding training in varying age groups of normally achieving children. Moreover, there are numerous investigations with academically deficient children in which metacognitive treatments are employed, but success is measured on nonacademic cognitive tasks (e.g., Barkley, Copeland, & Sivage, 1980; Denney, 1975; Palkes, Stewart, & Freedman, 1972; Snyder & White, 1979). All of these investigations, however, are excluded from the present review.

Delineation of Training Studies

The training studies reviewed in the present chapter are delineated on two bases. The first concerns the children targeted: training studies are grouped in terms of whether or not there is indication that the underachieving children have attentional deficits. The second broad basis concerns the general type of instructional program designed: training studies are grouped in terms of whether they predominately employ mechanical self-monitoring procedures or verbal-elaborative procedures (Loper, 1982). The rationale for this categorization follows.

Target Population

Many types of children have been described as academically deficient: LD, hyperactive, impulsive, underachieving, and behaviorally disordered children can all be seen as underperformers. The present review considers any and all of these categories to represent underachievement, the one stipulation being that the children are academically behind.

One of the foremost difficulties in interpreting this literature is the lack of operational criteria uniformly characterizing experimental subjects. Even within a given diagnostic subset (e.g., LD), there is scant evidence of consensus on what would be considered the critical psychological or educational features (Keogh, Major, Omori, Gandara, & Reid, 1980; Lovitt & Jenkins, 1979; Senf, 1977).

It is not likely that delineation of the present series of investigations according to stated diagnoses will be helpful. While the majority of investigations specify a generic label that characterizes the trainees, lack of consistent operationalization makes it unclear whether different designations represent essentially different groups. For example, several investigations target "learning disabled children with attentional problems" (e.g., Gerber & Hall, 1981; Hallahan, Lloyd, Kosiewicz, Kauffman, & Graves, 1979). These children may well resemble those labelled as "hyperactive" in other investigations (e.g., Varni & Henker, 1979); Douglas and her associates have consistently argued for better operational delineation between hyperactivity and learning disability (Ackerman, Dykman & Peters, 1977; Douglas & Peters, 1979; Tant & Douglas, 1982). The labeling of children as either underachieving or LD has also been called into question. Summarizing 5 years of research concerning the assessment of learning disability, Ysseldyke and his associates have concluded that little psychometric basis exists for justifying the distinction between underachievement and learning disability in educational placement decisions (Ysseldyke, Thurlow, Graden, Wesson, Algozzine, & Deno, 1983).

As an alternative to grouping children according to stated diagnoses, training studies are grouped according to whether they do or do not indicate that the children in question have attentional difficulties. The fundamental goals of intervention with attentionally disordered children may vary from those for children without known attentional deficits. With attentionally disordered children, the principal focus may be on structuring an academic situation that induces the child to function at acceptable attentional levels; enhanced attention as well as academic improvement is the desired result. On the other hand, goals for underachievers who do not suffer attentional problems may be more focused on qualitative changes in academic performance.

A few investigations classify their underachieving children as being "behaviorally disordered." This description defies the attention–nonattention distinction. While it is probable that some of these children evidence attentional difficulties, it is not clear that all do. However, in the interest of preserving as much homogeneity as possible, these are included in the studies that intervene with attentionally disordered children. These cases are noted.

Training Approach

Training approaches can be distinguished in terms of their instructional format. Two broad approaches that characterize the literature under review are the elaborative approach and the mechanical approach (Loper, 1982). The principal structural difference between the approaches relates to the desired response from the trainee. If the trainee is required to repeat a predetermined sequence of self-instructions and responses, the treatment is termed *mechanical*. If the treatment requires employment of an open-ended sequence of self-instructions and responses, it is termed *elaborative*.

A mechanical approach is characterized by the use of instructional techniques that are routinely repeated throughout the instructional sequence and that call for a limited range of acceptable responses. The form of the response does not change over time or over items. An example of a mechanical response would be to place checkmarks after each line in a social studies quiz, indicating that the question had been answered and rechecked. The child might be required to ask him- or herself after each item "Was this correct?" The appropriate responses would consist of checkmarking and answering "yes" or "no." The self-verbalization and overt activity would not change according to item.

Contrary to this approach, an elaborative training strategy involves invocation of unique situation-specific responses in order to self-regulate behavior. This could involve a series of open-ended questions that theoretically would have limitless possible responses. For example, instead of placing checkmarks and asking a restricted "yes–no" question, the child taking the social studies quiz could be instructed to ask him- or herself "What is the main idea in this question? Do I know any other things about the material in this question? What other way could the teacher have asked this question? How would I answer those questions?" and so forth. This training approach would be designated as elaborative because of its invocation of a wide range of responses that are unique to the particular question. Occasionally, an intervention under review includes both mechanical and elaborative features. In these cases, the intervention is grouped according to the component given relatively more emphasis by the authors of the intervention.

The structural difference has methodological and perhaps conceptual implications. Data from the two approaches often are suitable for different types of scrutiny. For example, while the accuracy of employing mechanical self-checking routines may be estimated by simple frequency counts and comparisons of self-assessments to externally observed assessments, elaborative techniques may require more qualitative analyses concerning the content of the elaborations. In addition, each format may be more suitable for a particular goal. For example, a mechanical approach with its programmed emphasis upon repetition may be desirable when the goal of treatment is to develop automatic self-checking routines (Loper, 1982).

Experimental Designs Used in Interventions

The combination of these two categorical bases results in four grouping of children: (1) mechanical and (2) elaborative interventions with attentionally disordered children and (3) mechanical and (4) elaborative treatments for children without specified attentional deficits. Although this categorization makes some conceptual sense, the methodologies employed across the groups of studies vary considerably. With the exception of one investigation (Gerber & Hall, 1981) all of the interventions reviewed with attentionally disordered children utilize single-subject methodology (Hersen & Barlow, 1976; Kratochwill, 1978). These studies scrutinize the performance of a small number of children using repeated measurements, usually on a daily basis. The investigations may last for a fairly long time period (e.g., several months). While a wide variety of designs are employed, most of the inquiries examined in the present review utilize either a reversal design or multiple-baseline design. In *reversal designs*, baseline measurements are initially taken (Phase A) before any treatment is introduced; this is followed by the intervention phase (B), followed by a withdrawal of treatment (return to Phase A), and then subsequent reintroduction of the treatment (B). If the child's targeted performance (e.g., reading rate) shows shifts that parallel the presence of the intervention, a case is made for the effectiveness of the treatment in inducing desired change. In multiple-baseline designs, intervention is sequentially applied to either different behaviors of the same individual or to the same behavior across several individuals.

These procedures seem well suited to intervention concerns. The necessity for detailed and frequent measurement of performance makes it more likely that assumed trends are stable. Within a given treatment, single-subject designs may be quite useful in isolating particular aspects of a treatment that are most critical to success; the series of investigations carried out in Hallahan's laboratory concerning self-monitoring are a case in point (Kneedler & Hallahan, 1984). The design also may mesh well with school curricular needs. Children can, for example, be tested repeatedly on seatwork that is a realistic approximation of the daily drill they would ordinarily be assigned.

A possible weakness of such an approach concerns the difficulty of readily generalizing across studies. Of the studies reviewed in which an attention deficit was specified, no two studies targeted children with identical sets of characteristics (age, diagnosis, and academic weakness); nor is this surprising given the hodgepodge of children who may be characterized as underachievers. It can be argued that general improvement across diverse children exposed to different treatments attests to the strength of self-regulatory procedures, in general, with underachievers. However, ascertaining the important key commonalities and differences that mediate the trend can sometimes become difficult.

Unlike the studies that target attentionally disordered children, the studies reviewed that do not specify attentional characteristics have more of a mix of both single-subject and group-design procedures, with group designs being more frequently employed. The group studies tend to contrast either the effects of a treatment with underachievers versus regular achievers or the effects of different aspects of treatment within groups of underachievers. The advantages of such approaches tend to complement those of single-subject designs. The replication of the same procedures with a sizeable group reduces the probability that effects are idiosyncratic, and enables an estimate of the variability of the effects of the treatment within large sets of individuals. The ability to specify the precise component or components of a particular treatment which are most responsible for change, however, are not as efficiently addressed, and the validity and reliability of the fairly infrequent measures may be questionable. To some degree, much of the difficulty of drawing firm conclusions concerning this literature relates to the diversity of designs, and concomitant weaknesses, across the various investigations.

The self-regulatory interventions reviewed are summarized in Tables 1 and 2. (Table 1 focuses on studies with attentional deficits specified; Table 2 focuses on those without.) Elaboration on specific investigations follows.

Elaborative Self-Regulatory Instruction with Attentionally Disordered Children

Meichenbaum and Goodman Elaborations

The model for a large portion of the elaborative approaches can be traced to the self-instructional sequence developed by Meichenbaum and Goodman (1971). The approach, originally intended to reduce impulsivity, consists of several stages:

1. *Cognitive modeling*—an adult models self-instructional routines
2. *Overt, external guidance*—the child imitates the adult's self-instructional routine
3. *Overt self-guidance*—the child performs the task while verbalizing self-instructions aloud
4. *Faded self-guidance*—the child performs the task while whispering self-instructions
5. *Covert self-instructions*—the child performs the task while covertly self-instructing.

The modeling provided by the adult includes problem definition ("What is it that I am supposed to do?"), focused task-specific self-instructions, and self-reinforcement and self-correctional verbalizations. The approach has been demonstrated to be effective in improving the self-regulatory skills of a wide variety of clinical populations (Meichenbaum, 1977).

Several investigations have utilized the Meichenbaum and Goodman sequence in attempts to modify the academic behavior of attentionally disordered children. Results are somewhat inconsistent, and suggest that external reinforcement may play an important role in the utilization of the approach with attentionally disordered children.

Friedling and O'Leary (1979) designed a replication of an investigation conducted by Bornstein and Quevillon (1976), which employed the Meichenbaum and Goodman (1971) sequence as a method of training overactive preschool children. The Bornstein and Quevillon investigation, which had focused on attentional behavior alone, suggested that the self-instruction enhanced attention in a generalized classroom situation. Friedling and O'Leary's replication targeted the academic performance of older hyperactive children. Predictions concerning the benefits of the approach were not confirmed: with the exception of easy problems, academic and on-task performance were not detectably affected. Friedling and O'Leary subsequently introduced a token system whereby children were administered tangible rewards for on-task behavior. Results indicated enhanced on-task performance, but no effect on academic behavior.

Another elaborative self-regulatory training program that achieved mixed results undertook a component analysis of the effects of self-instruction, self-monitoring, and self-reinforcement with 3 hyperactive children (Varni & Henker, 1979). During the self-instructional phase, the children were taught to apply Meichenbaum and Goodman (1971) verbalizations to academic and nonacademic material. During the self-monitoring phase, the children were given wrist counters to enable them to assess how long they persisted at reading tasks. In the final phase, the children utilized self-monitoring in conjunction with self-reinforcement (redeemable tokens for good performance). Results indicated that the effects of the first two phases were negligible: Apparent improvement was not maintained in the absence of a supervising adult. The final phase, which employed a combination of self-monitoring and self-reinforcement, was superior to the other phases in terms of improving both academic performance and on-task behavior. However, it was not a clear win. While there was an overall trend toward improvement, there was also considerable bounce, or fluctuation, during this final phase.

A very mild reinforcement was sufficient to induce distractible preschool underachievers to efficiently utilize self-instruction in an intervention undertaken by Bryant and Budd (1982), which employed the Meichenbaum and Goodman (1971) strategy. Three preschoolers were targeted: All were of low-average academic ability, showed poor performance on an academic readiness test, and were teacher-referred as "highly distractible." A multiple-baseline design was used to compare children's academic performance in the classroom during the intervention phases. In the first phase (baseline), no training was implemented. During the second Table 2 focuses on those without. Elaboration on specific investigations

Table 1

Self-Regulatory Interventions with Academically Underachieving Children: Attention Deficit Specified

Author	Subjects	Targeted academic area	Intervention	Major results
Cameron & Robinson, 1980	3 hyperactives with academic deficiency (7–8 years)	Math Oral reading[a] On-task[a]	Self-instruction[b] Self-correction External reinforcement	Improved math, oral reading and on-task; maintenance with external reinforcement withdrawn
Bryant & Budd, 1982	3 distractible children with poor academic readiness (4–5 years)	Preschool skills	Self-instruction[b] External reinforcement	Improved accuracy No change in completion rate without external reinforcement
Dubey & O'Leary, 1975	2 hyperactives with poor reading comprehension (8–9 years)	Reading	Oral reading of passage	Greater reading comprehension with oral reading than with silent reading
Friedling & O'Leary, 1981	8 hyperactives No information re: achievement level (6–8 years)	Reading Math[a] On-Task[a]	Self-instruction[b] External reinforcement	No changes in academics Improved on-task with external reinforcement
Gerber & Hall, 1981	32 LD children (9–10 years)	Spelling	Prediction Self-questioning Self-evaluation	Improved accuracy for lower level spellers
Hallahan et al., 1979	1 LD boy (7 years)	Handwriting[a] Math[a] On-Task	Self-monitoring	Improved on-task and academic productivity
Hallahan et al., 1982	1 LD boy (8 years)	Math[a] On-Task	Self-monitoring Teacher-monitoring	Improved on-task and math productivity in both conditions Greater on-task with self-recording
Heins, 1980	4 LD boys (7–9 years)	Math[a] On-Task	Self-recording either at external or internal cue	Improved math in both conditions Greater on-task with external cue

Study	Subjects	Target	Procedure	Results
Kosiewicz et al., 1982	1 LD boy (9 years)	Handwriting	Overt verbalization of handwriting process; Self-correction	Improved accuracy with either procedure
Lloyd et al., 1982	4 LD children (9–10 years)	Math[a]; On-task	Self-recording; Self-assessment	Greater changes in on-task behavior with self-recording than self-assessment; Inconsistent academic change
Lloyd et al., 1981	3 LD children (8–10 years)	Decoding	Overt verbalization of decoding strategy	Negligible
Lovitt, 1973	16 children with school problems (8–10 years)	Math and reading; Disruptive behavior	Various combinations of self-timing, self-correcting, self-charting and self-specification of contingencies (7 experiments)	Improved academic productivity; Reduced disruptive behavior
Lovitt & Curtiss, 1968	1 behaviorally disordered boy with math deficiency (11 years)	Math	Overt verbalization of problem before responding	Improved math accuracy
McLaughlin et al., 1981	6 behaviorally disordered boys reading deficiency (10–12 years)	Reading	Self-recording (unchecked); Self-recording (checked against teacher recording)	Greater improvements in reading accuracy when self-recording checked against teacher recording
Paquin, 1978	1 behaviorally disordered girl with academic problems (9 years)	Reading comprehension; Math; Phonics[a]; Disruptive behavior[a]	Self-chart	Improvement in reading comprehension, math and disruptive behavior; No change in phonics
Varni & Henker, 1979	3 hyperactive LD boys (8–10 years)	Reading; Math; On-Task[a]	Self-instruction[b]; Self-monitoring; Self-reinforcement	Self-instruction or self-monitoring alone not as effective as when combined with self-reinforcement

[a]Observed only. No direct intervention.
[b]Procedure based on Meichenbaum and Goodman, 1971.

241

Table 2

Self-Regulatory Intervention with Academically Underachieving Children: No Attention Deficit Specified

Author	Subjects	Targeted academic area	Intervention	Major results
Lesgold et al., 1975	62 children—75% were reading deficient (Grades 3–4)	Reading comprehension	Self-imagery	Improved reading comprehension No changes on standardized test scores
Levin, 1973	54 good and poor readers (Grade 4)	Reading comprehension	Self-imagery	Improved reading comprehension for good readers and poor readers without vocabulary problems
Malamuth, 1979	33 poor readers (Grade 5)	Reading comprehension On-task[a]	Self-instruction[b]	Improved reading comprehension and on-task
Palincsar & Brown, 1981	4 poor reading comprehenders (Grade 7)	Reading comprehension	Self-verbalization to synthesize information Corrective feedback	Greatest improvements in reading comprehension if corrective feedback produced instruction in self-verbalization
Pflaum & Pascarella, 1980	40 LD children (8–13 years)	Oral reading Reading grade level[a]	Identify and correct own oral reading errors and determine relative impact of errors on meaning	Improved reading grade level scores Effects negligible before second grade achievement level

Study	Sample	Target behavior	Strategy	Results
Pressley, 1976	54 good and 32 poor readers (Grade 3)	Reading comprehension	Self-imagery	Improved reading comprehension
Robin et al., 1975	30 children with handwriting deficiency (Kindergarten)	Handwriting	Self-instruction	Improved handwriting on targeted letters; Poor generalization effect
Schumaker et al., 1982	9 LD adolescents (12–18 years)	Ability-level paragraph writing; Grade-level paragraph writing[a]	Self-questioning; Self-correction	Improved accuracy; Generalized to grade-level paragraphs
Spates & Kanfer, 1977	45 children with math deficiencies (6–7 years)	Math	Self-monitoring; Criterion-setting; Self-evaluation	Self-instruction *before* performance (criterion setting) is critical component for treatment success
Swanson, 1981a	1 LD boy (11 years)	Decoding	Self-recording with and without praise contingent on accurate self-recording	Greater oral reading accuracy when praise is contingent on accurate self-recording
Swanson, 1981b	3 LD children (8–9 years)	Decoding; Reading comprehension	Self-recording; External-reinforcement	Improved accuracy on behaviors targeted by self-recording and reinforcement
Wong & Jones, 1982	60 LD children (Grades 8–9); 60 non-LD children (Grade 6)	Reading comprehension	Self-questioning	Improved reading comprehension in trained LD children; No change for non-LD

[a] Observed only: no direct intervention.
[b] Procedure based on Meichenbaum & Goodman, 1971.

and Goodman strategy to task worksheets. In the final phase (mild class-room intervention), children were explicitly reminded and encouraged to apply the self-instructional procedures in the classroom; stickers were given to the children for completing their work on time. Results indicated that although the self-instruction produced increased accuracy during class-room performance, it did not have any apparent effects on the frequency with which children completed work on time. However, the introduction of the mild classroom intervention raised task completion to acceptable levels.

The preceding investigations introduced tangible reinforcement after self-instructional procedures proved ineffective. A training program de-vised by Cameron and Robinson (1980), which was undertaken with three 7- to 8-year-old hyperactive children who were academically behind, sug-gests that reinforcement may be useful at the beginning of an interven-tion. After a no-treatment baseline, children were trained in the Meichenbaum and Goodman self-instruction; during this phase, children were also required to check their own worksheets and to assign points to themselves. Special activity time was given by the trainer, contingent upon accuracy of math responses. Children were subsequently exposed to a self-management phase, during which no external intervention or reinforce-ment was employed. Results indicated that the first training phase resulted in increased levels of on-task and academic performance relative to the baseline condition; moreover, when the reinforcement was subsequently removed (self-management phase), the performance showed a small but consistent improvement.

Taken as a whole, these investigations cast doubt on any simple for-mulation concerning the overall role of reinforcement in elaborative self-regulatory intervention with attentionally disordered children. It is worth noting that although all of these procedures employed tangible reinforce-ment in some capacity, its use across studies was far from uniform. When improvement was apparent, it was not consistently clear-cut. The pres-ence of considerable fluctuation mars several effects. One viable hypoth-esis is that reinforcement served to focus the children's attention on the relevant appropriate response. The erratic effects may reflect the varying levels of attentional deficiency in the children and/or the degree to which the reinforcement was associated with particular targeted behaviors. How-ever, the data is insufficient for drawing this conclusion with assurance. An unknown element in most intervention studies, including the afore-mentioned, concerns the children's previous exposure to reinforcement treatments. The degree to which some hyperactive children have been trained (inadvertently, perhaps) to attend only when reinforcement is forthcoming is unascertainable.

Task-Specific Elaboration

All of the preceding investigations employed a variation of the Meichenbaum and Goodman (1971) sequence of self-instructions. The content of these self-guiding questions is broad and capable of being employed in a variety of settings with multiple tasks. For example, the question "What is it that the teacher wants me to do?" can be used for any sort of academic material. This feature serves to increase the potential generalizability of the program. During the modeling phase, children are taught how to respond to these questions with very explicit task-specific self-instructions; the more explicit these instructions are, the more probable the treatment success (Meichenbaum, 1977). A possible source of the variability of treatment success may relate to the actual specificity of self-instructions employed. Children with attentional disorders may be more prone to fade out the specific self-instruction, and replace them with broad platitudinous responses. As most of these training studies are designed to induce the child to self-monitor covertly, systematically evaluating the merits of this hypothesis is not an easy matter.

As an alternative, elaborative training programs can be designed with more direct, task-specific instructions. (The cost of these programs may be in reduced generalizability [Loper & Hallahan, 1982]). Gerber and Hall (1981) developed a task-specific elaborative training program designed to improve spelling performance in LD children with attentional deficits. Before intervention, children were evaluated in terms of their qualitative spelling performance. Children were designated as either phonetic or transitional spellers, depending upon the type of spelling error typically committed. Although transitional spellings were incorrect, they accounted for every phoneme with a conventional letter or letter combination and showed knowledge of orthographic rules. The less mature phonetic spellings represented every phoneme but were eroneous in representation of tense vowels and certain syllables by single letters whose articulation approximated the phoneme (e.g., *egl* for *eagle*). The LD children were assigned either to a training or to a control group. Controls were given time with the trainer, during which they were given general interviews and admonished to check their work carefully. The children assigned to the training condition were taught how to (1) predict ability to spell words, (2) employ a self-guided proofreading routine, and (3) check off uncertain parts of a spelling attempt. The self-guided proofreading scheme consisted of the following questions:

1. Have I ever heard this word before?
2. Do I know what this word means?
3. Do I know how to spell any words that sound like this word?

4. Which part(s) of this word am I not sure about?
5. What are some other ways I could try to spell this word?
6. Does this word look correct?

Results indicated that the treatment increased the probability of self-cor-rection attempts by all of the LD children. Trained LD phonetic spellers were almost 6 times more successful, in terms of final spelling accuracy, than the untrained phonetic spellers. Training effects, in terms of spelling accuracy, were not evident for the more mature spellers; however, all chil-dren who recieved training showed desirable qualitative shifts in spelling performance.

Several features are noteworthy in the Gerber and Hall (1981) study. Unlike other elaborative approaches with attentionally disordered chil-dren, the Gerber and Hall self-instructions targeted a particular academic skill: the self-instructions applied to spelling alone. The specificity of the instruction may have served to place a very structured demand on the children, which in turn may have offset the attentional deficits. A second interesting feature of the program is the total absence of back-up reinfor-cers. Of the elaborative procedures reviewed that target attentionally dis-abled children, this is the only investigation that induced change purely through internal regulatory activities. The origin of this benefit may relate to the previous point: By designing a program that very directly targets a particular skill, the possible signalling functions of external reinforcement may not be necessary. Finally, it is worth noting the absence of clear-cut training effects with the transitional spellers. A recurrent finding in much of the training literature concerns the apparent best match between a child's skill level and the training approach. The point is more fully dis-cussed in a following section.

Mechanical Self-Regulatory Training with Attentionally Disordered Children

Self-Monitoring of Attention

Hallahan and his associates have conducted a series of intervention studies that utilize mechanical self-monitoring with attentionally disor-dered LD children. In the first of this series, an LD boy with attentional problems was taught to self-monitor his own on- and off-task behavior (Hal-lahan et al., 1979). The treatment required the child to perform academic seatwork (math computation and handwriting exercises) while keeping track of when he was paying attention. The child was given a self-moni-toring sheet on which he placed checkmarks indicating whether or not he was paying attention. A tape recorder with a random interval tone served to signal the child to ask himself "Was I paying attention when I heard the tone?" Upon hearing the tone, he recorded his response ("yes or no") on the self-recording sheet. Results indicated sharp increases in on-task behavior (determined by external observer) and improvement in his rate of correctly completed math and handwriting seatwork assignments. Subsequent to the training condition, the external apparatus (tape recording, recording sheet) were faded out; the child continued to maintain treatment effects. No back-up reinforcers were employed at any point during treatment.

A subsequent investigation from Hallahan's laboratory attempted to evaluate the relative importance of the self-assessment and self-recording aspects of the treatment (Lloyd, Hallahan, Kosiewicz, & Kneedler, 1982). The component that consisted of the child's asking himself if he was paying attention was termed self-assessment, and the component that consisted of the child's marking his response on an answer sheet was termed self-recording. Academic productivity, or number of correct math "movements" (component of the math problem) per minute, served as the dependent variable. Results indicated that self-recording was essential for achieving improved levels of on-task behavior. Unlike other investigations from Hallahan's laboratory, this study did not show detectable improvement in academic productivity under either treatment.

Other intervention studies undertaken using the self-monitoring procedures developed by Hallahan suggest that the method may be effectively used in group instruction (Hallahan, Marshall, & Lloyd, 1981), that self-recording results in more beneficial effects than does teacher-recording (Hallahan, Lloyd, Kneedler, & Marshall, 1982), and that the presence of the tape-recorded cue results in greater on-task performance than a non-cued condition (Heins, 1980).

It should be emphasized that the self-monitoring instructions in all of the Hallahan studies target attention. Improvement in academic skills, while measured, is not directly targeted by the self-regulatory procedure. Rather, the procedure serves to heighten the child's awareness of his or her own level of attention, resulting in more efficient and task-directed use of time. Component analyses seem to suggest that benefits are maximized when the monitoring procedures are overt and intrusive.

Benefits of Intrusiveness

The benefits of clearly observable and intrusive self-guiding strategies with attentionally disordered children have been observed in other investigations. Requiring children to overtly verbalize academic material appears to be superior to allowing covert verbalization for increasing academic accuracy (Dubey & O'Leary, 1975; Kosiewicz, Hallahan, Lloyd, & Graves, 1982; Lovitt & Curtiss, 1968). In interpreting the mechanism for the superiority of overt verbalization with hyperactive children, Dubey & O'Leary suggested that the overt responding presented the advantages of demonstrating to the child a procedure that is controlled by the child him- or herself, that can take its effect immediately, and that helps to facilitate attentional behavior.

Paquin (1978) reduced the disruptive behavior of a 9-year-old girl with learning difficulties by requiring her to self-graph her academic accuracy; concomitant improvements in accuracy were demonstrated. As in the Hallahan investigations discussed previously, effects were demonstrated without the presence of back-up reinforcers. The approach was most effective in reading, which was the child's strongest competency area. As in the Hallahan investigations, the suggestion was made that the procedure was most effective in imparting needed consistency and efficiency to a skill that was already apparently in the child's range (Kneedler & Hallahan, 1984).

Accuracy in Self-Recording

The importance of the accuracy of a child's self-recording is in question. For instance, several of the mechanical self-monitoring and self-recording interventions have demonstrated reactivity effects even in the absence of self-recording accuracy. In the Hallahan investigations, some children tended to be inaccurate in their self-assessments of on- and off-task behavior; inaccuracy did not appear to detectably affect treatment results (Hallahan, Lloyd, Kauffman, Loper, 1983). An investigation conducted by McLaughlin, Burgess, and Sackville-West (1981), however, indicated that requiring accuracy in self-recording may enchance reactivity effects. Six behaviorally handicapped underachieving children placed in a self-contained special education classroom were required to self-record their study behavior. During the self-recording phase, students marked an answer sheet to indicate whether or not they were studying; the intervals between recording were random and student-determined. Following this phase, the children again were required to self-record their own study behavior, but with the additional condition that their recordings had to match those of their teacher. Results indicated greater academic accuracy during the condition in which the student's evaluations had to match the teacher's. These results are consistent with other studies that have concluded that accurate self-recording is necessary for reactivity (Crow & Mayhew, 1976; McLaughlin & Malaby, 1979) and are inconsistent with those that have concluded that reactivity occurs in the absence of accurate self-monitoring (Kneedler & Hallahan, 1984; Nelson, 1977; Nelson, Hay, Devany, Koslow-Green, 1980).

In terms of the present consideration of attentionally disordered children, some of the variability may relate to the intrusiveness of other features of the self-monitoring routine. In an analysis of the Hallahan et al. (1979) procedure, Heins (1980) suggested that benefits were maximized if children self-recorded at the cue of an external tone rather than at child-selected intervals, as was the case in the McLaughlin et al. (1981) investigation. Greater behavioral change was also evident when children were required to self-record attentional behavior by placing checkmarks on an answer sheet than when they were allowed simply to question themselves about their attention (Lloyd et al., 1982). These findings support other evidence that the intrusiveness of a self-recording procedure is related to reactivity (Nelson, Lipinski, & Boykin, 1978). It is possible that if the self-recording procedure is not sufficiently intrusive to engage the child's attention, some additional external monitoring, such as checking for accuracy, will be needed. The relative paucity of investigations that have examined this issue with attentionally disordered underachievers makes it difficult to draw firm conclusions; further examination of the role of accuracy in self-monitoring interventions is in order.

Elaborative Self-Regulatory Training for Children without Stated Attentional Disorders

Meichenbaum and Goodman Elaborations

Malamuth (1979) employed a modified version of the Meichenbaum and Goodman (1971) procedure with fifth-grade children identified as poor readers. Half of the children were assigned to a self-monitoring condition whereby they were instructed to study picture cartoons with and without written words; training procedures required the children to analyze the instructional task, using the Meichenbaum and Goodman self-instructions. The remaining children were assigned to the control group in which they observed a model employ the same self-monitoring strategies taught to the training group; however, they were not explicitly taught to employ the procedures themselves. Results indicated superior reading performance from the children receiving the self-management training. In addition, the children trained in employing the self-monitoring procedures evidenced greater inhibitory control on a subsequent measure of sustained attention. This finding is consistent with other investigations that have demonstrated that attentional gains may be made through academic interventions (Holman & Baer, 1979).

Robin, Armel, and O'Leary (1975) employed self-instructions modeled after the Meichenbaum and Goodman (1971) sequence in an attempt to improve the performance of kindergarten children with handwriting deficiencies. Children were assigned to a self-instruction condition, to a direct-training condition (during which the children received social reinforcement and feedback—the experimenter scored the letter with a transparent overlay and described how the child's letter compared with a sample), or to a no-treatment control condition. Results indicated that both training procedures were superior to no treatment, and that the self-control procedure was more effective than the direct-training procedure in terms of improving performance on target letters. However, none of the procedures appeared to be useful in improving performance on nontargeted (generalized) letters, leading the authors to conclude that the procedure, while statistically effective, was practically burdensome and not worth the trouble.

The children in the Robin et al. (1975) intervention were kindergarteners with writing deficiencies. Because handwriting is normally far from perfect at this grade level, the children targeted may have been quite deficient in their basic skills (see Kosiewicz et al., 1982). Intensive drill and practice may be more beneficial at such a level. It is clearly essential for self-regulatory training programs to specify the optimal level of preskills that are necessary for maximization of treatment effects (Pflaum & Pascarella, 1980).

Elaborations that Induce Preparedness

Several investigations have suggested the benefits of introducing self-elaboration early in the training sequence as a way of inducing the children to plan for upcoming cognitive activity. Spates and Kanfer (1977) designed a self-regulatory intervention to aid children in performing math-fact calculations. Forty-five first-grade students who were deficient in math were selected; all selected children had demonstrated sufficient knowledge of minimal math facts. Children were assigned to one of four training conditions that manipulated the point at which, during math computation, each child employed an elaborative self-verbalization. Depending upon condition, the child (1) simply read the numerals out loud (control), (2) verbalized the math process as it was being done (self-monitoring), (3) verbalized the process before it was done (criterion setting), or (4) employed a combination of criterion setting with self-monitoring or self-reinforcement. Their data suggested that the critical component of the treatment was the criterion-setting phase, during which the child verbally elaborated the procedures she or he was going to need in order to solve the problem.

These results suggest the benefits of employing elaboration as a mechanism for planning behavior beforehand. Spates and Kanfer (1977) targeted arithmetic accuracy; similar conclusion have been drawn concerning reading processes, as well. In particular, some investigations have suggested that supplying reading deficient children with comprehension questions before they read a passage serves to improve comprehension performance (Maier, 1980; Wong, 1979). Trainers in the Wong investigation posed questions that taped thematically relevant information; in the Maier study, children were directed by the trainer to look for particular events in the reading passage.

In a follow-up of her questioning study, Wong designed an intervention that taught children how to self-question (Wong & Jones, 1982). LD and normally achieving children were assigned either to an experimental or a training condition. In the training condition, children were instructed to formulate and answer comprehension questions. As expected, the procedure served to enhance the comprehension performance of LD children; of equal interest was the finding that the procedure had a slightly debilitating effect on the comprehension of the normally achieving children. The authors suggested that, while the procedure helped to activate the LD children to focus on relevant material, it served to undermine the performance of the children who were already competent in reading comprehension.

An old-fashioned technique designed to aid children in developing effective studying and comprehension skills is the SQ3R *method* (Survey, Question, Read, Recite/Write, Review) designed by Robinson (1946). Long before metacognition was fashionable, Robinson suggested that children be trained to first survey reading material by skimming the content and noting important headings, italicized words, and so forth. The children were induced to form a question that would seem to summarize the important information within a passage. Finally the children executed the three "R's" of the formulation by reading to find the answer to the question, reciting and writing important notes concerning the answer, and reviewing the material.

Robinson's (1946) method was applied by Schumaker, Deshler, Alley, Warner, and Denton (1982) to eight LD adolescents. The program was taught by a 10-step instructional sequence, which included, among other components, a rationale for the approach, modeling of the strategy, and corrective feedback concerning the child's use of the technique. Results indicated that children were able to successfully generalize training procedures to grade-level textbooks; in addition, they received higher grades on textbook quizzes subsequent to training.

Informed Feedback

Training in the use of the SQ3R adaptation devised by Schumaker et al. (1952) included two corrective feedback periods during which the child was supplied with information concerning his or her proficiency in using the self-regulatroy strategy. Several investigations that are outside the range of the present review have emphasized the importance of giving children feedback concerning the utility of a cognitive strategy (Kennedy & Miller, 1976; Paris, Newman, & McVey, 1982; Ringel & Springer, 1980).

Brown has repeatedly argued that cognitive training must make provision for instructing the child in the utility of the strategy training (Brown, 1978; Brown & Campione, 1978; Brown & Palincsar, 1982). She distinguishes between blind and informed training: while *blind training* keeps the child ignorant of the purposes of procedures, *informed training* gives children specific feedback concerning the reason why their work is or is not improving.

Palincsar and Brown (1981) developed a training sequence for four seventh-grade students who were at the seventh percentile in reading comprehension for their grade level. Two conditions were imposed for each of the children. In the corrective feedback condition, children were given information concerning their correct and incorrect responses to comprehension questions. Students were shown how to trace back to the passage to find the correct answers. The second condition, strategy training, involved treaching the children to synthesize information from a passage after it was read. Children were instructed how to paraphrase information from the text, classify relevant details, predict possible questions that could be formed from the text, and hypothesize about the possible content of subsequent passages. Accuracy on passage-comprehension tests served as the dependent variable. After a no-treatment baseline, children received one of two treatment orders: two children received the corrective feedback training for a number of days, followed by the strategy treatment; the treatment order for the remaining two children was reversed. All four children evidenced an improvement in reading comprehension performance with either treatment order. However, the imposition of the corrective feedback prior to strategy training appeared to be more beneficial. In order to get the performance level of children in the strategy-first condition up to the level of those in the feedback-first condition, strategy training had to be reintroduced; with this modification (which produced the optimal feedback before strategy ordering) academic performance improved.

These results underscore the relevance of designing training programs with built-in mechanisms for impressing an awareness upon the child of the need for the intervention. It is significant that this heightened awareness was induced by intentionally allowing the children to falter at a task. This procedure slightly resembles the Meichenbaum and Goodman (1971) recommendation for inclusion of a modeling of flawed performance during training as a way of demonstrating to children how to cope with errors. However, the Palincsar and Brown (1981) investigation purposively allowed the children to make errors and then structured an intentional period designed to highlight to the children when they had made an error. This design resulted in a better comprehension of the need and/or rationale for the subsequently introduced self-regulatory strategy.

Imagery Elaboration

All of the investigations described thus far in this section have employed verbal elaboration as a self-regulatory technique. Another elaborative technique that has been used involves training children to use imagery in order to improve reading comprehension. Pressley (1976) trained 8-year old children to create a mental image of reading material. Training involved showing the children slides that illustrated information relayed in a reading passage; a control group of children was instructed to try to remember the information as best they could. Children were divided into good readers, who were above reading level, and average to poor readers, who were either at or below reading level. Results indicated that the imagery improved comprehension for both reading levels.

A self-imagery intervention designed by Levin (1973) combined good and average readers into a group and contrasted their performance to children who were below grade level. The expected reading level by treatment interaction was still not present. Among the poor readers, a trend was noted whereby children were unable to benefit from the program unless they possessed adequate vocabulary skills. The suggestion (which by now should be familiar) was made that a self-regulatory procedure is effective only if sufficient preskills are present. Along similar lines, Lesgold, McCormick, and Golinkoff (1975) improved the reading comprehension of underachieving third and fourth graders by training them to imagine and construct cartoon representations of written material.

It is noteworthy that while self-imagery has been employed as a method of enhancing the comprehension of underachieving children without specified attention deficits, little has been done with attentionally disordered children using this approach. Perhaps the procedure is not sufficiently overt and directive to engage children with attentional deficiencies. Apparently, however, this possibility has not been formally evaluated. This hypothesis merits formal evaluation.

Mechanical Self-Regulatory Training for Children without Stated Attentional Disorders

Much of the early interest in teaching children with school problems how to self-monitor was generated as a result of research conducted within Lovitt's laboratory (1973). Lovitt implemented seven self-management interventions for children with academic or social disabilities. Included were treatments to self-record, self-schedule, self-correct, self-time, self-chart, and self-evaluate. Unfortunately, he did not specify which children primarily exhibited academic difficulties, and which exhibited social problems; no criteria were presented by which children were classified into either designation. The weight of the diverse projects implied that a wide range of self-regulatory activities could be used to increase academic productivity and decrease undesirable behaviors. It should be recalled that at the time of this investigation, relatively few researchers were examining the effects of self-regulatory treatments with special education children; emphasis on academic change was rarer still.

Generally, self-regulatory training approaches that have targeted reading comprehension have employed elaborative techniques. This is not surprising. Elaborative techniques encourage children to reflect on a variety of possible alternatives that are available for a situation. This emphasis fits well with training in comprehension. One exception to this trend is a mechanical self-monitoring intervention from Swanson's laboratory (1981a), designed to evaluate the importance of directly targeting desired behaviors in self-regulation. In the first experiment, children kept track of and were reinforced for correct oral pronunciation of reading assignments; although the procedure improved oral pronunciation, it did not improve reading-comprehension performance. In the second experiment, children recorded and were reinforced for speed of reading an oral passage and accurate responding to comprehension questions; results indicated speedier reading performance, but nonconclusive changes in comprehension. In the third experiment, children self-recorded and were reinforced for correctly answering comprehension questions; results indicated improved reading comprehension performance. These effects are consistent with the conclusion previously drawn in this chapter concerning the importance of overtly targeting the specific behavior that is to be changed.

Unfortunately, Swanson did not include a condition whereby self-monitoring of correct comprehension performance was evaluated without any concomitant reinforcement. This decision may have been prompted by his interpretation from an earlier investigation (Swanson, 1981b) that an intervention that combines praise and self-recording is superior to a praise-only intervention. However, such a direction would seem fruitful. The Hallahan self-monitoring procedures effected results without any concomitant external reinforcers (Kneedler & Hallahan, 1984). It is the present authors' hunch that external reinforcement is less likely to be needed when the monitoring procedure is sufficiently intrusive and direct. If additional external reinforcement is not demonstrably needed to induce change, then omitting it seems sensible.

Unlike the many interventions that specifically direct children's attention to their own correct performance, some investigations have successfully induced change by training children how to detect their own errors. The Gerber and Hall (1981) intervention that was previously discussed taught a spelling proofreading strategy to attentionally deficient LD children. Pflaum and Pascarella (1980) required LD children to listen to tape recordings of their own oral reading and to detect decoding errors that did and did not affect passage meaning. Results indicated that children who were reading above a second-grade reading level benefited from the procedure. In one of the few self-regulatory interventions targeting the performance of adolescent LD children, Schumaker, Deshler, Alley, Warner, Clark, and Nolan (1982) demonstrated the effectiveness of an error-monitoring procedure in which children learned to detect errors concerning capitalization, overall legibility, punctuation, and spelling (COPS) in their written compositions. Utilizing a multibaseline design across three students and then replicating twice with additional sets of three students each (nine children total), the authors presented persuasive evidence for the benefits of the approach.

Error-monitoring would seem to be a particularly fruitful direction for future research. An important issue to be addressed is the relative benefits of directing the child's attention toward his or her errors, as opposed to correct performance. In two of the error-monitoring interventions, the treatment was effective only at certain skill levels (Gerber & Hall, 1981; Pflaum & Pascarella, 1980). It is conceivable that the appropriateness of requesting a child to focus on his or her erroneous, instead of correct, performance will depend on the child's maturity, skill sophistication, and/or the nature of the task itself. Further research would be welcome in expanding our understanding of the benefits of error self-monitoring.

Conclusions: Self-Regulatory Interventions
with Academically Deficient Children

Need for Comparable Studies

Interest in developing training interventions that place responsibility on underachieving children to regulate their own behavior is rapidly increasing. A welcome trend that has recently emerged is an emphasis on measuring outcome in terms of academic gain.

The results from the large majority of these interventions are very promising. Nevertheless, a need for additional, well-controlled studies is clearly indicated. Problems with the current body of metacognitive research primarily involve insufficient descriptive information within studies and inconsistent methodological practices among them. A variety of metacognitive learning strategies—such as self-monitoring, self-questioning, and self-instruction—have been developed; although different investigators have labeled their treatments similarly, however, there may be substantial differences between the approaches (e.g., "self-monitoring" as utilized by Spates & Kanfer [1977] versus that described by Hallahan et al. [1979]). Moreover, the strategies have not been applied uniformly across studies: the kinds of tasks to which they are applied differ, ranging from various reading comprehension assignments to on-task behavior. In some cases, the strategy and/or the task is not described in sufficient detail to allow for replication. Furthermore, generalization and maintenance data are frequently unreported.

Insufficient descriptions of the children identified by each investigator are also a major weakness of the metacognitive literature. While the present review attempted to suggest, for example, how treatment interventions may be differentially effective with children with attentional disorders, the conclusions are weakened by the lack of operationalization of attentional disability. Along similar lines, all too many investigators failed to report sufficient information on the academic skill levels of targeted children, again making comparisons difficult. As a result of these limitations and the relatively small number of investigations that have focused on academic performance, drawing firm conclusions is not possible. Nevertheless, several trends are evident that suggest viable hypotheses appropriate for more thorough investigations.

Need for Match of Intervention to Population

The research suggests, upon initial inspection, that mechanical self-regulating interventions are more successful than elaborative techniques with attentionally disordered children. The apparent superiority of mechanical interventions with this population may be attributable to the structure of the approach: mechanical routines are characterized by regularity and repetition, which encourage the development of automatic self-regulation. Mechanical self-monitoring allows children to conserve and focus attention with regularity and consistency. For children whose academic performance is suppressed primarily because they do not attend long enough to accomplish tasks efficiently, mechanical self-monitoring—particularly at the automatic level—is obviously useful.

Contrasting the relative benefits of elaborative and mechanical interventions with academic underachievers who were not identified as attentionally disordered is difficult because very few studies employing mechanical techniques have been undertaken with this group. The elaborative procedures that were conducted, however, were generally successful in increasing academic accuracy. Additional research is clearly warranted in this area.

Need for Match of Intervention to Task

It would seem unwise to conclude that mechanical self-regulating training is always more desirable than elaborative interventions with attentionally disordered children or that only elaborative techniques should be used with nondisordered underachievers. Additional factors, which may have prompted the differential results, underline the need to determine the best fit between the targeted task and the treatment approach.

In terms of the apparent benefits of mechanical training with attentionally disordered children, the selection of tasks was not consistent across populations. The majority of the elaborative interventions designed for children not specifically designated as having attentional disorders targeted fairly complex tasks such as reading comprehension; these interventions were consistently successful. The elaborative procedures involving attentionally disordered children, however, tended to target rote tasks such as math computation or oral decoding; these produced less-clear results. Elaboration, which would seem to be suitable for tasks requiring reflection on a variety of alternatives, may not be an efficient method of teaching basic skills. The more consistent positive results that were obtained in the mechanical interventions for children with attention problems may therefore be attributable to a more desirable task-to-treatment match-up. Additional elaborative self-regulatory interventions that target reflective analysis on a wider range of skills with attentionally disordered children are indicated. (Abikoff, personal communication, November 1982, for example, has begun work on a project to explore the usefulness of reflective self-regulatory procedures on the long- and short-term academic performance of stimulant-treated hyperactive children. Initial results look promising.)

Need for Specification of Strategy, Task, and Outcome

Several of the studies explored have addressed the need to overtly emphasize for children the particular metacognitive strategies that will help them perform specific academic tasks. The benefits of making the self-regulation explicit are more apparent with mechanical approaches than with elaborative ones. The implementation of mechanical training requires the targeting of a specific behavior, along with instruction in some mechanical monitoring, such as self-recording. Elaborative procedures, on the other hand, are open-ended and therefore involve less direct matching. The finding that back-up reinforcement increases the effectiveness of elaborative strategy training with attentionally disordered children (Bryant & Budd, 1982; Friedling & O'Leary, 1979; Varni & Henfer, 1979) suggests that reinforcement may help the child to identify his or her target behaviors. Other research suggests that when a self-monitoring procedure is sufficiently overt and intrusive, accuracy of self-recording may not be critical to treatment success (Kneedler & Hallahan, 1984; Nelson et al., 1978).

Moreover, there is a need to include techniques that help children to relate these behaviors to their newly acquired metacognitive strategies. Heightening children's awareness of the usefulness of particular strategies, for example, has been found to enhance self-regulatory interventions (Brown & Palinscar, 1982).

Need for Match of Intervention to Skill Level

Another pervasive theme in the literature under review is the need to fit the intervention to the skill level of the student. The importance of requisite preskills to metacognitive training has been recognized by a number of investigators employing a variety of self-regulatory interventions across several different subject areas (Kosiewicz et al., 1982; Levin, 1973; Lloyd, Saltzman, & Kauffman, 1981; Pflaum & Pascarella, 1980; Spates & Kanfer, 1977). In studies of reading comprehension, for instance, subjects with inadequate vocabulary skills (Levin) and relatively low reading-achievement grade levels (Pflaum & Pascarella) did not benefit as much from strategy training as did those with more advanced preskills. Similarly, Lloyd and his colleagues found that only when instruction in basic multiplication and division preskills preceded strategy training did correct performance generalize to other problems. At the other end of the spectrum are indications that particular self-regulatory interventions will be less effective if a child's achievement is beyond a certain level (Gerber & Hall,

1981; Wong & Jones, 1982). Most interventions will probably be useful within a general range of competency. Careful determination of the range appropriate to a specific procedure, however, is essential to ensuring its effectiveness.

Several investigators have also noted that treatment was most effective with those skills that were within a child's repertoire but were not being reliably exhibited (Friedling & O'Leary, 1979; Kneedler & Hallahan, 1984; Paquin, 1978). This finding has a familiar ring. Much of the formal interest in developing metacognitive treatments for underachieving children grew from research concerning cognitive behaviors such as impulsivity, attention, and memory. The literature has consistently demonstrated that academically deficient children have difficulty in accessing information, and that simple instruction in appropriate strategies can rapidly improve their performance. Implicit in the contention that underachieving (and younger) children have a production deficiency (Flavell, 1970) is the assumption that necessary structures are present but are not being activated. It is delightful to discover that self-regulatory interventions—which can trace at least part of their heritage to this line of metacognitive research—are producing effects in concordance with theory.

Summary

In conlusion, the research reviewed demonstrates that interventions designed to induce underachieving children to regulate their own academic behavior can improve task performance. The time-honored advice concerning the wholesomeness of self-awareness finds support. Reported positive treatment effects include more-rapid and more-accurate task completions, enhanced quality of responses, and more-consistent utilization of those academic skills that are within a given child's repertoire. The need for continued circumscription of the limits of self-regulation, however, are clearly in order. The success of these interventions with individual students depends in part upon the appropriate matching of treatment approach to task, as well as the child's preskill mastery, attentional level, and awareness of the potential benefits of employing self-regulatory strategies.

References

Ackerman, P. T., Dykman, R. A., & Peters, J. E. Teenage status of hyperactive and nonhyperactive learning disabled boys. *American Journal of Orthopsychiatry*, 1977, 47, 577–596.

Arter, J. A., & Jenkins, J. R. Differential diagnosis—prescriptive teaching: A critical appraisal. *Review of Educational Research*, 1979, 49, 517–555.

Arter, J. A., & Jenkins, J. R. Examining the benefits of prevalence of modality considerations in special education. *Journal of Special Education*, 1977, *11*, 281–298.

Barkley, R. A., Copeland, A. P., & Sivage, C. A self-control classroom for hyperactive children. *Journal of Autism and Developmental Disorders*, 1980, *10*, 75–89.

Bauer, R. H. Memory processes in children with learning disabilities: Evidence for deficient rehearsal. *Journal of Experimental Child Psychology*, 1977, *24*, 415–430.

Bauer, R. H. Memory, acquisition, and category clustering in learning disabled children. *Journal of Experimental Child Psychology*, 1979, *27*, 365–383.

Bornstein, P. H., & Quevillon, R. D. The effects of a self-instructional package on overactive preschool boys. *Journal of Applied Behavior Analysis*, 1976, *9*, 179–188.

Bos, C., & Filip, D. Comprehension monitoring skills in learning disabled and average students. *Topics in Learning and Learning Disabilities*, 1982, *2*, 79–85,

Brown, A. L. Knowing when, where, and how to remember: A problem of metacognition. In R. Glaser (Ed.), *Advances in instructional psychology*. Hillsdale, NJ: Erlbaum, 1978.

Brown, A. L., & Campione, J. C. Permissible inferences from the outcome of training studies in cognitive development research. *The Quarterly Newsletter of the Institute for Comparative Human Development*, 1978, *2*, 46–53.

Brown, A. L., & Palincsar, A. S. Inducing strategic learning from texts by means of informed, self-control training. *Topics in Learning and Learning Disabilities*, 1982, *2*, 1–17.

Bryant, L. E., & Budd, K. S. Self-instructional training to increase independent work performance in preschoolers. *Journal of Applied Behavior Analysis*, 1982, *15*, 259–271.

Cameron, M. I., & Robinson, J. J. Effects of cognitive training on academic and on-task behavior of hyperactive children. *Journal of Abnormal Child Psychology*, 1980, *8*, 405–419.

Crow, R., & Mayhew, G. Reinforcement effects on accuracy of self-recording behavior of elementary students. In T. A. Brigham, R. Hawkins, J. Scott, & T. F. McLaughlin (Eds.), *Behavior analysis in education: Self-control and reading*. Dubuque, IA: Kendall/Hunt, 1976.

Cullinan, D., Epstein, M. H., & Silver, L. Modification of impulsive tempo in learning disabled pupils. *Journal of Abnormal Child Psychology*, 1977, *5*, 437–444.

deHirsch, K., Jansky, J., & Langford, W. S. *Predicting reading failure*. New York: Harper, 1966.

Denney, D. R. The effects of exemplary and cognitive models and self-rehearsal on children's interrogative strategies. *Journal of Experimental Child Psychology*, 1975, *19*, 476–488.

Digate, G., Epstein, M., Cullinan, D., & Switsky, H. Modification of impulsivity: Implications for improved efficiency in learning for exceptional children. *Journal of Special Education*, 1978, *12*, 459–468.

DiVesta, F. J., Hayward, K. G., & Orlando, V. P. Developmental trends in monitoring text for comprehension. *Child Development*, 1979, *50*, 97–105.

Douglas, V. I., Parry, P., Marton, P., & Garson, C. Assessment of a cognitive training program for hyperactive children. *Journal of Abnormal Child Psychology*, 1976, *4*, 389–410.

Douglas, V. I., & Peters, K. G. Toward a clearer definition of the attentional deficit of hyperactive children. In G. A. Hale & M. Lewis (Eds.), *Attention and cognitive development*. New York: Plenum Press, 1979.

Dubey, D. R., & O'Leary, S. G. Increasing reading comprehension of two hyperactive children: Preliminary investigation, *Perceptual and Motor Skills*, 1975, *41*, 691–694.

Egeland, B. Training impulsive children in the use of more efficient scanning techniques. *Child Development*, 1974, *45*, 165–171.

Engelmann, B. A., Granzin, A., & Severson, H. Diagnosing instruction. *Journal of Special Education*, 1979, *13*, 355–363.

Flavell, J. H. Developmental studies of mediated memory. In H. W. Reese & L. P. Lipsitt

(Eds.), *Advances in child development and behavior* (Vol. 5). New York: Academic Press, 1970.

Flavell, J. H. Metacognition and cognitive monitoring: A new area of cognitive-developmental inquiry. *American Psychologist.* 1979, *34,* 906–911.

Friedling, C., & O'Leary, S. G. Effects of self-instructional training on second and third grade hyperactive children: A failure to replicate. *Journal of Applied Behavior Analysis,* 1979, *12,* 311–319.

Garner, R. Monitoring of understanding: An investigation of good and poor readers' awareness of induced miscomprehension of text. *Journal of Reading Behavior,* 1980, *12,* 55–63.

Garner, R., & Reis, R. Monitoring and resolving comprehension obstacles: An investigation of spontaneous text lookbacks among upper-grade good and poor comprehenders. *Reading Resource Quarterly,* 1981, *16,* 569–582.

Gerber, M. M., & Hall, R. J. Development of orthographic problem-solving in learning disabled and normally achieving children. Unpublished monograph, University of Virginia, 1981.

Hagen, J. W. The effect of distraction on selective attention. *Child Development,* 1967, *38,* 685–694.

Hagen, J. W., Barclay, C. R., & Newman, R. S. Metacognition, self-knowledge, and learning disabilities: Some thoughts on knowing and doing. *Topics in learning and learning disabilities,* 1982, *2,* 19–26.

Hagen, J. W., & Sabo, R. A developmental study of selective attention. *Merrill-Palmer Quarterly,* 1967, *13,* 159–172.

Hallahan, D. P., & Kauffman, J. M. *Introduction to learning disabilities: A psycho-behavioral approach.* Engelwood Cliffs, NJ: Prentice-Hall, 1976.

Hallahan, D. P., Kauffman, J. M., & Ball, D. W. Selective attention and cognitive tempo of low achieving sixth grade males. *Perceptual and Motor Skills,* 1973, *36,* 579–583.

Hallahan, D. P., Lloyd, J. W., Kauffman, J. M., & Loper, A. B. Academic problems. In R. J. Morris & T. R. Kratochwill (Eds.), *Practice of child therapy: A textbook of methods.* New York: Pergamon Press, 1983.

Hallahan, D. P., Lloyd, J. W., Kneedler, R. D., & Marshall, K. J. A comparison of the effects of self- versus teacher-assessment of on-task behavior. *Behavior Therapy,* 1982, *13,* 715–723.

Hallahan, D. P., Lloyd, J. W., Kosiewicz, M. M., Kauffman, J. M., & Graves, A. W. Self-monitoring of attention as a treatment for a learning disabled boy's off-task behavior. *Learning Disability Quarterly,* 1979, *2,* 24–32.

Hallahan, D. P., Marshall, J. K., & Lloyd, J. W. Self-recording during group instruction: Effects on attention to task. *Learning Disability Quarterly,* 1981, *4,* 407–413.

Hallahan, E. P., & Reeve, R. E. Selective attention and distractibility. In B. K. Keogh (Ed.), *Advances in special education* (Vol. 1): *Basic constructs and theoretical orientations.* Greenwich, CT: Jai Press, 1980.

Heins, E. D. Training learning disabled children's self-control: Cued and non-cued self-recording in the classroom. Unpublished doctoral dissertation, University of Virginia, 1980.

Hersen, M., & Barlow, D. H. *Single case experimental designs.* New York: Pergamon Press, 1976.

Holman, J., & Baer, D. M. Facilitating generalization of on-task behavior through self-monitoring of academic tasks. *Journal of Autism and Developmental Disorders,* 1979, *9,* 429–446.

Johnson, D., & Myklebust, H. *Learning disability: Educational principles and practices.* New York: Grune & Stratton, 1969.

Kagan, J., Rosman, B., Day, D., Albert, J., & Phillips, W. Information processing in the significance of analytic and reflective attitudes. *Psychological Monographs*, 1964, 78(No. 1).

Kennedy, B. A., & Miller, D. J. Persistent use of verbal rehearsal as a function of information about its value. *Child Development*, 1976, 47, 556–569.

Keogh, B. K., Major, S. M., Omori, H., Gandara, P., & Reid, H. P. Proposed markers in learning disabilities research. *Journal of Abnormal Child Psychology*, 1980, 8, 21–31.

Kneedler, R. D., & Hallahan, D. P. Self-monitoring as an attentional strategy for academic tasks with learning disabled children. In B. Gholson & T. Rosenthal (Eds.) *Applications of cognitive developmental theory*. New York: Academic Press, 1984.

Kosiewicz, M. M., Hallahan, D. P., Lloyd, J., & Graves, A. W. Effects of self-instruction and self-correction procedures on handwriting performance. *Learning Disability Quarterly*, 1982, 5, 71–78.

Kratochwill, T. R. *Single subject research*. New York: Academic Press, 1978.

Lesgold, A. M., McCormick, C., & Golinkoff, R. M. Imagery training and children's prose learning. *Journal of Educational Psychology*, 1975, 67, 663–667.

Levin, J. R. Inducing comprehension in poor readers: A test of a recent model. *Journal of Educational Psychology*, 1973, 65, 19–24.

Lewidge, B. Cognitive behavior modification: A step in the wrong direction? *Psychological Bulletin*, 1978, 85, 353–375.

Lloyd, J. W., Hallahan, D. P., Kosiewicz, M. M., & Kneedler, R. D. Reactive effects of self-assessment and self-recording on attention to task and academic productivity. *Learning Disability Quarterly*, 1982, 5, 216–227.

Lloyd, J. Saltzman, N., & Kauffman, J. Predictable generalization in academic learning by preskills and strategy training. *Learning Disability Quarterly*, 1981, 4, 203–216.

Locke, E. Behavior modification is not cognitive—and other myths: A reply to Lewidge. *Cognitive Therapy and Research*, 1979, 3, 119–125.

Loper, A. B. Metacognitive training to correct academic deficiency. *Topics in Learning and Learning Disabilities*, 1982, 2(1), 61–68.

Loper, A. B., & Hallahan, D. P. A comparison of the reliability and validity of the standard MFF and MFF20 with learning disabled children. *Journal of Abnormal Child Psychology*, 1980, 8, 377–384.

Loper, A. B., & Hallahan, D. P. A consideration of the role of generalization in cognitive training. *Topics in Learning and Learning Disabilities*, 1982, 2(2), 62–67.

Lovitt, T. C. Self-management projects with children with behavioral disabilities. *Journal of Learning Disabilities*, 1973, 6, 138–150.

Lovitt, T. C., & Curtiss, K. A. Effects of manipulating an antecedent event on mathematics response rate. *Journal of Applied Behavior Analysis*, 1968, 1, 329–333.

Lovitt, T. C., & Jenkins, J. R. Learning disabilities research: Defining populations. *Learning Disability Quarterly*, 1979, 2, 46–50.

Maccoby, E. E., & Hagen, J. W. Effects of distraction upon central versus incidental recall: Developmental trends. *Journal of Experimental Child Psychology*, 1965, 2, 280–289.

McKinney, J. D., Haskins, R., & Moore, M. G. *Problem solving strategies in reflective and impulsive children*. Final Report: National Institute of Education, Department of Health, Education, and Welfare, Project No. 3–0344, Washington, DC, July, 1977.

McKinney, J. D., & Haskins, R. Cognitive training and the development of problem-solving strategies. *Exceptional Education Quarterly*, 1980, 1, 41–51.

McLaughlin, T. F., Burgess, N., & Sackville-West, L. Effects of self-recording and self-recording plus matching on academic performance. *Child Behavior Therapy*, 1981, 3, 17–28.

McLaughlin, T. F., & Malaby, J. E. Modification of student-determined performance standards in elementary special education. *Education and Treatment of Children*, 1979, 2, 31–41.

Mahoney, M. J., & Kazdin, A. E. Cognitive behavior modification: Misconceptions and premature evacuation. *Psychological Bulletin*, 1979, 86, 1044–1049.

Maier, A. S. The effect of focusing on the cognitive processes of learning disabled children. *Journal of Learning Disabilities*, 1980, 13, 143–147.

Malamuth, Z. N. Self-management training for children with reading problems: Effects on reading performance and sustained attention. *Cognitive Therapy and Research*, 1979, 3, 279–289.

Meichenbaum, D. *Cognitive behavior modification: An integrative approach*. New York: Plenum Press, 1977.

Meichenbaum, D. J., & Goodman, J. Training impulsive children to talk to themselves: A means of developing self-control. *Journal of Abnormal Psychology*, 1971, 77, 114–126.

Messer, S. B. Reflection–impulsivity: A review. *Psychological Bulletin*, 1976, 83, 1026–1052.

Nelson, R. O. Assessment and therapeutic functions of self-monitoring. In M. Hersen, R. M. Eisler, & P. M. Miller (Eds.), *Progress in behavior modification* (Vol. 5). New York: Academic Press, 1977.

Nelson, R. O., Hay, L. R., Devany, J., & Koslow-Green, L. The reactivity and accuracy of children's self-monitoring: Three experiments. *Child Behavior Therapy*, 1980, 2, 1–24.

Nelson, R. O., Lipinski, D. P., & Boykin, R. A. The effects of self-recorders' training and the obtrusiveness of the self-recording device on the accuracy and reactivity of self-monitoring. *Behavior Therapy*, 1978, 9, 200–208.

O'Leary, S. G., & Dubey, D. R. Applications of self-control procedures by children: A review. *Journal of Applied Behavior Analysis*, 1979, 12, 449–464.

O'Connell, J., & McKinney, J. D. Problem solving strategies of learning disabled children. Paper presented at the Southeastern Psychological Association, New Orleans, March, 1979.

Owings, R. A., Peterson, G., Bransford, J. D., Morris, C. D., & Stein, B. S. Spontaneous monitoring and regulation of learning: A comparison of successful and less successful fifth graders. *Journal of Educational Psychology*, 1980, 72, 250–256.

Palincsar, A. S., & Brown, A. L. Training comprehension monitoring skills in an interactive learning game. Unpublished manuscript, University of Illinois, 1981.

Palkes, H., Stewart, M., & Freedman, B. Improvement in maze performance of hyperactive boys as a function of verbal training procedures. *Journal of Special Education*, 1972, 5, 337–342.

Paquin, M. J. The effects of self-graphing on academic performance. *Education and Treatment of Children*, 1978, 1, 5–16.

Paris, S. G., Newman, R. S., & McVey, K. A. From tricks to strategies: Learning the functional significance of mnemonic actions. *Journal of Experimental Child Psychology*, 1982, 34, 490–504.

Pflaum, S. W., & Pascarella, E. T. Interactive effects of prior reading achievement and training in context on the reading of learning disabled children. *Reading Research Quarterly*, 1980, 16, 138–158.

Pressley, G. M. Mental imagery helps eight-year-olds remember what they read. *Journal of Educational Psychology*, 1976, 68, 355–359.

Ringel, B. A., & Springer, C. J. On knowing how well one is remembering: The persistence of strategy use during transfer. *Journal of Experimental Child Psychology*, 1980, 29, 322–333.

Robin, A. L., Armel, S., & O'Leary, K. D. The effect of self-instruction on writing deficiencies. *Behavior Therapy*, 1975, 6, 178–187.

Robinson, F. P. *Effective study*. New York: Harper & Row, 1946.

Schumaker, J. B., Deshler, D. D., Alley, G. R., Warner, M. M., & Denton, P. H. Multipass: A learning strategy for improving reading comprehension. *Learning Disability Quarterly*, 1982, 5, 295–304.

Schumaker, J. B., Deshler, D. D., Alley, G. R., Warner, M. M., Clark, F. L., & Nolan, S. Error monitoring: A learning strategy for improving adolescent academic performance. In W. M. Cruickshank & J. W. Lerner (Eds.), *The best of ACLD: Coming of age* (Vol. 3). Syracuse, NY: Syracuse Press, 1982.

Senf, G. M. A perspective on the definition of LD. *Journal of Learning Disabilities*, 1977, 10, 537–539.

Snyder, J. J., & White, M. J. The use of cognitive self-instruction in the treatment of behaviorally disturbed adolescents. *Behavior Therapy*, 1979, 10, 227–235.

Spates, C. R., & Kanfer, F. H. Self-monitoring, self-evaluation and self-reinforcement in children's learning: A test of a multistage self-regulation model. *Behavior Therapy*, 1977, 8, 9–16.

Sullivan, J. Comparing strategies of good and poor comprehenders. *Journal of Reading*, 1978, 21, 710–715.

Swanson, L. Modification of comprehension deficits in learning disabled children. *Learning Disability Quarterly*, 1981, 4, 184–202. (a)

Swanson, L. Self-monitoring effects on concurrently reinforced reading behavior of a learning disabled child. *Child Study Journal*, 1981, 10, 225–232. (b)

Tant, J. L., & Douglas, V. I. Problem-solving in hyperactive, normal and reading disabled boys. *Journal of Abnormal Child Psychology*, 1982, 10, 285–306.

Thomas, J. W. Agency and achievement: Self-management and self-regard. *Review of Educational Research*, 1980, 50, 213–240.

Torgesen, J. K. Memorization process in reading disabled children. *Journal of Educational Psychology*, 1977, 69, 571–578.

Torgesen, J. K. Factors related to poor performance on memory tasks in reading disabled children. *Learning Disability Quarterly*, 1979, 2, 17–23.

Torgesen, J. K. Conceptual and educational implications of the use of efficient task strategies by learning disabled children. *Journal of Learning Disabilities*, 1980, 13, 364–371.

Torgesen, J. K., & Goldman, T. Verbal rehearsal and shortterm memory in reading disabled children. *Child Development*, 1977, 48, 56–60.

Varni, J. W., & Henker, B. A self-regulation approach to the treatment of three hyperactive boys. *Child Behavior Therapy*, 1979, 1, 171–192.

Wepman, J. M. The perceptual basis for learning. In E. C. Freerson & B. Barbe (Eds.) *Educating children with learning disabilities: Selected readings*. New York: Appleton-Century-Crofts, 1967.

Willows, D. M., & Ryan, E. B. Differential utilization of syntactic and semantic information by skilled and less skilled readers in the intermediate grades. *Journal of Educational Psychology*, 1981, 73, 607–615.

Wong B. Increasing retention of main ideas through questioning strategies. *Learning Disability Quarterly*, 1979, 2, 42–47.

Wong, B. Activating the inactive learner: Use of questions/prompts to enhance comprehension and retention of implied information in learning disabled children. *Learning Disability Quarterly*, 1980, 3, 39–47.

Wong, B. Strategic behavior in selecting retrieval cues in gifted, normal achieving and learning disabled children. *Journal of Learning Disabilities*, 1982, 15, 33–37.

Wong, B., & Jones, W. Increasing metacomprehension in learning disabled and normally achieving students through self-question training. *Learning Disability Quarterly*, 1982, *5*, 228–240.

Ysseldyke, J. E., Thurlow, M., Graden, J., Wesson, C., Algozzine, B., & Deno, S. Generalizations from five years of research on assessment and decision making: The University of Minnesota Institute. *Exceptional Education Quarterly*, 1983, *4*, 75–93.

Zelniker, T., & Oppenheimer, L. Modification of information processing of impulsive children. *Child Development*, 1973, *44*, 445–450.

Zelniker, T., Jeffrey, W. E., Ault, R., & Parsons, J. Analysis and modification of search strategies of impulsive and reflective children on the Matching Familiar Figures Test. *Child Development*, 1972, *43*, 321–335.

CHAPTER 7

Children's Ability to Cope with Failure: Implications of a Metacognitive Approach for the Classroom

Joy L. Cullen

Introduction

The current focus of cognitive psychology on the active constructive role of the learner (e.g., Brown, Bransford, Ferrara, & Campione, 1983; Calfee, 1981; Wittrock, 1979) is illustrated clearly in investigations of children's metacognition. Initially defined as "one's knowledge concerning one's own cognitive processes or products or anything related to them" (Flavell, 1976, p. 232), the concept of metacognition is now generally considered to encompass the cognitive-monitoring processes (Flavell, 1981) and strategic actions (Brown & DeLoache, 1978) that are believed to facilitate effective human performance.

Since the mid-1970s, the psychological research on metacognition has engendered considerable interest in the relevance of the construct for understanding learning failure. Torgesen (1977), for instance, has proposed that the inefficient and inactive task performance of learning disabled (LD) students may be accounted for by deficiencies at the meta level rather than by specific cognitive deficits. This position has been bolstered by extensive literature on attention and memory in LD students (Hallahan & Reeve, 1980; Torgesen, 1980; Torgesen & Kail, 1980). Torgesen's (1977) theory has stimulated a number of investigations designed to enhance the use of efficient task strategies in LD children (e.g., Wong, 1979, 1980). A

267

similar line of research with mildly retarded children (Brown & Campione, 1978; Campione & Brown, 1977) is developing procedures to enhance the use of trans-situational strategic behaviors, in order to reduce the widespread phenomenon of production deficiencies (Flavell, 1976) in the task performance of retardates.

Metacognitive training studies are developed on the assumption that the growth of organized strategic behaviors in the inefficient learner will, in turn, promote more effective academic learning. They have been largely concerned with the domain of activity termed by Brown et al. (1983) as "academic cognition." According to these writers, *academic cognition* comprises the cold (i.e., unemotional), effortful, and isolated dimensions of cognitive activity in contrast to "everyday cognition" which incorporates emotional, effortless, and social dimensions. Thus, the metacognitive studies have focused primarily on behaviors such as study strategies or checking procedures that are assumed to contribute directly to the learner's efficient use of cognitive strategies.

A separate body of research also has contributed to our understanding of learning failure since the mid-1970s. This line of inquiry has focused on motivational and personality variables that affect children's learning (e.g., Hamilton, 1976; Ruble & Boggiano, 1980; Stipek & Weisz, 1981; J. Thomas, 1980). Work in this field includes (1) investigations of children's locus of control, self-concepts, and expectations and attributions for success and failure; (2) studies of the phenomenon of learned helplessness; and (3) the investigation of a variety of procedures for developing self-management in children. In their recognition of the dynamic relationship between achievement and motivational variables, these studies appear to have ventured into the realm of everyday cognition in which people, situations, and emotions are significant elements of the learning encounter.

Although the two traditions have developed independently, it is today possible to identify several overlapping interests. J. Thomas (1980) has noted their common concern with behaviors that are, first, strategic in nature, and, second, propaedeutic (introductory) rather than prerequisite to learning. Further, both bodies of research are concerned with enhancing the learner's control in achievement situations. Brown and Campione (1978), for instance, have argued that metacognitive training studies should improve the child's feelings of personal competence and control. From a motivational perspective, Stipek and Weisz (1981) have summarized studies from three theoretical perspectives—social learning theory, attribution theory, and intrinsic motivation theories—in order to emphasize the relationship between achievement and perceptions of control. Finally, the importance of the learner's achievement-related cognitions has been emphasized in both bodies of research. Several reviews concerned with academic motivation (e.g., Dweck & Goetz, 1978; Maehr, 1978; Nicholls, 1979a; A. Thomas, 1979) have discussed the role of task-oriented cognitions in sustaining motivation long enough to reach a task solution. Because cognitive monitoring processes are also believed to facilitate progress toward cognitive goals (Flavell, 1981), they bear a strong similarity to the task-oriented cognitions identified by motivation theorists (e.g., Maehr & Nicholls, 1980; Nicholls, 1979a).

The evolution of the concept of metacognition itself demonstrates a broadening of the concept to incorporate an affective dimension. Flavell's (1979, 1981, in press) more recent analyses of metacognition touch upon many issues pertaining to motivation. For example, Flavell now considers the following to be legitimate forms of inquiry for metacognitive researchers: the monitoring of emotions and social cognitions, as well as the effects of subjective experiences such as pain and anxiety or cognitive and affective metacognitive experiences (e.g., curiosity or puzzlement) on performance. Torgesen (1977), too, has indicated the usefulness of the concept of metacognition for considering the interface of affective and cognitive development, although his theory appears to have engendered little in the way of direct investigation of the affective dimensions of metacognitive acquisitions. Similarly, Brown et al.'s (1983) analysis of metacognition, although restricting metacognitive activity to the realm of academic cognition, has at the same time acknowledged the potential significance of affect (e.g., see the section *Beyond Cold Cognition*, Brown et al., 1983). Further, Brown (1978) has focused on the possible interface of metacognitive impairment and negative affect in her perceptive analysis of the difficulties that face disadvantaged children when they commence formal schooling.

Although there is a growing awareness of the interrelationship of children's understanding of task requirements and their feelings, beliefs, and attitudes about the task, there is, according to a review of children's research on learning and cognition (Sigel, 1981), a need to study the interface between cognition and affect. With Sigel's injunction in mind, this chapter first aims to review an area of research that emphasizes the contiguity of cognition and affect: children's ability to cope with failure. Specifically, it is intended to explore the relationship between metacognition and learned helplessness as two areas of research concerned with promoting the learner's control in achievement situations. Second, the affective dimensions of metacognitive activity are examined with particular reference to the study of children's ability to cope with task failure. In this regard, J. Thomas (1980) has hypothesized that students who have been given responsibility for the management of their own learning may be more likely to use strategic behaviors. If this hypothesis is correct, then it is probable that instructional conditions will affect the acquisition and maintenance of children's task-related strategies. A final objective of the chapter, therefore, is to consider instructional conditions that are likely to activate (or inactivate) metacognitive activity in failure situations.

Learned Helplessness and Metacognition

The theory of learned helplessness (Abramson, Seligman, & Teasdale, 1978; Seligman, 1975) has attained considerable popularity for explaining the behavior of children who routinely give up in the face of failure. According to the learned-helplessness perspective (Dweck & Goetz, 1978; A. Thomas, 1979), these children are helpless because they believe failure to be insurmountable. Thus helpless children generalize failure experiences to other achievement-related situations because they attribute failure to uncontrollable factors such as lack of ability, task difficulty, or teacher bias. On this basis, several researchers have developed procedures to teach children to attribute failure to insufficient effort, thereby increasing task persistence in the face of failure (Andrews & Debus, 1978; Chapin & Dyck, 1976; Dweck, 1975; Fowler & Peterson, 1981; Schunk, 1981).

Although the attribution-training studies have achieved considerable success with their objectives, there remains an inherent weakness in their rationale—the assumption that effort renewal alone will improve performance. In this regard, Bandura (1977), on the basis of clinical evidence, has suggested that continued exhortations to try harder may even serve to increase helplessness if the individual does not possess the personal resources for coping with the task. Further, developmental studies have shown that children eventually learn that effort is an insufficient prerequisite for academic success (Nicholls, 1976, 1978, 1979b).

The complex role of effort attributions has been illustrated in a study (Schunk, 1982) that attempted to clarify the role of effort attributional feedback in achievement contexts. Schunk found that linking past achievement with effort (e.g., You've been working hard) promoted task involvement, skill development, and perceptions of self-efficacy, whereas stressing the value of future effort (You need to work hard) did not promote achievement behaviors above what could be expected from additional training with the task. Schunk's findings are a further indication that, for maximum benefit, effort attributions may need to be associated either with past successes or with specific strategies for coping with the task. If this assumption is correct, given strategies for trying again after a failure and the experience of success following renewal of effort, children would be less likely to respond with helpless reactions in future achievement contexts. With these qualifications to the role of effort renewal in mind, Cullen and Boersma (1982) attempted to devise procedures for minimizing helpless reactions to failure by integrating effort attributional feedback with specific task strategies for coping with failure.

Cullen and Boersma (1982) selected 30 LD fourth-grade boys who were placed part of the time in resource-room programs on the basis of 1½ or more years deficiency in reading and/or language achievement, and 30 normally achieving boys who were randomly selected from the same regular classrooms as the LD children. The two groups did not differ significantly on standardized measures of quantitative or nonverbal abilities but did differ in verbal abilities and grade point average with the LD boys receiving lower scores. The 60 boys were given failure experiences on a problem-solving task (unsolvable network puzzles), following which they received either tutor assistance or self-instructional training to induce success in coping with failure, or a no-training condition. It was expected that tutor-assistance training, which emphasized the use of external resources for coping with failure, would be more effective for reversing helplessness deficits with LD boys who tend to be inactive learners (Torgesen, 1977) and to hold external perceptions of success (Chapman & Boersma, 1979; Pearl, Bryan & Donahue, 1980). Conversely, normally achieving boys who are more internally oriented in successful achievement situations (Chapman & Boersma, 1979; Pearl, Bryan & Donahue, 1980) were expected to perform more effectively following self-instructional training that emphasized the child's personal resources for coping with failure.

The two training conditions differed only in the nature of the instructions and the type of activity engaged in by the child to reach a solution. For the self-instructional condition, the child was told "If you are having trouble there is something you can do. You can check the cue cards to help you to work out the sequence," whereas in the tutor-assistance condition the child was told "If you are having trouble there is something you can do. You can ask me to help you work out the sequence." The task required the child to form a logical sequence from a choice of attribute cards. On the first five trials, failure was manipulated by interruption after 20 seconds when the child was told he had exceeded the time usually taken by children his age to solve the problem. Children in the self-instructional condition were then reminded to check the cue card, whereas children in the tutor-assistance condition were told the appropriate card. The following five trials were success trials on which the instructional conditions were gradually withdrawn. Children in the no-training condition were left to work independently with the training task materials for an equivalent period of time (the neutral task). Training effects were assessed on a subsequent problem-solving task (solvable tangram puzzles) administered immediately following the training, and on a measure of continuing motivation (choice of similar problems or an alternative neutral activity to take home).

As expected, the tutor-assistance condition was more effective in minimizing the effects of failure with the LD boys, thereby supporting the view that LD children are dependent learners. With the normally achieving children, both conditions were effective for minimizing the disruptive effects of failure, indicating, perhaps, that the experience of coping with failure on the training task contributed to feelings of competence regardless of the condition. For the purposes of the present discussion, the most interesting results pertain to the untrained children who, in accordance with the learned helplessness paradigm, were expected to show signs of helplessness. Consistent with this hypothesis, performance decrements were shown by the untrained normal achievers who required a significantly longer mean time to reach task solution. Of particular interest, however, was the evidence that these boys were able to recover spontaneously from the initial failure through the use of independent and constructive strategies. They made active constructive use of the materials on the neutral task when left to work independently; they persisted with the subsequent problem-solving task to reach a solution despite longer working times; and they showed motivation to continue with similar problem-solving tasks at home. Furthermore, they used task-oriented verbalizations, which apparently focused their efforts on alternative strategies for coping with the task. In sum, the performance of the untrained normal achievers suggested that they had developed a variety of strategies for coping with failure.

In contrast, the untrained LD boys made only passive use of the neutral task materials, quickly gave up on the subsequent problem-solving task, attributed their failure to task difficulty, and failed to show interest in continuing with the tasks at home. These behaviors are consistent with a helplessness explanation of LD children's reactions to failure, but, further to this, point to an impairment at the metacognitive level of functioning. The apparent dependency of the LD children who received tutor-assistance may also point to this conclusion, although the fact that these children were motivated to continue with the experimental tasks at home does suggest that more independent behaviors could be fostered with appropriate instructional conditions.

The findings of the Cullen and Boersma (1982) study thus raise the possibility that the manifestation of learned helplessness is partially determined by the availability of metacognitive strategies for coping with failure. While this explanation of learned helplessness in terms of metacognitive deficits contrasts with the commonly accepted attributional explanation of helplessness, it is by no means inconsistent with an attributional approach and it is possible to reinterpret some of the findings from the helplessness studies in metacognitive terms. Studies by Diener and Dweck (1978, 1980), for instance, have documented patterns of reactions to failure that are highly consistent with Cullen and Boersma's view.

Diener and Dweck (1978, 1980) designated children as either helpless or mastery oriented, according to whether they attributed failure to lack of ability or lack of effort. After receiving failure feedback on a number of discrimination problems, mastery-oriented children maintained or improved performance, but helpless children deteriorated in their performance. When achievement-related cognitions were elicited, it was found that mastery-oriented children engaged in self-instructions and self-monitoring designed to bring about success, whereas helpless children made ability attributions (Diener & Dweck, 1978). Also, helpless children, compared to mastery-oriented children, underestimated their number of successes and overestimated their number of failures (Diener & Dweck, 1980). In line with these findings, Pearl, Bryan, and Herzog (1983) hypothesized that lack of success would cue non-LD children to explain their performance in analytic, strategy-specific terms while LD students would be more likely to become helpless following failure. After playing a laboratory bowling game for which they received either predominantly high or low scores the children explained why they had achieved their scores. Results were consistent with the view that LD children are less likely to become mastery-oriented in response to failure. Whereas failure seemed to stimulate the non-LD children to cognitively analyze a task, the responses of the LD did not differ over conditions of high or low success. Further, the LD tended to attribute failure to external factors while the non-LD attributed low scores to lack of effort.

Given the tendency of non-LD students (Pearl et al., 1983) to cognitively analyze a task in strategy-specific terms, and the effective utilization of cognitive monitoring skills by mastery-oriented children, (Diener & Dweck, 1978) it seems likely that the initial effort attributions of these children referred not so much to generic effort renewal but to the renewal of effort in terms of specific strategies. Cullen and Boersma (1982) also found that when attributions were elicited by open-ended questions rather than the more usual forced-choice measures, normally achieving children referred to specific strategies rather than to general effort renewal. Methodological differences, therefore, may well account for the greater emphasis placed on general effort renewal in many of the earlier learned helplessness studies (e.g., Butkowsky & Willows, 1980; Dweck, 1975; Dweck & Reppucci, 1973; Weisz, 1979).

The importance of cognitive processing has been noted also in studies concerned with promoting persistence. Fowler and Peterson (1981), in a study designed to increase reading persistence and alter attributional styles of helpless children, found some support for the use of self-instructional internal speech as a technique for increasing persistence and modifying attributions. Children who received direct attribution retraining appeared to be more actively involved and to make greater use of self-instructions than groups receiving indirect attribution retraining. Direct attribution retraining constituted listening to a recording of a child making effort attributions and practicing the same, and similar statements, while indirect attribution retraining constituted the more usual attributional feedback from experimenter or teacher. Given the reported use of self-instructions in the direct attribution condition, it seems plausible that the procedure actually constituted a self-instructional technique that served to focus the child's cognitions on ways of dealing with the task. In accordance with this view, Harris (1982) has demonstrated that the use of task strategies and persistence can be improved in both LD and normally achieving children through the use of cognitive training procedures designed to elicit verbal self-instructions (private speech). Consistent with Torgesen's (1977) hypothesis that LD children are inefficient learners, this study found that the proportion of task-irrelevant private speech was greater with LD than with normally achieving children in both training and control conditions. Of particular interest is the finding that cognitive training substantially increased the proportion of task-relevant private speech with the LD children. The differential use of self-instructions by successful and unsuccessful learners also has been reported by Peterson, Swing, Braverman, and Buss (1982) who used a stimulated recall procedure to elicit children's reports of their cognitive processes during direct classroom instruction. These researchers found that high-ability students were more likely to report the use of specific cognitive strategies than were the low-ability students, and that the reported use of strategies was related to attending behaviors, seatwork outcomes, and achievement test scores.

Overall, the evidence does point to the significance of cognitive-monitoring processes for maintaining appropriate achievement behaviors, and for the alleviation of learned helplessness in children. The present evidence, however, is not entirely clearcut. The data cited do not indicate whether the inactive behavior of the low ability, LD, and helpless students results from metacognitive deficits or merely the failure to activate strategies. Pearl et al. (1983) have expressed some caution about the assumption that LD children fail to produce task-appropriate strategies solely because of difficulty in retrieving or applying a particular strategy. They point out that when the LD children in their study attributed their low success to task difficulty or to luck, the failure experience may have indicated that they just had to wait until the task or their luck changed. Such an interpretation of failure would effectively interfere with any attempt to activate task strategies. Similarly, Dweck (1981, p. 329) has emphasized that the difference between helpless and mastery-oriented children is not that of possessing or not possessing the requisite skills but of displaying these skills when they are called into question. These issues are relevant to the question of whether metacognitive deficits are a determinant of learned helplessness. Reference to Flavell's (1981) distinction between cognitive and metacognitive strategies possibly provides some insight into the nature of helplessness deficits. If it is assumed that impaired performance occurs just at the metacognitive level there is no reason to assume, in addition, the presence of specific cognitive deficits. This is a point convincingly argued by Torgesen (1977) in his analysis of the inactive learning styles of LD students.

Further qualifications to the role of achievement-related cognitions in the manifestation of learned helplessness have been expressed by Weisz (1981), who replicated Diener and Dweck's (1978) think-aloud technique with retarded children and failed to obtain a clear relationship between children's verbalizations and task performance. Weisz's results may be an indication that the mechanisms of helplessness differ with different populations. Possibly the private speech of retarded children is not sufficiently developmentally advanced to regulate behavior effectively. Further, the overt helpless reactions to failure that have been observed in children with learning disabilities, a naturally acquired form of helplessness (Johnson, 1981), and those exhibited by helpless children who have been identified on the basis of ability attributions for failure (e.g., Diener & Dweck, 1978, 1980) or the experimental induction of helplessness (Dweck & Reppucci, 1973) need not necessarily share the same causal mechanisms.

Despite ambiguity about the meaning of the passivity exhibited by helpless learners, the results of these studies do indicate the potential value of cognitive-monitoring procedures for reducing helpless responses to failure. In this regard, cognitive monitoring may have two important functions in alleviating helplessness. First, it directs the learner to alternative strategies for coping with the task. Second, it contributes to the learner's sense of control or agency in the learning situation. As such, it illustrates an integral link between affective and cognitive dimensions of learning.

In regard to the second function, the perspective of clinical studies that have developed coping procedures as a vehicle of change may usefully be cited. Bandura (1977), for example, who has brought a cognitive social-learning perspective to bear on the issue of learned helplessness, has emphasized that an individual's feelings of self-efficacy, or sense of control, in threatening situations is dependent on the acquisition of the requisite skills for coping with a task. Bandura's analysis is not dissimilar to developments within cognitive-behavior modification theory (Meichenbaum, 1977). Initially concerned with the use of self-instructional training to enhance the self-control of impulsive and hyperactive children, the extension of cognitive-behavior modification procedures to academic tasks has highlighted parallels between the findings of cognitive-behaviorists and the metacognitive researchers (Meichenbaum & Asarnow, 1979). In particular, the centrality of the construct of control in the more recent writings of Bandura and Meichenbaum has been echoed in the metacognitive literature. Brown (1978, p. 79) has identified "conscious executive control" as a critical variable that makes strategic activity possible in a range of problematic situations. Similarly, Flavell (in press) has considered the sense of self as an active causal agent for promoting monitoring and regulatory processes.

To conclude, the concept of control, be it couched in terms of effort renewal, coping strategies, strategic behaviors, executive processes or sense of agency, has emerged as an integral feature of several theoretical formulations concerned with the facilitation of effective academic performance. It was the apparent congruence of these diverse positions that led me to investigate children's knowledge of strategies for coping in school failure situations.

Children's Styles of Responding to Failure

Do children differ in their awareness of strategies for coping in school failure situations? To answer this question, ninety 8-year-old children from three urban schools in New Zealand were interviewed about a variety of hypothetical situations in which the child was confronted with a failure situation (Cullen, 1981). For example, the child was asked: "You are working on a math problem in school and you get stuck. What would you do then?" In the same session, a behavioral measure of the child's persistence on a novel problem-solving task was obtained by recording the number of times the child withdrew from a problem before reaching either a solution or the 3-minute time limit. The problem-solving task comprised two sets of puzzles, networks, and tangrams. Half the sample was given the tasks in the order networks, interview items, tangrams, whereas half the sample received the tasks in the order tangrams, interview items, networks. Spontaneous verbalizations about the task were elicited by asking the child to say out loud what he or she was thinking while working on the puzzles.

There were no effects of task order on either the verbal or the behavioral data.

To assess children's styles of responding to failure, the interview data were coded according to the following criteria: coping responses (i.e., active and constructive attempts to deal with the failure); neutral responses (i.e., passive reactions that indicated neither active attempts to cope nor negative reactions that interfered with coping responses); and negative responses (i.e., reactions that interfered with constructive attempts to deal with the failure). The majority of responses were categorized as either coping responses or negative responses. Children's knowledge of coping was derived from the number of coping responses reported by each child. Each interview item received a score of 1 for the presence of a coping response regardless of the frequency of coping responses, yielding a maximum coping score of 10. On this basis, 29 children (32%) were identified as high scorers who received coping scores of 8 to 10, and 27 children (30%) were identified as low scorers who received scores of 1 to 5.

High and low scorers were subdivided further on the basis of qualitative differences to form four comparison groups. Qualitative differences in coping responses were established according to the following criteria: social resource and general effort responses were defined as *low-level coping responses* for 8-year-old children; specific effort, learned skill, study skill, and cognitive responses were defined as *high-level coping responses*. Whereas high-level responses revealed the child's awareness of what he or she could do to control performance, low-level responses suggested recourse to immediate action and the absence of reflective processing skills. Negative affective responses were subdivided into *anxiety responses* (defined as affective reactions that suggested anxiety, embarrassment, or guilt about failure) and *anger responses* (which suggested the presence of anger, aggression, or frustration about failure).

Figure 1 illustrates the major response categories on which the comparison groups were differentiated: high-level coping, low-level coping, affective (anxiety and anger), and withdrawing from the task.

Strategy-oriented children were high scorers who used predominantly high-level coping responses that comprised strategies such as the use of study skills or renewing effort in terms of a specific checking or monitoring strategy.

Action-oriented children also scored high on the coping measure but used predominantly low-level coping responses such as general effort renewal and asking for help.

Anxiety-oriented children were low scorers on the coping measure, using predominantly negative affective responses that suggested anxiety, embarrassment, or guilt about failure.

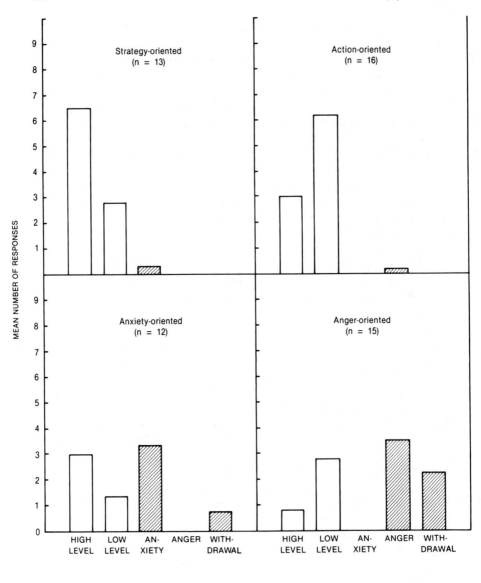

FIGURE 1. Mean number of high-level coping, low-level coping, anxiety, anger, and withdrawal responses for each of the four groups of children. *Source:* Cullen, J. L. Children's reactions to school failure. *New Zealand Journal of Educational Studies*, 1981, 16, 63.

Anger-oriented children were low scorers who used predominantly negative responses that comprised either withdrawing from the task or statements suggesting anger, aggression, or frustration about failure.

While the use of hypothetical failure situations may place some qualifications on the validity of the verbal data, similar verbal responses were revealed when the spontaneous verbalizations were examined. Strategy-oriented children typically monitored their progress with statements such as "Perhaps I should try the medium triangle. That fits," while action-oriented children made frequent use of generic self-instructions to "try again." Anxiety-oriented children did reveal some self-monitoring of progress but were also highly conscious of the interviewer's surveillance. This was evident in their use of statements such as "I'm not doing it properly, am I?" Anger-oriented children spoke very little but when this did occur primarily indicated their intention to "give up" on the task, or their belief that they were "no good" at puzzles.

To investigate the role of coping strategies in the manifestation of learned helplessness, the four groups were compared on the basis of persistence on the problem-solving task, and school achievement (teacher ratings and standardized achievement test scores). Parental socioeconomic status (SES) was also recorded. On the basis of these analyses, the four groups were characterized in the following way. Strategy-oriented children were high achievers, highly persistent, and came from above-average-SES homes. Action-oriented children were low achievers, highly persistent, and mostly came from below-average-SES homes. Anxiety-oriented children were also above-average achievers, highly persistent, and from above-average-SES homes, whereas anger-oriented children were low achievers, failed to persist with problems, and came from below-average-SES homes.

Coping Strategies and Effective Performance

Cullen's (1981) findings provide considerable support for the hypothesized relationship between metacognitive activity and the ability to cope with failure experiences. The high-level coping responses expressed by the strategy-oriented children probably reflect a more general level of metacognitive knowledge, and this appears to be associated with efficient cognitive monitoring on problem-solving tasks as well as with successful school achievement. Conversely, the anger-oriented children who produced few coping responses were poor achievers and revealed helpless reactions to failure on the problem-solving task. Thus, they gave up in the face of failure, and when verbalizations did occur, tended to give ability attributions for failure. While the findings do not indicate whether the limited coping responses of the anger-oriented children resulted from an absence of strategies or the failure to activate them, the passivity of these children on the problem-solving task does suggest the presence of metacognitive impairment. The expression of anger and frustration by these 8-year-old children also clearly indicates the disruptive effects school failure can have on children who possess few strategies for coping with a failed task.

A parallel can be drawn between the contrasting styles of the strategy-oriented and anger-oriented children, and that of Diener and Dweck's (1978) mastery-oriented and helpless children. In Diener and Dweck's study, cognitive monitoring and ability attributions, elicited by the think-aloud technique following failure feedback, were differentially associated with maintenance or improvement in performance in the case of the mastery-oriented children and performance decrements in the case of the helpless children. Considered together, the two studies provide clear support for the view that effective achievement behaviors are facilitated by the availability of a range of strategies for coping with ambiguity and error. In addition, Cullen's (1981) findings suggest that, at least with some children, metacognitive knowledge is associated with strategic performance. Such a connection has found only tenuous support in earlier studies of metacognition (e.g., Cavanaugh & Perlmutter, 1982).

Discontinuities between metacognitive knowledge and actual performance were, however, evident in the responses to failure of the action-oriented and the anxiety-oriented children. In the case of the action-oriented children, the availability of low-level coping strategies was associated with high persistence on the problem-solving task, but with low achievement on academic tasks. Thus, the presence of low-level coping strategies alone was apparently insufficient to produce effective academic performance, although these children did appear to hold generally positive attitudes to schoolwork. In the case of the anxiety-oriented children, while present achievement is clearly satisfactory, it seems likely that negative affect will interfere with effective cognitive monitoring and efficient academic performance once these children are exposed to more formal evaluation procedures at the upper levels of the school. Both cases point to basic issues concerning the development and maintenance of metacognition: the socialization experiences of the child, and the influence of affect on children's use of strategic behaviors.

Socialization and the Growth of Strategic Behaviors

Flavell (in press) has suggested that some experiences may be heuristic or propaedeutic to metacognitive development, and it may be that the low-level coping responses of the action-oriented children, together with their ready persistence in problem-solving situations, may actually constitute this type of experience. If this is so, the question arises as to why a child with positive reactions to failure experiences should fail to acquire the reflective forms of control revealed by the strategy-oriented children, or to succeed on school tasks. It is, of course, possible to argue that these children possess a generally lower level of ability and that the poor achievement of the action-oriented children relates to this factor. An alternative explanation, consistent with a socialization perspective on metacognitive development, places less emphasis on ability and more on experiential factors, particularly those concerned with childrearing practices in the formative preschool years.

Accounts of the emergence of self-regulative capacities (Brown et al., 1983; Kopp, 1982; Wertsch, 1979) have drawn upon Vygotsky's (1978) theory of the development of speech, language, and thought, to develop the hypothesis that metacognitive development is associated with a gradual shift from other-regulation to self-regulation. According to this position, the child experiences other-regulation in the form of adult-child interactions in early childhood, and it is on the basis of these experiences of directed problem-solving that self-regulative capacities gradually emerge. While nonverbal forms of other-regulation have been considered (e.g., Wertsch, McNamee, McLane, & Budwig, 1980), a central place has been given, in both the Russian and the metacognitive formulations, to the function of adult-child dialogue in this process. A major conclusion of the work in this field (Kopp, 1982) is that caregivers are important mediators of individual differences in self-control in children. In accordance with this position, it is probable that the metacognitive deficits that seemed to mark the performance of both the action-oriented and the anger-oriented children in Cullen's (1981) study are associated with socialization experiences in early childhood. The SES of the action- and anger-oriented children differed significantly from that of the strategy- and anxiety-oriented children—the two groups who revealed some evidence of metacognitive activity. Fathers of the two former groups were more likely to hold unskilled or semiskilled occupations, while parental occupations of the latter groups were more likely to be represented at professional or managerial levels.

To postulate SES differences in childrearing practices is, of course, a contentious issue, as the continuing dialogue on the topic of SES differences in child language attests. (See, e.g., Wells, 1981a, for a refutation of the position.) Nevertheless, the results of many investigations of children's language indicate that children from the extremities of the SES range (i.e., the difference between unskilled and professional occupations) are likely to grow up with differing experiences of the use of language for thinking, for problem solving, and for communication, particularly in the context of parent–child dialogue (e.g., Blank, Rose, & Berlin, 1978; Francis, 1974; Tizard, Carmichael, Hughes, & Pinkerton, 1980; Tough, 1977; Wootton, 1974). With this body of research in mind it is plausible to argue that the low-SES action- and anger-oriented children have commenced school with language and experiences that do not readily facilitate the growth of metacognitive activity or directly contribute to the acquisition of the literacy-related activities that are fundamental in the early school years. Brown (1978) similarly has argued that metacognitive impairment in disadvantaged children may impede the transition from the informal preschool learning environment to formal school learning.

Further to Brown's view, the present discussion focuses in particular on the significance of the child's early experiences of language with an interactive adult. It is assumed that these early interactive learning experiences have an important influence on the learning strategies and attitudes the child subsequently develops in the school context (Wells, 1981b). Some support for the contention that disadvantaged children commence school with impaired self-regulatory capacities comes from a New Zealand study (Cullen, 1983) of 5-year-olds in their first year at school. Teachers of Year 1 classes in five urban elementary schools were asked to nominate children who were considered to have adjusted well to school learning or who were poorly adjusted to school learning after one term at school. (In New Zealand, children commence school at the age of 5 years.) Fourteen well-adjusted and poorly adjusted pairs from the same classrooms were identified. The children's use of language for reporting, directing, reasoning, predicting, and projecting was recorded in two learning contexts in the natural classroom settting: an unstructured free-choice situation and a structured teacher–child situation. The structured situation was defined as an interactive learning situation in which the teacher used questioning to engage the child in conversation about a story or picture. An unstructured situation was defined as an episode in a free-choice activity program in which the child could self-select activities (e.g., puzzles, blocks, craft activities) and interact informally with other children. Observers, who were unaware of the teachers' nominations, each gathered language samples from one well-adjusted child and one poorly-adjusted child in the two situations.

The results showed that in the unstructured situation the well-adjusted children were more likely to use self-directing language than other-directing language, while the reverse pattern occurred with the poorly adjusted children. In the structured situation, although there were no significant differences in the frequency of response, well-adjusted children were more likely to engage in complex combinations of language use, while poorly adjusted children tended to respond with brief or one-word utterances, and rarely initiated conversation. Thus, the two groups clearly differed in their ability to monitor their own activities and to interact with an adult in a learning situation. Both abilities could be said to relate to early experiences with an interactive adult and to reflect aspects of metacognitive development.

Subsequent analysis of SES data on the two groups revealed a significant difference in SES background, with the poorly adjusted children predominantly represented at the unskilled and semiskilled levels. The study thus provides some indirect support for the view that at least with some low-SES children, early adult–child interactions have failed to facilitate metacognitive growth, and that these deficiencies are evident in the child's performance at school entry. It is possible, of course, that the poorly adjusted low-SES children's general lack of ease with the teacher contributed to the teacher's initial nominations of poor adjustment. However, teachers were not aware of the nature of the observations to be gathered at the time the nominations were recorded. Further, significant differences in language use as well as in midyear reading progress were obtained between the two groups, indicating that teachers were accurate in their assessment of the capacities required for adjustment to school learning in 5-year-old children. The possibility that teachers' initial nominations influenced teaching behaviors toward the two groups, thereby independently affecting reading progress, cannot, of course, be entirely eliminated. However, the interest shown by the teachers in the use of the language data for remedial purposes when it was discussed with them at the completion of the study does seem to indicate that expectancy effects associated with SES were not a significant factor in the study. Finally, if children's early experiences with an interactive adult do subsequently influence their relationships with teachers, this may be an important source of negative school-related affect in the at-risk child. New entrants to school perceive teachers in a powerful and pervasive role (Cullen, 1984), hence, an uneasy teacher–child relationship may well affect the growth of more general attitudes toward school.

Other New Zealand studies have obtained data on Maori children, which indicate that metacognitive impairment may be a precursor of the low school achievement of Maoris. Podmore (1978) observed new entrant (5-year-old) Maori, Polynesian, and Pakeha (New Zealanders of European extraction) children in the natural classroom setting and found that the Maori and Polynesian children were less likely to attend to the teacher or to comply with her or his instructions. Ritchie (1978) found that attendance at an experimental preschool improved Maori children's learning-to-learn skills, (e.g., attending behavior) upon school entry. The intervention program enjoyed a favorable adult–child ratio and emphasized the use of language experiences, of developmental activities, and of shared reading with English and Maori-language books—all conditions that seem likely to promote interactive learning experiences.

Older Maori children are also less likely to use verbal and direct help-seeking behaviors with a teacher, and are more likely to use nonverbal help-seeking behaviors (McKessar & Thomas, 1978). This behavior pattern could have the effect of reducing further opportunities for practicing metacognitive activity, because teachers who fail to understand cultural differences may interpret the nonverbal mannerisms of Maori children as negative personal characteristics (Metge & Kinloch, 1978). In turn, teachers are likely to develop negative expectations for the academic performance of Maoris (St. George, 1983), thereby contributing to the negative academic self-concepts held by low-achieving Maori children (Chapman, 1984; Chapman & Boersma, 1982).

The failure of Maori children to attain early language facility is also consistent with the traditional Maori childrearing style in which older siblings care for toddlers when a new baby is born (Garrett, 1971; Ritchie & Ritchie, 1979). Thus, Maori children may lack adult models and interactive learning experiences in the early years. Further, in a structured teaching situation with older children, Maori mothers are less likely than Pakeha mothers to talk during the task, and Maori children are more likely to exhibit off-task behaviors (D. Thomas, 1978). The available evidence on the socialization of Maoris, therefore, is consistent with the view that young Maori children are less likely to experience forms of other-regulation with an interactive adult and that this is likely to result in impaired self-regulatory capacities upon entry to school.

An Australian study (Bunday, 1982) also has pointed to some of the early learning origins of differences in self-regulatory capacities of low-SES children. Twenty 6-year-old children who were in their first year of attendance at a priority school in a low-cost housing area were identified as either high or low attenders on the basis of teacher ratings and independent observations of each child's performance on an assigned task. (Schools are designated priority on the basis of high incidence of low SES or migrant, or Aboriginal students and are eligible for special funding.) *High attenders* were children who revealed a high incidence of attending behaviors such as renewal of effort while engaged in individual seatwork. Conversely, *low attenders* were children who were frequently off-task. Mothers of the children were subsequently interviewed to ascertain the extent to which childrearing practices encompassed literacy-related activities and activities that would be likely to promote persistence and attending. Bunday found that mothers of low attenders were less likely than the mothers of high attenders to read books with their children or to have books in the home, to provide puzzles and other problem-solving activities, or to take their children on family excursions. The families of low attenders were also more likely to live in low-rental housing and to have changed homes frequently, conditions suggesting that family instability may be affecting both the nature of the parent–child relationship and the child's adjustment to school. In school, the low attenders were making poorer progress in reading and language activities when compared with the high attenders. Thus, a link between poor achievement, metacognitive impairment and home background, similar to that obtained in Cullen's studies (1981, 1983) was identified. In particular, the paucity of activities for promoting literacy and problem-solving in the homes of the low attenders is a further indication that individual differences in self-regulatory capacities are associated with socialization practices in the early childhood years. A comprehensive developmental literature is now available to bolster the belief that the child's ability to cope and be competent is related to early childrearing practices. (See, e.g., Turner, 1980, for a review of clinical, experimental, and observational data that support this view.)

The Role of Negative Affect

The late 1970s have shown a revival of interest in the role of affective variables in school learning (e.g., Bloom, 1976; Messick, 1979). In the field of learning disabilities, there is considerable documentation of the association between negative affect and poor school achievement, although the causal mechanisms involved are far from clear (Chapman, Cullen, Boersma & Maguire, 1981). Boersma and Chapman, for example, have reported that LD children hold relatively negative self-perceptions of ability and lower expectations for future achievement compared to normally achieving children (Boersma & Chapman, 1981; Boersma, Chapman, & Battle, 1979; Cullen, Boersma, & Chapman, 1981). They also hold more external locus-of-control orientations (Chapman & Boersma, 1979) and attributions that suggest learned helplessness (Dunn, Pearl, & Bryan, 1981; Pearl, Bryan, & Donahue, 1980). These relative differences seem to hold regardless of whether the LD children receive no special educational services (and therefore are not labelled as LD, e.g., Dunn, Pearl, & Bryan, 1981) or are receiving remedial assistance in resource room programs (e.g., Boersma & Chapman, 1981).

Given the widespread acknowledgement of the affective characteristics of failure-prone students, the emergence of negative affect in the context of Cullen's (1981) study of school failure is not unexpected. Two features of this study are, however, noteworthy. First, the study highlighted the presence of anxiety, frustration, and anger about school learning in children as young as 8 years who had only just completed the more informal years of their elementary schooling. Such findings are of grave concern for the educators of young children. The development of a learning set of helplessness in the early school years must surely have lasting implications for the effectiveness of later schooling. Second, there is a strong suggestion that negative affect may interfere with the effective use of children's existing repertoires of metacognitive strategies, as well as impeding further metacognitive development.

In the case of the anger-oriented children, metacognitive deficiencies were apparent in their poorly expressed knowledge of coping strategies and passive performance on the problem-solving task. Their low school achievement also suggested that school learning is customarily an unrewarding experience for these children. These characteristics seem unlikely to nurture the acquisition or maintenance of metacognitive activity, because it is assumed that the activation of metacognitive strategies is most likely to occur when the individual is not inhibited by emotional responses (Flavell, in press). The helplessness exhibited by the anger-oriented children is usually associated with a belief in the uncontrollability of achievement outcomes (Dweck & Goetz, 1978). Given the low SES of these children and the prevalence of societal attitudes that lead working-class children to accept lack of ability as sufficient explanation of their lower academic and occupational performance (Freeman-Moir, 1981; Nash, 1981), the prognosis for the anger-oriented children appears gloomy in the absence of appropriate educational intervention. Stipek (1981) has shown that SES differences in locus of control at school entry can be reduced during the first year of school. This goal could well be the aim of all teachers of young children. The development of an internal locus of cognitive control is, according to Flavell (in press), likely to promote the monitoring and regulation of cognitive enterprises.

The anxiety-oriented children in Cullen's (1981) study responded to failure with anxiety, guilt, and embarrassment, and on the problem-solving task were acutely aware of the researcher's presence, glancing frequently at her and commenting about their performance, usually in denigratory terms. These children were high achievers and did report some high-level coping strategies. Further, cognitive monitoring and regulation were also evident in their systematic approach to the problems. It is probable, though, that the anxious reactions of the anxiety-oriented children would interfere eventually with effective metacognitive activity. Even at the age of 8 years, error and ambiguity were cues for anxiety about performance for these children, although they subsequently persisted with alternative strategies to reach a solution.

Anxiety about achievement had not yet depressed the school progress of these 8-year-olds. The fact that anxiety develops in the context of the informal learning environment that typifies the early school years in New Zealand does, however, suggest that more formal teaching practices and evaluative procedures in subsequent years could have the effect of raising anxiety to disruptive levels. High levels of anxiety could be manifest in underachievement, thereby reducing the possibility of failure by lowering aspirations, or by adopting an overcautious style of learning, which could avoid exposure to threatening situations. Either response is likely to reduce opportunities for the exercise of independent and active learning styles, and to place limits on achievement. The high SES of the anxiety-oriented children further suggests that parental pressure to achieve could exacerbate this process. In this way, everyday experiences of success and failure, pressure to achieve from parents and teachers, and children's anxiety about performance may reciprocally interact to inhibit metacognitive activity.

To summarize this section, several important conclusions follow from the preceding discussion. Children's metacognitive knowledge is differentially associated with styles of responding to failure, and, with some children, academic achievement. Second, it seems likely that early socialization experiences, in particular the child's experiences with an interactive adult, contribute to metacognitive development and assist the child's adjustment to school learning. Further, it is probable that negative affect associated with school failure impedes both children's metacognitive development and their efficient use of available metacognitive strategies. Finally, the association of children's metacognitive activity and negative affect with school-related tasks suggests that teachers may play an integral role in the acquisition and use of metacognitive strategies in the school context. This seems particularly apposite with regard to the early school years when interactive learning experiences based on the adult–child situation may assist the transition from the informal preschool learning environment to the formal learning environment of the school (Cullen, 1983).

The Influence of Inappropriate Teaching Practices

Nicholls and Burton (1982) have proposed that children's task involvement, regarded by these authors as the optimum motivation for intellectual development, is influenced by social and personal factors contributing to classroom climate. Motivation that is task oriented (Nicholls, 1979a) places the locus of student effort in the student's interest and in the desire to master a task rather than in the desire for external rewards (extrinsic motivation) or the maintenance of self-esteem (ego, or self-enhancing motivation). Task orientation was demonstrated by Diener and Dweck's (1978) mastery-oriented students and the strategy-oriented children in Cullen's (1981) study who were clearly applying their metacognitive abilities to the solution of a challenging problem. It is probable that task involvement, by focusing on the learner's task behaviors, is the form of motivation most likely to promote metacognitive activity.

According to Nicholls and Burton (1982), factors such as the organizational strategies adopted to facilitate learning and specific feedback from teachers influence children's task involvement. As an example of the first factor, task-oriented motivation on a challenging task can be transformed to extrinsic motivation by the use of rewards or surveillance (Lepper & Greene, 1978). With respect to the second factor, teachers may be able to enhance student involvement through the use of interest attributions ("Well, you certainly are interested in . . . .").

The identification of the learning conditions that would activate and maintain task involvement has obvious implications for educators. In this regard, the 8-year-olds in Cullen's (1981) study spoke of a variety of everyday teaching practices when they responded to questions about school failure. These spontaneous comments about teachers yielded a rich source of children's perceptions of classroom practices. When these verbal data were coded on the basis of empirically derived categories, it was clear that the children were referring to practices that were likely to inhibit their use of self-directed strategies to cope with failure experiences. Each of these practices suggested the influence of a specific teacher behavior on the child's reaction to failure, either through direct instruction or by allowing a practice of the child's to continue unchecked. The teacher behaviors, deemed by Cullen and Carver (1982) to be inappropriate teaching practices were grouped as follows:

1. Omit example: general instruction to omit difficult example or leave until another child or teacher can help.
2. Erase example: child permitted to erase incorrect work and recommence without checking or identifying error.
3. Teacher response failure: teacher fails to follow up incorrect written or verbal response.
4. Presentation of work: over-emphasis on appearance of work, to the detriment of content mastery.
5. Extrinsic material rewards: over-emphasis on points, stars and other devices which can devalue the task's intrinsic interest and stress presentation.
6. Substitute activity: Child encouraged to change to an "easier" task.

Although such practices may well contribute to the smooth running of the classroom and to the goals of the "hidden curriculum" (LeCompte, 1978), in the present context they are regarded as inappropriate in that they are likely to interfere with children's self-directed learning. Many of these everyday classroom practices are known to have detrimental effects on student learning. For example, the use of peer tutors has recently been questioned. Ellis and Rogoff (1982) found that child and adult tutors used very different teaching strategies and that learners performed better with adult tutors. The practice of allowing other children to help a child in difficulties is, then, likely to lead to less effective learning as well as to remove the responsibility for coping from the child. The use of rewards, in the form of points, stars, or other devices, is a practice that is likely to reduce subsequent interest in a task (Lepper & Green, 1978). The 8-year-old boy who would not attempt to correct a problem because "It's not worth marks. It's not like stars" (Cullen, 1982) vividly portrayed the negative side of a reward system in the classroom.

Cullen and Carver (1982) found that 39% of the total sample of 90 children referred to at least one of the inappropriate teaching practices. When the data were analyzed according to style of responding to failure, strategy-oriented children were least likely to refer to one of the practices, while approximately half of the anxiety- and anger-oriented children and one-third of the action-oriented children did so. On the basis of these data it appears that children, such as the strategy-oriented group, who engage in effective cognitive monitoring are less likely to be influenced by inappropriate teaching practices, while children with some degree of impairment or affective blocking of metacognitive activity are more vulnerable to the effects of teacher influence. It seems then, that many everyday teaching practices could be examined critically to ensure that children are not regularly exposed to learning situations that encourage passivity or nonstrategic responses. Cullen and Carver's data also provide some support for Rohwer's (1980) hypothesis that initially more proficient students enhance their proficiency at a relatively faster rate than the less proficient because they receive relatively little prescriptive instruction.

There are broader influences too, evolving from the content of school learning, which are likely to permeate the classroom learning environment. When the child commences school and is introduced to the structured activities of the formal learning environment of the school, he or she will probably perceive many tasks and assignments as meaningless. Holt (1969) has vividly described the sense of failure that can develop in children for whom school tasks do not make sense. More-recent observational studies have commented on the apparent meaninglessness of many school activities. Anderson (1981), for example, has recorded incidents in the natural classroom setting, suggesting that first-grade students viewed the purpose of assignments in terms of a content-coverage orientation rather than that of content mastery. In order to complete assignments, low-achieving students developed strategies that contributed to task completion, but that did not necessarily contribute to the mastery of the content or to the acquisition or maintenance of adaptive learning-to-learn skills. For example, one low-achieving child was able to complete an assignment that required her to copy statements off the board and illustrate them, by copying from a neighbor's drawing and asking "What do we do here?" She was, however, unable to read the sentences to confirm that she understood what she was doing. Durkin's (1978–1979) observation that children are encouraged to view reading as completing worksheets suggests that use of such strategies to complete assigned tasks may not be uncommon among low-achieving children. Similar observations have been made by King (1978) in a study of British infant schools. The large-scale ORACLE study of classroom processes in British primary schools (Galton & Simon, 1980; Galton, Simon, & Croll, 1980; Simon & Willcocks, 1981) also highlights many practices that are likely to interfere with task-oriented motivation. Such practices include the low levels of problem-solving and inquiry activities in classrooms, the repetitive use of work cards, and the emphasis teachers give to busyness.

Anderson's (1981) study suggests that low-achieving children would be less likely than high achievers to respond to an error or ambiguity with cognitive monitoring skills, because they would be less able to identify errors in tasks that are customarily meaningless. Unable to see the sense of the task, and deprived of coping strategies or metacognitive assistance from the teacher, such children are likely candidates for learned helplessness. Teachers who are alert to opportunities for developing children's coping responses will use a variety of strategies that provide children with metacognitive assistance. These include the use of questions, prompts, and examples to encourage children to ask questions, to persist with a task, to check instructions, and to find appropriate aids. Cullen's (1983) finding that the language uses of poorly adjusted 5-year-olds differed in quality with the presence or absence of an interactive adult in structured and unstructured learning contexts also suggests that the sensitive use of extended conversation with young children, in situations that arouse their interest and motivation, could be a fruitful means of promoting the use of language for thinking and self-regulation.

With some children who commence school with impaired self-regulatory capacities, it may be desirable for teachers to take over the tutor function of the preschool parent (Wood, Bruner, & Ross, 1976; Wood & Middleton, 1975), for whom effective instruction comprises a dynamic interactive process. A critical feature of this process is the gradual diminishing of the tutorial function as the child develops independence in problem solving. Unrequested help-giving may eventually yield negative perceptions of ability in the recipient (Meyer, 1982), thereby leaving the learner vulnerable to the effects of learned helplessness.

The excessive anxiety experienced by some of the high-achieving children also may be reduced by practices that encourage a task orientation and focus on the problem-solving process rather than on evaluation of the product. A learning environment that aims to foster a task orientation and to minimize debilitating negative affect would first deemphasize competition and social comparison, and second accept ambiguity and error as a normal part of learning. The use of classroom-management procedures that place the responsibility for learning on the student rather than the teacher (e.g., Matheny & Edwards, 1974; Wang & Stiles, 1976) is an approach that seems likely to provide these conditions of learning.

Teaching Metacognitive Strategies

The implications of a metacognitive approach to learning are not restricted to the regular classroom. Reviews concerning children with learning problems (Brown & Campione, 1978; Kauffman & Hallahan, 1979; Kendall & Finch, 1979; Meichenbaum & Asarnow, 1979) have noted the potential of cognitive-monitoring procedures in the remedial setting. Along these lines, a remedial program for teaching metacognitive strategies in conjunction with the mathematics curriculum has been devised (Carver, 1981) in order to investigate the role of metacognitive strategies in reducing learned helplessness.

Carver selected twelve 10-year-old children from the same classroom in a New Zealand urban school, on the basis of teacher ratings on a checklist that tapped the behavioral manifestations of helplessness (e.g., persistence, response to task failure, use of strategies) and of low achievement in mathematics. Each child was interviewed about his or her reactions to the result on a class mathematics test, to assess knowledge of metacognitive strategies and attributions for failure. The children were then divided into two matched groups, treatment and control, on the basis of helplessness ratings, attributions, knowledge of strategies, and mathematics attainment.

Each group worked with the investigator for two 30-minute sessions per week for 6 weeks. Most of each session was concerned with assigned book work from the normal mathematics program conducted by the classroom teacher. The investigator's role was to give individual help with concepts that had been introduced by the classroom teacher. For the treatment group, this consisted of helping children to use metacognitive strategies such as checking to overcome their difficulties. Charts were used in the strategy training to elicit checking and monitoring strategies. For example:

> *Stuck?*
> Before you yell "Help!"
> STOP What can you do first?
> 1. Read the question again.
> 2. Study the top of the page.
> 3. Look in the index.
> 4. Think back to what the teacher said.
> (Carver, 1981, p. 56)

The prompt to study the top of the page referred to the format of the mathematics text, in which information necessary for working the examples and a worked example were contained in a box at the top of the page.

For the control group, assistance consisted of the type of content-based help typically provided by teachers. This included pointing out mistakes and explaining the error with individual children, as well as some oral blackboard teaching sessions on the concepts with the group. Comparable group contact with the treatment group focused on the use of the strategy charts.

Following completion of the program, interviews based on a second mathematics test were conducted to assess attributions for failure and metacognitive knowledge and to provide a correction task on which strategy use could be observed. Strategy use was also observed on a new mathematics task by an assistant who was unaware of which children had received the strategy training, 3 weeks after the completion of the training. All posttreatment interviews were tape-recorded, and running records were made of the child's behavior to permit qualitative analysis of strategy use. In addition to recording the type of strategy used (e.g., checking worked examples at the top of the page) strategy use was assessed at three levels: *unprompted* (child shows independent use of strategies); *general prompt* (child is asked to correct an example); *specific prompt* (child is reminded to use a specific method or strategy).

Carver found that children who had received strategy training showed a more strategic approach on both the correction task and the new mathematics task and showed greater ability to respond to prompts on the new mathematics task, when compared with controls. All the treatment children were able to verbalize specific strategies for coping with difficulties in mathematics, whereas the control-group children said that they would ask for help. In addition, only one treatment child referred to lack of ability as the reason for failure on the second mathematics test, compared with five control children who gave ability attributions for failure.

Although these findings are limited by the exploratory nature of the study and the small numbers of children involved, the investigation has identified some useful procedures for small-group teaching in either the classroom or the remedial setting. Further, Carver's results provide promising support for the usefulness of metacognitive training for reducing helpless reactions to initial failure on a task. There are, however, several practical issues arising from the investigation, which highlight the difficulties of improving children's metacognitive strategies in a remedial setting when the metacognitive aims of the program are not fully articulated with everyday practices in the regular classroom. Carver (Cullen & Carver, 1982) has noted that the evaluative atmosphere of the classroom appeared to interfere with metacognition. This was illustrated by the child in the first interview who stated that he would not do anything to correct a wrong example because that would be cheating and you just had to face up to getting it wrong. The teacher's practice of marking examples at the end of the mathematics period, when little time was available for practicing correction skills was similarly opposed to metacognitive goals of learning.

Carver also had difficulty integrating a strategic approach to task performance with a mathematics program that was organized on a content-coverage model. The teacher's practice was to assign one or two pages of the mathematics book daily, thereby limiting the time available for extra work on difficult concepts in each group session. Carver found that strategy training was of limited value when children did not have at least some basic competence with the mathematics content. The two treatment children who gained least from the strategy training experienced considerable difficulty with the content of the mathematics curriculum. For these children, checking and monitoring strategies were apparently of little help when the content itself did not make sense. This finding is consistent with Brophy's (1977, p. 383) injunction that the use of learning-to-learn skills depends upon the knowledge of rudimentary tool skills in the basic subject content. Thus, a child who is still struggling with the meaning of a subtraction operation is unlikely to be cued by an error to make use of checking skills.

Of interest also is the treatment children's greater ability to respond to prompts on the new mathematics task. This finding illustrates the importance of teachers providing metacognitive assistance to maintain newly acquired strategies. This implication holds for both remedial and regular class teachers. Richey, Miller, and Lessman (1981) have found that LD students differ in learning behaviors between resource and classroom settings, and suggest that this may relate to student uncertainty about which behaviors are regarded as appropriate by classroom and resource teachers. In the light of these findings, it seems that unless teachers increase their own metacognitive awareness, metacognitive training procedures may have only limited effectiveness as a remedial technique. If remedial programs of strategy training are to be maximally effective, the classroom learning environment must actively reinforce and extend the strategies acquired in the remedial setting.

Conclusion

There are now sufficient data available to support the proposed relationship between metacognitive deficits and learned helplessness. Whether a helpless response to failure results from retarded metacognitive development or the failure to activate existing repertoires of strategies is unclear. It may be that different mechanisms are involved with different populations of children. What does seem clear is that the learner's affective state is likely to interfere with efficient metacognitive activity. Further, the negative affect that accompanies impaired metacognitive performance appears to be strongly associated with a variety of everyday classroom procedures.

These conclusions hold implications for both the metacognitive researcher and the classroom teacher. The studies of children's ability to cope with failure have revealed the interface of affect and cognition in the domain of metacognitive activity. It follows, then, that future research on metacognition will need to encompass the study of affective variables if it is to explain adequately children's everyday learning behaviors. Only then, it is suggested, will metacognitive research have the potential to attain complete educational relevance. But educational relevance is a goal in which teachers are also critically involved. It remains for the classroom teacher to create a learning environment in which the acquisition and use of strategies for coping with initial failure on a task is an everyday phenomenon. Such an environment will likely incorporate metacognitive goals of learning, and provide a supportive, noncompetitive atmosphere in which children's initial task failure does not evoke debilitating negative affect. In sum, an essential aspect of metacognitive activity is to retain the child's desire to cope with the task.

References

Abramson, L. Y., Seligman, M. E. P., & Teasdale, J. D. Learned helplessness: Critique and reformulation. *Journal of Abnormal Psychology,* 1978, 87, 49–74.

Anderson, L. M. *Student responses to seatwork: Implications for the study of students' cognitive processing.* Paper presented at the annual meeting of the American Educational Research Association, Los Angeles, April, 1981.

Andrews, G. R., & Debus, R. L. Persistence and the causal perception of failure: Modifying cognitive attributions. *Journal of Educational Psychology,* 1978, 70, 154–166.

Bandura, A. Self-efficacy: Toward a unifying theory of behavioral change. *Psychological Review,* 1977, 84, 191–215.

Blank, M., Rose, S. A., & Berlin, L. *The language of learning: The preschool years.* New York: Grune and Stratton, 1978.

Bloom, B. S. *Human characteristics and school learning.* New York: McGraw-Hill, 1976.

Boersma, F. J., & Chapman, J. W. Academic self-concept, achievement expectations, and locus of control in elementary learning disabled children. *Canadian Journal of Behavioral Science,* 1981, 13, 349–358.

Boersma, F. J., Chapman, J. W., & Battle, J. Academic self-concept change in special education students: Some suggestions for interpreting self-concept scores. *Journal of Special Education,* 1979, 13, 433–442.

Brophy, J. E. *Child development and socialization.* Chicago: Science Resource Associates, 1977.

Brown, A. L. Knowing when, where, and how to remember: A problem of metacognition. In R. Glaser (Ed.), *Advances in instructional psychology* (Vol. 1). Hillsdale, NJ: Erlbaum, 1978.

Brown, A. L., Bransford, J. D., Ferrara, R. A., & Campione, J. C. Learning, remembering, and understanding. In P. H. Mussen (Ed.), *Handbook of child psychology: Vol. 3. Cognitive development.* New York: Wiley, 1983.

Brown, A. L., & Campione, J. C. Memory strategies in learning: Training children to study strategically. In H. L. Pick, H. W. Leibowitz, J. E. Singer, A. Steinschneider, & H. W. Stevenson (Eds.), *Psychology: From research to practice.* New York: Plenum, 1978.

Brown, A. L., & Deloache, J. S. Skills, plans, and self-regulation. In R. S. Siegler (Ed.), *Children's thinking: What develops?* Hillsdale, NJ: Erlbaum, 1978.

Bunday, M. *A study of the relationship between children's attending behaviour, their development of literacy skills and socioeconomic and environmental factors.* Unpublished manuscript, Graduate Diploma in Early Childhood Studies, Western Austrilian College of Advanced Education, 1982.

Butkowksky, I. S., & Willows, D. M. Cognitive-motivational characteristics of children varying in reading ability: Evidence for learned helplessness in poor readers. *Journal of Educational Psychology,* 1980, 72, 408–422.

Calfee, R. Cognitive psychology and educational practice. In D. C. Berliner (Ed.), *Review of research in education* (Vol. 9). American Educational Research Association, 1981.

Campione, J. C., & Brown, A. L. Memory and metamemory development in educable retarded children. In R. V. Kail & J. W. Hagen (Eds.), *Perspectives on the development of memory and cognition.* Hillsdale, NJ: Erlbaum, 1977.

Carver, J. *The influence of metacognitive training on learned helplessness.* Unpublished masters research paper, University of Canterbury, 1981.

Cavanaugh, J. C., & Perlmutter, M. Metamemory: A critical examination. *Child Development,* 1982, 53, 11–28.

Chapin, M., & Dyck, D. G., Persistence of children's reading behavior as a function of N length and attribution retraining. *Journal of Abnormal Psychology*, 1976, 85, 511–515.

Chapman, J. W. The self-concept of Maori school pupils revisited: A critique of Ranby's study and some new data. *New Zealand Journal of Educational Studies*, 1984, 19, 45–54.

Chapman, J. W., & Boersma, F. J. Learning disabilities, locus of control, and mother attitudes. *Journal of Educational Psychology*, 1979, 71, 250–258.

Chapman, J. W., & Boersma, F. J. *The Student's Perception of Ability Scale: Cross-national validation of an instrument for measuring academic self-concept.* Paper presented at the annual meeting of the Australian Psychological Society, Melbourne, August, 1982.

Chapman, J. W., Cullen, J. L., Boersma, F. J., & Maguire, T. O. Affective variables and school achievement: A study of possible causal influences. *Canadian Journal of Behavioral Science*, 1981, 13, 181–192.

Cullen, J. L. Children's reactions to school failure. *New Zealand Journal of Educational Studies*, 1981, 16, 58–68.

Cullen, J. L. Learning to cope with failure in the early school years. *set*, 1982, (1, Item 6).

Cullen, J. L. The influence of the context of learning on young children's use of language. *Australian Journal of Early Childhood*, 1983, 8, 17–22.

Cullen, J. L. *Relating to authority in the primary school years.* Paper submitted for publication, 1984.

Cullen, J. L., & Boersma, F. J. The influence of coping strategies on the manifestation of learned helplessness. *Contemporary Educational Psychology*, 1982, 7, 346–356.

Cullen, J. L., Boersma, F. J., & Chapman, J. W. Characteristics of third-grade learning disabled children. *Learning Disability Quarterly*, 1981, 4, 224–230.

Cullen, J. L., & Carver, J. *The educational relevance of metacognition: Some preliminary issues.* Paper presented at the Second National Child Development Conference, Melbourne, August, 1982.

Diener, C. I., & Dweck, C. S. An analysis of learned helplessness: Continuous changes in performance, strategy, and achievement cognitions following failure. *Journal of Personality and Social Psychology*, 1978, 36, 451–462.

Diener, C. I., & Dweck, C. S. An analysis of learned helplessness (II): The processing of success. *Journal of Personality and Social Psychology*, 1980, 39, 940–952.

Dunn, G., Pearl, R., & Bryan, T. *Learning disabled children's self evaluations.* Manuscript submitted for publication, 1981.

Durkin, D. What classroom observations reveal about reading comprehension instruction. *Reading Research Quarterly*, 1978–1979, 14, 481–533.

Dweck, C. S. The role of expectations and attributions in the alleviation of learned helplessness. *Journal of Personality and Social Psychology*, 1975, 31, 674–685.

Dweck, C. S. Social-cognitive processes in children's friendships. In S. R. Asher & J. M. Gottman (Eds.), *The development of children's friendships.* Cambridge: Cambridge University Press, 1981.

Dweck, C. S., & Goetz, T. E. Attributions and learned helplessness. In J. H. Harvey, W. Ickes & R. F. Kidd (Eds.), *New directions in attribution research* (Vol. 2). Hillsdale, NJ: Erlbaum, 1978.

Dweck, C. S., & Reppucci, N. D. Learned helplessness and reinforcement responsibility in children. *Journal of Personality and Social Psychology*, 1973, 25, 109–116.

Ellis, S., & Rogoff, B. The strategies and efficacy of child versus adult teachers. *Child Development*, 1982, 53, 730–735.

Flavell, J. H. Metacognitive aspects of problem solving. In L. B. Resnick (Ed.), *The nature of intelligence.* Hillsdale, NJ: Erlbaum, 1976.

Flavell, J. H. Metacognition and cognitive monitoring: A new area of cognitive-developmental inquiry. *American Psychologist*, 1979, *34*, 906–911.

Flavell, J. H. Cognitive monitoring. In W. P. Dickson (Ed.), *Children's oral communication skills*. New York: Academic Press, 1981.

Flavell, J. H. Speculations about the nature and development of metacognition. In R. H. Kluwe & F. E. Weinert (Eds.), *Metacognition, motivation, and learning*. In press.

Fowler, J. W., & Peterson, P. L. Increasing reading persistence and altering attributional style of learned helpless children. *Journal of Educational Psychology*, 1981, *73*, 251–260.

Francis, H. Social background, speech and learning to read. *British Journal of Educational Psychology*, 1974, *44*, 290–299.

Freeman-Moir, D. J. Employable and quiet: The political economy of human mis-development. *New Zealand Journal of Educational Studies*, 1981, *16*, 15–27.

Galton, M., & Simon, B. (Eds.), *Progress and performance in the primary classroom*. London: Routledge & Kegan Paul, 1980.

Galton, M., Simon, B., & Croll, P. *Inside the primary classroom*. London: Routledge & Kegan Paul, 1980.

Garrett, E. M. *The Maori adolescent*. Unpublished manuscript, Massey University, 1971.

Hallahan, D. P., & Reeve, R. E. Selective attention and distractibility. In B. K. Keogh (Ed.), *Advances in special education* (Vol. 1). Greenwich, CT: JAI Press, 1980.

Hamilton, V. Motivation and personality in cognitive development. In V. Hamilton & M. D. Vernon (Eds.), *The development of cognitive processes*. London: Academic Press, 1976.

Harris, K. R. *The effects of cognitive training on private speech and task performance during problem solving among learning disabled and normally achieving children*. Paper presented at the annual meeting of the American Educational Research Association, New York, March, 1982.

Holt, J. *How children fail*. Harmondsworth, Middlesex: Penguin, 1969.

Johnson, D. S. Naturally acquired learned helplessness: The relationship of school failure to achievement behavior, attributions, and self-concept. *Journal of Educational Psychology*, 1981, *73*, 174–180.

Kauffman, J. M., & Hallahan, D. P. Learning disability and hyperactivity (with comments on minimal brain dysfunction). In B. B. Lahey & A. E. Kazdin (Eds.), *Advances in clinical psychology* (Vol. 2). New York: Plenum, 1979.

Kendall, P. C., & Finch, A. J. Developing nonimpulsive behavior in children: Cognitive-behavioral strategies for self-control. In P. C. Kendall & S. D. Hollon (Eds.), *Cognitive-behavioral interventions: Theory, research and procedures*. New York: Academic Press, 1979.

King, R. *All things bright and beautiful? A sociological study of infants classrooms*. Chichester: Wiley, 1978.

Kopp, C. B. Antecedents of self-regulation: A developmental perspective. *Developmental Psychology*, 1982, *18*, 199–215.

LeCompte, M. Learning to work: The hidden curriculum of the classroom. *Anthropology and Education Quarterly*, 1978, *9*, 22–37.

Lepper, M. R., & Greene, D. (Eds.). *The hidden costs of reward*. Hillsdale, NJ: Erlbaum, 1978.

McKessar, C. J., & Thomas, D. R. Verbal and non-verbal help-seeking among urban Maori and Pakeha children. *New Zealand Journal of Educational Studies*, 1978, *13*, 29–39.

Maehr, M. L. Sociocultural origins of achievement motivation. In D. Bar-Tal & L. Saxe (Eds.), *Social psychology of education: Theory and Research*. Washington, DC: Hemisphere, 1978.

Maehr, M. L., & Nicholls, J. G. Culture and achievement motivation: A second look. In N.

Warren (Ed.), *Studies in cross-cultural psychology* (Vol. 2). New York: Academic Press, 1980.

Matheny, K. B., & Edwards, C. R. Academic improvement through an experimental classroom management system. *Journal of School Psychology*, 1974, *12*, 222–232.

Meichenbaum, D. *Cognitive-behavior modification*. New York: Plenum, 1977.

Meichenbaum, D., & Asarnow, J. Cognitive-behavioral modification and metacognitive development: Implications for the classroom. In P. C. Kendall & S. D. Hollon (Eds.), *Cognitive-behavioral interventions: Theory, research, and practice*. New York: Academic Press, 1979.

Messick, S. Potential uses of noncognitive measurement in education. *Journal of Educational Psychology*, 1979, *71*, 281–292.

Metge, J., & Kinloch, P. *Talking past each other: Problems of cross-cultural communication*. Wellington: Price Milburn, 1978.

Meyer, W-U. Indirect communications about perceived ability estimates. *Journal of Educational Psychology*, 1982, *74*, 888–897.

Nash, R. Schools can't make jobs: Structural unemployment and the schools. *New Zealand Journal of Educational Studies*, 1981, *16*, 1–14.

Nicholls, J. G. Effort is virtuous, but it's better to have ability: Evaluative responses to perceptions of effort and ability. *Journal of Research in Personality*, 1976, *10*, 306–315.

Nicholls, J. G. The development of the concepts of effort and ability, perception of academic attainment and the understanding that difficult tasks require more ability. *Child Development*, 1978, *49*, 800–814.

Nicholls, J. G. Quality and equality in intellectual development: The role of motivation in education. *American Psychologist*, 1979, *34*, 1071–1084. (a)

Nicholls, J. G. Development of perception of own attainment and causal attributions for success and failure in reading. *Journal of Educational Psychology*, 1979, *71*, 94–99. (b)

Nicholls, J. G., & Burton, J. T. Motivation and equality. *Elementary School Journal*, 1982, *82*, 367–378.

Pearl, R., Byran, T., & Donahue, M. Learning disabled children's attributions for success and failure. *Learning Disability Quarterly*, 1980, *3*, 3–9.

Pearl, R., Bryan, T., & Herzog, A. Learning disabled and nondisabled children's strategy analyses under high and low success conditions. *Learning Disability Quarterly*, 1983, *6*, 67–74.

Peterson, P. L., Swing, S. R., Braverman, M. T., & Buss, R. Student's aptitudes and their reports of cognitive processes during direct instruction. *Journal of Educational Psychology*, 1982, *74*, 535–547.

Podmore, V. N. *Polynesian and Pakeha new entrant school children's behaviour: An observational study*. Unpublished masters thesis, Victoria University of Wellington, 1978.

Richey, D. D., Miller, M., & Lessman, J. Resource and regular classroom behavior of learning disabled students. *Journal of Learning Disabilities*, 1981, *14*, 163–166.

Ritchie, J. *Chance to be equal*. Whatamonga Bay, NZ: Cape Catley, 1978.

Ritchie, J., & Ritchie, J. *Growing up in Polynesia*. London: Allen & Unwin, 1979.

Rohwer, W. D. How the smart get smarter. *Educational Psychologist*, 1980, *15*, 35–43.

Ruble, D. N., & Boggiano, A. K. Optimizing motivation in an achievement context. In B. K. Keogh (Ed.), *Advances in special education* (Vol. 1). Greenwich, CT: JAI Press, 1980.

Schunk, D. H. Modeling and attributional effects on children's achievement: A self-efficacy analysis. *Journal of Educational Psychology*, 1981, *73*, 93–105.

Schunk, D. H. Effects of effort attributional feedback on children's perceived self-efficacy and achievement. *Journal of Educational Psychology*, 1982, *74*, 548–556.

Seligman, M. E. P. *Helplessness: On development, depression, and death.* San Francisco: Freeman, 1975.

Sigel, I. E. Child development research in learning and cognition in the 1980s: Continuities and discontinuities from the 1970s. *Merrill-Palmer Quarterly,* 1981, *27,* 347–371.

Simon, B., & Willcocks, J. (Eds.). *Research and practice in the primary classroom.* London: Routledge & Kegan Paul, 1981.

St. George, A. Teacher expectations and perceptions of Polynesian and Pakeha pupils and the relationship to classroom behavior and school achievement. *British Journal of Educational Psychology,* 1983, *53,* 48–59.

Stipek, D. Social-motivational development in first grade. *Contemporary Educational Psychology,* 1981, *6,* 33–45.

Stipek, D. J., & Weisz, J. R. Perceived control and academic achievement. *Review of Educational Research,* 1981, *51,* 101–137.

Thomas, A. Learned helplessness and expectancy factors: Implications for research in learning disabilities. *Review of Educational Research,* 1979, *49,* 208–221.

Thomas, D. Communication patterns among Pakeha and Polynesian mother–child pairs: The effects of class and culture. *New Zealand Journal of Educational Studies,* 1978, *13,* 125–132.

Thomas, J. W. Agency and achievement: Self-management and self-regard. *Review of Educational Research,* 1980, *50,* 213–240.

Tizard, B., Carmichael, H., Hughes, M., & Pinkerton, G. Four year olds talking to mothers and teachers. In L. A. Hersov, M. Berger & A. R. Nicol (Eds.), *Language and language disorders in childhood.* Oxford: Pergamon, 1980.

Torgesen, J. K. The role of non-specific factors in the task performance of learning disabled children: A theoretical assessment. *Journal of Learning Disabilities,* 1977, *10,* 27–34.

Torgesen, J. K. Conceptual and educational implications of the use of efficient task strategies by learning disabled children. *Journal of Learning Disabilities,* 1980, *13,* 364–371.

Torgesen, J. K., & Kail, R. V. Memory processes in exceptional children. In B. K. Keogh (Ed.), *Advances in special education* (Vol. 1). Greenwich, CT: JAI Press, 1980.

Tough, J. *The development of meaning.* London: Allen & Unwin, 1977.

Turner, J. *Made for life: Coping, competence and cognition.* London: Methuen, 1980.

Vygotsky, L. S. *Mind in society: The development of higher psychological processes.* (M. Cole, V. John-Steiner, S. Scribner & E. Souberman, Eds. & Trans.). Cambridge, MA: Harvard University Press, 1978.

Wang, M. C., & Stiles, B. An investigation of children's concept of self-responsibility for their school learning. *American Educational Research Journal,* 1976, *13,* 159–179.

Weisz, J. R. Perceived control and learned helplessness among mentally retarded and nonretarded children: A developmental analysis. *Developmental Psychology,* 1979, *15,* 311–319.

Weisz, J. R. Learned helplessness in black and white retarded children identified by their schools as retarded and nonretarded: Performance deterioration in response to failure. *Developmental Psychology,* 1981, *17,* 499–508.

Wells, G. *Learning through interaction: The study of language development.* Cambridge: Cambridge University Press, 1981. (a)

Wells, G. Some antecedents of early academic attainments. *British Journal of Sociology of Education,* 1981, *2,* 181–200. (b)

Wertsch, J. V. From social interaction to higher psychological processes: A clarification and application of Vygotsky's theory. *Human Development,* 1979, *22,* 1–22.

Wertsch, J. V., McNamee, G. D., McLane, J. B., & Budwig, N. A. The adult–child dyad as a problem-solving system. *Child Development,* 1980, *51,* 1215–1221.

Wittrock, M. C. The cognitive movement in instruction. *Educational Researcher*, 1979, 8, 5–11.

Wong, B. Y. Increasing retention of main ideas through questioning strategies. *Learning Disability Quarterly*, 1979, 2, 42–47.

Wong, B. Y. Activating the inactive learner: Use of questions/prompts to enhance comprehension and retention of implied information in learning disabled children. *Learning Disability Quarterly*, 1980, 3, 29–37.

Wood, D., Bruner, J., & Ross, C. The role of tutoring in problem solving. *Journal of Child Psychology and Psychiatry*, 1976, 17, 89–100.

Wood, D., & Middleton, D. A study of assorted problem solving. *British Journal of Psychology*, 1975, 66, 181–191.

Wootton, A. J. Talk in the homes of young children. *Sociology*, 1974, 8, 277–295.

Author Index

Numbers in italics refer to the pages on which the complete references are cited.

Subject Index